ZURCHUNGPA'S TESTAMENT

༄༅། །བྱར་རྒྱུང་ཟལ་གདམས་བསྐྱུད་ཆུའི་མཆན་འགྲེལ་ཞེ་ཆེན་
རྒྱལ་ཚབ་པདྨ་རྣམ་རྒྱལ་གྱི་གསུང་རིན་པོ་ཆེའི་ཕྱེང་བའི་ཡང་འགྲེལ་
སྐུབས་རྗེ་རིལ་མ་ཁྱེན་རྡོ་རྗེ་འཆང་གྲིས་ཕ་རན་སིའི་སྐྱབ་སྟེ་
ཐེག་མཆོག་འོད་གསལ་ཆོས་སྐྱིང་དུ་ཆུ་བའི་
མ་ན་ང་སྐྱིང་པོའི་ཡང་བཅུད་
བཞུགས།

པདྨ་ཀུ་རའི་སྐུ་བསྒྱུར་མཐུན་ཚོགས་ནས་
སྐུ་བསྒྱུར་ཞུས།།

The Padmakara Translation Group gratefully acknowledges the generous support of the Tsadra Foundation in sponsoring the translation and preparation of this book.

♦ ♦ ♦ ♦ ♦

Zurchungpa's Testament

A COMMENTARY ON ZURCHUNG SHERAB TRAKPA'S
Eighty Chapters of Personal Advice

by Dilgo Khyentse Rinpoche
Based on Shechen Gyaltsap's Annotated Edition

Translated by the
Padmakara Translation Group

SNOW LION PUBLICATIONS
ITHACA, NEW YORK • BOULDER, COLORADO

Snow Lion Publications
P. O. Box 6483
Ithaca, NY 14851 USA
(607) 273-8519
www.snowlionpub.com

Printed in U.S.A. on acid-free recycled paper.

ISBN-10 1-55939-264-9
ISBN-13 978-1-55939-264-8

Library of Congress Cataloging-in-Publication Data
Rab-gsal-zla-ba, Dil-mgo Mkhyen-brtse, 1910-1991
   Zurchungpa's testament : a commentary on Zurchung Sherab
Trakpa's Eighty chapters of personal advice / by Dilgo Khyentse Rinpoche,
based on Shechen Gyaltsap's annotated edition ; translated by the
Padmakara Translation Group.
      p. cm.
   Translated from an oral presentation in Tibetan.
   Includes bibliographical references.
   ISBN-13: 978-1-55939-264-8 (alk. paper)
   ISBN-10: 1-55939-264-9 (alk. paper)
   1. Śes-rab-grags-pa, Zur-chuṅ, 1014-1072. Źal gdams pa brgyad bcu pa.
2. Rdzogs-chen. 3. Spiritual life—Rñiṅ-ma-pa (Sect) I. Źe-chen rgyal-tshab
padma-'gyur-med-rnam-rgyal, 1871-1926. II. Śes-rab-grags-pa, Zur-chuṅ,
1014-1072. Źal gdams pa brgyad bcu pa. English.   III. Padmakara
Translation Group. IV. Title.
BQ7662.4.S463R33 2006
294.3'444—dc 22
                                                              2006029734

Line drawings by Olivier Philippot
Designed and typeset by Gopa & Ted2, Inc.

Contents

Foreword

THE GREAT eleventh-century Tibetan master Zurchung Sherab Trakpa was someone who, by practicing the Buddha's teachings throughout his life, attained the highest possible level of spiritual realization. Shortly before he left this world, he shared his extensive experience of Buddhist practice with his disciples in a series of instructions, the *Eighty Chapters of Personal Advice*. Beginning with basic topics such as faith, impermanence, and renunciation, these simple yet profound instructions cover the path of the three trainings—discipline, concentration, and wisdom—and culminate in the extraordinary view, meditation, and activity of the Great Perfection.

Our teacher Dilgo Khyentse Rinpoche, who was a living embodiment of the path that Zurchungpa describes, gave this teaching to a group of practitioners in retreat to be used as an aid for their practice, basing his explanation on a commentary on Zurchungpa's text by his own teacher, Shechen Gyaltsap Rinpoche.

I am delighted that it will now be available to a wider public, and I am sure that all those who sincerely put this teaching into practice will derive enormous benefit, both for themselves and for anyone whom they encounter.

Jigme Khyentse
Dordogne 2006

Translators' Introduction

A NOTABLE FEATURE of Tibetan Buddhist literature is the number of pithy and easily memorized texts that condense the classical teachings into practical instruction manuals. Often cryptic in style, they provide the practitioner with keys that serve as reminders opening up a complete range of teachings to be put into practice. Garab Dorje's *Hitting the Essence in Three Points*, Atisha's *Seven-Point Mind Training*, Gyalse Thogme's *Thirty-seven Practices of the Bodhisattva*, and Padampa Sangye's *Hundred Verses of Advice* are just a few examples of such works that have become important classics in their own right.

Less well known is Zurchung Sherab Trakpa's *Eighty Chapters of Personal Advice* (*zhal gdams brgyad bcu pa*)—personal not only because they represent the distillation of a lifetime's experience of practice by a highly accomplished master, but also because they answer the needs of individual practitioners at different stages of the path. Each chapter deals with a particular topic and contains between three and thirty-four single-sentence instructions.

The Vajrayana teachings brought to Tibet by Padmasambhava, Vimalamitra, and other masters in the eighth century AD have come down to us by means of two kinds of lineal transmission: the short lineage of the treasures (*terma*), which were hidden by these great teachers and later rediscovered by the emanations of their disciples; and the long lineage of oral transmission (*kama*), in which the teachings have been transmitted from master to disciple until the present day. The early masters of this *kama* lineage belonged principally to four families, namely the So, Zur, Nub, and Nyak clans, and of these, the Zur family is noted for three outstanding masters: Zurpoche Shakya Jungne (the Great Zur), his uncle's grandson Zurchung Sherab Trakpa (the Little Zur), and Zurchungpa's own son, Zur Dropukpa Sakya Senge. These three masters of the Zur lineage had such mastery over mind and matter that, to judge from His Holiness Dudjom

Rinpoche's account in his *History of the Nyingma School*,[1] there was no distinction in their lives between the miraculous and the everyday. We read of them levitating, walking on water, flying through the air on the rays of the sun, passing through rock, lengthening a temple pillar that was too short, and performing numerous other feats. When, after a year-long retreat, Zurpoche performed a tantric dance, his foot sank up to the ankle in a rock. Zurchungpa, prostrating to the footprint of his guru, left the imprint of his own topknot and dangling earrings.

Nowadays, with the abundant use of special effects in cinema and television playing to our fascination with the supernatural, it is all too easy for us to be dazzled by the Zur masters' superhuman lifestyles and to forget that their miraculous displays resulted from years of genuine spiritual endeavor. They were fully enlightened beings who had completely transcended the feats they displayed. Their stories are intended to serve as inspirational models, and from reading them we can learn how to follow in their footsteps. In particular Zurchungpa's life story teaches us two things: that he earned his extraordinary degree of spiritual attainment by carrying out every one of his teacher's instructions to the letter; and that everything he did, however spectacular, was simply a manifestation of his enlightened activity for the sake of beings. His flying through the air, for example, enabled him to travel long distances swiftly and thus give three sessions of teaching in one day, each in a remote location many tens of miles from the last. His sole purpose in this was to benefit beings and spread the teachings more expeditiously. And although such impressive feats undoubtedly inspired devotion in his disciples, enabling them to receive blessings and progress on the path, he never used them in order to become famous.

✦✦ Zurchung Sherab Trakpa (1014–1074) ✦✦

Zurchung Sherab Trakpa was born to the accompaniment of wondrous signs. He learned to read and write in his seventh year, and in his ninth year he learned to chant the ritual of the peaceful and wrathful deities. A disagreement with his fiancée in his thirteenth year upset him deeply, and he left home determined to meet Zurpoche Shakya Jungne and to devote his life to practicing the Dharma. When he arrived, Zurpoche asked him what clan he came from. Not daring to admit that he was the Guru's second cousin, Zurchungpa replied "I am just a very small Zur (*zur chung*)." The name stuck. Despite the fact that he had only his wolf-skin coat to offer, he was accepted as a disciple by Zurpoche and immediately began studying. He underwent numerous austerities, at first refusing any material aid from his teacher, even though he was too poor to afford the supplies for copying books. Through his total devotion to Zurpoche, and by studying and practicing day and night in remote hermitages, he attained an extraordinary level of realization. Although he resolved to remain for twenty-four years in continuous retreat at the hermitage Zurpoche had given him at Mount Trak Gyawo, he was obliged for two main reasons to break his retreat after thirteen years, and was therefore prevented from actually attaining the rainbow light body—the ultimate accomplishment of the Great Perfection, where the practitioner's body dissolves into light. The first reason was that his attendant disturbed him during a long period of solitary practice: seeing that his master's mouth and nose were covered with cobwebs and thinking that he had passed away, he cried out loud and broke Zurchungpa's concentration. The second reason was that his active presence was required in order to ensure the preservation of the teachings.

Zurchungpa was famed and respected not only by Nyingmapas but also by followers of the New Tradition. On one occasion a geshe well-versed in dialectics sent his student to challenge Zurchungpa to a debate. "Let this pillar be the topic of debate," he declared. Zurchungpa accepted by passing his hand through the pillar, to the astonishment of the student, who subsequently became his disciple. Not that Zurchungpa lacked the necessary dialectical skills to defeat his opponents. His debate with four others sent by another geshe was carried out more on their terms, but it was soon over: his replies to their questions left them with no hope of a rejoinder. They later became his four principal disciples.

The epoch of these three Zur masters was a golden age for the Mantrayana. At that time, these teachings were only given to carefully selected disciples, who then devoted themselves to intensive practice, following their teachers' instructions to the letter and thereby attaining the highest accomplishment. By the nineteenth century, these secret teachings were much more widely taught, to the extent that Patrul Rinpoche could write (in *The Words of My Perfect Teacher*), "In Tibet these days there cannot be a single lama, monk, layman, or laywoman who has never received an empowerment." As a result, the teachings began to lose their subtle force and directness, and the proportion of tantric practitioners who attained accomplishment declined over the centuries. Yet even as late as the mid-twentieth century, there were still a few who attained the rainbow light body, leaving behind no physical trace. And a considerable number of masters of the Great Perfection passed away to the accompaniment of sounds, light, earthquakes, and other remarkable phenomena, dissolving most of their bodies into light and leaving remains which, when cremated, yielded *ringsel* and other extraordinary relics. One such master was Shechen Gyaltsap Pema Gyurme Namgyal, on whose annotated edition of Zurchungpa's *Eighty Chapters* Dilgo Khyentse Rinpoche based his commentary.

✦ Shechen Gyaltsap Pema Gyurme Namgyal (1871-1926) ✦

Shechen Gyaltsap, also known as Jamyang Lodrö Gyamtso Drayang, the name by which he refers to himself in the colophon of the present text, was the heart-son of Ju Mipham Namgyal Rinpoche (1846-1912) and was largely responsible, with Khenchen Kunzang Pelden (c.1870-c.1940), for continuing Mipham Rinpoche's teaching tradition. He studied with the greatest teachers of his day, including Jamyang Khyentse Wangpo (1820-1892), from whom he received teachings on the present text, and Jamgön Kongtrul Lodrö Thaye (1813-1899). He was undoubtedly one of the most learned lamas of his time, and his collected writings fill thirteen volumes, which include an extensive commentary on Atisha's *Seven-Point Mind Training*, a detailed explanation of the preliminary practice, and a treatise on the nine vehicles. He was also one of the most accomplished practitioners. He once completed what was intended to be a three-year retreat in only three months and left the imprint of his foot in a rock at the entrance to his hermitage. It is said that when Shechen Gyaltsap's body was cremated, it vanished without a trace, and that where the smoke settled on the leaves in the surrounding countryside, crystal relics were found.

Shechen Gyaltsap Rinpoche was the first of Dilgo Khyentse Rinpoche's principal teachers, for it was he who recognized and enthroned him as the incarnation of Jamyang Khyentse Wangpo's mind. His many disciples included Jamyang Khyentse Wangpo's activity emanation, Dzongsar Khyentse Chökyi Lodrö (1896-1959), who was also one of Dilgo Khyentse Rinpoche's most important teachers.

✦✦ Dilgo Khyentse Rinpoche (1910-1991) ✦✦ [2]

Kyabje Dilgo Khyentse Rinpoche was one of the last of the generation of great lamas who completed their education and training in Tibet. He was the senior lama of the ancient Nyingma tradition, the guru of the royal family of Bhutan, and an outstanding upholder of the Practice lineage, having spent twenty-two years of his life meditating in retreat and accomplishing the fruits of the many teachings he had received.

He also composed numerous poems, meditation texts, and commentaries—twenty-five volumes in all—and was a *tertön*, a discoverer of spiritual treasures, whose visionary revelations bring Padmasambhava's profound oral pith instructions directly to us. Renowned for his ability to transmit the teachings of each Buddhist lineage according to its own tradition, he was the exemplary exponent of Tibet's Rime, or nonsectarian, movement and the venerated teacher of many lamas of the four major Tibetan schools. He was also one of the leading masters of the pith instructions of Dzogchen, the Great Perfection, and one of the principal holders of the Longchen Nyingtik tradition. His Holiness the Dalai Lama has said that he regards Khyentse Rinpoche as his principal Dzogchen teacher.

Scholar, sage, and poet, Rinpoche never ceased to inspire all who encountered him through his extraordinary presence, simplicity, dignity, and humor.

Khyentse Rinpoche was born in 1910 in East Tibet's Denkhok Valley. His family descended from the royal lineage of the ninth-century king Trisong Detsen; his father was a minister to the king of Derge. When still in his mother's womb, he was recognized as an extraordinary incarnation by the illustrious Mipham Rinpoche, who later named the infant Tashi Paljor and bestowed a special blessing and Mañjushri empowerment upon him.

Even as a little boy, Rinpoche manifested a strong desire to devote himself entirely to the religious life. But his father had other ideas. His two elder sons had already left home to pursue monastic careers; one had been recognized as an incarnate lama and the other wanted to become a doctor. Rinpoche's father hoped that his youngest son would follow in his own footsteps and manage the extensive family estates, and he could not accept that he might also be a *tulku*, or incarnate lama, as had been indicated by several learned masters.

At the age of ten, the boy was taken severely ill; he was bedridden for nearly a year. Knowledgeable lamas advised that unless he was allowed to embrace the spiritual life he would not live long. Yielding to everyone's entreaties, his father agreed that the child could follow his own aspirations in order to fulfill his destiny. Thus it was that, aged eleven, he entered Shechen Monastery in Kham, East Tibet, one of the six principal monasteries of the Nyingma School. There, his root guru, Shechen Gyaltsap, Mipham Rinpoche's Dharma heir, formally recognized and enthroned him as an incarnation of the wisdom-mind of the first Khyentse Rinpoche, Jamyang Khyentse Wangpo, the peerless lama who—along with the first Jamgön Kongtrul— set in motion a Buddhist renaissance throughout Tibet. All contemporary Tibetan masters draw inspiration and blessings from this movement.

Khyen-tse means wisdom and love. The Khyentse *tulkus* are incarnations of several key figures in the development of Tibetan Buddhism. These include Longchenpa, the brilliant fourteenth-century Dzogchen master whose prolific writings illuminate the entire range of Buddhist knowledge; Jigme Lingpa, who in the eighteenth century founded the Longchen Nyingtik tradition; and King Trisong Detsen and Vimalamitra who along with Guru Rinpoche brought tantric Buddhism to Tibet in the ninth century.

At Shechen, Khyentse Rinpoche spent much of his time studying and meditating with his root guru in a hermitage above the monastery. During this time Shechen Gyaltsap gave him all the essential empowerments and instructions of the Nyingma tradition. Rinpoche also studied with many other great masters, including the renowned Dzogchen Khenpo Shenga, who imparted to him his own major work, The Thirteen Great Commentaries. He received extensive teachings and transmissions from more than fifty teachers in all.

Before Shechen Gyaltsap passed away, Khyentse Rinpoche, then aged fifteen, promised his beloved master that he would unstintingly teach whoever asked him for Dharma. From then until he was twenty-eight, he spent most of his time meditating in silent retreat, living in isolated hermitages and caves or simply under the shelter of overhanging rocks in the mountainous countryside near his birthplace. His mastery of the mystic heat (*tummo*) practice was such that the inside of his cave was warm even during the icy Tibetan winters. He also left the imprint of his foot in a rock below one of his hermitages.

Dilgo Khyentse Rinpoche later spent many years with Dzongsar Khyentse Chökyi Lodrö (1896-1959), who was also an incarnation of the first Khyentse. After receiving from Chökyi Lodrö the many empowerments of the Rinchen Terdzö, the collection of Revealed Treasures (*termas*), Rinpoche told him he wished to spend the rest of his life in solitary meditation. But Khyentse Chökyi Lodrö's answer was, "The time has come for you to teach and transmit to others the countless precious teachings you have received." From then on, Rinpoche worked constantly for the benefit of beings with the tireless energy that is the hallmark of the Khyentse lineage.

During the 1970s and '80s, despite his age, Khyentse Rinpoche travelled all over the Himalayas, India, Southeast Asia, and the West transmitting and explaining the teachings to his many disciples. He was often accompanied by his wife, Sangyum Lhamo, and his grandson and spiritual heir, Rabjam Rinpoche.

Wherever he was, he used to rise well before dawn, praying and meditating for several hours before embarking on an uninterrupted flow of activities until late into the night. He accomplished a tremendous workload with total serenity and apparent effortlessness.

Rinpoche made three visits to Tibet between 1985 and 1990. There, he inaugurated the rebuilding of the original Shechen Monastery, destroyed during the Cultural Revolution, and oversaw the restoration of Samye Monastery, which he consecrated in 1990.

In Nepal, Khyentse Rinpoche transplanted the rich Shechen tradition to a new home—a magnificent monastery in front of the great stupa of Boudhanath. This became his principal seat, housing a large community of monks, led by their abbot Rabjam Rinpoche. It was Khyentse Rinpoche's particular wish that this should be a place where the Buddhist teachings would be continued in their pristine purity, just as they were previously studied and practiced in Tibet, and he invested enormous care in the education of the promising young lamas capable of continuing the tradition.

Other projects dear to him included the building of stupas and monasteries in sacred places, which he said would help promote world peace, further Buddhist values and practice, and help avert conflict, disease, and famine. In India, he built a new stupa at Bodhgaya, the site of Shakyamuni Buddha's enlightenment beneath the Bodhi Tree. Preserving Tibet's extraordinary heritage of Buddhist literature was particularly important to him. After the systematic destruction of books and libraries in Tibet by the Chinese, many works existed in only one or two copies. Thanks to Khyentse Rinpoche's efforts, almost three hundred volumes of texts that might otherwise have been lost forever have been published.

Through his extensive enlightened activity, Khyentse Rinpoche unsparingly devoted his entire life to the preservation and dissemination of the Buddha Dharma. His greatest satisfaction was to see the Dharma actually practiced.

He made a number of teaching visits to the West during the last fifteen years of his life, including two North American tours. At his European seat, Shechen Tennyi Dargyeling in Dordogne, France, where people from all over the world received extensive teaching from him, he guided several groups of students in traditional three-year retreats. It is a measure of his contribution to establishing Tibetan Buddhism in the West that no fewer than five hundred disciples from Europe and North America attended his cremation in Bhutan in 1992.

No factual account of Dilgo Khyentse Rinpoche's life can fully convey who he was. Those who had the immense fortune to spend any time with him knew they were in the presence of an authentic living Buddha, for he completely embodied the teachings he propagated and the great spiritual masters whose lineages he held. Even strangers were profoundly touched by his presence and instinctively sensed his exceptional humanity and spiritual qualities. His whole life was a true continuation of the lineage that had come down to him through Zurchung Sherab Trakpa and Shechen Gyaltsap Rinpoche, and which he passes on to us in this teaching on the *Eighty Chapters of Personal Advice*.

⁕⁕ Zurchungpa's *Eighty Chapters of Personal Advice* ⁕⁕

The *Eighty Chapters* were Zurchungpa's last teaching, the testament he gave to his disciples before passing away. It is hardly surprising, then, that he concerns himself exclusively with practice, and although a few of his instructions assume some basic theoretical knowledge of such topics as the five aggregates, the eight consciousnesses, the ten actions, and so on, the emphasis is on how to put such knowledge into practice. There is little here that has not been written elsewhere, but that is not to say that Zurchungpa's text lacks originality. What is striking about his presentation of the Great Perfection is that while he often appears to repeat himself, he shifts slightly each time, lending contrast and perspective to the teaching and adapting his angle to the particular needs and intellectual capacities of his individual students.

The *Eighty Chapters* are divided into five main sections. The first of these is a short introductory section on faith and devotion, which are essential qualities for anyone who wishes to understand the teachings and put them into practice. This is particularly true in the Mantrayana, where realization depends on being open to the teacher's blessings. The bulk of the text comprises three main sections, each dealing with one of the Three Trainings, which encapsulate the whole of the Buddha's teaching—discipline, concentration, and wisdom. The training in discipline, for Zurchungpa, is not merely a question of observing lists of do's and don'ts. While these things are certainly important, for him the essential point is to create circumstances that will help inner realization to blossom and to avoid those that will hinder such realization. A sincere desire to get out of samsara, a constant awareness of impermanence, and a vigilant mind are more important to him than the wearing of monastic robes. The section on the training in concentration deals not so much with how to concentrate, but rather with how to undistractedly keep in mind the view of the Great Perfection. And the realization of that view is the subject of the section on the training in wisdom. These are exceptionally profound instructions that need to be repeatedly heard from a qualified master. Some readers may find the later chapters difficult to understand, but those who have already received some "mind" teachings will hopefully be able to use these chapters as reminders that help to deepen their practice and understanding. The fifth and final section contains a single chapter summarizing the whole text.

On their own, even the most approachable instructions in the *Eighty Chapters* are not always immediately comprehensible. While it does not require a great deal of imagination to guess why "faith is like a wishing-gem," as we read in the second chapter, Zurchungpa's incitement in the forty-ninth chapter to "always strip naked" and to "commit suicide" calls for some explanation, as does "'slander the *yidam*" in Chapter Twenty. This is why Shechen Gyaltsap Rinpoche intercalated the lines of Zurchungpa's original text with his own notes, usually in the form of a short sentence for each instruction. In some cases he merely inserted a qualifying word or phrase; in others he found it useful to add one or more paragraphs. He also included a structural outline based on the teachings that Jamyang Khyentse Wangpo had given him on this text and on a detailed commentary, which unfortunately we have been unable identify. In our translation of Dilgo Khyentse Rinpoche's commentary, Zurchungpa's root text appears in bold typeface, Shechen Gyaltsap's introduction, notes and structural outline in italics, and Khyentse Rinpoche's commentary in normal typeface. In the earlier sections, these different elements (root text, notes, and commentary) mostly appear separately, though they must be read together; in the later chapters, they are largely intermingled.

⁘ The History of This Teaching ⁘

In the summer of 1986, Dilgo Khyentse Rinpoche made one of his regular visits to the Dordogne in France, during which he gave a series of teachings to the three-year retreatants at Chanteloube, who had just completed the preliminary practices and were starting the "main" practice of the sadhanas and mantra recitations. The teachings he gave therefore included numerous empowerments, along with the oral transmission of a number of important texts, including some by his root teacher, Shechen Gyaltsap Rinpoche. In particular he gave a detailed teaching on the latter's annotated edition of Zurchungpa's *Eighty Chapters of Personal Advice*, which he began by telling us, "While it is very important to receive empowerments to mature one's being, as we are engaged in practice it is also crucial to have the liberating instructions—the explanations on the practice. I will therefore give an explanation of these few pieces of spiritual advice."

We mention the background of this teaching not merely for historical interest but because it is important for readers to understand Khyentse Rinpoche's teaching within the context in which it was given. Zurchungpa's text contains profound instructions that will be difficult to put into practice effectively without first having received the necessary empowerments and blessings from a qualified teacher. Although times have changed and the Dzogchen teachings are given more openly than they were a thousand, or even fifty, years ago, it is certainly no less true that progress in the practice of Dzogchen depends exclusively on the blessings of the lama. Readers who wish to get the most out of Zurchungpa's advice need to use it hand-in-hand with the guidance of their own teacher.

Khyentse Rinpoche's manner of teaching consisted of reading the text—that is, Zurchungpa's root text and Shechen Gyaltsap's notes—interspersed with his own oral commentary. In some of the later chapters especially, he gave little or no commentary and read out the text on its own. Many of these sections consist of so-called pith instructions, seemingly simple phrases used by the enlightened masters of the Great Perfection to convey their profound realization to individual disciples, in quite specific situations. The words they used, often in relatively nontechnical language, were tools used as a support for transmitting ideas that completely transcended the literal meaning of the words themselves. The impact of these oral instructions is naturally lessened when they are confined to the printed page. And they are diluted even further in the process of being translated into English (with the syntactical constraints that translation implies and the possibility of errors in the interpretation of their stylistic peculiarities) by individuals whose spiritual realization could never begin to match that of the original authors.

Khyentse Rinpoche gave this teaching in Tibetan, and it was from recorded tapes that Matthieu Ricard subsequently made an oral translation for the benefit of the Chanteloube retreatants. The recording of this translation was then transcribed. Later the transcription was edited and a fresh translation was made of Shechen Gyaltsap's original text. Two editions were used. One was published by Dilgo Khyentse Rinpoche at Shechen Monastery in Nepal and was the edition he taught from. The other was a photocopy made by Matthieu Ricard of an original woodblock edition brought back in 1989 from Shechen Monastery in Tibet. Both editions contain mistakes, but since the Nepalese edition omits some words and even whole sentences present in the woodblock edition, we have generally taken the latter as the more reliable and have done our best to incorporate the corrections into our translation.

A text of this sort contains much repetition of technical terms such as "absolute nature" and "unborn." For stylistic reasons we have occasionally used synonyms for some of these words. These and other technical terms are briefly explained in the Glossary. A deeper understanding of many of them may be obtained by reading books dealing with the graded path (*lam rim*), in particular Jigme Lingpa's *Treasury of Precious Qualities*, Patrul Rinpoche's *The Words of My Perfect Teacher*, and Gampopa's *Jewel Ornament of Liberation*.

Many of the points that Khyentse Rinpoche mentions in his teaching would have been impossible to index satisfactorily, and we have therefore attempted to summarize them thematically in the Table of Contents. Readers who simply wish to refer to the titles of the eighty chapters will find them listed on pages 385–387.

✦✦ Acknowledgments ✦✦

The Padmakara Translation Group is deeply grateful to the following lamas who patiently gave their time to solving certain difficult points in the printed text: the late Kyabje Dilgo Khyentse Rinpoche, Taklung Tsetrul Pema Wangyal Rinpoche, Jigme Khyentse Rinpoche, Alak Zenkar Rinpoche, Lopon Nyima Dondrup, and Yangchen Chozom. We are especially indebted to Matthieu Ricard, without whose translation of the oral commentary the teaching in this book could never have been published. His translation was transcribed and edited by Stephen Gethin, who also revised the translation of the text with Helena Blankleder. Special thanks are due to Jill Heald, who entered the bulk of the handwritten transcript into a computer; to Jennifer Kane for her suggestions on the earlier chapters; and to Kali Martin and Anne Paniagua, who kindly read through the manuscript and suggested numerous improvements.

Dilgo Khyentse Rinpoche's Commentary

on Shechen Gyaltsap's Annotated Edition
of Zurchung Sherab Trakpa's
Eighty Chapters of Personal Advice

Introduction

AMONG THE MASTERS of the Nyingma tradition there are a number of great lamas that belonged to the Zur family, the most important being the Great Zur, Zurchen Shakya Jungne, and the Little Zur, Zurchung Sherab Trakpa. A third lama of the Zur family is sometimes referred to as the Middle Zur.

This text is a collection of pieces of advice written by Zurchung Sherab Trakpa. My root teacher, Shechen Gyaltsap Rinpoche, received the transmission from Jamyang Khyentse Wangpo, who also explained the text to him. Later, Shechen Gyaltsap wrote this annotated edition, interspersing Zurchung Sherab Trakpa's *Eighty Chapters of Personal Advice* with commentary in the form of notes.

◆◆ The Title ◆◆

"An annotated edition of Zurchung Sherab Trakpa's precious oral instructions on the three trainings, *The Eighty Chapters of Personal Advice*, entitled *A Necklace of Jewels*." The subtitle is: "Pith instructions comprising the essence of the Pitakas in general and of *Epitome, Magic, and Mind* (in particular)." The latter refer to the three main tantras of the inner Mantrayana, namely the *Epitome of Essential Meaning*, the *Net of the Magical Display*, and the Eighteen Tantras of the Mind Section.[3]

A Necklace of Jewels is similar to Gampopa's *Four Themes*, one of the best known teachings of the Kagyu tradition, composed of spiritual advice given according to the stages on the path. I shall explain all I know of it.

The most important thing when one is practicing in retreat is to develop a feeling of disillusionment with samsara so that one can progress on the path, and for this one needs to receive the pith instructions for the path. Here then are these instructions, set out clearly and concisely, for those who have been through the preliminary practice properly and are now doing the main practice.

✦✦ The Text ✦✦

The text begins with homage:

NAMO RATNA GURU BHYA

NAMO means "homage" or "obeisance." RATNA is "jewel" or "rare and supreme."⁴ GURU is "the Teacher." BHYA⁵ indicates the action of paying homage. It therefore means:

I pay homage to the precious Teacher.

The text opens by saying:⁶

Bowing down to the teacher who is Vajrasattva in reality,
I shall thread a Necklace of Jewels,⁷
The Eighty Chapters of Personal Advice
Laid out in detail with a structural outline—
A treasury of gems of the three trainings.

This is a homage to Zurchung Sherab Trakpa, who was someone who had completely renounced wordly affairs and become a fully enlightened siddha. He was in no way different from Vajrasattva, so it is to him that homage is paid.

What do we mean by the three trainings? Whether we practice the sutras or tantras, we cannot avoid going through the trainings of discipline, concentration, and wisdom. As Jamgön Kongtrul Lodrö Thaye himself said when he wrote his vast treatise known as the *Treasury of Knowledge*, everything contained in this encyclopedia is included in the three trainings. The text we are studying now is like a treasury of jewels that condenses the most precious points of the three trainings. It includes many pieces of advice, arranged in eighty chapters. And in the same way that one makes a necklace by threading the jewels one after another, the author is now going to present this text in full.

The Buddha, having considered the various mental capacities
of sentient beings,

As far as the Buddha himself is concerned, only the teachings of the ultimate meaning are necessary: he does not need to teach the expedient meaning. But as far as sentient beings are concerned, different kinds of teaching are necessary to suit their various mental capacities, whether modest, middling, or exceptional. Some beings have very vast minds; they can understand the most profound and vast teachings. Some have less open minds, and others are extremely narrow-minded. There are thus teachings for all levels—the Great Vehicle, the Basic Vehicle, and so forth—that the Buddha has taught according to beings' ability to understand and assimilate them. However elementary or essentialized such teachings may be, their purpose in all cases is to set beings on the path to liberation, and the final destination is the same irrespective of the point of departure.

Take the example of a mother feeding her baby. She starts by giving only milk, which is very easy for the newborn baby to take. If she were to give solid food, the infant would not even be able to swallow it, let alone digest it. But when the child grows a little bigger, it can start having slightly more solid food like the three white foods and the three sweet foods, yogurt, and so on. Then gradually, as it grows bigger, it is able to eat solid food of all kinds.

Similarly, the Buddha has given the teaching in stages covering the whole path of the sutras and tantras. He first gave the teachings for beings on the Shravaka level and the teachings for the Pratyekabuddhas. Then, for those beings who have a vaster mind he gave the Mahayana teachings. That is not to say that there are fundamental differences in the way the Buddha himself taught: his teaching can, rather, be likened to falling rain. When rain falls from the sky, it falls in exactly the same way over the whole land, but what the water becomes when it reaches the ground depends on the kind of container into which it falls. If it falls on a lake with very pure water, the rainwater will remain as it is, very pure and transparent. If it falls into a dirty pit or muddy pool, it will take on the color and appearance of the dirt or mud. In the same way, although the mind of the Buddha always expresses the ultimate truth, depending on the level of the beings receiving his teachings he set forth the absolute truth on a variety of levels, which we term "vehicles." This is why he

taught the various vehicles of the Dharma.

According to the Nyingma tradition there are nine such vehicles—three lesser vehicles, three intermediate ones, and three higher ones. More generally, we speak of three vehicles: that of the Shravakas, that of the Pratyekabuddhas, and that of the Bodhisattvas.

From these Deshek Gyawopa teased out the wool of the sutras and the tantras.

Deshek (*Sugata* in Sanskrit) means "a Buddha." *Gyawopa* means "the man who lives in Gyawo Trak," *Gyawo Trak* being the name of Zurchungpa's mountain retreat. *Deshek Gyawopa* refers to Zurchung Sherab Trakpa, the teacher who is one with the Buddha, and means "the Sugata who dwells in Gyawo." What did he do? He carefully studied all the teachings of the sutras and tantras in the same way that one prepares wool for weaving by teasing it and fluffing it out, removing the bits of grass and other dirt in it.

He churned the milk of the Three Pitakas.

If you churn milk thoroughly for a long time, you get butter; by churning curd you obtain cheese and whey. In the same way, by going over the meaning of the instructions in the Three Pitakas—the Vinaya, Sutras, and Abhidharma—again and again, Deshek Gyawopa extracted the quintessence of the teachings, like butter from milk.

He drank the words of the learned ones like water.

The Dharma was originally introduced to Tibet from the supreme land of India. The great panditas from India were invited to Tibet, and together with the Tibetan translators they translated the scriptures from Sanskrit into Tibetan. According to the teachings of the Ancient Tradition, although the great panditas like the Abbot Shantarakshita and the great translators appeared in human form, they were not in any way ordinary people; they were fully realized beings. Translators like Vairotsana, Chogro Lui Gyaltsen, and Kawa Paltsek were emanations of Ananda and other close disciples of the Buddha who took rebirth in Tibet in order to spread the teachings. Guru Rinpoche himself used to say such-and-such a translator was the reincarnation of such-and-such an Indian pandita. So they were not like ordinary translators, they were not ordinary beings. They had full realization of the whole of the Dharma and their minds became inseparable from Guru Rinpoche's wisdom mind. Thus it was that in the inconceivable, spontaneously accomplished temple of Samye, at the request of King Trisong Detsen, who turned all his wealth into gold and offered full measures of gold each time he requested the teaching, the great panditas headed by Guru Rinpoche and Vimalamitra, and the great translators headed by Vairotsana, translated the scriptures from Sanskrit into Tibetan. Through Guru Rinpoche's blessings, the works translated included not only well known texts from India but also hitherto unknown teachings that had been kept as treasures by the dakinis. This is a special feature of the Nyingma tradition.

At a later period, the translator Ngok Loden Sherab[8] travelled to India, where he worked on a translation of the *Ornament of the Sutras*. In this he came across a passage where the word "to be attached" occurs three times together. Wondering how he could translate the same word three times, he consulted Vairotsana's old translation and found that Vairotsana had translated it as referring to the three tenses, past, present, and future,[9] with the sense of "hesitation."[10] The passage actually meant "there is no hesitation in the past, present, or future." When he saw this, Loden Sherab became fully confident that the ancient translators were true Buddhas and praised them, saying,

> Vairotsana is like the sky,
> Ka and Chog are like the sun and moon,
> Rinchen Zangpo is like the morning star,
> And I myself am like a firefly.

He explained this as follows. Vairotsana's knowledge and wisdom are so vast that he is like the sky. Kawa Paltsek and Chogro Lui Gyaltsen are like the sun and the moon. Rinchen Zangpo,[11] who is without peer among all the translators of the New Translation tradition, is like the morning star, meaning Venus, which shines very brightly at dawn. And he himself, he said, had been given the title *lotsawa*,[12] but counted for no more than one of the fireflies one sees on a summer night.

Nowadays we can go to India very quickly and easily, but in the days of the great translators it was much more difficult. They had to travel on foot, carrying all their belongings on their backs and enduring the heat and numerous dangers on the way. Once they had arrived in India, in order to study with the panditas translators had to obtain permission from the local kings, who in those days were very jealous and unwilling to let others study the precious teachings, employing guards to prevent these teachings from being taken away to Tibet.

Vairotsana, for instance, went to India for the first time at the age of thirteen, and we can read in his life story of the immense difficulties and hardships he had to go through to receive the teachings. The translators visited not only Bodhgaya but also all the great universities and seats of learning like Vikramashila and Nalanda, where there might have been five hundred or a thousand panditas. Very few of these panditas, however, were panditas of the Mahayana, and of these even more rare were panditas versed in the Secret Mantrayana. Moreover it was by no means easy for the translators to make inquiries in the local language to find out which panditas might be holders of the secret pith instructions. It was only through his own clairvoyance and the blessing and predictions of protectors such as Ekajati that Vairotsana was able to know which teachings to look for and find the panditas who held them. The translators of the New Translations also had to endure great hardships in order to receive the teachings, as we can see in the life story of the great translator Marpa, who travelled three times to India and four times to Nepal, each time carrying everything on his back.

He savored the realization and experience of former masters like salt.

Just as adding salt to food improves its taste, Zurchung Sherab Trakpa savored the pith instructions of the previous lineage masters, their profound wisdom and understanding, their experience and realization; and his hearing, reflecting, and meditating on the teachings was like adding salt to the teachings themselves.

Looking at appearances as in a mirror,

—meaning that he looked at the appearances of samsara and nirvana as if looking at reflections in a mirror, beautiful or ugly—

he saw that whatever one does there is nothing but suffering.

In the three worlds of samsara, whatever one does with one's body, speech, and mind, it is only the cause of suffering. This means that any samsaric action[13] is the cause of suffering. At present we can eat good food, wear nice clothes, and have a comfortable place to stay, and we feel this is quite a happy situation. But to obtain that, we have in fact done nothing but accumulate negative actions, which are the cause of future suffering. From the moment we are born from our mother's womb, we cannot but set off in the direction of death. Then, when we finally meet with death, even if we are very powerful, we cannot influence death; however rich we are, we cannot bribe death; however beautiful we are, we cannot seduce it.

Look at the ordinary activities of beings in samsara: they are involved in protecting those who are dear to them, in getting the better of those who are not dear to them, in ploughing fields and conducting business and trade. If you examine all these actions, they are all linked with negativity. There is hardly anything in them that is virtuous. Acting only in this negative way is like eating food mixed with poison: it may taste delicious at the time, but it will have deadly consequences.

Therefore,

He saw that the concerns of this world are to be given up.

He saw that it is better to completely give up all one's endless plans and projects that involve thinking, "If I do this or that, in the future I will be able to enjoy good food, have good clothes, and be in such-and-such a pleasurable situation."

He saw that besides accomplishing something meaningful for future lives, nothing is of any use.

Why? Because there is not a single being born who will not die. And there is not a single being who dies and does not take another rebirth. When we leave this life, however rich we are, we cannot take even a handful of food. Though we may have many fine clothes, we cannot take a single thread of them. Even this body, which we have cherished so much, we will have to leave behind as a corpse. What we cannot avoid taking is the burden of our positive and negative actions. After we have crossed the threshold of death with this burden, the place in which we will find ourselves will not be somewhere pleasant and agreeable where we can feel comfortable and relaxed. It will be like coming to a huge plain, a place of complete desolation in which we do not know where we are or where we can go. We will be like a small child that is too young to walk, abandoned in the middle of a vast plain, where it will either die or be eaten by wild animals. Each and every one of us will end up in this situation, with this fear. But we remain blind to it. We cannot see it coming. We cannot see beyond this present life and spend our time complaining about our house, our food, and our possessions. We think that keeping our friends and getting rid of our enemies is the most important thing. But actually it only brings us harm. That is why the text continues,

He saw that status and fame have to be thrown away like spit and snot.

Some individuals become very famous, and people say of them, "They are very learned, they are very powerful, they are very clever." But when death comes, it will be of no use to them. They will be obliged to give up all their fame and wealth, discarding it like snot without being able to ask themselves, "Should I keep it or should I throw it away?"

> *He saw the need to rid himself of retinue and bustle—for it is hard to make everyone happy—and to meditate alone.*

In ordinary life we are always having to concern ourselves with other people. If we have a family, wife, husband, and children, we are concerned with what will happen to them; we have to do everything to protect them, to ensure that they prosper. This involves endless activity, and in the process our entire human life runs its course. We never ask ourselves whether all this will be truly useful or whether it will do us harm in the future. We should now see that these things are, in fact, a disturbance, and just as we would wish to get rid of an enemy, we should want to get rid of these distracting conditions. If someone were to be hostile to our children or other members of our family, for example, we would think only of how to get rid of him, and even imagine using violence or killing him. But in truth there is no way one can subdue all one's enemies, and there is no end to the number of enemies one can have. The only way is to completely give up all these worldly concerns. One needs to go to a secluded place, a lonely mountain retreat, and turning one's thoughts inward, to work hard at putting the teachings into practice.

Deshek Gyawopa saw this, and he therefore went to the place known as Trak Gyawo, as we can read in the account of his life in the *History of the Nyingma School.*[14]

> *At Trak Gyawo he practiced intensively*[15]

throughout his life, just as Milarepa did. As a result of his practice, he achieved realization for himself and for others, and opened the way for spreading the teachings of the Ancient Tradition, expressing his full realization in the form of spontaneous spiritual advice for beings of the future:

> *He himself made a living experience of these* Eighty Chapters of Personal Advice *on how to practice the whole of the Dharma.*

These are oral instructions that essentialize all the Buddha's own words and the commentaries on them, which are extremely vast and difficult to understand. They are presented in a way that is easy to assimilate, like food that a child can digest, and are given directly into our hands, in the form of eighty pieces of advice. They are not empty utterances, but instructions that he himself followed. As he said, the reason he was able to get out of samsara, the ocean of suffering, and attain the level of Vidyadhara, taking a place on the seat of enlightenment, was that he practiced instructions like these.

For those who fear birth and death, this is a practice for today.

There are two great sources of fear in samsara, the moment of birth and the moment of death. The suffering and fear experienced at these two times have to be faced completely alone; there is no one who can really help us. The only thing that can help alleviate those sufferings is the practice of the supreme Dharma. Nothing else can do so. But we do not know how to practice it: we have only become clever at doing worldly things. From an early age we have learned how to make things comfortable for ourselves and how to avoid being uncomfortable. This sort of attitude has resulted in a high degree of material achievement. We can fly through the sky in airplanes, and so on, and we have made life very easy from the material point of view. But actually we are just like children running after a rainbow. These things do not really help us. We need to turn our minds toward the Dharma by reflecting on these sufferings of birth and death. By doing so, we enter the path, going first through the preliminaries, and then proceeding to the main practice. As we practice, we will gradually get a true taste of what it means to become disillusioned with worldly affairs and to progress on the path. This is something that will come with experience. But we must not postpone it, thinking, "I will do this practice next month or next year . . . ." If we have received a teaching today, it is today that we should start putting it into practice, for it is only from the moment we actually plant a seed that it will start to sprout.

He gave this as a spontaneous teaching, out of love, as direct heartfelt advice.

Deshek Gyawopa spoke these words for the sake of the many beings who would come in the future, so that if they were to hear this teaching and reflect and meditate on it, it might be of some help to them.

Parents who love their children give them all sorts of helpful advice, telling them what is right and what is wrong: "If you do this, you will get into trouble; if you do that, it will help you," or "If you associate with that sort of person, he will help you, but be careful not to go around with that other person as he will trick you." The same is true for this extraordinary instruction by Deshek Gyawopa, which will aid us both in this life and in the next. If we fail to follow this advice, we will get into trouble and be harmed both in this life and in subsequent ones.

He gives this advice as if he were opening his heart, expressing his deepest, innermost thoughts for our benefit. It is like a final testament given to one's children as one is dying. Afterwards the children will think, "These were my parents' last words," and they will have all the more respect for what those words mean. Similarly, if we practice in accordance with the meaning of this, his final testament, it will greatly help us in the future. The way to do so is gradually, day after day, to reflect and meditate one by one on each of the pieces of advice in this series he has given us. Then they will be like flowers, which emerge as shoots in spring and grow day after day, finally coming into full bloom in summer.

> There are five topics. As we find in the scriptures:
> Having cultivated firm devotion,
> In the field of pure discipline
> Sow the seed of concentration,
> And see the harvest of wisdom ripen.

If we wish to practice the Dharma authentically but we do not have faith, however much we listen, reflect, and meditate, it will not bear fruit. Our practice will be without light, like the world before dawn when there is no sun.

We also need to use the field of pure discipline. To practice the Dharma, it is essential to have the solid foundation of the Pratimoksha, Bodhisattva, and Secret Mantrayana vows. Without these it is impossible to practice the Dharma, just as it is impossible to build a big house without having firm ground to build on.

Once we have this well-prepared field, we can plant in it the seeds of concentration from which experiences and realization will grow. We also have to take care of the field properly, to till the earth, spread manure, and water it; and the sun must shine on the field to warm it.

If all these conditions are brought together properly, then the crop of wisdom will grow without difficulty. And just as a good harvest brings wealth, with these three trainings, the trainings of discipline, concentration, and wisdom, it is certain we will attain liberation.

Accordingly, there are the instructions on faith, the gateway.

When you want to enter a house, you go in through the door, not through the window. In the same way, faith is the door through which we should go in order to set out on the path of the Dharma. Then there are

The instructions on discipline, the basis,

which shows the need for firm discipline in the practice. Discipline alone is not sufficient. We need to sow the seeds of concentration, so there follow

The instructions on concentration, the means,

which includes meditation on sustained calm and profound insight. These again have to be reinforced or permeated with wisdom:

The instructions on wisdom, the essence.

Wisdom is the essence of both discipline and concentration. Without it the path will not work in leading us to omniscience, that is, enlightenment. The fifth section is

To conclude, a summary of the above.

This is the basic structure of Zurchungpa's *Eighty Chapters of Personal Advice.*

I. Faith

THE FIRST SECTION, on faith, *has five chapters.*

$$\bullet\bullet\ 1\ \bullet\bullet$$

Showing the importance of faith as a prerequisite—

without faith there is no way one can even begin to practice the Dharma—

and the fault in not having faith,

for without faith one is not a suitable vessel for the teachings.

Son, since it is a prerequisite for the whole of the Dharma, it is important to recognize the fault in not having faith and the virtues of having it.

Here "Dharma" means "that which will lead us to liberation from samsara and to ultimate omniscience and enlightenment." The word "Dharma" derives from a root that means "to correct." Just as when one makes a statue out of clay, first sculpting a rough form and then carefully correcting all the small defects to make a perfect representation, when we practice the Dharma, it corrects all our imperfections and brings all our good qualities to perfection.

Another meaning of Dharma is "to hold," or "to catch." For instance, when a fish is hooked, it cannot but be taken out of the sea and end up on dry land. Once one has entered the door of the Dharma and been "hooked" by the Dharma, even if one does not practice very much, the blessing of the Dharma is such that one can only be benefited and drawn toward liberation. Of the many different kinds of activity, the Dharma, which is the activity aspect of the enlightened Buddha, is the most important. And when we take refuge in the Buddha, Dharma, and Sangha, the ultimate refuge is, in fact, the Dharma.

The Dharma has two aspects, transmission and realization—the teachings in the scriptures of the Tripitaka, which we can study, reflect upon, and practice; and the experiences and realization that grow out of such practice. These two aspects include all the Three Jewels. The Buddha is the one who expounds the Dharma; the Sangha comprises the companions on the path who accompany us in practicing the Dharma. Of all the different meanings of the word "dharma,"[16] the most important is this Jewel of the Dharma, the vast and profound teaching of the Buddha.

One might wonder whether the scriptures are the Jewel of the Dharma. They are not the ultimate realization,[17] but they are nevertheless the Jewel of the Dharma. This is because they are the support for that realization. Just as, on the physical plane, a statue or other image of our Teacher[18] inspires devotion when we look at it, and through generating devotion we receive blessings and can progress along the path, similarly the scriptural Dharma sustains our realization. This is why, when Lord Buddha passed into Nirvana, he said that the Dharma would be his representative. Through studying the Dharma one can know what the Buddha himself is like and what the teaching is like; one can know the path to enlightenment. The Dharma is thus a likeness of the dharmakaya; it is the dharmakaya made visible.

In order for us to practice the Dharma, faith must come first. We need to know what are the drawbacks of not having faith and what are the qualities and benefits that come from having it. Faith, disillusionment with the world, and the desire to get out of samsara are not things that everyone has naturally, from the beginning. But they can be developed, for every sentient being has the tathagatagarbha, the buddha nature, within himself or herself. The presence of the buddha nature naturally helps all good qualities to grow, just as the presence of the sun in the sky naturally dispels darkness over the earth. It is this tathagatagarbha that is pointed out through the instructions of Mahamudra and the Great Perfection, and because of this buddha nature that we have within us, it is quite easy for faith, determination to be free, and so forth to arise on their own within our minds. To help these qualities grow in us, we need to receive teachings from our teacher, to follow him, and to reflect on the enlightened qualities we can see in him. As we do so, we will naturally understand the drawbacks of not having faith.

Now we may talk about faith, but unless we know what we mean by faith, it will merely be an empty word.

The essence of faith is to make one's being and the perfect Dharma inseparable.

When the Dharma and one's being have truly mingled, then there is perfect faith. Faith also implies aspiration, a sense of longing. When we long to become very rich, for example, we do everything necessary, undergo great hardship, and expend a lot of energy to achieve this goal. The same is true for wishing to become famous or to achieve any other worldly goal: if our aspiration and determination are strong enough, we will manage to achieve what we want. This is a very powerful quality. Similarly, with faith there is a strong motivation and wish to achieve something, and a natural understanding of the drawbacks of not having this sort of aspiration. When faith has become truly blended with one's mind and become part of it, then one's Dharma practice naturally becomes genuine and pure. This is what is meant by the "perfect Dharma."[19] This clear aspiration to practice the Dharma is what we call faith.

The etymology of the word "faith" is: the aspiration to achieve one's goal.

When we hear about all the qualities of the past Buddhas, the lives of the great teachers, and the realization they achieved, we may aspire to achieve such qualities ourselves and to set out on the path. This longing is what we call yearning faith. We may, for instance, think that the Dharma is something valuable and therefore start to learn Tibetan. As we gradually begin to understand the language, our longing to understand the teachings will grow more and more. This is the fruit of our aspiration. If we were to distinguish different kinds of faith,

The categories of faith are three: vivid faith, yearning faith, and confident faith.

The first of these, vivid faith, is the natural interest and vivid joy we feel when we hear about the lives of Guru Rinpoche and the great siddhas, and the miracles they performed.

Yearning faith is the longing and hope we have when we then think, "If I practice the teachings, then in this life or at least in a future life I myself will achieve the level of Guru Rinpoche and the siddhas." We may also experience yearning faith when we hear of the qualities of Buddhafields such as the Pure Land of Bliss and aspire to be reborn there.

Confident faith is the confidence that gradually builds up when we have both vivid and yearning faith and we think, "If I practice these teachings, there is no doubt that I will be able to attain Buddhahood myself." It is the certainty that as in the past beings were able to gain realization through the Dharma, so it will be in the future. It is confidence in the truth of the teachings. It is confidence in death—in its fearfulness, imminence, and unpredictability—and in all the other aspects of the teachings.

There are six faults that come from not having faith.

If we do not have faith, we will not be suitable vessels for the teachings.

Without faith one is like a rock at the bottom of the ocean—

the Dharma will not benefit one's being.

A rock on the bottom of the sea may remain there for thousands of years but it never gets any softer. It stays as hard as ever. Similarly, if we do not have faith, the Dharma will never penetrate our being and benefit us.

One is like a boat without a boatman.

If the ferryman or boatman is absent, there is no way one will be able to cross a big river or lake. In the same way, without faith

one will not be able to cross to the other side of samsara.

One is like a blind person who goes into a temple—

he is unable to see the precious relics and sacred objects, such as statues, that represent the Buddha's body, speech, and mind; and since he cannot see them he cannot give rise to faith, respect, and devotion.

Similarly, if one has no faith,

one will be unable to understand the words and their significance.[20]

One is like a burnt seed—

the sprout of enlightenment—devotion, diligence, and compassion—*will not grow.*

Without faith

One is like a sheep stuck in a pen

or like a sheep that has fallen into a steep-walled pit with no way to climb out:

there is no liberation from suffering in the ocean of samsara.

One is like a maimed person who has landed on an island of gold.

Someone with no hands, even if he lands on an island filled with gold and precious jewels, is unable to bring anything back with him. Similarly, although in this life one may have obtained a precious human existence, met a spiritual teacher, and entered through the gateway of the Dharma, if one has no faith, one will not be able to reap any of the achievements or qualities of the path:

one will return empty-handed at the end of this precious human life—

the freedoms and advantages will have been squandered.

◆◆ 2 ◆◆

The virtues of faith.

Son, there are six virtues of faith.

Faith is like a very fertile field.

When a fertile field has been well ploughed and tilled, each grain the farmer sows, whether wheat, rice, or any other kind, will yield thousands more grains, and the farmer will become very prosperous. In the same way,

the whole crop of virtue will grow.

When one has faith, one will naturally feel a great longing to practice the Dharma, and through this one will be able to achieve all good qualities. As the Buddha said, faith is like a jewel or treasure. It is the root of all other trainings and practices.

Faith is like a wishing-gem—

it fulfills all one's own and others' desires.

Someone who finds a wishing-gem and places it on top of a victory banner will have all his wishes and prayers fulfilled. All the clothes, wealth, food, and valuable things he could want will be effortlessly provided, not only for him but for everyone else in the region who prays and makes wishes before that wishing-gem. Similarly, if we have faith, everything we desire to achieve in our Dharma practice, such as being able to listen to the teachings, to reflect on them, and to meditate on them, will be effortlessly granted, along with all the good qualities that arise from these.

Faith is like a king who enforces the law.

He makes himself and others happy.

As a result of faith, we naturally recognize that all happiness comes from observing the law of cause and effect, from acknowledging that negative actions lead to suffering and that positive actions lead to happiness. We develop mindfulness and vigilance, distinguishing between what is to be avoided and what is to be adopted, and we then become suitable vessels for the qualities of the Dharma. When a king enforces the laws he has decreed, there is peace throughout the kingdom and there are no quarrels, feuds, or bandits. Similarly, when we have faith, not only are we happy, we are able to make others happy too. The spiritual qualities that we gain from having faith will be perceived and shared by the people around us. And like a medicinal tree that heals anyone who touches it, our own faith will inspire others to endeavor in the Dharma and to seek liberation.

Faith is like someone who holds the stronghold of carefulness.

He will not be stained by defects and he will gather qualities.

A temple or mansion that is built on the solid rock of a mountain is extremely safe and invulnerable to attack from hostile forces. Inside it feels very secure and one can collect within it all sorts of valuable things. Similarly, if we have faith, we will gradually be able to gather and store safely the whole treasury of precious qualities of the Dharma, such as those of listening, reflecting, and meditating. Sakya Pandita said that if one studies one verse a day, one can gradually become very learned, like a bee gathering honey. Even though a bee has a tiny mouth, by collecting the nectar it is slowly able to amass a large quantity of honey. Likewise, by studying gradually with the mouth of faith we will be able to gather the qualities of the Dharma—disillusionment with the world and diligence directed toward liberation.

Faith is like a boat on a great river.

It will deliver one from the suffering of birth, old age, sickness, and death.

With a boat one can cross even a very wide river. One has little difficulty in safely carrying oneself across and transporting all sorts of goods and valuables. In the same way, if we have faith, we can recognize the defects of our condition in samsara, where we are afflicted by the sufferings of birth, old age, sickness, and death. Moreover, we gradually recognize that the only remedy for this is the Dharma, and through practicing the Dharma we are able to free ourselves from these four root sufferings of samsara.

When Buddha Shakyamuni's disciples encountered problems, the Buddha used to explain how these difficulties had come about through actions they had committed in their past lives. By this means, his disciples naturally began to understand the workings of the law of cause and effect and the fact that nothing in samsara is beyond suffering. As a result, they rapidly attained the level of Arhat. Faith has the power to dispel any of these four main sufferings. To illustrate how it dispels the suffering of old age, there is a story from ancient India about an old man of ninety years who requested ordination from Lilavajra. Lilavajra told him that since he was so old and did not even know how to read or write, it was too late for him to take ordination and to begin the path of Dharma in the usual way. But there was a special practice he could do, and he gave him the empowerment and instructions on the sadhana of White Mañjushri. Because the old man had great faith and possessed the appropriate karma, within seven days he had a vision of White Mañjushri and attained the accomplishment of immortal life. It is said that to this day he dwells in Payul Phakpachen. So through faith one can even overcome the suffering of old age. One can equally alleviate the suffering of sickness. By meditating on the Medicine Buddha and reciting his dharani, one can purify the negative actions that are the cause of one's illness and thus be cured of disease.

Faith is like an escort in a dangerous place.

It will free us from the fears of samsara and its lower realms.

Through faith we acquire confidence in the Dharma. We acknowledge the defects of samsara and we realize that the cause of our suffering in samsara is our past negative actions, which in turn arise from afflictive emotions. This leads us to exert ourselves in practicing the Dharma, and as a result we are naturally freed from the lower realms. This is why it is very important to repeatedly generate faith in our minds.

++ 3 ++

The causes that nurture faith and its qualities.

Having recognized the fault in not having faith and the advantages of having it, we now have to see how to develop faith and make it grow. Faith is not something that beginners naturally have right from the start. It has to be developed through different causes and conditions.

Son, there are ten causes that give rise to faith.

You need to know that there is no happiness in your present way of life and circle of friends.

In all our previous lives until now we have constantly wandered in samsara. With our body, speech, and mind we have accumulated all sorts of negative actions. We have always clung to those dear to us and hated those we have perceived as enemies. We have been completely distracted by the eight ordinary concerns.

It is important to realize that all this has been pointless. As a result of it all, we find ourselves in our present condition: though we want to be happy, all we manage to achieve is suffering. However affectionate and well-intentioned our parents, relatives, and friends may be, if we listen to what they say, there is no way we will be led to practice the Dharma. They themselves have been caught in samsara for such a long time that the only advice they can give us is how to get the better of our enemies, how to plough the fields and grow crops, and how to get rich by doing business. They are friends leading us in quite the wrong direction. There is a saying:

> Don't ask your father's opinion,
> Don't discuss things with your mother,
> Tie your own nose rope around your head,
> Use the Dharma to get your head into the sun.[21]

The same is true of relationships with others: they are devoid of any happiness. This does not mean we suddenly have to regard all our friends as enemies. It is simply that we need to stop alternating between hatred for so-called enemies and excessive attachment to our friends. We should be free from attachment and hatred. We should feel only loving-kindness and compassion for those whom we perceive as enemies, and in the best case we should be able to introduce both friends and those who were formerly our enemies to the Dharma. Bear in mind that introducing beings to the Dharma is a way of repaying their kindness. It is said that even if one were to carry one's parents on one's shoulders all the way round the earth, one would still not be able to repay their kindness. So the best way to repay the kindness of beings, who have all been our parents, is to introduce them to the Dharma. To repay his mother's kindness, Buddha Shakyamuni went to the Heaven of the Thirty-three, where she had been reborn, and stayed there for the duration of the summer retreat,[22] expounding the Dharma. The teachings he gave there are recorded in the Kangyur in the *Sutra in Repayment of Kindness.*[23]

Where Shechen Gyaltsap's note says

> *Ultimately these are the cause of suffering,*

he means that if we follow worldly ways, we may become quite successful, we may be rich and influential or have the command of a large army, but in order to achieve that we will have committed exclusively negative actions involving deceit, lies, and malice. These are the very cause of suffering, and it is for this reason that Lord Buddha and his followers left home and became renunciants. They lived in secluded hermitages and devoted their lives to practicing the Dharma, living on food given to them as alms and free from the negativity that comes from all the things one normally does to earn a living.

You need to have confidence in the law of cause and effect,

> *for it can never ever fail.*

The root of faith is confidence in the law of cause and effect. We should never think that small positive actions have no effect. Just as by collecting drops of water one can gradually fill a huge vessel, by reciting the six-syllable mantra a thousand times every day, for example, you will gradually accumulate a large number of recitations and acquire the excellent qualities associated with the mantra. On the other hand, never think there is no harm in doing a negative action, even a very small one. Even a tiny spark can burn a haystack as big as a mountain. Nor should we underestimate the power of a tiny negative thought. We might think, "I have not harmed anyone physically, I haven't spoken harshly. This is just a little thought; it is not that serious. It is not as if I had killed someone. And anyway, I can purify it through confession." But as it is said, a thought of anger arising in the mind of a Bodhisattva for even a sixtieth of the time it takes to snap one's fingers is enough to make that Bodhisattva fall into the Hell of Ultimate Torment as many times as there are such instants of anger. We have to be constantly vigilant, watching what the mind is doing, looking to see whether our virtuous thoughts have increased, whether we can cultivate them further, and whether we need to apply the right antidote. We must be continuously aware of our good and bad thoughts, like children at school who are marked up or down depending on whether they have given the right or wrong answer.

There was once a brahmin in India called Ravi. In order to train his mind in virtue he made two piles of pebbles, one with white pebbles and one with black. Each time he had a bad thought or did something wrong he would put a black pebble aside. And each time he had a pure, virtuous thought he would put a white pebble aside. At the end of the day he counted these white and black pebbles. In the beginning he found he had almost only black ones, but by being mindful and applying the proper antidotes day after day, he reached a stage where half the pebbles were black and half were white. Gradually there came a day when he could hardly find any black pebbles; he had had only pure thoughts and actions during the day. This is how we can change our minds: because thoughts are compounded and conditioned, they can be changed. Thus even someone like a butcher can suddenly become deeply disillusioned with suffering, with samsara, and giving up all negative actions, enter the path of liberation and ultimately achieve enlightenment.

Then there is the story of the hunter Kyirawa Gonpo Dorje. In the beginning he was such a fanatical hunter that he would kill any animal within sight. Until he met Milarepa, his arrow never missed a single animal that caught his eye. Then he met Milarepa and felt tremendous devotion to him. He gave up everything and in a single lifetime was able to go to a pure realm.[24] Understanding the law of cause and effect is thus very important. It is what the Buddha Shakyamuni taught when he first turned the Wheel of Dharma. He showed that suffering and the cause of suffering are what have to be discarded and that the path and the fruit of the path are what have to be achieved. To develop faith it is necessary to have confidence in the law of cause and effect. If we do so, our faith will necessarily lead to a result.

In ancient India there was a very learned Tirthika philosopher called Durdharsakala, whose knowledge of the ten branches of science was unrivalled. "No one in India is as learned as I am," he thought to himself, and he set out for the monastic university of Nalanda, where there were five hundred Buddhist panditas. So learned was he that when he engaged these Buddhist panditas in debate, he defeated most of them. He was on the point of defeating them all when the great pandita Aryadeva appeared and, sitting on a rock, took on Durdharsakala. In the debate that ensued, Durdharsakala was defeated. His punishment, as decreed by the local king, was to have both his hands cut off, and he was left to sit at the gates of Nalanda with a novice monk to feed him. From where he was sitting he could hear the Nalanda panditas reciting the Tripitaka. One day, as he listened, he realized that the passage being recited clearly concerned himself, for it was a prediction by the Buddha about a certain Tirthika sage who would come to Nalanda, be defeated in debate, and finally gain faith in the Dharma, becoming an active proponent of the teachings. He suddenly felt tremendous confidence in the truth of the Buddha's teachings. Asking the young novice attending him to bring him the volume of the Tripitaka and place it on his head, he made the following prayer: "If this prediction is true, then by the power of that truth may my hands be restored and may I be diligent in spreading and benefiting the Dharma. If it is not true, may I die here, right now." Through the blessings of the Buddha—for the prediction was true—as he uttered these words, he found his hands restored. Not only did he enter the path of the Buddhadharma, but he also went on to become famed as Lopön Pawo, one of the four most illustrious masters in the history of Indian Buddhism.[25] This story also appears in a work by Patrul Rinpoche on the benefits of reading the Mahayana sutras, which contains numerous examples showing clearly and simply how the law of cause and effect functions.

When we gain this sort of confidence in cause and effect, we will find it impossible to indulge in negative actions and quite natural to perform positive ones. Like a sick patient, once we are sure that a medicine is making us better, we will not hesitate to take it, however sour or bitter it may be.

You need to remember death and impermanence.

There is no certainty when you will die.

Although one has this precious human body, it is utterly impermanent. There is no doubt we will lose it to death and resume wandering in samsara. For in samsara, all that is born will die, all that is gathered will be exhausted, all that comes together will be separated, and all that is high will fall down.

Yet the time of death is quite uncertain. Moreover, the circumstances that might bring death are unpredictable. When we consider how many of the people we have met in our life are already dead, or seriously sick or suffering, we can see clearly how impermanence works. This sort of reflection on death will induce us to go to a lonely place and devote our lives to spiritual practice. It is why Jetsun Milarepa himself went to a deserted place and spent his whole life in ascetic practice—because he was constantly aware of the suffering and imminence of death.

You need to remember that you will depart without your retinue or wealth.

When you die, you have to leave them all behind, so they are no use to you.

There was once a universal monarch named King Mandhata. As a universal monarch he had all the seven attributes of royalty and travelled through the sky on a cloud, preceded by the golden wheel, which gave him dominion over everywhere he went. King Mandhata ruled the four continents as well as the abodes of the Four Great Kings. He became so powerful that he ascended to the Heaven of the Thirty-three and shared the throne with Indra. But then it occurred to him that it would be nice if he could sit on that throne alone. As a result of this negative thought, he fell back to the lowest states of existence and became a common beggar with nothing at all. Just like him, however much wealth we may accumulate, there will be nothing we can take with us at death. Even if our fame spreads far and wide like the roar of a thousand dragons, it will not follow us through death, nor will it help us at all at the moment of death, however flattering it is now. Even if we become as rich as Vaishravana, we will not be able to take any of our wealth with us at the time of death. We will not even be able to take our own body with us. All these things we will have to leave behind. We will be taken out of the midst of all our wealth, fame, and power like a hair plucked out of a block of butter: it comes out alone without a single particle of butter sticking to it. This is true not only for ordinary beings and for universal monarchs like King Mandhata, but even for enlightened beings like the Buddha. He could fly through the sky accompanied by his whole following of Arhats, Shravakas, and Pratyekabuddhas, but now he has departed from this ordinary world, and apart from the account of his life and enlightenment there is nothing to be seen of him. Nor can we say to ourselves, "I'm not worried: when I die, I will go to a Buddhafield," because this is not something that we can just predict or decide.

You need to bear in mind that you are powerless to choose your next rebirth.

There is no knowing where the force of your actions will take you.

Unless we have accumulated positive actions, there is no way we can go to the higher realms. And if we have committed negative actions, however powerful we may be, there will be no escaping their influence when we die. Like the body and its shadow, we can never separate from the result of our actions. The imprints of our positive and negative actions are like a huge burden on the shoulders of the consciousness, and as we enter the intermediate state this is the only thing that will not get left behind—it is certain to follow us. If we have spoken a single harsh word to someone, it will be there on our consciousness. If we have felt devotion for a single instant, it will be there on our consciousness. So if we have performed vast positive actions, we will be reborn in a Buddhafield, where we can meet the Buddha in person and receive teachings; or at the very least we will be reborn in the higher realms of samsara among gods or humans. But if negative actions predominate, then whether we like it or not, we will be thrown like a stone into the lower realms.

The point is that we are blind to the existence of future lives. We spend most of our time endeavoring to become rich, attempting to get rid of anyone who prevents us achieving our worldly ambitions, and trying to look after those dear to us. And when we succeed in these, we are really proud of ourselves and think, "What a clever person I am." But this will not help at all. We tend to think we are safe in our fortress, but this is not the case. We will have to go where our actions take us, and there is no certainty where we will be reborn. We are unaware that it all depends on our actions.

You need to remember how hard it is to obtain a fully endowed human body such as this.

It is difficult to bring together the freedoms and advantages and their multiple causes.

At present we have this human body, we have met a spiritual teacher, we have crossed the threshold of the Dharma, and we have received the teacher's instructions. So we have in our hands all the conditions that make it possible to achieve Buddhahood within a single lifetime. Truly this human existence is like a golden vessel. But if we do not put it to proper use, death could snatch it out of our hands at any moment, and who knows if in our next life we will meet the Buddha's teachings? Even if we happen to come into contact with the Buddhadharma in our next life, who knows whether we will be interested in it or whether we will be able to meet a spiritual friend? So it is now, when all the right conditions have come together, that we should make use of our human body. When people who are very sick manage to find a doctor—one, moreover, who has the right medicine—they do everything they can to continue receiving treatment, however difficult it may be for them. We are in the same situation. We have met the doctor, who is the spiritual teacher, and have received the medicine, his nectarlike instructions. We now have everything we need to practice. Rather than throwing away such an opportunity, we must make full use of it. Then, if we have practiced perfectly during our lives, the moment of death will consist of nothing other than recognizing the clear light of dharmakaya. If our practice has been of middling quality, we can confidently expect to be reborn in a Buddhafield, where we will be able to continue on the path. Failing that, we should at least have the confidence to be able to say to ourselves, "I have done this much practice, so I will certainly not be reborn in the lower realms."

It is not enough to simply have been born a human—this is not what is meant by a precious human life. There are billions of beings in this world who have a human body, but theirs is not the precious human body. What we call the precious human body is one endowed with the five individual advantages and the five circumstantial advantages. Beings without these are like people who have no eyes, nose, or tongue with which to see, hear, or taste. They have a useless human life.

In spring the farmers work late into the night ploughing the fields, sowing seed, and tilling the soil, because it is the right moment, and if they miss it, they will not get a crop. For us too it is the right moment: we have these eight freedoms and ten advantages and we have met a spiritual teacher. We have gathered all the right conditions, so rather than falling prey to indolence and laziness we must seize this opportunity to practice the Dharma.

You need to bear in mind that the whole of samsara is suffering,

It is never anything other than the three kinds of suffering.

Why should we want to get out of samsara? Because when we examine samsara, we can see that nothing in any of the six realms is beyond suffering. Beings in the hells suffer from heat and cold; those in the preta realms from hunger and thirst; and animals suffer from being enslaved, from stupidity, and from being eaten by others. Human beings suffer from birth, old age, sickness, and death, from meeting enemies, from separating from loved ones, from encountering what they do not want, and from not getting what they do want. The asuras suffer from jealousy and from fighting with the gods. And the gods suffer from losing the perfect conditions they have enjoyed for so long. So there is not one of these six realms that transcends suffering. We in samsara should feel like a prisoner who has been thrown into jail and whose only thought with every passing hour is "When can I get out? Will I be set free tonight? Tomorrow morning?" Once we realize the extent of the suffering in samsara, our only thought will be, "How can I find a way to get out of samsara? When can I manage to free myself? What is the quickest way to get rid of all the actions that make samsara go on and on?"

You need to see the immense qualities of the Three Jewels,

What can help us get out of samsara? It has to be something that is itself free from samsara. And this quality is only to be found in the Buddha, Dharma, and Sangha, which we know as the Three Jewels or the Three Precious Refuges. "Buddha" means someone who has rid himself of all defects and acquired all good qualities. He is like someone very rich and at the same time highly altruistic, who by virtue of his wealth can help an enormous number of people. As a result, if we feel even a single instant of faith in the Three Jewels or perform a single prostration toward them, they will naturally be there in front of us without our needing to invoke them. The blessings of the Three Jewels are so powerful that simply hearing their names can free us from the lower realms. And yet the chance to hear those names is still something very rare and precious, not to be had unless one has gained the appropriate merit. One might spend a billion gold coins but one could never buy the opportunity to hear the names of the Three Jewels. If beings immersed in intense suffering—animals, hell beings, and even those who experience the unbearable agony of the Hell of Ultimate Torment—were to remember the names of the Three Jewels for a single instant, this would suffice for them to find themselves in that same moment in a Buddhafield. But such a thought never occurs to them. Why? Because they do not have the right merit for such a thought to arise in their minds; in their past lives they have never had any interest in practicing the Dharma. On the other hand, even small children born in a place where the Buddha came and taught have the good fortune to have a connection with him. From a very early age they know how to say, "I pay homage to the Teacher, to the Buddha, the Dharma, and the Sangha." Through this connection they are able to follow the path of the Dharma throughout their series of rebirths.

It is certain that they forever protect us from the suffering of samsara.

Once one has been taken under the protection of the Three Jewels, samsara will recede further and further, and nirvana will come closer and closer. The wisdom minds of the Buddhas are so filled with compassion that whoever makes a connection with them will eventually be set on the path to liberation. To take a present-day example, the Chinese have destroyed many temples and statues in Tibet, thus committing negative actions whose results they will have to experience as suffering. Yet the mere fact that they have seen those precious representations of the compassionate Buddha and have thus made a connection with him will eventually lead in some future life to their practicing Dharma and being liberated. The same is true for beings—even wild animals or birds—who hear the sound of the Dharma. Even if they do not understand anything, feel faith, or gain realization when they hear the scriptures of the Tripitaka being read, that sound is so full of blessings that those beings will find the gates of the lower realms closed and will be brought onto the path.

Now who can show beings these great qualities of the Three Jewels and guide those who have understood these qualities along the path? It is the spiritual master.

You need to look at the lives and deeds of the Holy Beings.

The activities of their Body, Speech, and Mind are unstained by faults or defects.

When one meets a great scholar, out of admiration one naturally feels like studying and becoming learned oneself. And when one meets a very accomplished being, one feels like practicing in order to become as realized as he is. Thus, meeting learned and accomplished beings creates a spontaneous desire to acquire the same qualities as they have. Look at the life of Jetsun Milarepa: his story—how he renounced the world, followed his teacher, and underwent much hardship to attain enlightenment—is well-known even to non-Buddhists and is a universal source of admiration and respect. Similarly, anyone who reads about Guru Rinpoche's deeds— how he protected beings from the lower realms, establishing them on the path to liberation, and how he subdued all the negative forces in Tibet— feels like taking refuge in Guru Rinpoche.

Whatever we see of the physical aspect, the words, or the mind of a spiritual teacher will inspire us to practice the Dharma. Physically, he might be a perfect monk wearing the three monastic robes, and we will naturally feel joyful and think, "Here is someone who has given up all worldly affairs, who is free from all family ties, who has no family to support, who can spend all his life practicing the pure Dharma." We might hear the teachings or read the lives of great teachers such as Shabkar Tsogdruk Rangdrol—hearing how they renounced the world and stayed in mountain retreats—and we will naturally feel inspired to do the same and devote ourselves to Dharma practice.[26] As for the teacher's mind, when we receive teachings from him and reflect on their meaning, we will realize that the preliminary practice helps us develop disillusionment, determination to be free, and confidence; that the main practice leads to experiences and realization; that hearing the names of the Buddhas frees us from the lower realms; and that all these are due to the qualities of the teacher's enlightened mind, which has transmitted this understanding to us. The teacher is therefore like a stainless, perfectly pure jewel. Like the Norbu Jitaka gem whose radiance alone makes the turbid water in a muddy pool completely clear, a true spiritual master can turn everyone around him to virtue and to the authentic Dharma by the sheer radiance of his enlightened qualities.

You need to keep the company of excellent friends who abide by virtue.

Their good ways will naturally rub off on you, and faith and other virtuous qualities will increase.

Ideally we should be like a wounded animal, staying in solitary retreat without any companions. But if this is not possible, we should at least keep the company of friends with whom we have a pure connection, who are disciples of the same teacher, and who are inclined to virtue. Their presence will serve as a reminder if ever we find ourselves forgetting the Dharma. And they can help us clarify any doubts or questions we may have about the meaning of the teachings. When all the monks and nuns in a monastery are very mindful and careful in observing their vows, the atmosphere in the monastery is naturally harmonious. If we live with spiritual companions, their qualities will automatically rub off on us.

•• 4 ••

Counseling yourself with thirteen teachings on things to be regarded with distaste.[27]

Son, there are thirteen things to be abhorred.

Unless you turn your back on your fatherland, you will not vanquish the demon of pride.

As long as we stay in our native country there will be no end to disliking our enemies and being attached to our loved ones. In our own country, we meet people who are well disposed toward us and we become attached to them. This leads us to engage in all sorts of actions based on attachment. Then there are people who obstruct us and we think of them as enemies. It is impossible to avoid attachment and hatred. When we manage to get the better of our enemies, we feel very brave and successful. In our dealings with those we like, we indulge in attachment and busy ourselves with all sorts of different activities. When we are able to help others and show affection for those to whom we are attached, we feel we are good people. In either case, whether we are bravely subduing our enemies or virtuously helping others, we feel very proud of ourselves.

Wholeheartedly adopt foreign lands.

If you go somewhere where you do not know anyone, there is no cause for either attachment or hatred. In foreign countries you can wander indifferently. Even if you are an accomplished being, no one will know you; if you are a great scholar, nobody will recognize you. So there will be very few causes for distraction.

Unless you give up the activities of a household, you will never find the time to practice the Dharma.

When you are responsible for a household, you have to plough the fields or engage in commerce and look after the affairs of the house. You never have a chance to practice the Dharma. People in this situation may think or talk of practicing the Dharma but they are so busy they never have any leisure to actually do so, and their aspirations are merely words. That is why Shechen Gyaltsap adds,

Put aside the business of running a household.

In other words, you should drop all plans and projects for making your household more prosperous or for increasing it.

If you do not practice the moment faith arises, there will be no end to the jobs you have to do.

We have had the good fortune to meet a teacher and to receive some teachings, but this will not go on happening forever. When we have the chance to hear the teachings, reflect on them, and meditate, we should do so immediately because this opportunity may never come again. Otherwise, out of indolence and laziness we may think, "I have received all these precious instructions, I will definitely start putting them into practice in the future," and we will keep postponing our practice. When the hunter Kyirawa Gonpo Dorje met Milarepa, he felt great devotion and an ardent desire to practice the Dharma. He told Milarepa that he would return home just one last time to tell his family of his intention to practice the Dharma and then come back. Milarepa answered, "If you do that, you will probably change your mind. Start practicing now." And in his *Hundred Verses of Advice*, Padampa Sangye says, "People of Tingri, while you're thinking of it, practice straight away." So

Cut through your indecision.

In other words, you should think, "Now I am determined to practice the Dharma, I shall attend this teacher, I shall receive his instructions, and I shall put them into practice." This is something you have to decide by yourself and then actually implement.

Do not blame others for your own lack of faith.

If we do not feel much devotion, it is not because there is something wrong with one of our teachers or because our companions have affected us adversely. It is purely because of our own defects and wrong way of perceiving things. The teacher is placing in our hands all the means for achieving enlightenment, so we should see perfection in everything he does and says. If we think he is truly the Buddha, whatever he does is perfect. This sort of devotion will cause our impure perception, in which we see defects in the teacher, to give way to pure perception, in which we see his enlightened activities as they actually are. Unless we have faith, we will see defects in the teacher, as did Sunakshatra,[28] who declared that the Buddha's teachings were simply designed to fool beings, and Devadatta, who despite being the Buddha's cousin, spent his life trying to harm him. So examine your own mistakes and defects and

Wind the nose rope around your head—

that is, the rope Tibetans use to lead animals by the nose. In other words, mind your own mistakes.

Unless you cast your possessions to the wind, you will never exhaust your worldly ambitions.

As long as we remain preoccupied with delicious food and comfortable clothes, wherever we are we will never be satisfied. However much we have, it will never be enough and we will always want more. On the other hand, if we can be content with just enough food to fill our stomachs and sufficient clothing to protect us from the cold, then whether or not we live in pleasant surroundings, whether or not we have friends, we will be free to progress along the path to enlightenment, and that is more than enough.

Whatever you have, use it to make offerings to the teacher and to the Three Jewels.

If you are wealthy, the best way to use your wealth is to serve the Sangha and to offer money for building temples and making objects that represent the Three Jewels.[29] You should also practice the three ways of pleasing the teacher. The best way to please him is through your own practice and accomplishment. The middling way is to do everything you can to serve him physically, verbally, and mentally. The least beneficial way to please him is to make material offerings.

Wealth is like an illusion, but if we offer it and use it for meritorious purposes, we will gather merit. Merit too is like an illusion, but it helps lead to enlightenment, for such merit never disappears. There was once a young country boy who was extremely poor. One day he saw the Buddha Vipashyin passing, begging for alms. He was suddenly filled with faith and wanted to offer him something, but because he was so poor he had nothing to offer except seven peas he was holding in his hand. With great devotion he threw the peas before the Buddha as an offering. Four of them fell in the Buddha's begging bowl, two touched his heart, and one fell on top of his head. As a result of the complete faith he had when he made this offering, he was later reborn as King Mandhata. Because of the four peas he had offered, he ruled the four continents. Because of the two peas that touched the Buddha's heart, he had dominion first over the realm of the Four Great Kings and later over the Heaven of the Thirty-three. And because of the pea that fell on the Buddha's head, he had the good fortune to share Indra's throne.

Everything depends on one's attitude. The boy's offering was very small but was made with a very pure attitude and therefore had a great result. On the other hand, an offering made simply with the intention of appearing important or gaining fame, or made with the competitive aim of being better than anyone else, will bring hardly any benefit, no matter how big it is. That is why we should have the same attitude to worldly possessions as Jigme Lingpa did: "Seeing all possessions and wealth as impermanent and without essence, seek the wealth of the seven noble riches." The seven noble riches are faith, discipline, a sense of shame in one's own eyes, a sense of decency in others' regard, and so forth. When we have them, all good qualities will grow from within. But if we accumulate a lot of wealth and hoard it greedily, we are simply creating the cause for rebirth as a preta.

Unless you distance yourself from your relatives, there will be no interruption in your attachment and aversion.

Stay far away from your relatives and friends, for when someone is good to you, it is very difficult to avoid becoming attached. Similarly, if someone wrongs you, it is difficult to avoid feeling aversion. And this leads to all sorts of different activities. It is therefore important to stay away from them, like a wounded animal, which seeks an isolated place where it can recover from its wounds:

> *Always rely on solitude.*

Unless you act now, you cannot be sure where you will go next.

At this moment we are truly at a crossroads, so now is the time to practice. We might think, "I will meet the teacher again next year and receive teachings, and I will practice then," but we cannot be sure that we will be able to do things as planned. We do not know what could happen even a short time from now.

> *Now, when all the favorable conditions have come together, you should do anything to get free from samsara.*

When one is thrown into jail by the authorities, one's only thought is, "How can I get out? Who can help me?" Similarly, when one is sick, one only thinks of finding a doctor and taking his medicine. One will do anything to get rid of one's predicament. So now that we have gathered the conditions for doing so, we should be constantly preoccupied with getting further and further away from samsara. We should be prepared to do anything to get even a millimeter further away from samsara.

Doing nothing now when you have the means, the prayers you make for future lives are empty chatter.

You might say, "Right now I have to finish my work, I have such-and-such business to attend to, but I'll pray that in a future life I will be a very good practitioner." But these are just meaningless words. Who knows what will happen in the next life? If we are caught up in so much attachment to friends in this life, then in the next life our attachment will be even greater. Attachment to our wealth and activities is the very cause for rebirth in the lower realms. And if we cannot get rid of animosity toward enemies, it will cause us to be reborn in the hells in the next life.

> *If you have the ability and you do not act, you are letting yourself down.*

When one has a garden that has been prepared for growing flowers and one does nothing about it, one is simply letting oneself down. Now, when it is possible for us to practice the Dharma, we should realize that this is an extremely rare and precious opportunity that should be used immediately, because things will change and it will not last forever.

Without lying to yourself, practice the Supreme Dharma.

If you think that being dishonest with yourself is all right, then that is fine. You might as well carry on with all your worldly activities—doing business and cheating others, crushing your enemies and promoting your friends. But if you think this is not actually the right way to benefit yourself, you will realize that you have only been harming and deceiving yourself. So instead,

take your own mind as a witness.

Jetsun Milarepa said, "The root of samaya is not to be ashamed of oneself." There is no way the mind can lie to itself. We know what we have been doing. We can easily see whether we have followed the teacher properly and whether we have put his instructions into practice or not. The mind can see the smallest things perfectly well—there is nothing it can hide from itself. If one has made a little progress or gained a few good qualities, the mind will know. But while it is very easy for one to know what is happening in one's own mind, it is difficult for others to judge from one's external appearance and behavior. So the only real witness to how you are thinking and acting should be your own mind.

Forsake now what you will have to give up anyway, and it will become meaningful.

However much wealth you have accumulated, you will not take even a tiny bit of it with you through the door of death. All the delicious food you are always eating merely turns into excrement. Status and fame will have to be left behind when you die. But right now you can choose to give all these things up deliberately. You can give them away and devote yourself to practicing the Dharma. For when death comes, you will have to abandon them all anyway—against your will. Your friends and relatives will gather round weeping, and it will be tremendously hard to leave them. You will have to draw up your testament, leaving all your possessions behind. And on top of all that, you will not have acquired any spiritual qualities.

So it would be far better to use your wealth to serve the Sangha, to make offerings to the teacher, and to offer it for worthy purposes.

At the time of the Buddha there was a householder called Anathapindaka who decided to give away all his land to build a vihara in which the Buddha and his disciples could stay. One day he was with the Buddha's disciple Shariputra marking out the ground for the vihara, and he noticed Shariputra smile. An Arhat does not smile without reason, so he asked Shariputra what had pleased him. Shariputra replied, "I have just seen that there is a palace already waiting for you in one of the Buddhafields." That is how infallible the law of cause and effect is. At present Anathapindaka is in the Heaven of the Thirty-three enjoying the pleasures of the gods. And as predicted by the Buddha, during this kalpa of a thousand Buddhas, Anathapindaka will come as a Bodhisattva, appearing as each Buddha's patron, building a vihara for him, and being reborn each time in a Buddhafield.

> *Whatever you have, your body and wealth, give it away*
> *for the Dharma.*

Jetsun Milarepa, for example, offered a big copper pot to Marpa, and through this offering he made the proper connection for becoming a fit vessel for the whole of Marpa's teaching.

> **Rather than concerning yourself with things you obviously**
> **cannot complete, concern yourself with making an experience**
> **of what you definitely can complete.**

Whatever you do, there are things that you will never be able to cope with. You might think of subduing enemies and manage to get the better of a few around you, but there is no end to those enemies. You could never subdue all the enemies on earth. Similarly, you may be attached to some people, but you could never be equally attached to all the sentient beings on this earth even though they have all been your parents. There is no end to ordinary attachment. But what you really can do at present is to decide to practice the Dharma and devote all your energy to that. That is something manageable—something you can cope with. Therefore,

> *For the sake of the Dharma, be prepared for austerity and forbearance.*

> **Instead of preparing for next year —when you cannot be sure**
> **whether or not there will be a next year—prepare for death, which**
> **is certain to happen.**

How can we say, "Next year I shall do this or that, I shall conduct such-and-such business, I shall accomplish such-and-such a task"? You might just as well go to a dry riverbed, set a few nets, and put out lines and hooks in the expectation of catching some fish. That is why Shechen Gyaltsap notes,

Time is short, curtail your plans.

Starting from this very moment, we should make a heartfelt aspiration to meet the teacher, to receive his teachings, to begin the preliminary practice, and, having completed it, to continue immediately with the main practice, going through the generation and perfection phases and the practices of the Great Perfection without pausing between one stage and the next. If we have the deep intention to practice like this, then everything will happen accordingly and there will be immeasurable benefits. Jigme Lingpa himself says in his teaching on the preliminary practice that those who complete the five stages of the preliminary practice without any major downfall are certain to take rebirth in the Copper-Colored Mountain.[30] But there is no time to lose for we cannot be sure when death will come.

As you practice, food and clothing will take care of themselves, so do not have great hopes or fears.

If you begin by saying, "I want to practice, but first I must find somewhere nice to stay and buy food and provisions," this will only delay you. Once you decide to practice and start doing so, the blessings of the Three Jewels will take care of your most basic needs in terms of food and clothing. The Buddha himself declared that you will never find the bones of a Dharma practitioner who has died of hunger and cold. So

For those who practice the Dharma it is very important to give up all concern for this life.

The thirteen points in this chapter concern things for which we should feel distaste. What do we mean here by distaste? Like a jaundiced patient who has no appetite at all for greasy food, a genuine Dharma practitioner is said to be someone who is completely uninterested in possessions, achievement, fame, or glory in worldly life. Like someone thrown alive into a pit of fire, as *The Words of My Perfect Teacher* puts it, he has no desire at all for the things of this life.

++ 5 ++

Thirteen important points that show the unmistaken path.

Son, there are thirteen things that are very important.

If we observe these thirteen important points related to body, speech, and mind, we will have no difficulty practicing. The first one concerns the teacher:

His realization is like space, beyond all partiality.

Those whose realization has become as vast as the sky have no bias. They do not see samsara as something to be rejected, nor do they see the qualities of nirvana as something to be preferred and obtained. They have realized that all the afflictive emotions and the negative actions in samsara are by nature the kayas and wisdoms of the Buddhas.

In the causal vehicle of characteristics, absolute truth is considered as that which has to be realized, while the phenomena of relative truth are considered as impure and to be rejected. But this sort of discrimination, this dual perception of pure and impure, of something to be obtained and something to be rejected, is not the correct view of the Secret Mantrayana. Why? The root of our wandering in samsara is the five gross aggregates. According to the Mantrayana, which distinguishes between the way things appear and the way things are, these aggregates, along with the elements, sense organs, and sense objects, may appear as our relative perceptions. But with regard to the way they are, they are the pure three seats—that is, they are by nature the five Dhyani Buddhas and their consorts, the eight male and female Bodhisattvas, and so on. When we fail to recognize this and cling to the gross aggregates, we give rise to the afflictive emotions. The aggregates thus become the cause for wandering in the three worlds of samsara. Mantrayana practitioners are able to dispel this deluded perception of the aggregates and so forth and allow their true nature, the way it is, to appear clearly. They thus achieve the perception of infinite purity. Theirs is realization without any bias, in which there is no distinction between samsara as something to be rejected and nirvana as something to be preferred and obtained.

His experience is constant and level like the ocean.[31]

Realization comes through three stages: understanding, experiences, and realization. The first of these is theoretical understanding, which comes from learning the teachings. Of course it brings some benefit, but it is not very stable. It is like a patch sewn onto a piece of clothing: it can come off again. Although we have some theoretical understanding, it may not be very reliable in the face of different circumstances and might not help us cope with difficulties.

Experiences are like mist: they will fade away. Practitioners who spend their time practicing in seclusion are certain to have many different experiences, but these experiences are very unreliable. As it is said, experiences are like rainbows, but the great meditator who runs after them like a child will be deceived. We may occasionally have flashes of clairvoyance, seeing things we cannot ordinarily know. We may have signs of accomplishment, or predictions from the deity or the dakinis. But such experiences in most cases give rise to hope and expectation. They are none other than the tricks of demons: they simply cause obstacles.

When true realization dawns in one's mind, it is like the king of mountains, Mount Meru, which no wind can shake. This means that in a thousand good circumstances the mind does not become attached and in a thousand adverse circumstances the mind feels no aversion. It is said that for those who attain the level of Arhat it does not make the slightest difference whether on one side there is a beautiful person waving a sandalwood fan and on the other side a fearsome person threatening to kill them with an axe. They feel neither attachment to the one nor aversion to the other. This is the quality of realization one achieves through the so-called Lesser Vehicle, so how much vaster should the realization of the Great Vehicle be. And in the Great Perfection we speak of the "exhaustion of phenomena in the expanse of dharmakaya." "Exhaustion" here does not mean the extinction of phenomena but rather the exhaustion of all *deluded* perceptions. In that state, what is ordinarily perceived as suffering arises as perfect bliss and all distinctions between good and bad have vanished. All circumstances, whether good or bad, thus become helpers, friends on the path.

His compassion shines evenly, like the sun and the moon.[32]

When we have proper devotion and confidence in the Three Jewels and the teacher, their compassion is always present, like the sun and moon that move constantly over the four continents. It is unthinkable that the sun and moon might ever stop shining, or that they might stop shining over one particular place. If your devotion to your root teacher and the Three

Jewels is sound, you can be sure that they are watching over you with compassion constantly, day and night, through happiness and suffering.

> **To a teacher who has these three qualities, it is very important to be respectful.**

You should respect such a teacher with your body, speech, and mind. It is said that in the beginning one has to be skillful in finding the teacher, in the middle one has to be skillful in following him, and in the end one has to be skillful in putting his instructions into practice. Someone who succeeds in these three ways will travel the whole path without difficulty.

To enter the path of Dharma, we have to be properly prepared and very sure of what we are doing. In ordinary life, people who are about to start an important project, get married, or build a house begin by carefully considering the different elements of the situation. Similarly, if we want to practice the Dharma, we first have to find an authentic teacher, and for this we should not rely on how famous he is. Then having found an authentic teacher, we have to follow him properly and practice his instructions. In following the teacher, it is said we should be like a belt that cannot be felt when worn; that is, we should never be a source of discomfort for him or disturb him. Like salt, which readily dissolves in water, we should be able to adapt to all circumstances and not be bothered by them. With our body, speech, and mind we should follow the teacher without causing trouble, doing whatever pleases him and never, even secretly, doing anything that might displease him. We should be like a swan or duck gliding between the lotus flowers, picking at the flowers and feeding, but without disturbing the surface of the water or making the water muddy. Like this, if we please the teacher throughout our life, then when death comes, our mind will readily become one with the teacher's mind in the same way that Jigme Lingpa merged his mind with Longchenpa's.

> *As the teacher is the root of the path, follow him, pleasing him in the three ways.*

He is the "root of the path" because without a spiritual teacher there is no way one can progress along the path. Of the three ways of pleasing the teacher, the best is to put his teachings into practice. He gives teaching not because he expects any sort of recognition, remuneration, power, or fame, but simply because he can see how beings are deluded in samsara and how they suffer on account of delusion. He gives instructions as a remedy for delusion, hoping that beings can thereby free themselves from ignorance. He does this out of sheer compassion like parents who kindly advise their children to do certain things and warn them against doing other things purely for their own good, hoping their children will lead happy lives. If the Buddha turned the Wheel of the Dharma three times, it was not because he was restless and had nothing better to do. Neither was it because he hoped to become famous. It was simply out of his intention to dispel the ignorance of beings, and because he wished to set beings on the path to enlightenment. As a result of his kindness, we can now hear the names of the Three Jewels and read the teachings in the Three Pitakas that show what is positive and what is negative. Thanks to his kindness, the practice of Dharma is accessible to us.

Do not do anything disrespectful, even in a dream.

It is said that if you dream you commit a negative act like killing, lying, or stealing, even though it is a dream, when you wake up, you must regret what happened in the dream and confess it. Likewise, if you feel disrespect for the teacher, even in a dream, as soon as you wake up you should deeply regret it and confess. Remember, too, that the more you pray to the Three Jewels and to the teacher, the greater will be the blessings you receive.

It is very important to give instructions to disciples who are proper vessels.

Someone who has faith in the Three Jewels and the teacher, who is interested in hearing, reflecting, and meditating, and who is very diligent should be given the teachings without reserve, for this will bring great benefit. "Instructions" here refers to major instructions—the profound instructions that lead to liberation and enlightenment—and not to minor instructions for curing sickness, dispelling obstacles, and creating prosperity in this life. What then are the benefits that will come from giving such instructions to those who are suitable vessels?

They will hold the lineage and benefit themselves and others, and the teachings and beings.

In the best case, disciples will become lineage holders, like the Seven Patriarchs who held Buddha Shakyamuni's teachings: they became equal to the Buddha himself and continued his activities, holding, expounding, and preserving the Dharma. Among Milarepa's disciples there were

Gampopa, who was like the sun, and Rechungpa, who was like the moon, and eight who were able to go to the pure realms in their lifetime, in the very same body. These disciples were the true representatives of their teacher. It is through the kindness of such lineage holders, teachers who are fully enlightened holders of the teaching, that the different instructions of the eight great chariots can still be given and practiced today, despite the Buddha having taught the Dharma over two thousand years ago.[33]

Do not be miserly with the teachings.

Someone who is truly concerned with the next life and interested in the Dharma should be shown all the texts and given all the instructions, without hiding anything. Of course, there is no need to reveal texts and instructions on black magic since these can be harmful, but anything that is helpful for the disciple's practice should be given.

It is very important to give up attachment to things, externally and internally.

Practitioners who have full confidence in the Three Jewels need never worry about food and clothing. These will come their way anyway. When the sun shines in summer, it does not need to think about what it is doing— making the forests and meadows turn green, the flowers blossom, and fruits ripen, and warming everyone on the earth. It does all this naturally. Likewise, if you practice the Dharma sincerely, people will naturally be disposed toward you and will help you in your practice. Those who renounce the world and take ordination are naturally respected by their families and others, who are happy to support them. Those who are very learned do not have to talk about it; they easily win respect. And siddhas who have attained a high degree of accomplishment do not have to claim they are siddhas. Their accomplishment is evident and they are venerated for it. So we need not be preoccupied or obsessed with external necessities; they will come our way naturally. And in no event should we be attached to such things, otherwise we will be influenced by the eight ordinary concerns and be led into all sorts of activities in order to procure and keep them.

Remember the defects of attachment to the pleasures of the five senses.

When we crave beautiful forms, we become like moths, which are attracted to light and get burnt by the flame. However much enjoyment we may derive from the pleasures of the senses, there will never come a time when we have had enough. The more we indulge in them, the more they become like honey smeared on a razor, cutting our tongues as we try to lick it off.

> The pleasures we desire will bring us ruin,
> They're like the *kimba* fruit, the Buddha said.[34]

So remembering these defects give up desire as much as you possibly can.

In practicing the instructions, it is very important to think in the long-term.

In practicing the Dharma, the longer we maintain our diligence, the more good qualities will grow within us and the deeper our understanding of the Dharma will be. To really benefit from the teachings and develop good qualities, it is not enough to simply hear them. We have to be like the great teacher Vasubandhu: although he had developed the power of infallible memory and knew ninety-nine hundred thousand treatises by heart, he would still read them daily. He even used to recite them all night, seated in a large oil jar to protect him from the wind. Jigme Lingpa said that truly diligent Dharma practitioners remain diligent even when they get old; they become less distracted and busy. This is a sign of the real practitioner, who has not been "touched by frost."[35]

Even if it takes very long, your days and life must be spent practicing. Jetsun Milarepa said, "Do not expect quick results; spend your time practicing—in a race with death." It makes no sense to think, "I have practiced for one year; will I obtain realization? I have practiced for three years; will I obtain realization?" Simply think, "If I die, that will be that, but until then I am going to practice." As you become more and more acquainted with the Dharma, your understanding will naturally become deeper and good qualities will grow. When the Dharma hits the mark, it becomes more and more effective.

It is said that Dharma practitioners start out with suffering and end up with happiness. When we start practicing, we have to go to a secluded place where we have very little food and must endure heat and cold. Moreover, the practice is difficult to begin with, there seems to be little progress, and we do not have any signs of experience or realization. But then as we persevere in the practice and the Dharma gradually becomes part of us, our minds feel more and more confident and serene. In the beginning we are bound to have obstacles, but with time we will feel happier and happier in the practice.

With worldly activities it is just the opposite: everything is very pleasant to begin with, but the end is very painful. We may start off happy, with wealth, a comfortable existence, and all life's pleasures. But in order to achieve that, we will have accumulated mainly negative actions and can therefore only end up suffering in this life and for many lives to come. This is why we must not view our Dharma practice in the short term. Never think, "I've practiced so hard for months and years, and I've still not had any result." Otherwise you will get discouraged when, after one, two, three or more years, you have still not had any experiences. Take the example of Asanga. He meditated for twelve years, praying to Maitreya, and in all that time never had the slightest sign of accomplishment. Finally he had an experience of genuine and overwhelming compassion, and at that moment Maitreya appeared to him in person. "I've been praying to you all these years and you never showed any sign of your presence," complained Asanga. Maitreya replied, "I have been next to you from the moment you began practicing, but on account of your obscuration you did not realize I was present." So

> With regard to the Dharma, do not be impatient. You need
> to accompany the teacher for a long time.

To follow the teacher for a long time is of great value and it is otherwise difficult to obtain all his qualities. Just as on a gold mountain all the trees, bushes, and flowers turn golden, if you follow the teacher like a shadow, you will become like Ananda: he never left the Buddha's side and eventually obtained all the qualities of his body, speech, and mind.[36] And just as all the gods and nagas take great care of the wishing-gem and make it their crown ornament—that is, they recognize its great value—you should never separate from your teacher even for an instant.

Do not be skittish

Do not be superficial and inconstant, thinking that following the teacher and receiving his teachings will make you famous or that receiving only a few words of instruction and making a "Dharma connection" will suffice.

It is very important to develop fervent devotion to the yidam deity and the Three Jewels.

The essence of the Buddha's teachings is to be found in the Three Jewels and in the yidam deity, so you should have the intention to do the practices related to them, praying and reciting the mantras over a long period of time. If you do, the yidam will always be close to you, you will receive blessings and eventually meet the deity face to face. In the *Mani Kabum*, Songtsen Gampo describes how to accomplish all the ordinary and supreme activities of pacifying, increasing, controlling, and fiercely subduing. He explains that for this one can do no better than to rely on Avalokiteshvara as one's yidam. He himself was able to meet Avalokiteshvara as if shaking hands with him, and it is through Avalokiteshvara's blessings that the Land of Snows was protected and the Dharma introduced to Tibet. Similarly, Lama Mipham[37] practiced all his life on Mañjushri as his peaceful yidam and on Yamantaka as his wrathful one, and through this practice his mind became united with the enlightened mind of Mañjushri.[38]

All this depends on the strength of our devotion. The stronger our devotion, the greater the blessings. But to have no devotion is like hiding oneself in a house with all the doors and shutters closed. The sunlight will never get in. Without devotion, even if we spend all our time near the teacher, his blessings will never enter us. At the time of Lord Buddha, there were Tirthika teachers who spent some time in his presence and heard him teach, but since they had no faith they did not receive his blessings and could not attain enlightenment.

> *Without fervent devotion, blessings will not enter.*
> *At all times be diligent in taking refuge,*

because the root of all the Dharma is the refuge; it is the ultimate object of meditation of both the sutras and tantras.

It is very important to cultivate diligence in the practice of virtue.

It is said that if the Buddha Shakyamuni could become a fully enlightened Buddha after accumulating merit and wisdom for three measureless kalpas, it was from having brought the transcendent perfection of diligence to its ultimate point. He spent countless lives thus accumulating merit and in thirty-two of these was reborn as a universal monarch, each time accumulating boundless merit. As a result of this constant diligence, he finally became the Buddha, whom beings could know and meet. And it was with this sort of constant diligence that Jetsun Milarepa was able to reach the level of Vajradhara within a single lifetime.

Act like a beautiful woman whose hair has caught fire.

A beautiful woman whose hair was on fire would not waste a second trying to put the fire out. With that sort of diligence there is nothing you would not be able to accomplish.

Do not fall under the influence of laziness,

Without applying yourself, you will never succeed at anything. If you are truly interested in listening, reflecting, and meditating, you should always be thinking, "There is so much to do, and no knowing when I might die," and you should not waste a single instant on distracting activities.

It is very important to steer clear of negative actions.

To do so you need to be very mindful and vigilant. Be aware of whether your actions are positive or negative. Once you know what has to be taken up and what has to be avoided, you must avoid even the minutest negative action. If you find you have committed a negative action physically, verbally, or mentally, you must acknowledge it immediately, confess, and repair the downfall. And if you see that you have done something positive, make a prayer: "May I do even more, may I increase in virtue."

Think of their fully ripened effect and avoid them as you would
a speck of dust in your eye.

It is important to examine your actions very closely. Particularly with minor negative actions, we do not see what the result will be immediately, but it is certain that those actions will mature and that we will have to experience the result. Enlightened beings can see this very clearly. For them even the most minute negative action is like a speck of dust in one's eye—one has to get rid of it immediately. We ordinary beings, on the other hand, are unable to see the consequences of our actions. We are unaware of our minor deeds and lose track of them like an arrow shot into a thick forest. We act without understanding where our actions will lead. But if we had the vision of an enlightened being, we would see that even the minutest action has a result.

It is very important to rely on the absence of thoughts
in your mind.

The root cause that makes us wander in samsara is the chaining of our thoughts, and it is said that discursive thought is the "great ignorance" that makes us fall into the ocean of samsara. Unless we do something about it, this chaining of thoughts will go on and on forever. So it is very important to employ the correct remedy, and here the main remedy is to cultivate the state free from wandering thoughts.

Let the thoughts related to the five poisons dissolve by themselves.

For ordinary beings, thoughts related to the five poisons will keep on coming up in the mind. Nevertheless, we should not let these thoughts dominate us. Our approach to this can take different forms. In the Basic Vehicle one applies the appropriate antidotes for such thoughts. For example, the antidote for anger is to meditate on patience, the antidote for attachment is to meditate on disgust, and the antidote for ignorance is to meditate on the law of cause and effect and on interdependence, understanding how ignorance leads to samsara, and so on. In the Great Vehicle one investigates the five poisons and comes to the conclusion that they are like a dream or illusion: their ultimate nature is emptiness. Once one knows this, one cannot be influenced by them. In the Mantrayana one realizes that the basic nature of the five poisons is wisdom and, thus transformed, one uses them on the path of liberation and the path of skillful means.

In the postmeditation period, it is very important to rely on compassion and bodhichitta.

Whether we are practicing virtue or giving up negative actions, we should think that our sole purpose is to benefit sentient beings—all beings, without excluding a single one. As we realize the extent of beings' suffering and of our own inability to help them, we should develop the firm intention to do everything necessary to benefit them and dedicate all our physical, verbal, and mental actions to them. Otherwise, if we practice only with the self-centered intention to be comfortable in this life and to avoid being reborn in the lower realms in future lives, any virtuous practice we do will have very limited results. Unless we begin with the altruistic attitude and end by sharing the merit with all sentient beings so that they can attain enlightenment, our practice is not the genuine Mahayana. We may call it the "Great Vehicle," but there is nothing great about it. The root of the Great Vehicle is that for the preparation one generates bodhichitta, for the main practice one is free from concepts, and for the conclusion one dedicates the merit to all sentient beings. Without these three supreme methods it is impossible to practice the Mahayana. The principal practice of Bodhisattvas is to leave aside their own interests and consider others more important. We should follow their example.

This is the root of the Great Vehicle and is therefore indispensable.
Train in considering others more important than yourself.

The Buddha manifested countless times in this world as different Bodhisattvas. He did not do this in order to repeatedly win fame and glory, nor was it merely to have food and clothes. It was simply due to his universal compassion—his wish to help beings he saw snared by ignorance and to free them from their suffering.

It is very important to develop the conviction that the instructions are unmistaken.

When you receive authentic instruction, you should concentrate first on hearing it, then on reflecting on its meaning, and finally, through meditation, making it part of you. As you do so, you will gain the conviction that the instruction you have received is truly undeceiving and become confident of its excellence.

If you have no doubts, accomplishment will be swift in coming.

The boundless benefits of putting the instructions into practice—meditating on the yidam, reciting the mantra, and so forth—are described in the relevant scriptures. Do not have any doubts about the truth of these and you will swiftly achieve such qualities. But as long as you doubt and hesitate—wondering, "Does mantra recitation really have such power?" or "Can I really gain siddhi if I do the yidam practice?"—it will be impossible for you to achieve realization or accomplishment.

Furthermore, the root of attaining accomplishment is careful observance of the three vows: the Pratimoksha vows of the Basic Vehicle, the Bodhisattva precepts of the Great Vehicle, and the samayas of the Vajrayana. This is why Zurchungpa says,

It is very important to observe the vows and samayas.

This is the well-tilled, fertile field in which good crops naturally grow. Therefore,

*Do not let your mind be stained by the downfalls and faults related
to the three vows.*

The three vows refer to the outer vows of the Pratimoksha, the inner precepts of the Bodhisattvas, and the secret precepts of the vehicle of the Vidyadharas. As a lay practitioner, you might think you have never taken a Pratimoksha vow, but although you may not have been through the full Pratimoksha ritual, any Vajrayana empowerment you have received will have included Pratimoksha vows as an integral part of the empowerment. There is no empowerment in which one does not take the three vows, one after another. How do we receive the Pratimoksha vows in that case? Through the kindness of the teacher we give rise to deep disillusionment with samsaric affairs. This is already part of the Pratimoksha vow, the essence of which is to realize the sufferings and shortcomings of samsara and to develop a strong determination to be free.

In the same way, if you have received a Vajrayana empowerment, there is no way you cannot have taken the Bodhisattva vow, even if you did not go through the formal ritual. At the beginning of an empowerment the teacher says, "These teachings should be received and practiced for the sake of all beings, as numerous as the sky is vast." This is the essence of the Bodhisattva vow, arousing bodhichitta. Likewise for the samayas, the Vajrayana precepts: the empowerment introduces one to the realization that all forms are the deity, all sounds are the sound of the mantra, and all thoughts are the display of the absolute nature. For the body, we receive the vase empowerment with the image of the deity. For our speech, we repeat the mantra and receive the secret empowerment. For the mind, we receive the third empowerment with the deity's symbolic attributes. So in a Vajrayana empowerment all the Vajrayana vows are complete. We have all received Vajrayana empowerment,[39] so we have taken these three vows. It is therefore very important to keep them and to avoid all faults and downfalls related to them, as such faults and downfalls are extremely negative.

The essence of all these vows is summed up in this saying from the sutras:

Abandon evildoing,
Practice virtue well.

Give up all negative actions and you will be keeping the three vows. Cultivate positive actions and again you will be practicing the essence of the three vows.

However, if in performing positive actions—following the teacher, listening to his teachings, and putting them into practice—and in giving up negative actions you feel self-satisfied or proud and think, "What a good deed I've done," this sort of clinging is a great defect. You should always be completely free from clinging and see everything as a dream, as an illusion. Although you are following a teacher, in truth the absolute teacher is the dharmakaya, which is the nature of your own mind. The outer manifested teacher you are following at present is himself like a dream. His manifested body is not permanent and he will again leave this world. The true inner dharmakaya teacher is never separate from you. So even if on the relative level you follow a teacher, practice, and do lots of positive actions, you must do so without any clinging, seeing all these as illusory by nature.

It is very important to establish the unborn nature of the mind.

As your mind and appearances are the display of the absolute
nature, come to the clear conclusion that the nature of mind
is unborn like space.

In short, all the infinite phenomena of samsara and nirvana are nothing else than the projection of one's own mind and are therefore an illusion. Nothing is truly existent and permanent. When you understand this, you will realize that everything is unborn like space, that its nature is emptiness. It is with this realization—that you yourself, the teacher, and all phenomena are like a dream and illusion—that you should practice the meditation on the wisdom deity and recite the mantra. And if you ever have a sign of accomplishment, even a vision of the yidam, you should continue to recognize its illusory nature and avoid the error of feeling attached or proud. To be conceited and think, "I have achieved a sign of accomplishment" is an obstacle, a demon. However high your realization may be, you must never be proud of any signs such as clairvoyance that you may experience, but remain free from clinging and see their dreamlike nature. Otherwise, if you are attached to such things, it will be impossible for even the most basic qualities of the path to develop in your mind. As the great siddha Saraha said, "Wherever there is attachment, there will be a downfall." Even the husk of a sesame seed's worth of attachment will create great suffering in the mind. So if you have any result in your practice, you should simply think that it is the natural consequence of doing the practice and not be proud of it. As we read in *Parting from the Four Attachments*, the

four-line teaching that Mañjushri gave in a vision to the great Sakyapa teacher Jetsun Trakpa Gyaltsen:

> As long as there is clinging, there is no view.

**It is very important not to give the secret pith instructions
to an improper vessel.**

Profound teachings such as those of Mahamudra and the Great Perfection have to be given to a suitable disciple, for they are like the milk of the
snow lioness, which can only be collected in a container made of gold or a
similar precious substance. To worthy disciples, as has already been stated
in this text, the teachings should be given and not concealed, for they will
benefit them. But to give the teachings to someone who is not worthy is a
pure waste, just as pouring the snow lioness' milk into an earthenware pot
results in the pot being broken and the milk being wasted as well. The
greater the extent to which the pith instructions are kept secret, the swifter
the results in the practice. In ancient times in the supreme land of India,
the Vinaya teachings were widely taught. But all the practices of the Secret
Mantrayana were kept completely secret. In a gathering of a thousand panditas, no one would ever know which of them were practicing the Secret
Mantrayana, who their yidams were, or what mantras they were reciting.
It was only if one of them started flying through the sky or performing
some other miracle that people would realize he had been practicing the
Mantrayana. In Tibet, however, the Mantrayana teachings have gradually
spread and are now known to everyone. As result, the proportion of practitioners who actually attain accomplishment and realization is much
smaller.

> *Divulging the secret teachings leads to criticism, so be careful:*
> *take pains to check the worthiness of the disciple.*

This is why the teacher should know how to recognize the disciple's
potential. To someone worthy he should give all the instructions without
holding anything back. But to disciples who do not have the appropriate
qualities he should give teachings that will benefit them in accordance
with their real capacity—first the teachings for beings of lesser capacity,
then the teachings for those of middling capacity, and so on, thus gradually transforming them into suitable vessels. In your own practice, too,
you should apply the same principle. Practice in accordance with your

capacity and see everything as dream and illusion. If you do so, you will reap great benefit.

> **This was the first section from the *Eighty Chapters of Personal Advice*, the instruction on firm faith, the gateway.**

In this section the immense qualities and importance of faith have been shown and expressed by teachers who were both very learned and highly accomplished and who were therefore able to condense the teachings into this essentialized instruction while retaining all their profound meaning.

II. Discipline

*Instructions on the jewel-like superior training in discipline,
the perfect foundation.*

JUST AS IT IS IMPOSSIBLE for the continents and mountains in the universe to exist without the ground as a foundation, in order to travel the path perfectly we need a perfectly pure foundation, namely the superior training in discipline.

There are eighteen chapters.

✦ 6 ✦

An instruction on timeliness in the practice.

If you practice the Dharma when the time is right, you can be sure that the practice will follow its proper course and that it will act as a marvelous method for perfecting experiences and realization.

Son, there are ten facts.[40]

If the continued existence of the Buddha's teaching and your having faith coincide, it is simply that you accumulated merit in past lives.

What is the relationship here between faith and the Buddha's teaching? It is that the Buddha's teaching is the right object of our faith. We have to distinguish between those objects that are worthy of our faith and those that are not. Worthy objects are the Three Jewels: the fully enlightened Buddha, the sublime Dharma, and the Sangha. Unworthy ones are worldly gods like Indra or Brahma, or spirits like *tsen* in whom people take refuge. Even if we take refuge in them sincerely, these unworthy objects do not have the power to protect us since they are not free from samsara themselves. Now the Buddha may have taught, but if his teachings had not endured until the present day, we would have no teachings to receive and put into practice. While they continue to exist, you have the chance to hear and reflect upon the sublime Dharma. So if the teachings are present and you have confidence in them, it is a sign that you accumulated merit in your past lives.

> Now that for once you have acquired the freedoms and advantages, do not squander them.

If you do not have great diligence and you fail to make use of this present opportunity, there is no certainty that in your next life you will be reborn somewhere where the Buddha's teaching exists or that you will be interested in it and have faith. So you must not waste this opportunity by rendering this human life useless and empty. The most important thing for making use of such an opportunity is to have a keen interest in the Dharma. Unless you are interested, even though the teachings are there, you will never start practicing them. You will be like a dog presented with grass— it is not interested in eating it.

However, even if you are interested, there is a risk you will not get to the very heart of the teachings, so you need to follow an authentic teacher. A beggar goes to a rich man for alms, not to another beggar who has nothing to give.

If you are interested in the Dharma and meet a master who possesses the instructions, it is simply that the blind man has found the jewel.

If a blind person were to find a wishing-gem in the dust on a path, it would be something to marvel at. All his wishes would be fulfilled and he would be able to fulfill the wishes of all beings. And in this life he would have food and clothes and be wealthy and prosperous. But to find the instructions of the Dharma is even more precious, for while the wishing-gem can give us all we want in this life, the Dharma can provide all we could wish for in this life and in all our future lives. Thus a faithful disciple who meets an authentic teacher has the means for attaining enlightenment in one lifetime.

Later it will be hard to find such a teacher repeatedly, so stay
with him for a long time without separating from him, like the
eyes in your forehead.[41]

In general, wherever we go, day and night we take great care of our body,
but we are especially careful about our eyes. We should have the same kind
of concern for this precious human body and the teacher's instructions and
stay with the teacher over a long period of time, for it will be very difficult
to find such an opportunity again.

If faith, diligence, and wisdom coincide in a body free of defects, it
is simply that these good qualities are the karmic result of having
trained in the Dharma.

Once we have this precious human body, which is free from the eight
intrusive circumstances and the eight incompatible propensities, we
should make use of it to practice the Dharma. At the same time, if we have
faith, diligence, and wisdom, we have the three qualities required for entering the Vajrayana. In the Vajrayana, which is the highest and most profound of all the vehicles, the teacher first guides disciples who have faith
by means of the ten outer empowerments that benefit. Then, to disciples
who also possess diligence, he gives the five inner empowerments that confer ability. To disciples who additionally possess keen wisdom, he bestows
the three profound secret empowerments. These three qualities are equally
necessary in the Sutrayana: without faith it is impossible to progress along
the path; without diligence there will be no result in the practice even if
one starts to listen, reflect, and meditate; and without keen intelligence and
wisdom one will never get the vital point of the teachings, however much
effort one makes. If you have these three, it is a sign that in your past lives
you have already trained in the Dharma and developed such qualities. So

Be diligent in the methods for making these three grow.

Ordinary beings' minds are utterly fickle, quaking like *kusha* grass, which
bends in whichever direction the wind blows. You must therefore be very
diligent, following the example of the great sages of the past who continuously applied themselves to increasing their faith, diligence, and wisdom.
Otherwise you will be unable to prevent yourself from falling back and will
be carried away in the ocean of suffering. This is why the root text says,

If your being born in samsara coincides with relatives scolding you,[42] it is simply that you are being exhorted to practice.

Decide for yourself and practice the Dharma.

However well-meaning your relatives and friends may be, their advice and pleas will only greatly increase your attachment and involvement in samsara—and it is because of your afflictive emotions and past actions that you were in samsara in the first place. This is why listening to all their propositions will hinder your practice. You must make your own decision. If you really want to practice the Dharma correctly, the only person who can give you proper advice is a spiritual teacher; the only advice you can really rely on is the Buddha's teachings. While there is nothing the teacher says that does not accord with the Buddha's teachings, any advice our parents and family may give us, though of course motivated by love and affection, is based on ignorance, for they are still enveloped in the gloom of samsara. Unfortunately they can only tell us how important it is to protect our kin and get rid of those who might harm us; how courageous we will be if we get the better of our enemies; and how proud they will be if we succeed in this. So you must make a definite decision not to follow the advice of anyone but your teacher and remain like a drop of mercury in the dust, which stays perfectly clean and does not mix with the dust around it.

If your having things and your being delighted to give them away coincide with a beggar, it is simply that generosity is coming to perfection.

In order to practice generosity, when you have things like food, clothes, money, and so on, you should be eager to offer them to the Buddhas or give them to beggars. Then, if you meet a beggar, all the favorable conditions for an act of generosity will be present. You should take advantage of these three occurring together and give away as much as you can without being influenced by niggardliness. If you think, "I won't give now, I'll give later," or "This beggar doesn't look desperate enough, I'll give to one who is more in need," you will never manage to be generous. Look at the bees, who gather so much honey and store it only to have it taken away in the end by someone else. And mice, who spend their time hoarding grains that are then taken by others. Look at the many immensely rich people in this world who still never think of making an offering to the Three Jewels or giving to the needy.[43] Their wealth is piled up for no purpose; it is a complete waste. Someone who is very poor who offers just a single butter lamp with a pure intention will have inconceivably greater merit when he dies than an apparently rich person who is unable to give anything away and make offerings. Therefore,

> *Without being trussed by the knot of miserliness, give away*
> *impartially.*

Do not be selective in your generosity, thinking that it is better to give to one cause than to another. All forms of offering and giving are equally good. You should not imagine that making an offering to the Buddha is something very superior and dignified while giving to a beggar is very limited ("He will just eat what I give him, and that will be the end of it"). The Buddha himself became a Buddha by perfecting generosity and giving to the needy. It was because he was so generous that great compassion and wisdom grew in him. So there is no difference between making offerings to the Buddha and giving to the poor. In fact we should consider all the beings we meet, beggars and so on, as teachers showing us the path and helping us fulfill our wish to attain enlightenment. We should make offerings to them and give without discrimination.

> **If, when you are practicing, the dam of suffering bursts,**
> **it is simply that you are purifying your negative actions.**
>
> *Rejoice and give up wrong views.*

If you spend your whole life practicing alone in a mountain retreat, you will certainly have plenty of difficulties. You will fall sick, experience pain, and encounter many adverse circumstances. At such times do not think, "Although I am practicing the Dharma, I have nothing but trouble. The Dharma cannot be so great. I have followed a teacher and done so much practice, and yet hard times still befall me." Such thoughts are wrong views. You should realize that through the blessing and power of the practice, by experiencing sickness and other difficulties now, you are purifying and ridding yourself of negative actions you committed in past lives that would have led to rebirth in the hells and other lower realms in future lives. By purifying them now while you have the chance, you will later go from bliss to bliss. So do not think, "I don't deserve this illness, these obstacles, these negative influences." Realize instead that through the teacher's kindness and the power of the practice you can completely purify yourself of all your past negative actions. Experience your difficulties as the blessings of the Three Jewels. Furthermore, bear in mind that many, many beings are suffering in a similar way. Make a wish that the suffering you yourself are experiencing may take the place of all other beings' suffering, thinking, "May their suffering be exhausted in mine." So when you do experience such difficulties, you should be very happy and avoid having adverse thoughts like, "Why are such terrible things happening to me? The Guru and the Three Jewels don't care for me, they have no compassion, the practice doesn't help."

If people are hostile with a Dharma practitioner who has done nothing wrong, it is simply that they are setting him on the path of patience.

Avoid grudges and ill will; keep in mind the benefits of patience.

As Kunkhyen Jigme Lingpa said:

> An enemy repaying your good with bad makes you progress
>   in your practice.
> His unjust accusations are a whip that steers you toward virtue.
> He's the teacher who destroys all your attachment and desires.
> Look at his great kindness that you never can repay!

If someone criticizes or blames you even though you have not done anything wrong, do not get upset and angry or try to get even. Instead be grateful: regard it as an opportunity to purify your own actions from the past when you yourself blamed others. Don the armor of patience, reflecting on this verse:

> No evil is there similar to anger,
> No austerity to be compared with patience.
> Steep yourself, therefore, in patience,
> In various ways, insistently.[44]

Jigme Lingpa himself said that although many people accused and criticized him unreasonably, he always prayed, "May these people become my disciples in a future life so that I can benefit them." And indeed in his future lives he manifested as Do Khyentse Yeshe Dorje and as Jamyang Khyentse Wangpo.[45]

Here is a story that illustrates the benefits of patience. In one of his previous lives as a Bodhisattva, the Buddha was the rishi Patient Words. Although he was the brother of a king, he had long since forsaken worldly life and taken to a life of solitude and meditation in the forest. One day the king and his retinue of queens went into the forest for a picnic. The king fell asleep, and while he was sleeping, the queens wandered off and came across the rishi, Patient Words. When the king awoke and found that everyone had gone, he set out to look for his queens and eventually found them seated before the rishi listening to him teach. In a fury the king drew his sword and asked, "Who are you?"

"They call me Patient Words," replied the rishi.

"Let's see how patient you really are," cried the king, and with his sword he started cutting the rishi to pieces, slicing off his arms and legs. He was at the point of cutting off the rishi's head when the latter spoke:

"As you cut me up bit by bit, I vow that in a future life, when I attain enlightenment, one by one I will slice away all your afflictive emotions." Thereupon the king cut off the rishi's head. From the rishi's body, instead of blood, there flowed milk. The king suddenly realized that this was not an ordinary being he had killed, but a siddha.

"Who was this rishi?" he asked. When he learned that it was his very own brother who had become a great rishi by meditating in the forest, he felt deep remorse. He took the body of the rishi back to his capital, held an enormous offering ceremony, and constructed a stupa in which the relics were enshrined. When the rishi became the Buddha Shakyamuni, by the power of his prayer in that previous life the king became one of the first five disciples who received the Buddha's teaching at Varanasi. So a Bodhisattva is someone who takes refuge thinking, "May the harm that others cause me create a connection through which they may attain happiness."

If we achieve some results from our practice and find ourselves being respected by people, we must never be conceited or proud that our activities are increasing. See everything as a dream, as an illusion, and avoid getting attached to wealth and possessions, otherwise you will fall back into samsara and end up having nothing at all.

If your having consummate faith coincides with applying the instructions, it is simply that you have come to the end of karma.

The instructions are something we have to put into practice. Merely reading the doctor's prescription will never cure our illness. Our teacher's instructions are meant to be used when we encounter obstacles and difficulties. We should use them correctly and not miss the point. Just as the best way to kill someone is to stab him in the heart—he will not even survive one hour—if you apply the instructions correctly and hit the vital point, even one month of practice will be effective in dispelling your afflictive emotions and actions. Otherwise, however much you study and listen to the teachings, the instructions and your own being will go different ways. Unless you gain stability in your practice so that you really overwhelm your ego-clinging and afflictive emotions, any so-called advanced practice you do will be pointless, no more than an impressive-sounding name. But if you practice properly now,

> *In the future you will not be reborn in samsara.*

Like a hooked fish pulled out of the water, you will have been hooked by the compassion of the Buddhas. If in this life you are diligent and practice in the right way, even if you do not attain full realization, you will be reborn in a place where you can come across the teachings, meet the teacher, and continue to progress. The greater the connection you make with the Dharma in this way, the more you will benefit. It was through practicing the Dharma that all the sages in the past attained their level of realization.

> *The whole of the Dharma should serve as the antidote to attachment and aversion.*

Otherwise doing a lot of practice will only increase your pride; spending a long time in a cave or secluded place will just be a way to pile up possessions, and you will become an evil spirit. The practice will not have acted as an antidote to your attachment and aversion, it will not have been genuine Dharma.

> **If your own fear of death coincides with other people dying, it is simply that the time has come to turn your mind away from samsara.**

Once the Lord Buddha came across four strong men trying to split a huge rock blocking the road. However hard they tried they were unable to move it. Using his miraculous power the Buddha tossed the rock into the air with his toe, and when it landed again, he reduced it to gravel by pointing his finger at it. Everyone was amazed and said, "Surely there is no one in the world more powerful than you."

"Yes," replied the Buddha, "there is someone much stronger than me."

"Who can that person be?" they asked.

"When I pass into nirvana, I shall meet the Lord of Death. He is far more powerful than I am."

It is very important to constantly bear in mind that we are going to die, and that we will have to endure all the pain of dying. This does not apply only to us. Think how many people have died in the past month. And consider *how* they have died: some have died old, others have died young, and in all sorts of different circumstances. Where are all those people now, in which of the six realms have they ended up? Some of them must now be enduring the most terrible suffering. And we are bound to experience those very same sufferings too. When we reflect on all the torments that will befall us, it seems that nothing in this worldly life is of much benefit to us.

Do not be attached to happiness and comfort in this life.

However delicious the food is that we eat, it all turns into excrement. However beautiful the clothes we wear, they are only covering what is under the skin—foul components like flesh, blood, and lymph. So what is the point of dressing one's body up in brocades? This life is as fleeting as a cloud in the sky; it can vanish at any moment. No one can say how long they will live. And if they do live a certain amount of time, no one can say whether they will be happy and satisfied all their life. Nothing is certain— neither the circumstances of our death nor those of our life, so we should have no attachment to the things of this life. The only way to use our lives properly is to practice the Dharma, and to do so when we are young and our bodies and minds are in their prime. We might think, "For the next twenty years, or perhaps a bit less, I shall earn and save enough money to be able to stop working, and then I'll practice the Dharma." But who knows when we might die; who knows if in the meantime we might change our minds? This is why the root text says,

> **If you think you will finish your projects for this life first and after that practice a bit of Dharma, this is simply the demon's delaying tactics.**

It is very important not to fall under the influence of such a demon.

What we call a demon is not something with goggling eyes, a gaping mouth, sharp teeth, and a terrifying look. The real demon is our predilection for worldly activities, our attachment to friends and relatives, our aversion to enemies, and the fact that we are completely dominated by the eight ordinary concerns, together with the circumstances—both good and bad—that can make us stray from the Dharma. It is said that favorable circumstances are more difficult to deal with and use on the path because they are more distracting and make us forget the Dharma. So when we have everything we need—money, status, a comfortable home, food, and clothes—we should not be attached to these but view them as illusory, as things that appear in a dream.

Undesirable circumstances are relatively easier to deal with. It is relatively easier to meditate on patience when someone gets very angry with us or threatens us, and to practice when we are sick, because these are causes of suffering and suffering naturally reminds us of the Dharma. But when we are happy, when things are going well, these good circumstances have a tendency to blend very comfortably with our minds, like massage oil, which spreads easily over the body. When we enjoy good times, attachment rests easily on the mind and becomes part of our feelings. And once we are attached to good circumstances, the demon of the sons of the gods has arrived. Of the four demons, this is the one that creates pride: we become infatuated with success, fame, and riches. It is very difficult to rid the mind of such pride.

++ 7 ++

Thirteen instructions to put into practice.

Son, there are thirteen instructions.

As a spur to diligence in the practice, consider your own death and others'.

The time of death is uncertain, so give up all this life's pointless activities and projects.

For the Dharma, you need strong determination and diligence. Even if your life is at stake, the Dharma is something you must never give up. Just as one uses spurs to make a horse go faster, the main spur to diligence is to reflect on death. Think how many people in the world spend their time trying to defeat those they consider as enemies. They spend years and years fighting, and often die before they reach victory. For them the end result is rebirth in the hell realms. Others spend their time looking after the interests of their relatives and friends, but many die before being successful. And because of the attachment they have, they are reborn as pretas. If we were able to know precisely when we will die, we would be able to plan our lives and calculate exactly what we would do and when. But this is not the case. Some people die when they are going from one place to another. Others die when they are still in their mother's womb. Some die young, others die very old after going through all sorts of difficulties, illnesses, and all the sufferings of old age. There is no certainty at all about when we will die. And worldly activities are really very unimportant. So if you think you will complete all your ordinary projects first and practice the Dharma after that, you are not only wasting your time, but you also cannot be sure you will ever practice. It is said, "Worldly activities are like children's games. If we abandon them, there will be nothing more to do. If we continue them, they will never end." Moreover, it is important to realize how valuable the Dharma is and to realize that if you have had the chance in your present life to hear the teachings and reflect on them, this is only the result of your having accumulated merit in your past lives.

Just how precious and rare it is to receive the Dharma is illustrated in some of the former lives of the Buddha. In several of these lives he was reborn as a king in a place where there was no one teaching the Dharma. So great was the king's longing to receive teaching that he erected a high throne in front of his palace and offered his entire kingdom to anyone who would come and expound the Dharma. On one occasion, a rishi arrived and said he was willing to teach, but it would not be enough for the king to offer his kingdom: he should be ready to give his own life. The king replied that he would happily do so. The rishi therefore told him to make an offering of a thousand lamps by piercing a thousand holes in his body, placing a wick and some clarified butter in each hole. Without hesitating, the king proceeded to do so and lit all the lamps. The rishi mounted the throne and gave a single verse of teaching:

> Abandon evil doing,
> Practice virtue well,
> Subdue your mind:
> This is the Buddha's teaching.

Afterwards the rishi asked the king whether he had any regrets. The king replied, "I am filled with joy at having received this teaching." He was profoundly grateful and felt no pain at all. At that moment all the gods appeared in the sky and praised the king's determination to receive teaching. Through the blessing of his complete sincerity and joy in hearing the teaching and his total absence of regret in sacrificing himself, all his wounds were miraculously healed.

The king was required to undergo similar ordeals in other lives, like piercing his body with a thousand nails or jumping into a pit of fire. On each occasion, he did so without the slightest hesitation and each time, on account of his joy at receiving instruction, he was completely cured. All this shows just how precious it is to receive the teachings. We will always manage somehow to find food and clothing, but the Dharma is much more rare and precious, so it is important to have a deep respect for it.

If you want to cultivate extraordinary respect, examine the teacher's outer and inner qualities.

For us the teacher is the source of all good qualities and accomplishments. So you should examine him carefully to see the perfection in all his outer and inner qualities, and take them as examples to be followed. But in so doing, you must never have wrong thoughts or distorted views:

Avoid thinking of defects.

If you think the teacher has done something that seems not quite perfect, you should realize that this is simply your own deluded way of perceiving him, as was the case for the monk Sunakshatra who thought the Buddha only gave teachings in order to fool people. Even if you see a minute defect, realize that it is your own wrong perception: rid your mind of such thoughts and cultivate pure perception. As the note says:

Seeing faults reflects your own impure perception.

When Guru Rinpoche came to Samye, although he was a fully enlightened Buddha and displayed many marvelous deeds and miracles, there were still evil ministers who had wrong thoughts about him. They doubted his qualities and tried to obstruct his activities. Even King Trisong Detsen was prey to such doubts. Having received instructions from Guru Rinpoche, he went to Yamalung and meditated in a cave, practicing the sadhana of Amitayus. Through the blessings of this practice, Amitayus appeared in the sky before him and bestowed the empowerment from his own long-life vase: the king received the blessing for attaining immortal-

II. DISCIPLINE / 67
ity. He then returned to Samye riding a horse and arrived just as Guru Rinpoche was bestowing the empowerment of long life. The Guru was at the point of dispensing the long-life nectar when one of the evil ministers whispered to the king, "Who knows whether the liquor has been mixed with poison?" For a second the king hesitated, wondering whether it were true, and as a result the auspicious connection that would have secured the blessing he had received earlier was broken. This shows how important it is not to have wrong thoughts or doubts when there is actually nothing wrong.

If you want your conduct to concord with all, do not obstruct the efforts of others.

It is very important to maintain perfect harmony and good relations with all your Dharma companions, brothers, and sisters. You should be like a belt for them, like something one wears all the time but does not feel. You should be very adaptable, like salt, which readily dissolves in any kind of water, clear or muddy. Relating to the teacher alone will not do; you must be able to cope with other people. Otherwise, you will cause your samaya to deteriorate and upset the teacher. In everything you do, act in accordance with the Dharma and behave harmoniously with everyone. You can never become a genuine practitioner by relating poorly to people—upsetting everyone and acting contrary to their wishes.

Furthermore, of the Dharma's nine vehicles, practice the one that can truly help you in accordance with your present capacity and condition. Never dismiss the so-called lesser vehicles, thinking that they are too low for you. Each vehicle has teachings that can help us according to our capacity. So you should receive and examine the teachings of the Shravaka Vehicle properly, seeing the truth in them and practicing them as much as possible. Similarly, in the Bodhisattva and Mantra Vehicles you should learn whatever is beneficial for you and practice them as well as you are able. Thus, do not discriminate against lower vehicles or long to practice the so-called advanced teachings. Realizing that these teachings do not contradict each other, practice them in such a way that they truly help you to progress. Then everything will arise as teaching. The Buddha gave all the various teachings out of compassion, and they are all imbued with his wisdom: there is not a single word in them that can harm beings. Each one has the virtue of leading beings to liberation and enlightenment. So do not be sectarian and think, "Our teachings are far superior to those of other schools and philosophical traditions."

As all the vehicles are true in their own terms, do not have rigid opinions about paths or philosophical schools.

While we should never think that our own tradition is best and other traditions are inferior, there is no harm in genuine discussion and debate that is free of attachment and animosity, if it helps to clarify minor misunderstandings or incorrect interpretations in our own view. Likewise, misinterpretations of others' views can be corrected by discussions between learned siddhas.[46]

So as never to upset the teacher, practice hard.

It is very important not to upset the teacher or his other disciples. To have adverse views and act out of tune or disrespectfully with the teacher and those around him is not the way to please him, however much you might think you are practicing his teachings. Be fully determined to carry out the teacher's instructions exactly. Once you have received them, be diligent in practicing them as much as you can. If you do so,

You will acquire all good qualities without exception.

If there were a mountain of solid gold, all the birds—big and small—nesting on that mountain would naturally become golden in color. In the same way, if you stay with a spiritual teacher for a long time, his good qualities will naturally bring about a change in you, and you will acquire those same qualities. And if the teacher is pleased with your practice, accomplishment will be swift, since the yidam, the dakinis, and protectors are none other than the teacher's display.

If you want to attain accomplishment quickly, keep the Pratimoksha and Bodhisattva **vows and** Vajrayana **samayas without letting them degenerate.**

It is important to know what is permitted and what is not, to observe the precepts in accordance with your capacity,[47] and to be one-pointed in trying not to transgress them. When a king's subjects observe his laws carefully, the king is satisfied and his reign is peaceful: it is easy to run the kingdom and everyone benefits. In the same way, if we rely on the Buddha's words and the teacher's instructions, our ten negative actions and afflictive emotions will naturally decrease.

All the precepts boil down to giving up the ten negative actions and the five poisons as they are ordinarily experienced.[48]

So be diligent and single-minded in getting rid of these five afflictive emotions. As long as you do not do so, they will be the root of your wandering in samsara and you will be swept away as if by a big river, taken wherever the water carries you without being able to get to the bank. In the three worlds of samsara, the main sufferings are the four rivers of birth, old age, sickness, and death. Under their influence there is no freedom to practice. The crucial point you need to know is that to stop the flow of these four rivers one has to listen to the teachings.

If you want to halt the four rivers, you must ascertain the unborn nature of the ground-of-all.

The root of our wandering in the three worlds of samsara and the source of all actions and afflictive emotions is the erroneous perception of production where there is no production. We hold the unproduced ground to be produced, and this erroneous belief is the cause of our delusion. So we need to ascertain its unborn nature, to establish its empty nature.

When we speak of the "ground-of-all,"[49] it can refer to two things. One is the support of all the afflictive emotions and of the imprints of our actions. This is the deluded ground-of-all, which we have to be rid of. The other ground-of-all is the primordial ground from which both samsara and nirvana arise. It is the sugatagarbha or buddha nature present in every sentient being. It is what the "Prayer of Samantabhadra" refers to when it says, "There is one ground." This is what we are talking about here. When you recognize this ground, you will know the absolute nature beyond origin and you will thus realize that for all phenomena there is no coming into existence, no existing, and no ceasing to exist. Once you realize the unborn nature of the ground, you will no longer be swept away by the current of the four great rivers of suffering.

When you have understood the unborn nature of the ground-of-all, the continuous flow of birth and death will cease

and you will see the end of samsara. In the best case, you can put an end to samsaric rebirth in this very lifetime. And if not, through these precious instructions you should at least be able to free yourself from samsara within three lifetimes. In particular, those who practice the Mantrayana will in one life and one body attain the indestructible union body.[50]

If you want no obstacles to your accomplishing enlightenment, leave behind the distractions of this life.

For those who are able to practice diligently and one-pointedly it is possible to attain Buddhahood in a single lifetime. However, there are bound to be obstacles: outer obstacles, such as dangers related to the five elements—water, fire, wind, and so on; inner obstacles that cause physical illness, such as disorders of phlegm, bile, or energy; and secret obstacles caused by one's thoughts. These obstacles arise from attachment to the things of this life. If one has no attachment, it is impossible for such obstacles to occur. So it is very important to leave behind all the distractions of this life.

Trying to help others without having the ability is yet another distraction.

Unless you have fully realized the unborn, absolute nature yourself, to think of helping others will simply distract you and act as an obstacle to your own practice.

Do not try to benefit others when you yourself are not ready.

A Bodhisattva who has truly realized the ultimate, unborn nature of phenomena does not think of his own welfare for even an instant. Never is he not concerned with the welfare of others. But if you have not realized the absolute nature, what you may call benefiting others will merely be making you more busy. In fact, you will simply be creating more difficulties for yourself. There is a saying:

> Free yourself with realization,
> Liberate others with compassion.

So if you really wish to benefit others, the first step is to attain realization yourself. You must first mature your own mind, otherwise you will be incapable of helping others. Giving other people water is impossible unless you have a jug with water in it. If it is empty, you might make the gesture of pouring, but no water will come out. To take another example, when one lights a set of butter lamps using a lamp that is already lit, the latter must be full and burning with a bright flame in order to light the others.

II. DISCIPLINE / 71

You therefore need to have the genuine wish to help others and, with that attitude, to be diligent in the practice so that experience and realization can grow. This is why the root text says:

> **If you want to benefit others effortlessly, meditate on the four boundless qualities.**

To truly benefit others, you must have the precious bodhichitta fully developed in your being. Once you have it, you do not need to think of helping others or to make a deliberate effort to do so. It just happens naturally. The main thing that helps us develop the precious bodhichitta is to meditate on the four boundless qualities: love, the wish that all beings may be happy and have the causes of happiness; compassion, the wish that all beings may be free from suffering and the causes of suffering; sympathetic joy, the wish that all beings who are happy may remain so and become even happier; and impartiality, the wish that happiness may come to each and every sentient being without distinction, whether they are close to us or strangers. We call these four qualities "boundless" for four reasons. First, their benefits are boundless. Second, the number of beings to whom we should direct them is boundless, for sentient beings are as numerous as the sky is vast. Third, the qualities of enlightenment, which is the result obtained from meditating on them, are boundless. Fourth, the attitude we have when cultivating these four is boundless. Just as seed sown in a field that is properly tilled, watered, manured, and exposed to the sun will naturally produce a good crop, if you meditate sincerely and deeply on these four boundless qualities, the precious bodhichitta will certainly take birth in your being. Once you have trained your mind and experienced bodhichitta, even if you do not gather a lot of disciples and put on a performance of benefiting them, whatever you do directly or indirectly will naturally help others. So always keep in mind that the best way to benefit others is to meditate on the four boundless qualities.

If you train in bodhichitta, nothing you do will exclude others' welfare.

Someone who has such compassion is not only immune to harm from violent people and destructive spirits; he can, moreover, set them on the path to liberation.

> **If you are fearful of the three lower realms in your future lives, steer clear of the ten negative actions.**

It is important to be convinced that you will have future lives in which you can expect heat and cold in the hells, hunger and thirst among the pretas, and enslavement and slaughter in the animal realms. If you want to avert these miserable states, you have to avoid the ten unvirtuous actions and find antidotes for the five poisons in this life. If you can counteract anger, you will not be reborn in the hells. If you can counteract attachment, you will not be reborn among the pretas. If you can counteract bewilderment, you will not be reborn as an animal. Whether you avoid negative actions and cultivate positive ones is entirely in your hands. If you are able to do so, there is no way you will be reborn in the lower realms. But if you are not careful, and you indulge in all the negative actions while failing to cultivate positive ones, then, when you die, you will fall helplessly into the lower realms like a stone thrown into an abyss. So

Be careful, all the time.[51]

An ordinary being's mind is like a restless monkey. To tie this monkey so that it does not wander too far, we need to apply mindfulness (remembering what we have to do and what we have to avoid) and vigilance (keeping watch over our thoughts, words, and deeds). With mindfulness and vigilance, we will be aware of any unwholesome thoughts that arise and so be able to come up with the antidote to prevent them growing. As a result, we will be happy—even in this life. And if we have love and compassion, we will naturally be able to help others; in making others happy we will find our kindness returned and will be safe from harmful spirits and other nonhumans. With regard to future lives, if we have cultivated love, compassion, sympathetic joy, and impartiality in an ordinary way, we will be reborn in the celestial realms, like Indra's Heaven of the Thirty-three. And if we have cultivated the four boundless qualities with the aim of bringing all beings to Buddhahood, we will eventually attain full enlightenement.

If you want to be happy in this and future lives, be diligent in performing the ten positive actions.

The ten positive actions can be applied on different levels. While it is highly positive to refrain from negative actions, it is even more powerful to perform additional positive acts that are the opposite of the negative ones. Not only should we refrain from killing, for example, but in addition we should protect life by saving animals from being slaughtered. As well as refraining from stealing, we should give generously, and so on. To practice in this way, you have to become convinced of the truth of the law of cause and effect. Having gained this conviction, cultivate even the tiniest positive actions and avoid even the minutest negative actions. In this way you will gradually progress upwards through the different vehicles of the Shravakas, Pratyekabuddhas, and Bodhisattvas. Never think that the need to avoid negative actions and cultivate positive ones is a feature of the Basic Vehicle and that there is no such need in the Great Vehicle or in the Vajrayana. To do so is a fundamental error, which is why Shechen Gyaltsap's note says,

> Now, when you have the choice, do not confuse what is to be adopted with what is to be avoided.

While you have in your hands the freedom to act and you know which actions are negative, you should not err in the decisions you make and the way you behave.

If you want your mind to engage in the Dharma, you must experience the hardship of suffering.

To turn our minds to the Dharma we first have to realize for ourselves just what suffering in samsara implies. Unless we have a taste of samsaric suffering, our minds will never turn to the Dharma. Once we know what suffering is about, we will naturally try to find a way to be free from it. So we should understand the suffering inherent in samsara by studying the detailed explanations on the preliminary practice. Moreover, we need to be aware that by engaging in negative actions we are buying suffering in future lives. So we should be mindful, vigilant, and careful, and confess and repair our previous negative actions.

Beginners should also understand that when they start practicing the Dharma there is bound to be some difficulty. Trying to blend one's mind with the Dharma *is* difficult, but this is a very worthwhile kind of difficulty. There is a saying: "In experiencing difficulty one achieves something rare." It is only through great hardship that one can gain unique and worthwhile achievements. Buddha Shakyamuni, for instance, had to go through great difficulties accumulating merit over a period of three measureless kalpas, even though he himself said that the Great Vehicle was the vehicle for beings of superior capacity. And if the Vajrayana is said to be the path for attaining Buddhahood in a single lifetime, that is not to say that it is an easy path. Look at the hardships Jetsun Milarepa went through. For twelve years he meditated diligently, sitting on the bare ground in the cave of White Rock with neither a bite to eat nor a stitch of clothing. Without that sort of effort, the supreme accomplishment will never come on its own.

Reflect on the pointlessness of weary toil and develop deep determination. There has never been a spiritual path that is easy.

Look at the trouble and difficulty ordinary people go through in governing a country, for instance. They make such enormous efforts and yet it is all entirely pointless. If they were to make the same effort for a single day practicing the Dharma, that would bring them so much closer to liberation. But they have been wandering in samsara for so long their minds automatically go in the wrong direction. Their natural inclination is to take life, to steal, and to do all sorts of other negative actions like harming old people. They have never turned their minds toward the Dharma, let alone practiced it. This is why it takes many months and years of practice for us to develop a peaceful, happy mind. Because we still have so many wrong habits from previous lives, we do not gain peace and happiness easily. So with the momentous goal of attaining liberation in mind, turn your thoughts away from samsara and put your efforts one-pointedly into practicing the Dharma.

If you want to turn away from samsara, strive for unsurpassable enlightenment.

We need to remain diligent all along the path. Even if we have reached the level of Arhat as a Shravaka or Pratyekabuddha, we still have further to go to attain complete Buddhahood. "Unsurpassable enlightenment" refers to the ultimate result of the Great Vehicle, so this is what we should be seeking. And when Zurchungpa says, "strive," he means that we should think of being diligent for our entire life. It is no use thinking that it is a question of practicing for only a few months or years. We are heavily obscured by our afflictive emotions, so we have to practice diligently and one-pointedly until we have completely removed all our obscurations.

It is important to recognize the benefits of liberation and enlightenment according to the three vehicles.

To gain even a few of the qualities of liberation and enlightenment is to obtain something very precious. Bear in mind that realizing even a fraction of the Buddha's enlightened qualities brings immense benefit, whereas engaging in even a little worldly activity causes great harm. If you practice the teachings of the three vehicles in their entirety, you will acquire all their respective qualities and understand that these teachings are not contradictory. And as a result you will attain the three kayas—the dharmakaya, sambhogakaya, and nirmanakaya.

If you want to obtain the result, the three kayas, unite the two accumulations.

The two accumulations are the accumulation of merit—with concepts—and the accumulation of wisdom—without concepts. The former comprises the first five transcendent perfections—generosity, discipline, patience, diligence, and concentration—while the latter comprises the sixth perfection, transcendent wisdom. By diligently accumulating merit and wisdom together you will attain Buddhahood.

This will cause the stains veiling the three kayas to be removed.

The perfect buddha nature is in fact present within us, but it is obscured by afflictive emotions and by karmic and conceptual obscurations. We can remove these, as we have seen, by turning the mind toward the Dharma and cultivating the four boundless qualities.

++ 8 ++

Showing how to recognize what is not true practice: five things that are useless.

Son, there are five things that are useless.[52]

These five refer to what is not true Dharma: if you follow them, they will lead to your ruin.

No need to say you are interested in the Dharma if you have not turned your mind away from samsara.

Unless you feel deep down that samsara is a pit of burning coals, there is no point in saying, "I am practicing the Dharma, I am meditating, I am deep in samadhi." Without that profound conviction, you can only go in the opposite direction to the Dharma. Even if your practice leads to your gaining a good reputation, it will be completely in vain.

76 / ZURCHUNGPA'S TESTAMENT

If everything you do is for this life alone, you will not accomplish the Dharma.

With this sort of attitude it is impossible to practice the Dharma properly. You will simply get involved in things like protecting your relatives and friends and getting rid of your enemies; your life will run counter to the Dharma. Dharma and worldly activities are like fire and water. If you practice the Dharma genuinely, you cannot help giving up worldly activities. On the other hand, if you devote yourself to worldly activities, you will never be able to practice the Dharma properly. So cultivate a deep desire to abandon the things of this world and a strong determination to practice Dharma.

To practice the genuine Dharma, you have to counter attachment to samsaric perceptions.

The root of our repeatedly taking birth in samsara is the alternating desire and loathing we have for the objects of the five senses—forms, tastes, smells, sounds, and physical sensations—together with the perceptions our eight consciousnesses hold of these sense objects. When we feel attachment or, conversely, aversion to the experiences of the five senses, we sow the seed for rebirth in samsara. It all starts with attachment. If we had no attachment, there would be no reason for aversion. Because we are strongly attached to ourselves and to what is ours—our friends and relatives, our belongings, and so on—we feel aversion to anyone who might harm us or anything that is ours. But without attachment in the first place, there would be no aversion. Once attachment and aversion are present, however, we feel well-disposed to those who are good to us and we want to retaliate when people hurt us. This leads to a multitude of actions, which are the activities of samsara. Once our minds are dominated by attachment and aversion, any intention to practice the Dharma is eclipsed, so it is important to gain realization of emptiness.

No need to meditate on emptiness if you have not countered attachment to the things you perceive.

Meditation on emptiness implies a state like space. There is no occasion for thoughts like "I," "mine," "my body," "my mind," "my name," or "my belongings." This sort of clinging has no place in meditation on emptiness.

So if you have thoughts like "my possessions" and so on, there is no way your meditation and practice can be genuine.

One meditates on emptiness in order to release one's clinging, believing that things truly exist.

A genuine practitioner does not have this attachment to relatives and possessions, neither does he feel any aversion for enemies.

Unless you are free from this, emptiness is no more than a word,

it is quite useless.

No need to practice meditation if you do not turn your mind away from desire.

To say "I meditate" and at the same time still have an ordinary mind with desire and attachment will give no result.

Great meditators who end up sidetracked by village ceremonies risk dying as ordinary men.

Practitioners who have meditated in mountain retreats for a few years are often taken by ordinary folk to be very advanced meditators and many of them begin to believe the fools who speak of them as great meditators who have reached a high level of realization. They start accepting offerings and reverence from people, and they grow rich. They end up spending their time going from one village ceremony to another and behaving in a completely worldly way. This is no use at all.

No need for fine words if you have not assimilated the meaning yourself.[53]

If you want to practice the Bodhisattva path, whatever you do—be it a single prostration, one circumambulation, or just one recitation of the *mani*—you must do it for the sake of all sentient beings, with the wish that they all attain enlightenment. This is the true practice. On the other hand, practicing without such an attitude, mainly to become rich and happy and to achieve greatness in this life, while saying nice things and speaking as if one were a great Bodhisattva working for the benefit of others, is pointless.

There are many who are fooled by smart talk about the view, so hit the crucial point of the natural state.

To say things like "Everything is void," "There is no such thing as good or bad, virtue or evil," "All perceptions are spontaneously liberated as they arise," or "Afflictive emotions are liberated as they arise," without having true confidence in such a view and stability in one's practice, is known as merely carrying the view on one's lips. This is why Guru Rinpoche said to King Trisong Detsen, "My view is like space, but conduct must never slip toward the view, for if it does, it will be a wholly black, demonic view." He said that the view should be as high as possible but that one's conduct should comply with the most basic teachings. So it is important to get to the crucial point and master the true nature of things through your own experience and not merely in words. And regarding this, there is

No need to apply the instructions if you do not have devotion.

If you have great devotion, seeing the teacher as the Buddha himself, and maintain a lofty inner view while keeping your external conduct completely down to earth, all the qualities of experience and realization will grow effortlessly. Experiences and realization in fact come through the spontaneous devotion you have to your teacher, so when they occur, they are truly due to the teacher's kindness.

Any experiences, realization, or good qualities that occur depend on the teacher's blessing: without devotion the blessings can never possibly penetrate.

When Atisha was in Tibet, some people said to him, "Give us your blessing!" "Give me your devotion," replied Atisha. If you have devotion, you will receive the blessings; without it you can never do so.

++ 9 ++

Showing how to practice with determination and the great armor of diligence: five things one needs to do.

To accomplish the Dharma you should be ready to give your body and life a hundred times over. That is the sort of determination and courage it takes. If you practice sincerely even for a month, you will see some progress. But without determination, diligence, and energy you will not get much benefit.

Son, there are five things you need to do.

You need to have fervent devotion to the teacher, for then the blessings of the lineage will automatically rub off on you.

The first thing that illuminates the virtuous path[54] is devotion. If your devotion is such that you see your teacher as the Buddha in person, all the blessings of the lineage masters from Samantabhadra down to your own root teacher will enter you as naturally as water flowing down a slope, without your needing to seek or fabricate them.

The practice of the Secret Mantrayana is the path of devotion and blessings.

In the mantrayana one perceives all forms as the deity, all sounds as mantra, and all thoughts as the display of the absolute nature. The path for achieving this depends on receiving the teacher's blessings, and those in turn depend on devotion. The more you feel devotion, the more your confidence in the practice of Dharma will grow.

The root and lineage teachers are of one essence.

Many spiritual teachers have appeared in the past. Some were learned scholars, others were accomplished siddhas; some were monks, others were yogins; some appeared as deities like Vajrasattva, others appeared as dakinis like Lekyi Wangmo.[55] But whatever form they have taken, they are not different from one another in the way that ordinary beings are different. Their essential nature is exactly the same. They are in fact the display of a single teacher. The teachers from whom we ourselves have received teachings actually manifest the infinite array of tantric deities—the one hundred peaceful and wrathful deities, and so on. Just as space contains all the planets and other celestial bodies without overflowing, and the whole universe with its mountains and continents fits without difficulty into the infinite expanse of emptiness that is the absolute state of dharmakaya, so likewise all the Buddhas and lineage teachers are included in our own teacher. If we have firm devotion to our teacher, we will naturally receive the blessings of all the Buddhas:

See the teacher as the Dharmakaya Buddha. That way the blessings of all the Buddhas will enter you.

You need to accumulate exceptional merit, for then everything you wish for will work.

By putting into practice everything the teacher says, you will please him. And if you go through all the stages of the practice, such as the five sections of the preliminary practice and the offering of the seven branches, you will accumulate merit and thereby easily accomplish everything you aspire to in the Dharma.

The wishes of someone who has merit will be accomplished.

If you practice the Dharma properly, you will accumulate great merit and become like those with very good fortune: they have all the money they need to do whatever they want, they befriend influential people, and so on. It is merit that gives them the fortune to have all their wishes fulfilled. So if you have a great store of merit, to begin with you will always be reborn in the higher realms as a human or celestial being, and ultimately you will attain Buddhahood.

At all times offer the seven branches, backed by bodhichitta.

Of the many ways to accumulate merit, one of the quickest and most condensed is the offering of the seven branches. It includes all the methods for gathering merit and purifying obscurations—in short, for gladdening the Buddhas. And since we claim to practice the Great Vehicle, we must dedicate this and everything we do to the enlightenment of sentient beings without straying into thinking of our own welfare.

That way you will necessarily acquire a good heart.

If you have prepared your mind in this way, rendering it fit with mindfulness and vigilance so that negative thoughts do not occur and good thoughts grow, you will certainly develop extraordinary concentration:

You need to make your mind fit, for then extraordinary concentration will be born in your mind.

To make a lamp burn brightly, without flickering, one puts it inside a glass lantern to protect it from the wind. Similarly, to develop deep concentration we have to prepare the mind and still our thoughts with devotion and a correct attitude.

It is important to train perfectly in making the body and mind fit.

Through practice your body and mind will become fully trained and adaptable. As a sign of this, you may experience clairvoyance or be able to remain in meditation for days without feeling hungry or thirsty, and so forth.

You need to cultivate extraordinary concentration, for then the afflictive emotions will be overwhelmed.

When a lion roars, all the other animals naturally cower and flee. Likewise, when we develop genuine concentration, the afflictive emotions automatically diminish and shrink away. How do we achieve this? Ordinary people's minds are constantly ruffled by a multitude of thoughts. Unless we still these thoughts, it is very difficult to get rid of afflictive emotions. So first we need to stabilize our minds through the practice of sustained calm. Having tamed our wild thoughts and afflictive emotions with sustained calm we then eradicate them through the practice of profound insight. In this way concentration will grow.

Sustained calm is like a glass lantern protecting the flame inside from the wind. It quiets our thoughts and stops the mind from running after external objects. However, we cannot gain freedom from samsara with sustained calm alone. We need to extend it with profound insight. When we practice sustained calm, we will have the experiences of bliss, clarity, and absence of thoughts. If we cling to these experiences, desiring them and feeling a sense of achievement and pride when they happen, we will not progress. Profound insight completely frees us from clinging to the experiences of sustained calm. We therefore need to unite these two practices. When we do so,

> Sustained calm crushes the afflictive emotions, profound insight eradicates their seeds.

Unless we unite sustained calm and profound insight in this way, we will never succeed in realizing deep concentration.

You need to be free of afflictive emotions, for then you will quickly attain enlightenment.

On one occasion Padampa Sangye was asked, "Do negative actions tinge us once we have realized emptiness?" He replied that once we have realized emptiness, there is no reason for committing any negative action.

What do we mean by Buddhahood, or *sangye* in Tibetan? The first syllable, *sang*, implies waking up from the deep sleep of ignorance. Ignorance pervades all the eighty-four thousand afflictive emotions. Buddhahood is awakening out of all these afflictive emotions, which obscure the buddha nature—present and unchanging in every single sentient being—just as the clouds in the sky obscure the sun, so that we cannot see it. The reason it is possible for us to attain Buddhahood is precisely because we all have the buddha nature present within ourselves. Even a tiny insect on a blade of grass has it. So the path is simply a question of gradually unveiling our innate Buddhahood by practicing sustained calm and profound insight. It is not a search for something different from what we already have.

> *Besides your own mind divested of obscurations, there is no other enlightenment to be sought.*

✦✦ 10 ✦✦

Identifying counterfeit Dharma.

We may appear to be practicing the Dharma, but if it is not genuinely Dharma, our practice can lead us to the hells and the other lower realms. To say we are practicing the Dharma will simply be a lie.

Son, there are five things that become lies.

As long as you delight in the things of this world, saying you are afraid of birth and death becomes a lie.

People who are so totally involved in worldly affairs that they carry on working day and night in order to become rich, powerful, and famous, to look after their relatives and friends, and to get rid of anyone who gets in their way are telling a big lie when they say, "I am afraid of death."

> *Unless you are truly free from attachment, it is impossible to gain liberation from birth and death.*

The way to achieve freedom from attachment is the Dharma, so without practicing the Dharma there is no way you can be liberated from birth and death.

Unless you are afraid of birth and death, going for refuge becomes a lie.

When people are in difficulty, they seek protection. If they have broken the law, they ask to be pardoned. Why? Because they are afraid. In the same way someone who wants to get out of the cycle of birth and death goes for refuge in the Three Jewels out of fear. So to say, "I take refuge" without actually being afraid is to tell a lie. We might say, "I take refuge," or "Look on me with compassion," or "Teacher, you know everything, I am in your hands." But if we make such utterances simply on our lips without having a deep inner faith and without having realized the defects of samsara, our devout words may impress ordinary folk but they certainly will not convince enlightened beings.

The words alone will not help.

Unless you are rid of desire, saying you are a great meditator becomes a lie.

Although we speak of the Mantrayana as being the vehicle in which the object of desire is used as the path, it is still necessary to be free of attachment to that object. As long as you have attachment, the Mantrayana will not work, and you are lying to yourself if you think you will be able to attain enlightenment without giving up attachment. People who do not completely and purposefully give up all concern for friends, relatives, enemies, growing crops, building houses, and so on, and who at the same time think they are great meditators, end up as the old hermits one hears about, who merely accumulate things in their hermitages. If you really are a great meditator, you will know that,

> The end of all gathering is dispersing,
> The end of all living is dying.
> The end of all meeting is parting,
> The end of all rising is falling.

When you come to die, you will have to leave all your possessions behind; they will be of no use to you then. Neither should you be concerned with any external good qualities you might have such as a pleasing appearance or skill with words:

Attachment to anything, inside or out, is a cage imprisoning you.

Just as a bird in a bamboo cage can never get out, a mind caught by desire and attachment has no opportunity to escape onto the path of liberation.

Whether one is shackled with a golden chain or bound with a rope, it is the same

—one is immobilized, one cannot move one's legs. The Dharma is like gold, but if we do not practice it properly, it will tie us down in the same way as an ordinary rope. To practice genuinely we need to be deeply convinced about the law of cause and effect with regard to our actions.

Unless you have understood the law of karma, saying you have realized the view becomes a lie.

Without understanding the principle of karmic cause and effect, any Dharma practice you do will simply be a semblance of the real thing. As it is said, one's view should be as high as the sky, but one's conduct must be finer than flour. When you find yourself at the point of committing even a very minor negative action, you should not dare to do it because you know it will cause future suffering. And if you have the opportunity to perform even a tiny positive action, you should eagerly do so, knowing that it will help you accumulate merit and progress toward liberation. On the other hand, it will not help at all to think that negative actions do not matter because they can be purified by confession or because according to your lofty view there is no such thing as positive or negative, good or bad. A practitioner who has truly realized the empty nature of everything naturally has a much clearer understanding of interdependence and is convinced that actions inevitably produce effects. Saying one has realized the view without having understood the law of cause and effect is a lie, and so is saying that there is no need to avoid negative actions and undertake positive ones. This is why Shechen Gyaltsap notes,

You have to master the essential point that emptiness manifests as cause and effect.

The more complete one's realization of emptiness becomes, the more clearly one sees the infallible relationship of cause and effect in relative truth.

Unless you have abandoned the abyss of existence, saying you are a Buddha becomes a lie.

Without getting rid of the cause, the five poisonous emotions, you will never close off the abyss of samsara, their result. So be diligent in applying the antidote, the three trainings.

++ 11 ++

Practicing over a long period with determination, the armor
of diligence,[56] *and daring.*

It is important to keep up our determination under all circumstances. Obstacles should make us practice even harder. Even if we become seriously ill, we should put yet more effort into listening, reflecting, and meditating, and not let illness defeat us. Similarly, if we run out of food, we should continue with even greater diligence. As long as we are motivated in this way, everything will work out. So practice with devotion, great diligence, and wisdom.

Son, there are five things that are true.

It is true to say that without meditating one will never become a Buddha.

If you do not put the path into practice, even the Buddha catching
you with his hand cannot help you.

Just as it is impossible to buy anything without money or make anything without materials and tools, there is no way to attain enlightenment without practicing. Unless you practice properly, purifying your past negative actions and avoiding further downfalls, it is no good imagining that the Buddha will catch you with his hand and prevent your falling into the lower realms. It is true that no one in this world has greater compassion, wisdom, and ability than the Three Jewels, whose blessings are omnipresent. But if you do not have devotion and do not practice, you will not be open to the Buddha's blessings, and even if he holds you in his hands, he will not be able to help you. When King Trisong Detsen's daughter, Lhacham Pemasel, was dying, the King put her on Guru Rinpoche's lap, but even then the Guru said it would be impossible to save her from death. It takes more than simply being held in a Buddha's hands. Indeed,

This very universe rests on the palm of the Buddha Vairochana-
Himasagara.

We already dwell in the hands of the Buddha Vairochana-Himasagara, but despite this we are still in samsara. Resting on the universal Buddha Mahavairochana's two hands—folded in the meditation posture—is a jewelled alms bowl. In it is a great lake of nectar on which grows a lotus. Its twenty-five flowers are tiered one above the other from the alms bowl up to the Buddha's crown protuberance, and in one of these our whole universe is contained.[57] So we are there too, always dwelling in the hands of the universal Buddha, and yet that is still not enough. Why does it not help? Because we have accumulated all kinds of negative actions and afflictive emotions.

It is true to say that if you do not break the samaya, you will not go to hell.

Whatever you do, if you have not broken the samaya, you will not fall into the lower realms. There is a story about a disciple of the supreme physician, Gampopa. He was one of Gampopa's monks but later he gave up monastic ordination, married, and had many children. He made his living rearing pigs and over many years slaughtered a large number of them. One day he fell sick and was at the point of death. His wife summoned a Kadampa geshe who lived nearby to come and give him some last advice. "You have sinned greatly," the geshe told him, "now it is time to confess and repair your negative actions before you die. You must put your trust in the Three Jewels."

"What are the Three Jewels?" the dying man asked. "Are they outside or inside?"

"The Three Jewels are the Buddha, the Dharma, and the Sangha and they are outside," replied the geshe. Taking a statue of the Buddha he told him, "This statue is the Jewel of the Buddha." He then proceeded in similar vein to give an explanation of the Dharma and the Sangha.

"The Three Jewels are not outside, they are inside," said the sick man, "and the precious Gampopa told me they are present within one's mind; they are the nature of the mind. I have no need of your Three Jewels outside." At this the geshe became very upset and left. The old man then died, and when his body was taken to the cemetery and cremated, rainbows appeared everywhere and *ringsel* relics were found in the ashes. On hearing of this, Gampopa said, "The reason for this is that the old man never stopped practicing the essential instructions I gave him on Mahamudra. Although he committed many negative actions like giving up the robes and killing pigs, he maintained the flow of blessings from the practice I gave him, and he was therefore not stained by his negative actions and could attain a certain degree of realization at the time of death." So it is very important to preserve the samaya bond between oneself and the teacher.

Always take your own mind as witness and never part from
mindfulness and vigilance.

Jigme Gyalwai Nyugu had a disciple who was the head of a group of
hunters. When they went hunting wild yaks, he used to be content with just
the tails of the animals they killed. Having loaded the tails onto his horse,
he would look to the east. If he saw a cloud there, he would fold his hands
together and say, "My teacher Jigme Gyalwai Nyugu, who is Chenrezig in
person, is up there." The younger hunters used to scoff, "You can see how
devoted he is to Jigme Gyalwai Nyugu from the way he kills all those animals." On his deathbed he told them, "Jigme Gyalwai Nyugu has come in
person; I have met him." He prayed with great devotion and then said,
"Now Apu[58] will take me to Zangdopelri[59] and guide me there. There is
nothing to worry about."

This story shows how powerful devotion can be in purifying all one's
obscurations. Faith and devotion are like a universal medicine. Even
though Jigme Gyalwai Nyugu's disciple had committed many negative
actions like killing wild yaks, because of his faith and pure samaya with his
teacher he was able to attain liberation.

It is true to say that if you separate skillful means and wisdom,
you will fall to the Shravaka level.

"Skillful means" refers here to compassion; "wisdom" is the understanding of emptiness. Unless you have genuine bodhichitta and keep in mind
that everything you do is for the enlightenment of all beings, simply saying, "I am a follower of the Great Vehicle" or, "I am a Bodhisattva" or, "I am
a Vidyadhara" will not be of much use, nor will it be true. On the other
hand, if you constantly have the genuine wish to benefit others, even if you
do not say very much or do anything very spectacular, you will surely be
on the path of the Great Vehicle.

One who trains in the Great Vehicle must never separate skillful
means and wisdom.

How does one cultivate the skillful means of great compassion? All sentient beings without exception want to be happy, yet they fail to see that
the cause of happiness is cultivating positive actions. They do not want to
suffer, yet they do not realize that negative actions result in suffering. When
we think of all these beings, who without exception have been our kind

parents, and we see that out of ignorance they do the exact opposite of what would produce happiness, we feel enormous compassion for them. That is what is called the skillful means of great compassion.

The wisdom of emptiness involves seeing that all beings are ensnared by ignorance and deciding to perform positive actions with one's body, speech, and mind (for example, respectively prostrating and circumambulating, reciting prayers and mantras, and meditating on compassion), dedicating all the resulting merit for the sake of all beings—all this without any attachment.

If you can permeate the skillful means of compassion with the wisdom of emptiness, uniting the two, you will naturally be acting in accordance with what we call the six transcendent perfections.

Train in the path of the six transcendent perfections.

Whatever you do in practicing the Dharma revolves around view, meditation, and action. Of these, the view is of paramount importance. When you are traveling through a country, you have to know where to go, which form of transport to use, what the hazards are, and which routes are the safest. Similarly, on the path to enlightenment, you must have a clear view, understanding how to travel the path. Action is a companion for the view, but should never conflict with it. The view itself may be as high as you wish: it should be the attitude of the Great Vehicle and the view of the Great Perfection. But as far as your conduct is concerned, unless your view is completely stable, your actions should never be on the same level as the view. It is wrong to adopt lofty conduct on the basis of there being no such thing as the result of an action, no such thing as cause and effect, no such thing as good and bad. Keeping your actions very down to earth will never interfere with the loftiness of your view. But if your conduct is on a higher level than your view, this will constitute a real obstacle.

It is true to say that if you do not know how to unite view and conduct, you are on the wrong path.

As one traverses the nine vehicles, the view becomes increasingly advanced. The Shravaka's view, for instance, asserts the existence of indivisible particles and indivisible instants of consciousness. As a result of this view, Shravakas are unable to let go of their firm belief in the true existence of the material world. Although they have methods for purifying the obscurations of afflictive emotions, they are unable to purify the conceptual obscurations. Bodhisattvas, on the other hand, do not have the belief in the true existence of phenomena, and on this basis they accumulate merit and wisdom on a vast scale, infusing everything with the wish to help others. As a result, their view is much vaster than that of the Shravakas. Nevertheless, in the Sutrayana there is still the dualistic notion of samsara as something to be rejected and nirvana as something to be attained. There is no such dualistic concept for someone who has entered the Vajrayana and has full realization of emptiness, of the view of the inherent union of purity and evenness. When we have realized this, we are on the swift path to enlightenment. This is why it is important that the view should be as high as possible. But our conduct should match our capacity. In other words, our actions should suit the moment. For this, practitioners have to look inward and ask themselves whether what they are doing is appropriate to their level or not. If we are unable to judge our own capacity, we risk taking the wrong path.

Take heed that the view does not slide toward action, and that action does not slide toward the view.

Ultimately the view is not something to be sought outside: it has to be found within. So the text continues,

It is true to say that the mind is by nature perfectly pure and clear, unstained by defects.

When we speak of mind, the aware mind—with its many ceaseless thoughts—is not the ultimate mind. But once these thoughts have cleared away, there is left the true, ultimate mind whose essential nature is empty, whose natural expression is luminosity, and whose manifestation is all-pervading compassion.[60] This natural state of the mind, when realized, is like the sun in a cloudless sky dispelling darkness all over the earth. Until we realize this natural state of mind, our determination to be free, our compassion, and our contentment with what we have will all remain limited in scope.

This nature of mind is not something that some beings have and others do not. Even ordinary beings completely caught up in delusion have it. Even tiny insects have it. It is simply that they have failed to recognize it. The recognition of this natural state of mind constitutes the perfectly pure view completely free from any stains or defects. As it is said of the perfect view of the Middle Way, "I have no postulate, there is no flaw in my view."

Once all the clingings to samsara and nirvana have dissolved into the absolute expanse, one reaches the emptiness possessed of everything sublime, the view beyond all postulates of existence and nonexistence, and so forth. Kunkhyen Longchen Rabjam describes this as the ultimate view, the great purity and evenness. "Great purity" refers to the fact that there is no fundamental difference between samsara and nirvana; they are both, from the very beginning, the infinitely pure state of emptiness. "Great evenness" refers to the equality of all phenomena. It is pervaded by the unchanging great bliss, which is not the ordinary bliss obtained from the pleasures of the senses, like delicious food and so on, but the unchanging bliss that is the natural condition of the Buddha's enlightened mind.

This supreme great bliss is ever present in the Buddha's mind, so even if we were to look there, we would never find such a thing as suffering in his mind. Bodhisattvas who have realized this all-encompassing emptiness are completely free from expectation and apprehension. If someone is standing by their side with a sandalwood fan wafting a cool, sandal-scented breeze over them, they do not feel elated or attached to this. If someone insults them or blames them without cause, they do not feel any ill will. Even if someone threatens to chop off their head with a sword, as in the story of the rishi Patient Words, they feel neither fear nor anger. All this is the result of their having fully realized emptiness. But the emptiness they realize is not a mere blank, in which there is nothing at all. Its natural quality is clarity. The true view is the inherent union of emptiness and clarity.

This realization of emptiness completely destroys all the afflictive emotions. And it is not only the full realization of emptiness that has such power. According to Aryadeva, merely thinking just once that phenomena might possibly be empty—merely doubting their solid reality—is sufficient to tear the afflictive emotions to pieces. We ourselves may be quite a long way from realizing emptiness, but we can approach it by watching the nature of the mind and ascertaining its empty nature. That is what we call the path.

> *Mind is intrinsically radiant and has never been contaminated by adventitious impurities, so its natural expression is the great purity. This is the very reason exerting oneself on the path is meaningful. If it were intrinsically impure, there would be no transforming it into something pure, and there would therefore be no point in striving on the path.*

That very nature has never been fundamentally changed. It has always been there, and revealing it is known as the supreme accomplishment of Mahamudra, the ultimate goal. The reason Bodhisattvas have to accumulate merit and wisdom for three measureless kalpas is because they still have not recognized this Mahamudra. Otherwise there would be no need to continue. We keep going because that is the way to progress and to recognize the Mahamudra. Those who practice the three trainings on the path of the Shravakas and Pratyekabuddhas gain only partial realization of the ultimate emptiness, but this is already sufficient to rid themselves completely of afflictive emotions. Thus, striving on the path is worthwhile, because it brings us closer and closer to realizing emptiness. Without diligence, we will never realize emptiness.

Our efforts are also meaningful because we all have this buddha nature; it is fundamental to us. If the mind were not primordially pure, it would be quite impossible to make it pure, just as it is impossible to extract gold from ordinary rock, however much one breaks it up and tries to melt and refine it. But just as refining gold ore by washing, melting, and beating it will eventually produce gold, striving on the path will unveil the nature of enlightenment, which has been with us from the very beginning. This is precisely why we can attain enlightenment. If that perfectly pure absolute nature were not already present within us, there would be no way to create it by exerting ourselves on the path. Indeed, it is said in the Vajrayana that if one did not have the ground empowerment from the beginning, there would be no way to attain enlightenment. Unless the ground empowerment were present in the disciple's being, empowerment would not do any good. One cannot empower a grain of rice to be a grain of wheat. Giving empowerment to a pea or grain of buckwheat and telling it that it is now a grain of rice will not turn it into a grain of rice. But if it is already a grain of rice, then naturally it will grow and develop into a crop of rice.

In the same way, the view, meditation, and action related to the absolute nature are present within one's being. By unveiling this absolute nature through practice one can actualize Buddhahood. We all have the buddha nature. Now we need to recognize it through practice, like making fire by striking steel and flint in the presence of tinder. We can attain Buddhahood because its nature is intrinsic to us. It is important to understand this and put it into practice.

•• 12 ••

Son, there are five things that are pointless:

You might do them but the result will be wrong.

These refer to certain things we might do that do not liberate us from samsara or lead us to ultimate enlightenment. Like worldly activities, they produce the wrong result, the opposite of what we wish to achieve.

There is no point in following a master who does not have the nectar of the teachings.

It is important to check first whether he is authentic.

If the teacher himself does not possess the nectar of the teachings, even if you follow him very faithfully, there will be no result. All the effort you put into listening, reflecting, and meditating will be wasted because he cannot give you what he himself does not have. Conversely:

There is no point in accepting a disciple who is not a proper vessel.

If an authentic teacher pours the nectar of the teachings into an improper vessel, it is a waste for everyone. The teacher has given the teaching, but the disciple is unable to make use of it. It is wasted, like nectar poured into a broken or leaking pot so that it spills on the ground. Someone who is not a proper vessel may stay with the teacher and follow him like his shadow, but he will derive no benefit from the teaching and may even develop adverse views, like the monk Sunakshatra. He spent twelve years with the Buddha and learned the whole Tripitaka by heart, but because he had wrong views, he saw faults in the teachings and in the Buddha himself, and was subsequently born as a preta in a nearby garden.

Even if he follows you like your shadow, do not give him instruction. It will benefit neither you nor him.

There is no point in making a connection with someone who will not keep the samaya.

The samaya is the very life of the teaching and of one's relationship with the teacher, so there is no point in making a connection with someone who will not keep pure samaya. In as much as someone who cannot keep the samaya is not a proper vessel, the teacher, especially, should avoid making a connection with such a person.

> *The fault of his breaking the samaya will rub off on you, and he will not benefit either.*

Breaches of samaya can obscure us in two ways: first, they obscure the samaya breaker; second, they obscure anyone who associates with a samaya breaker. In the latter case, even if we have not committed any fault ourselves, simply associating or living with samaya breakers causes us to become obscured by their stain, just as a frog with contagious skin sores infects all the frogs in the same pond and a drop of sour milk makes fresh milk also turn sour. So making connections with those who have broken the samaya helps neither us nor them.

There is no point in performing positive actions that are mixed with negative ones.

For example, killing animals to earn money to build a temple or make representations of the Buddhas' body, speech, and mind,[61] or selling meat and liquor in order to sponsor the Sangha is tantamount to accumulating negative actions for the sake of the Three Jewels. It is quite contrary to the Dharma and does not help at all.

> *The preparation and conclusion must not be mixed with negative action.*

Anyone—a sponsor, for example—who performs a positive action should begin by having the pure intention to help the Dharma and to benefit all sentient beings. The beneficial act itself should be devoid of any negative deed, such as taking life or cheating other people in order to accomplish the so-called positive action. And after having performed a very virtuous deed like sponsoring the Sangha, one should not feel proud or look down on those who have not managed to do as much. Thus, to be genuinely positive, the action must be free from negativity in its preparation, main part, and conclusion. Otherwise, if white and black deeds are mixed, the positive action will be spoilt in the same way as delicious food is spoilt by mixing it with something unpalatable.

> *It is the nature of mixed actions that they mature as happiness and suffering separately.*

In other words, if an action consists of positive and negative deeds mixed together, one will experience both happiness and suffering in turn.

There is no point in knowing the teachings if you do not act accordingly.

If you know the teachings of the Dharma but do not practice them, they will be no more than empty words. Devadatta, for example, knew the whole of the *Avatamsaka Sutra* by heart, but he did not apply it to his conduct or integrate it with his mind. This is why the note says,

It is important, rather, to integrate everything you know with your being and to put it into practice.

Whatever you have heard and learned, do not leave it as empty words. Incorporate it into your mind so that your mind blends with the teachings. Then the teachings will act as a remedy for your afflictive emotions, and that is the point of the practice.

++ 13 ++

Putting the instructions into practice over a long period with determination, armor,[62] and daring.

It is said that with a single line of instruction one can attain complete Buddhahood. So even if you have not received many different teachings, you should greatly value any instruction. You should be prepared to give your life and all you have to receive it and practice it diligently, donning the armor of forbearance in the face of cold and heat, hunger and thirst, so that you can stay in isolated mountain retreats and devote your whole life to practice. And when you meet with obstacles or adverse circumstances, you should muster all your strength and apply yourself with even greater effort. If you do so over a long period of time, it is certain that your practice will bear fruit.

Son, there are eight instructions.

As you practice, cross the pass of attachment and aversion.

Begin by falling upon those bandits, the eight ordinary concerns.

The greater our diligence in listening, reflecting, and meditating on the teachings, the more we will deepen our realization and free ourselves from the fetters of attachment and aversion. To practice the Dharma, we have to be free from the eight ordinary concerns—pleasure and pain, fame and obscurity, and so on. In particular, we should never practice with the idea of becoming famous, nor should we be attached to any recognition we may gain from doing a lot of practice. Our minds should be completely rid of these eight ordinary concerns.

When you are studying the texts, don the armor of forbearance.

Earnestly put up with physical hardships and your inner fears regarding the profound meaning.

It is very difficult in the beginning to study all the various scriptures thoroughly and to put them into practice correctly. As ordinary people, our minds are full of afflictive emotions and are stained by past actions, which contradict what the Dharma teaches. Nevertheless, as we follow the teachings, our afflictive emotions and actions will gradually start to diminish. So it is important to put on the armor of forbearance, practicing with uninterrupted effort day and night. Even ordinary people do not mind going a whole day with nothing to eat or drink in order to attain mundane goals, making a lot of effort and undergoing great hardship. But in pursuing their worldly activities, they are involved in negative actions and are sowing the seeds of future suffering, so it is all for the wrong purpose. How much more meaningful it is to undergo similar difficulties—even for a day—for the sake of the Dharma, for it will purify our obscurations from the past and help us progress toward liberation. This is one kind of patience—putting up with difficulties in the practice. Another kind is to have the patience to accept the profound meaning. Mahamudra and the Great Perfection contain the highest teachings on the absolute nature and on emptiness, which are difficult for beginners to understand and accept. Indeed, some people feel afraid when they first hear the teachings on emptiness. Have the strength and openness of mind to accept these advanced and profound teachings, remembering that it was by practicing the teachings on this view as vast as space that all the great enlightened beings of the past attained realization.

When you are staying in sacred sites and secluded places, do not let your mind hanker after food and wealth.

Once you have received the teachings and diligently studied them, you need to integrate them with your mind by practicing in a secluded place, where there are few people and where your practice will not be disrupted by ordinary distractions. Your mind should be constantly on the watch, recalling what is the correct way to practice and then checking whether you are indeed practicing correctly. If you do something with your body, speech, or mind that is contrary to the teachings, you should confess it, repair it, and promise not to commit it again. If you do something that accords with the teachings, rejoice and dedicate the merit, thinking, "Through this may my obscurations be cleared away and may I eventually be able to benefit other beings."

What you must avoid doing, however, is thinking about the food you eat and worrying whether in the future you will have any food at all. It is particularly important to be content with what you have. It is said, "Those who know contentment have true wealth at their door." Be satisfied with having enough food to sustain you and enough clothing to protect you from the cold. Someone who is content with having just enough can adapt to any conditions and accepts things more easily. This is why

It is important to have few desires and be content with what you have.

Otherwise there will be no end to your desires, just as there is no end to a dog's appetite. One can feed a dog a large meal, but as soon as it has finished, it starts sniffing around for more. We are the same. We can eat a delicious meal and still want more. We can have all the clothes we need but still want to buy more. And there is no end to how much money we can have: if we have a million, we want two million; if we have two million, we want three. Unless we know how to be satisfied with what we have, our desires can never be fulfilled. A Dharma practitioner should be someone who knows how to have enough. Once you know how to be content in this way, you will realize that this is itself the greatest wealth one can have.

When you want the profound teachings, follow a master well-versed in them.

The highest teachings, such as those of the Great Perfection, are the most profound and quintessential teachings in Buddhism. If we wish to practice them, we have to rely on a teacher who has a real knowledge of these teachings. Students who follow someone overconfident, who explains such teachings in order to show off without really being certain of the genuine view, meditation, and action, will find it hard to understand the true meaning and even harder to put it into practice, let alone obtain the proper result. So for the teachings of the Great Perfection, we need a teacher who has a complete knowledge of the view, meditation, and action of the Great Perfection and who has directly experienced and realized these himself. Only a teacher who is qualified in this way can impart similar knowledge to the disciple.

Do not relegate the instructions to superficial knowledge: clear up all your doubts about them.

It is said, "Do not leave the instructions on the bookshelf." If you do so, and you let them remain superficial, theoretical items of knowledge, they will not help you to give up worldly activities or to feel the urge to free yourself from samsara. They will not lead you to practice genuinely, and there will be no growth in your experience or realization. So you must first be diligent in listening to the teachings. Then, having received them, go over the instructions point by point, and clear up any doubts you have concerning their meaning. Finally, integrate them and make them a direct inner experience. Having done this, go to a secluded place and make a firm commitment: "From now until I attain enlightenment I shall do nothing but put these instructions into practice."

When you meet a truly knowledgeable master, do all you can to please him and never upset him.

By doing so, you will gain all the qualities of his knowledge.

If you are able to please your teacher through your practice, you will make progress on the path. Look at Tilopa, who made Naropa undergo twenty-five great hardships, and at the Father Marpa who had Milarepa build the nine-storied tower several times. Because Naropa and Milarepa were convinced that their teachers were fully enlightened Buddhas, they did not have a single doubt. They followed their masters' instructions to the letter, and for this reason they were able to attain enlightenment themselves. If your teacher asks you to do something that you think is too burdensome or beyond your ability—even though it accords with the Dharma —and you fail to implement his advice, it will be an obstacle to your practice and will prevent your obtaining the qualities of realization. You should be like a skillful minister who knows how to fulfill the king's wishes. To always please the teacher with your practice and conduct is the best way to make progress on the path to liberation and the most certain way to attain realization. By always doing as the teacher says, you will gain the same qualities as he has, just as good quality clay in a flawless mold produces an image identical to the original.

Always be careful in your behavior.

Constantly apply mindfulness, vigilance, and carefulness in your physical, verbal, and mental actions, doing only what accords with the teacher's instructions. Never upset the teacher. Receive his teachings like a swan feeding off the various waterweeds and flowers in a lake without disturbing the water. It is important to know how to follow the teacher, listen to the teachings, and relate with the people around him, receiving what you need without causing any trouble.

When the Dharma gets difficult, stamp on your faint-heartedness.

For the sake of the Dharma, you should be ready to risk your life and body. Never think, when the teacher tells you to do something, "I dare not do this," or "It is too difficult for me." The Buddha himself said that even a bee could attain Buddhahood if it had faith, diligence, and compassion. So

With no concern for body and life, serve the Teacher and act with one taste

without distinguishing between pleasant and unpleasant or wishing you could be left to lead a quiet, comfortable life somewhere.

When your family disowns you, cut all attachment in your mind.

When you follow a teacher and receive teachings from him, your relatives may try to discourage you, saying, "It is not good to give up all worldly affairs; in the future you will fall on hard times." Though they may not be very happy that you are practicing the Dharma, reflect as follows: "They are caught up in the activities of samsara; they do not realize the benefits of liberation. I have encountered the Dharma, and this might be my only chance. Now that I have this opportunity, I shall practice whether they like it or not." In this way you should sever the ties of attachment in your mind.

Treat friends and enemies equally and let attachment and aversion be
liberated by themselves.

It is said,

No evil is there similar to anger.[63]

Falling under the influence of anger constitutes a real obstacle on the
path to liberation. It is therefore important to cultivate great patience with
regard to those who harm us and to arouse bodhichitta, wishing that they
may attain enlightenment. Similarly, excessive attachment to those who are
dear to us will simply draw us into an endless series of activities in caring
for them, and our Dharma practice will go to waste. So reflect on the fact
that enemies have been your friends or relatives in past lives and cultivate
love for them. Those who are dear to you have been your enemies in past
lives; excessive attachment to them will only prevent your encountering the
teachings and receiving instruction, and then your practice will be spoiled.
This is why it is important that all the ties of attachment and aversion are
loosened.

When you are straying into ordinary thoughts, bring your con-
sciousness back to the essence.

If the mind strays onto the object, afflictive emotions will grow,
so tether them with the rope of faith, diligence, mindfulness,
and vigilance.

When you encounter external circumstances, whether favorable or adverse, turn your mind inwards and apply mindfulness so that you are not
influenced by your habitual tendencies. Otherwise, each time you give in
to attachment and are seduced by beautiful forms, fragrant scents, or sweet
melodies, your afflictive emotions will grow. You will be going in exactly
the opposite direction to the Dharma. So instead, develop great faith in the
teachings, cultivate a yearning to practice them, and apply yourself diligently day and night. Remember clearly what you should and should not
be doing. Keep an eye on what your body, speech, and mind are doing, teth-
ering them with the rope of vigilance. In this way you will tame the wild
elephant that is your mind. Maintain your practice year after year, generating ever greater diligence and constantly checking your progress and
experience. In this way, the realization of Mahamudra and the Great Per-

fection will enter your being, and when that happens, all your deluded perceptions will be liberated by themselves.

> *Develop determination and endurance. Use the antidote of primal wisdom to let deluded thoughts be liberated by themselves. This is a crucial point.*

•• 14 ••

How to practice by applying whatever is necessary in the particular situation.

In this present age, beings have very short lives and a multitude of wild thoughts and gross afflictive emotions. We compound this by frittering away our lives in superficial, theoretical study. But the essence of the Dharma is to actually practice it and achieve inner realization. Before we can practice, therefore, we have to prepare ourselves with all the favorable conditions, just as someone who wants to travel somewhere begins by securing all the provisions and other things he will need on the journey.

Son, there are thirty-four pieces of advice.

> *If you are distracted outwardly by crowds and bustle, your virtuous activities will be dispersed.*

When our minds are distracted by different enjoyable experiences like going out with our friends, dancing, singing, drinking, and attending big public events, our practice becomes dispersed. It is not enough, however, to live alone in a retreat hut.

> *If you are distracted inwardly by thoughts, afflictive emotions will rise up.*

If inwardly we have a lot of wild thoughts and we are constantly recollecting all the samsara-oriented things we habitually did in the past, thinking of all sorts of things that might happen in the future, and letting our minds be disturbed by our likes and dislikes in the present, we will give rise to many afflictive emotions and fall under the influence of all these thoughts. We will wander and be distracted from our practice.

If you are otherwise distracted by your own magical powers and giving blessings, your own life will be threatened.

Coming in between outer and inner distractions, it may happen that, after spending a long time practicing, we attain a relative degree of realization, so that people begin to think we have great powers, can perform feats of magic, and give great blessings. If we become involved in practicing magic and so forth, in the end we create conditions that can harm our lives. Also, if people think we have great powers or realization, they will pay respect to us and serve us. This too can be a major source of distraction, ultimately affecting our lives and our very liberation.

For this reason,

As they are a source of obstacles, give up distractions.

However wealthy you are, even if you are as rich as Vaishravana, the god of wealth, with whole houses full of clothes, enormous estates, and lots of money, none of these things will help you one little bit when you die. So it is important to think to yourself, "Life is running away. I do not have time to get involved in all these activities. I only want to practice the Dharma."

When you are struck by death's poison, nothing will be of any use:

There is no time to tarry: quickly, meditate!

Do not be concerned with how you live

in this life, subduing enemies and protecting your kin;

be concerned with how you will die.

As Dharma practitioners, our job is not to defeat enemies and protect friends, but to find out how to rid ourselves of all our defects, prevent afflictive emotions from arising, and seek the quickest way to enlightenment. We should not concern ourselves with the ordinary things that may happen to us in this life, constantly thinking, "How can I become the bravest general and conquer as many countries as possible?" or "How can I become as rich as possible?" Rather, we should give up all such preoccupations and focus on what is going to happen to us at death and in the intermediate state—like someone who is seriously ill and knows he is going to die very soon: he does not go on making elaborate plans for the future.

Take the example of a young maiden's bangles.

When a young woman with three brass bangles on her wrists tries to wash her hands, the bangles jangle together unpleasantly. It is much easier and quieter for her to wash her hands if she removes them first. Similarly, if we try to practice in a place—even a so-called retreat center—where there are a lot of people, one person may start talking to another, who talks to a third person, and so on ad infinitum. It is much easier to stay completely alone with no one to talk to and no cause for distraction.

Practice alone without the luxury of attendants.

Otherwise you might think, "These people are helping me; I have to do something for them in return." Or you may find yourself being unhappy about the way they do things for you. If you stay completely on your own, there will be no cause for distraction and you will not need anything.

If you really must have companions, they should themselves possess the qualities of Dharma so that they help you progress. But companions whose main preoccupations are worldly activities, distractions, and even negative actions will cause you to stray from the Dharma, and you will no longer be able to benefit from practicing in a secluded place. Therefore,

In particular, avoid bad company.

As attachment to family is your own mind's

deluded perception, cast it aside.

If on account of excessive attachment you are unable to sever the ties with your relatives, you will be prevented from practicing the Dharma. You will not be able to achieve anything. It is important to realize that attachment to relatives and hatred for enemies are deluded perceptions. They are no different from the horses, chariots, and so forth that someone who has taken a psychedelic drug experiences as hallucinations, which can neither harm nor benefit him. But when we attach too great an importance to the delusions of ordinary life, we get caught up in them. The remedy for this is:

Do not indulge

in physical activities, talking, and thinking:

Too much of these gives rise to adverse circumstances.

Instead of spending your time with distracting activities like playing sports, attending public events, and working with all sorts of machines, devote your energies to doing prostrations and performing the various yogic exercises. And since the mouth is said to be the storehouse of afflictive emotions, rather than chatting carelessly and endlessly about everything that is happening all over the world, take a vow of silence and recite only mantras and prayers. As for thoughts, as long as you follow your thoughts, there will be no end to them. Indulging in excessive activities of this sort with your body, speech, and mind leads to adverse circumstances.

There is no need to be concerned with trying to please people:

You will be much happier having no one for company.[64]

We might feel that we need someone to support our practice and provide for our needs, but this can be another source of distraction, for we then feel obliged to keep our sponsors happy, giving them small presents and flattering them. In the process, we are diverted into wanting to become rich and receiving offerings that are stained by wrong attitudes. So rather than remaining in a place with lots of people to distract you, stay alone, be diligent in the practice and be content with the little you have. Then you will have no obstacles to your practice. You will find contentment in this life and finally attain ultimate bliss, enlightenment.

Thus attachment and aversion will not arise:

With no one to keep you company, there is no attachment or aversion.

Since sentient beings' desires are never satisfied,

It is impossible to make *everyone* **happy**—*even the Buddha could not do so*—**so stop trying to please people.**

Even when Lord Buddha was alive, there were non-Buddhist teachers who criticized him, who were not satisfied with his teachings, found fault with them, and developed wrong views. So if the Buddha was not able to keep everyone happy, how can we ordinary beings ever hope to do so? Give up being concerned with trying to keep people happy: it will simply interrupt your practice.

Here is a metaphor for being without thoughts related to attachment and aversion:

Stay alone like a corpse.

A corpse carried to the graveyard is not impressed or pleased by being given fine clothes or having nice things said about it. Neither does it feel cold if it has no clothes or get angry if one insults or scolds it. You should be like that, completely indifferent to good or bad conditions, to pleasant or unpleasant words, to being treated well or not.

Avoiding the abodes of attachment and aversion and thus being free from clinging and desire,

Do not enter a pit of thorns: stay in a place where you will be happy.

In places with a lot of people, one thought or word leads to another, and we build up a constant stream of attachment and aversion. Such places are like a pit of thorns. Instead, you should stay somewhere pleasant where there are no such causes for attachment and aversion, and where you will remain in a happy frame of mind.

Until now you have surrendered your bodies and lives to attachment and aversion.

From time without beginning we have been wandering in samsara. Countless times in our innumerable rebirths, our attachment has led us to give up our lives trying to fulfill our desires. Countless times our hatred has caused us to lose our lives trying to vanquish our enemies. If we were to collect all the tears we have shed in despair at not achieving our goals, they would more than fill the biggest oceans on this earth. And yet nothing of all this has brought us the slightest benefit.

Enough with the past, now stop such surrender.

Instead, make a promise that whatever difficulties you encounter, whether you are hungry or cold, you will give up ordinary activities and devote yourself to practicing the Dharma.

Now surrender your body and life to the Dharma.

Since all beings are endowed with the buddha nature

(they suffer because they have not recognized that buddha nature),

Do not consider people as enemies and friends; maintain primal wisdom.

Rather than holding on to the concepts of enemies and friends, which lead to our performing all sorts of karmic actions, regard them as helpers on the path to liberation. Better still, view everything from the point of view of wisdom.

Apply yourself eagerly to sameness.

Be assiduous in realizing the sameness of samsara and nirvana, of friends and enemies, of good and bad.

Do not look to fame *or to experiencing any others of the eight ordinary concerns;* **watch your own mind.**

That will be much more helpful.

Practice the ascetic discipline of guarding the mind.

There is no need for any other so-called ascetic practice.

Unless you are diligent *in this,* **you will go down.**

Even a single instant of negative thought creates the cause for being thrown into the lower realms.

Until now we have led ordinary lives spent mainly in trying to extend our possessions, build houses, run businesses, and raise families. We have worked very hard at these things, and yet they have not brought us much benefit. So now we should put our efforts into transforming our minds. Unless we do so, we will fall under the influence of all the different afflictive emotions that arise in the mind, and their destructive power is very great. As it is said, a single thought of anger arising in the mind of a Bodhisattva will completely destroy all the merit he has accumulated in three kalpas and cause him to be reborn in the hell realm for twenty intermediate kalpas.

Throughout the beginningless series of our lives, we have believed in the existence of things that do not exist. We have postulated the existence of an "I" where there is no "I" and of friends and enemies where there are no such things as friends and enemies.

From time without beginning, your belief in the reality of things has
fettered you in samsara. So now

Give up your wandering ways of the past.

There is no need to be concerned about the past. Irrespective of where
you were reborn previously, the main thing at present is that you have not
been born in one of the three lower realms. It is now time to give up all
your wandering in samsara.

It is important to know that

Of the seven noble riches, the foremost, the source of them all,
is being content.

Arhats, Pratyekabuddhas, and Bodhisattvas have no need for ordinary
riches such as gold, silver, and jewels. Their wealth is much more meaningful, for they have faith, discipline, generosity, learning, a sense of shame in
their own eyes, a sense of decency in others' regard, and wisdom. With
these, at each instant they come closer and closer to liberation. It is very
important to have these seven noble riches. If you lack faith, wisdom, and
so forth, you should cultivate them. As far as the Dharma and these seven
noble riches are concerned, you should never be satisfied: never think, after
doing a little practice, that you have exerted yourself enough. But as far as
ordinary wealth and possessions are concerned, you should be easily satisfied.

Go to the island in the ocean that has the riches you desire.

If you know how to be content, you will be truly rich, like the merchants
in ancient times who used to sail to jewel islands to gather all the precious
things there.

Without the capacity to be content, even a king is no better off than
a beggar,

because even if we are as a rich as Vaishravana, our wants never cease; we
never think we have enough, and, like beggars, we are always looking for
more. Instead,

Be satisfied with simply enough food and other necessities to stay alive.

If you reach this island, you will never return.

Once you reach the island of liberation and ultimate omniscience, you will never fall back into samsara. Those who have reached the sublime Bodhisattva levels and have little clinging to food and other things do not need gross material food. They are able to sustain themselves on the nourishment of concentration.

If you **have property, give it to your father.**

Get rid of all your belongings and give them to your parents and relatives without thinking of keeping or storing them. However, "father" here refers rather to one's spiritual father, the teacher.

If you please your teacher by offering him everything you have,
he will give you all the profound instructions,

for it is said that to offer a single drop of oil to anoint the teacher's body has greater merit than making boundless offerings to a thousand Buddhas. This is because it is the teacher himself who is able at this moment to establish you and all beings on the path of enlightenment; he is the most sublime of all objects of offering. So if you please him, he will give you all the instructions without holding anything back, as was the case with Marpa: he was so pleased by Milarepa's total dedication and diligence that he gave him the complete oral transmission.

If you make your old father happy, he will give you his heartfelt advice.

In an ordinary situation, when children are respectful and loving toward their father, he teaches them everything he knows so that they can be successful in the world, achieve their goals, look after their family, overcome difficulties, and so forth. Similarly,

The teacher too

Speaks to his son straight from the heart.

When the teacher is pleased with our conduct and practice, he will teach us how to defeat our enemies—not ordinary enemies, but our archenemies, afflictive emotions. He will teach us how to progress on each stage of the path to enlightenment, for he himself has made the same journey, and he therefore knows the path and has the necessary experience. Even a single word or sentence spoken by the teacher is of immense benefit. For the time being, it will give us joy and contentment; ultimately, it will bring us the bliss of enlightenment.

To a suitable vessel he gives the instructions in their entirety.

But to give the complete instructions to an unsuitable vessel would be wasting them, for the lineage would then be broken.

The disciple should guard them like his own heart and put them into practice

with one-pointed diligence.

When one comes across a wish-fulfilling jewel, there is no need to feel miserly, for it will freely grant everything one wishes or prays for—food, clothes, riches, whatever one wants. Likewise the teacher and his instructions will provide everything you need to attain liberation.

So **once you have found a gem, do not throw it away.**

Turn *the mind* **back** *from the deluded perceptions that are samsara* **and correct yourself:**[65]

Most activities in samsara are like children's games or the antics of a madman, so it is important to realize this and turn the mind away from such activities. If you happen to fall back into ordinary delusion, you must correct yourself immediately and return to the mind that is free from deluded perceptions.

Travel the highway to enlightenment.

Do not take the side roads of delusion: keep to the main highway, on which it is very pleasant to travel.

When your vajra brothers and sisters are assembled, think of yourself as the least important of them all.

When you are with them, hold them in high esteem and humbly consider your own qualities to be very few in comparison.

When your brothers and sisters are all together, listen to what they say and carry it out.

If you fear *your practice* **is being scattered, fence it in**

with mindfulness and vigilance, without which ordinary beings inevitably lapse into delusion and their practice becomes completely dispersed. Therefore,

Rely on mindfulness and vigilance and never be without them,

otherwise you will destroy the path to liberation.

If you fear you are running after *the objects of the six senses,* **hold yourself with the hook:**

Employ the watchman that is mindfulness.

Someone who has been captured with a hook has no option but to go wherever he is led. In the same way, if we catch hold of our mind—which risks being distracted by the objects of the six senses—with the hook of mindfulness, and with vigilance and carefulness, this will be of enormous benefit. We should use this watchman to constantly check how many positive or negative thoughts and actions we produce during the day. When we are able to control our minds through mindfulness, everything that appears in samsara and nirvana becomes an aid in our practice and serves to confirm the meaning of the teachings. All appearances are understood as being dharmakaya. We perceive everything in its natural purity, and there is nothing we can call impure:

Know that all perceptions are dharmakaya, and with that confidence—as though you had landed on an island of gold and jewels,

where you would not find ordinary stones even if you looked—

Make your view stand firmly on its own.

When we have confidence in our view and meditation, we can cope with any kind of circumstance and deal with any emotion that arises, since the effective antidote is always at hand.

Do not be ashamed in front of the deity, the teacher, or your own mind.

Observe discipline without hypocrisy.

The reason for practicing the Dharma is not so that others will have a good opinion of you. You should never practice in order to impress the yidam deity or the teacher or anyone else. Practice, rather, in such a way that you are never ashamed of yourself and can confidently say, "This is how I have practiced: my practice has not been tainted with negative actions or the eight ordinary concerns. I have practiced well." You know what goes on in your own mind, so make sure you are not uncomfortable with yourself. Then you will be able to conduct yourself according to the holy Dharma, observing the vows of the Basic Vehicle, the Great Vehicle, and the Mantrayana without hypocrisy. But if one moment you pretend to be a strict holder of the Vinaya and the next moment you let everything drop, this will not help.

Give generously and impartially,

and stop expecting anything in return or any karmic reward.

Do not think, "If I give a hundred now, I will get back one thousand tomorrow." And do not make distinctions, thinking, "I will only give to the sublime objects of refuge and not to ordinary beings—they are only ordinary, so they will not help me." Whoever they may be, good or bad, high or low, give generously.

Patiently bear with adversity,

providing help in return for harm.

If people harm you, instead of retaliating angrily make a wish that your connection with them will enable you in the future to bring them onto the path to liberation. Cultivating patience in response to their harming you helps you deal with all kinds of difficulties and adverse circumstances.

In particular, difficulties you may have when studying or practicing—sickness, aches and pains, hunger and thirst, and so on—are the result of negative actions you committed in the past. By experiencing them now, you are purifying these negative actions, so be joyful at having such an opportunity. On top of that, make a wish: "May all similar sufferings that other beings are experiencing be gathered into mine; may this suffering of mine replace theirs; may all their suffering thereby be exhausted." And practice the exchange, sending all your happiness and well-being to all beings.[66]

Put up with suffering when you are listening and reflecting:

readily accept such things as illness, pain, hunger, and thirst that you endure *for the sake of the Dharma, and take others' suffering upon yourself.*

However, even if you are diligent in listening and reflecting and you meditate for a long period of time, you must never think these will bring you renown. Even if you do become famous, do not indulge in expectation or attachment:

Do not cast your meditation into the mouth of fame

with hopes and so on of distinction and renown.

Your conduct should be such that you are not carried away by the demons

of the eight ordinary concerns. It is important to match it with your progress.

We need to carefully assess our level of experience and realization, and to match our conduct with that level. When we are beginners, for example, we should behave like bees, going from flower to flower to feed on the nectar. Then, when we have gathered a sufficient amount of teaching, we should proceed to the next stage, reflecting on the teachings we have received and experiencing them in order to extract their quintessence, just as we would churn milk to make butter. Finally, at the third stage, we should gain the ability to free ourselves from the afflictive emotions fettering us. On the other hand, if we fail to properly assess our level of realization, thinking that we are highly realized and can do exactly as we please, drinking alcohol, indulging in sex, and eating lots of meat, we will be going in quite the opposite direction to the Dharma.[67] Of course, if we truly have a high level of realization, whatever we do will directly benefit beings. So we need to be timely in our conduct. Mixing up our conduct and our level of realization will bring us no benefit.

According to the instructions of the Great Perfection, in the beginning one should be like a bee going from flower to flower searching for nectar. In the middle, one should go to an isolated retreat to practice the teachings, like a wounded wild animal that looks for a lonely, uninhabited spot in which to stay until its wounds are healed. In the end, having gained complete confidence in one's practice, one will be like a lion sleeping in a cemetery.

If you chase after the things you perceive, the demons that are the five poisonous thoughts will arise and

You will be beguiled by the demon of appearances.

You should understand that everything you perceive, beautiful or ugly, pleasant or unpleasant, is the display of primordial wisdom. As long as you do not lapse into being attracted to beautiful things and disgusted by ugly things, the mind will not be caught by outer phenomena.

It is important, therefore, that the mind does not chase after the object.

++ 15 ++

Six instructions for warding off defects.

Son, do not discredit the house of your forefathers.[68]

Where our parents and ancestors have set us an example in conducting themselves perfectly and so on, we should adopt the same ways. Otherwise we will bring shame on our family name. Similarly,

Do not bring shame on your own root teacher,

from whom you received so many instructions,

nor on the teachers of the lineage.

Do not taint your siblings and relatives.[69]

Avoid conflicts that prevent you from keeping the samaya with your brothers and sisters—those who have the same teacher as you and those in general *who have entered the Vajrayana.*

Do not throw dust on other relatives, close or distant.

"Other relatives" refers not only to blood relations but also to those with whom we have a connection through the Dharma—in other words, all other practitioners. So

Never speak harshly to others who practice the Dharma,

for among them there might be beings who are very learned or highly realized. It is important to recognize that practitioners from other Dharma traditions also have good qualities—qualities that we ourselves need to develop. Instead of disparaging them, try to follow their example. So never criticize those who follow other traditions, whether Sakyapa, Kagyupa, Nyingmapa, Gelugpa, or any other.

> **Without paying taxes to the king you cannot hope to be his subject.**[70]

When a king's subjects please him, he rules the country well, benefiting his subjects and bringing peace to the land. It is likewise when one pleases one's spiritual teacher. On the other hand,

> *If you do not please the teacher, his compassion and blessings will not flow.*

With regard to the teacher, we first have to check whether he is a qualified master. Then having made a spiritual connection with him and begun to follow him, we need to please him in three ways: the best way is by practicing his instructions; the second is by serving him with our body, speech, and mind; and the least effective is by offering him material gifts. However, if the teacher is displeased by our conduct, we will not receive his blessings, and without the Guru's blessings success in the practice is impossible. When Jetsun Milarepa was undergoing all those hardships building the nine-story tower, Marpa was so severe with him that his consort, Dakmema, took pity on him. Seeing that Milarepa had still not received any instructions from the master, she gave him a valuable turquoise and sent him to Marpa's principle disciple, Ngoktön Chökyi Dorje, with a forged letter asking him to give Milarepa instruction and let him practice. On reading the letter, Ngoktön Chökyi Dorje put Milarepa in retreat. After seven days, he came to Milarepa to check whether he had gained any realization and was astonished to find that Milarepa, who was obviously a very diligent practitioner, had made no progress. He left him in retreat for another week or so, at the end of which he again asked Milarepa if he had had any signs of realization. When Milarepa replied, "No," he could not believe it and realized that something must be wrong. Milarepa then explained that, since Marpa had not given him any instructions even though he had been with him such a long time, Marpa's consort, Dakmema, had sent him with the turquoise and the letter in the hope that Ngoktön Chökyi Dorje would teach him. "Now I understand," said Ngoktön Chökyi Dorje. "With the instructions I have given you it is impossible not to have some sign of realization within a week. The fact that you have not done so is simply because you have not received your teacher's permission." As this story shows, without the teacher's blessings any practice we do will be quite sterile.

Do not race downhill

toward negative actions,

otherwise you will find yourself tumbling into the lower states of existence, like a huge boulder rolling faster and faster down the mountainside.

Do not be clever in wrong ways

such as craft and pretence.

One's respect and devotion to the teacher should be completely genuine and sincere, right down to the marrow of one's bones. Always be free from any kind of deceit, not only with regard to the teacher but in everything you do.

•• 16 ••

An instruction on ten good and bad situations that do no harm—
if one can cope with them.

Son, there are ten things that do no harm.

Here "if you can cope" implies a choice: if you can cope, take it on;
if you cannot cope, do not take it on.[71]

If you put a heavy load on a horse or elephant, it can bear it. Similarly, if from among the Greater and Lesser Vehicles you choose the Great Perfection, you are making the right choice—provided you can handle it. But if you do not have the necessary prerequisites, like determination to be free, disillusionment with samsara, and acceptance by a qualified master, you must not overconfidently embark on the Great Perfection, for this will be harmful.

"Do no harm" means: if a particular situation does no harm, use it; if
it is harmful, don't.

People who are careful about their health, for example, avoid eating even small quantities of food that disagrees with them. Similarly, it is important to avoid anything that goes against the teacher's instructions, and to be able to put up with difficulties, hardship, and fatigue in order to accomplish anything that accords with those instructions.

> *So when you are able to take all adverse situations on the path without them affecting you adversely,*
>
> **If you can cope with the place, there is no harm in staying in your own country.**
>
> **If you can cope with those with whom you are connected,**
>
> *and do not develop attachment to friends and hatred for enemies,*
>
> **there is no harm in not leaving your family.**
>
> **If you can cope with the question of clothing,**
>
> *and have completely given up such things as worrying about how attractive you are or being embarrassed,*
>
> **there is no harm even in going naked.**
>
> **If you can cope with the problem of attachment and aversion**
>
> *and are able to take joy and sorrow on the path as one even taste,*
>
> **however you conduct yourself outwardly,** if inwardly you have confidence in the absolute nature, **you will not come to any harm.**
>
> *When you realize your own mind as being the teacher, all notions of difference are liberated by themselves. Thus,*
>
> **If you know how to handle the teacher, there is no harm in discontinuing respect.**

When one realizes that one's own mind is the teacher, such distinctions as "My teacher is good and dwells in dharmakaya; I am inferior and dwell in samsara . . ." are liberated by themselves. If, by avoiding such duality and getting rid of the concept of being separate, you can handle the teacher's instructions properly, you will naturally benefit disciples and Dharma brothers and sisters, and there will be no harm in discontinuing your efforts in things such as respect.[72]

When one uses reasoning to analyze samsara and nirvana, one finds that they are concepts. They do not have the slightest bit of true existence. They are simply the display or natural expression of the absolute nature. So

> *In realizing that there are no such things as the names of samsara*
> *and nirvana and that everything one perceives is self-arisen primal*
> *wisdom,*

**If you can cope with the ocean of suffering that is samsara,
even if you do not practice, you will not come to any harm.**

If you can cope with the lower realms

> *by liberating the mind and appearances into the absolute nature,*
> *so that there is no trace of the habitual tendencies* accumulated over
> such a long time in the past—at this level of realization,

**even if you perform negative actions, you will not come to
any harm.**

Put briefly, there are ten negative actions. You should avoid all of them, and on top of that you should save lives[73] and carry out other actions that help others, thereby performing the ten extraordinary positive actions. Nevertheless, at a high level of realization,

> *If it is for the sake of others, whatever one does is permissible.*

> *The absolute nature is free from effort and activity;*
> *The essential nature appears in different ways*
> *Yet the natural expression is free and nondual.*
> *When you know your own mind to be samsara and nirvana,*
> *Beyond the observance of all samayas to be kept,*

**you can cope with the hells, and there is no harm in not keeping
the samayas even if you have entered the door of the secret
mantras.**[74]

If you are confident in the view

that is beyond intellect and free from activity, and recognize that activities are delusion,

there is no harm in taking things easy and sleeping.

When we realize that all our activities are delusion and we seal everything with the awareness beyond the intellect, we gain the confidence of the view. We no longer feel the need to put our energies into worldly activities but simply remain in meditation.

If you can cope with the problem of residence

and are not attached to the quality of your dwelling—

if you make no distinction between a splendid mansion with lots of rooms and windows and fine things inside (to which its owner would normally be very attached) and a hovel that provides no more than protection from the wind and rain—

it does not matter where you live.

If you can cope with the problem of food

and are free from dualistic concepts of food being good or bad, pure or polluted,[75]

it does not matter what you eat.

If you can cope with the problem of the body

and have severed the ties of self-love,

even if you do not steer clear of contagious diseases, you will come to no harm.

++ 17 ++

Examining and deriding one's own faults and those of Dharma practitioners in general:

Son, there are eighteen objects of derision.

These are, in general, derisory behavior, erroneous practices, foolishness, and breaches of samaya; and there are eight things that prevent such faults from occurring.

It is important to be aware of our own faults. We should recognize them by comparing our own conduct with that of our teacher and Dharma companions, and by constantly checking whether our actions are positive or negative. Derisory behavior is behavior that is so completely wrong that one simply feels like laughing at it, as one would at a children's game. Erroneous practices include those of certain ascetics who, for instance, sit under the midday sun surrounded by four fires at the four cardinal points: they almost die of heat believing that they are thereby purifying themselves. An example of foolishness is someone who has understood nothing of the teaching but thinks he has understood it and even tries to teach others. Together with breaches of samaya, these all need to be avoided. There are eight things that help do so.

Someone good-natured who is competent to guide one;

Someone with a good nature—meaning someone open-minded, diligent, intelligent, and not distracted—is fully able to guide us and lead us along the path, taking us through all the various stages on the path of liberation.

A good friend who is clever at leading one;

By "good friend" we mean someone who is careful not to lapse into committing negative actions, who knows how to act in accordance with the Dharma, and is diligent in following the path to liberation.

A concern for future lives that stems from remembering death;

The most important way for us to keep the Dharma in mind is to think of the imminence and inevitability of death. This will spur us to be diligent and one-pointed in listening, reflecting, and meditating.

Careful avoidance of negative deeds stemming from the conviction that happiness and suffering are the result of actions;

If we are unhappy now, it is simply because we have harmed others in past lives or earlier in this life. And if we are happy and content now, this is the result of our having helped others. Once we realize the inevitability of this law of cause and effect, we will hesitate to do negative actions; should we happen to commit negative deeds, we will appreciate the need to confess and purify them. And when we do anything positive, we will dedicate it for the benefit of all beings.

A sense of shame in one's own eyes;

We need to feel a sense of shame with regard to ourselves, thinking, "I have followed such great teachers and practiced the sadhanas of the wisdom deities: how can I now have negative thoughts, words, and deeds? How can I behave like this when I have received all those teachings?"

A sense of decency in others' regard;

We should also feel a sense of shame at others' opinion of us: "What will the teachers and wisdom deities think of me?" For we must remember that when we do things contrary to or other than the Dharma, all the Buddhas and Bodhisattvas of the three times and ten directions, with their perfect omniscience, can see them clearly.

Great determination;

Once we know how to practice the Dharma, we should not waste a single moment but should practice day and night. As Jetsun Milarepa said, "Do not hope for swift realization; practice until you die."

Reliability, as in someone whose word can be trusted and who does not break his promise.

From the eight faults that are the opposite of these come derisory behavior and the rest.

Someone old, who sees people siding with their relatives and friends and trying to defeat their enemies, is inclined to laugh just as he would at a children's game, because he can see that all these things are so childish and vain—they do not lead to anything truly worthwhile or important. Similarly, whether we are practicing the Dharma or simply engaged in ordinary activities, without the eight conditions mentioned above, whatever we do is an object of derision.

> *An object of derision here is an object of scornful laughter or of contempt, something to be ashamed of both from the conventional point of view and from that of the holy Dharma.*

Now to explain these eighteen objects of derision, the first three concern faith.

In the beginning when faith is born,

and one feels devotion to the teacher and the Three Jewels,

one is ready to leap in the air.

> *When one receives the teachings, one does all sorts of things such as tearing one's hair out and weeping.*

Some people become so elated that they do all sorts of strange things, instead of listening properly, reflecting calmly, and sitting quietly in their Dharma robes with their eyes focused in front of their nose.

Later, torn by doubts, one fills desolate valleys with one's footprints

—meaning that one spends one's time going from place to place asking different teachers this and that.

> *Without having cleared up one's doubts about the instructions, one grows hesitant and wanders all over the place.*

Instead, you should find a qualified teacher and trustworthy spiritual companions to help you clear up all your doubts.

In the end, having completely lost faith, one becomes a mooring stone on the bottom of hell.

Once one starts to think that the teacher is not acting in the right way or one develops other wrong views of the teacher, one becomes like a stone that has sunk down to the deepest of the hells.

In the end one develops wrong views with regard to the Dharma and the teacher.

These are the three faults in not having firm faith.

The next three concern the teacher.

In the beginning, having found the master, one talks about all the teachings he has transmitted.

When we first meet the teacher, we entrust everything, our entire being,[76] to him. Then when we start to receive teachings, instead of keeping them for the purposes of our own practice, we repeat all the secret instructions to others, telling them how profound they are:

Having entrusted body and soul to him, one proclaims the secret teachings for all to hear, saying, "These are the most profound of my teacher's words."

Later, one tires of the master and criticizes him.

One regrets everything one offered before—

the material offerings one made and the effort one put into following him—

and one spreads rumors, claiming he has hidden defects.

In the end, one abandons the teacher and considers him as one's greatest enemy.

One makes new acquaintances and follows other teachers.

These are the three faults of following the teacher in the wrong way.

In the beginning, when one achieves a degree of concentration, one thinks, "There is no practitioner as good as I am."

Priding oneself on some small experience one has in sustained calm,

such as a flash of clairvoyance or paranormal insight, one thinks this is a sign of advanced realization; when one becomes infatuated with oneself in this way, *one gets the idea there is no greater meditator or better practitioner than oneself.*

Later, one gets tired of meditating and resembles an inmate in an open prison.[77]

We feel as if we were in prison doing practice, though without any great hardship, since we can let the time pass and sleep when we feel like it. At the same time, with this sense of imprisonment, we feel that our practice is not really leading anywhere:

In the hermitage one becomes bored during the day and fearful at night; at sunset one is glad to eat and sleep.

In the end, one gives up meditation and loiters in the villages.

If one does not integrate the Dharma with one's being and merely puts on a facade of Dharma, *one ends up performing village ceremonies or working as a hired laborer, a servant, and so forth.*

These are the three faults of failing to go through the practice properly.

In the beginning when experiences occur, one brags about them

like someone deranged

who thinks he can achieve great things but has nothing on which to base his confidence.

One is contemptuous of relative truth.

We do not follow the tradition because we have our own ideas concerning relative truth and the need for the methods and practices that belong to the relative level.

Later one gives up meditation and, as an expert in letters, takes to giving teachings.

Like someone who shows others the way when he himself has no idea which road to take, one explains the teachings to others without having any understanding or realization oneself.

If we ourselves do not know the path and have not reached the dry land of liberation, we cannot know all the dangers on the way. We cannot say, for example, "Here it is muddy, in that place there is a risk of fog, further on the path becomes dangerous." Without any true experience of the path, how can we guide others?

In the end when one abandons one's body, one dies in a completely ordinary state.

Like an ordinary being one dies without having really set out on the path.

These are the three faults of not obtaining any stability in the experience of the practice.

Next, unless we have clarified our view by following a realized teacher, receiving teachings from him, and clearing up all our doubts with him,

In the beginning, one develops but a faint conviction in one's realization of the view.

Having merely gained a vague and general understanding, one prides oneself on one's superb realization.

As a result of one's pride

One looks down on others

and ends up lapsing into distracting activities like frequenting crowded places, setting up a business, and engaging in all sorts of worldly activities.

Later, torn by doubts, one lies about one's knowledge and questions others.

Pretending to be knowledgeable when in fact one knows nothing, one pesters others with questions.

In the end, far from having the view, one is completely dominated by errors and obscurations.

Having fallen under the influence of eternalistic and nihilistic views like those of the Tirthikas, one never realizes the great evenness, the union state free from elaboration.

These are the three faults of not gaining the confidence of genuine realization.

When the result is lost in error, the windows of liberation are shuttered.

By failing to unite skillful means and wisdom, one misses the crucial point of the path and closes the door to nirvana, the result.

By blocking the windows of liberation, one will never interrupt the stream of birth and death.

Because of one's belief that everything that appears is real and the notion of one's body and mind as "I," one is fettered by karma and afflictive emotions, and there is no liberation.

As a result,

Unless one interrupts the stream of birth and death, one is powerless to choose where one will be reborn.

On account of one's actions and afflictive emotions, one cannot but take rebirth in existence.

These are the three faults or objects of derision where the result is utterly wrong.

They are derisory because sublime, realized beings who see us making such mistakes cannot help laughing.

Therefore, recognize these faults that come from not blending your mind and the Dharma, identifying them just as you would a criminal or thief, and do your best to avoid them.

✦✦ 18 ✦✦

Clarifying errors and obscurations: fifteen ways in which the practice goes wrong.[78]

When we fail to go straight to the vital point of the practice, we make mistakes and the practice goes wrong.

Having turned away from the holy Dharma, one follows ordinary, worldly ways while retaining the appearance of Buddhadharma.

This is what we call "wrong dharma." The word "dharma" or "way" can be used both for the worldly path taken by ordinary people and for the

II. DISCIPLINE / 125

spiritual path trodden by those who seek liberation. What we call a wrong path is that of someone who has the appearance of a spiritual practitioner but whose mind is dominated by ordinary concerns.

Son, there are fifteen ways in which the practice goes wrong.

The first of these is:

The view rushes into uncertainty.

Without having ascertained or directly experienced the view, we wrongly believe we have reached a high level of realization and start to seek celebrity, bearing out the saying that fools run after fame. We have only a superficial understanding but no sound realization, and we completely miss the crucial point of the view, which is the very root of attaining enlightenment. Instead of inner realization

one repeats others' words,

such as the sayings of scholar-siddhas that describe the view,

without having transformed one's own being.

The meditation gets lost in idiot meditation.

Unless we have clarified all our doubts and uncertainties concerning how to meditate, we may become complacent with only a vague, beginner's experience of sustained calm.

Without profound insight one does not destroy the foundation,
afflictive emotions: experiences and realization cannot take birth.

It is necessary to combine sustained calm with the view of profound insight, of emptiness, where there is no clinging. Otherwise, without profound insight, we can only crush the afflictive emotions somewhat, but we cannot eradicate them, and even if we spend many years in a mountain retreat, our practice will not give rise to meditative experiences and realization.

As a result of having failed to realize the view,

The action strays into wild, inappropriate conduct.

Acting in ways contrary to the Dharma, one behaves like a madman.

Without having gained firm confidence in the view, we engage in improperly considered actions, adopting a sham of Mantrayana conduct and thinking it is all right to drink beer, eat lots of meat, womanize, and so on. We fail to recognize the right time and the right way to act, and so end up behaving like a mad person. This is because

> *One has not recognized the crucial point of accumulation*
> *and purification.*

We think that as we progress toward realizing the absolute nature we no longer need to accumulate merit and wisdom and to purify our obscurations. In fact, the vaster our realization of the absolute nature becomes, the more clearly we understand the need for these two. It is said that even when we reach the stage where there is no difference between the meditation and postmeditation, we must still engage in practices that require effort. We still have to continue practicing in four sessions and so on, because our view may be as high as the sky but our conduct must be down to earth and as fine as flour.

The samaya gets lost in being undervalued.

We apply a measure to the samaya, thinking that we will keep the samaya up to a certain point beyond which there is no need to observe the minor details. But it is wrong to imagine that keeping the samaya is easy, that one need only keep the root samayas and that the branch samayas do not matter and can be overlooked.

> *Without knowing the precepts to be observed, one disdains the*
> *samaya, thinking there is no harm in spoiling it up to a point.*

The master is treated as one of one's own.

> *Thinking of him as an uncle,*[79] *one fails to develop faith or respect.*

Instead of seeing the teacher as the Buddha in person, we have the same feelings for him as we do for our family and friends. We feel affection for him but we do not see him as a true Buddha. As a result, his blessings cannot enter us.

The disciple attends teachings unwillingly.

> *If you listen to keep others happy or for fear of people criticizing,*
> *you will never understand the teachings.*

We attend the teachings unwillingly, without any real motivation save that of being concerned about other people's opinions of us (if we do not attend, they might think that we are not interested). Or fear that if we do not attend the teachings, people will criticize us or the teacher will be upset. We may also attend because we have heard that the teacher is very famous, and our attendance becomes more an indispensable social event. In either case, we are not deeply concerned with listening to the teachings, reflecting on them, and putting them into practice.

The practice is left for when one has the leisure.

By falling under the power of sleep and indolence, one will never obtain the result.

We practice the Dharma when we are in a happy frame of mind and our body is relaxed and comfortable, but at other times we drop it. However, Jetsun Milarepa said, "There's a long way to go, so practice without alternating between periods of being energetic and tense and of being loose and relaxed." For if we keep taking up the practice and then dropping it like this, we will not obtain the result—experience and realization.

One's experiences are ghost sightings.

Like a clairvoyant, one sees spirits and thinks of them more and more.

We become one of those people who can see nonhumans—ghosts, spirits, celestial beings, and the like—and instead of pursuing realization of the view and experiences in the practice, we lapse into thinking we are seeing ghosts and claiming that the dakinis have given us various predictions and so forth; we finally become obsessed by all these spirits and celestial beings. Such things are of little value in gaining realization, and when we become proud of them, they act as obstacles and are the sign of the demon. As the saying goes, "Obstacles are the sign of the demon; increase and decrease are the signs of meditative experiences." For it is the nature of experiences that they come and go.

The result of the practice **is the achievement of worldly fame.**

The attachment and aversion of the eight ordinary concerns increase and one is no different from ordinary people.

Instead of undoing the fetters of the afflictive emotions in our minds and giving birth to the wisdom of no-self, which is gained through sustained calm and profound insight, we err into running after worldly fame. We think, "I have spent years in solitary retreat. I have realized the Great Perfection. I have completely destroyed the eight ordinary concerns." And when we let others believe this, we start to gather a large following of disciples and to accept offerings and respect. This leads to many faults and takes us further and further away from the Dharma, while the eight ordinary concerns increase more and more.

One receives the instructions inauthentically.

Without serving the teacher or putting the teachings into practice,
one relies merely on having the texts and receiving the transmission.
Thus one does not throw oneself with real diligence into experiencing
the practice.[80]

We receive teachings but only superficially and not as suitable vessels who will be able to practice them in the right way and subsequently become holders of the teachings. At the same time, it may happen that a teacher who has only received the transmission of the text but has no proper experience of the practice gives the profound instructions to anyone who helps him or serves him, without considering whether that person is a suitable vessel who will practice and be able to hold the teachings. In this case he cannot transmit anything valuable to the disciple, and the latter will never develop a sound understanding of the view, meditation, and action.

Having obtained a human body in Jambudvipa,[81] one returns empty-handed,

like coming back empty-handed from an island of jewels.

Beings in this world of Jambudvipa have an exceptional opportunity to accumulate merit and wisdom and to purify their obscurations. If we do not use this privileged human existence to practice the Dharma or if we use it to practice the wrong way, we will be led to the lower realms. As the peerless Dagpo Rinpoche[82] said, if one does not get the crucial point of the teachings, even if one practices, the Dharma itself becomes the cause for falling into the lower realms. Similarly, for someone who travels to an island full of jewels and then comes away again without having taken any, all the difficulties he has gone through—sailing the ship, escaping from sea monsters, and so on—will have been in vain.

> *From the bed of a Dharma practitioner they remove the corpse of an ordinary person.*[83] *There was no point in obtaining a human body.*

Whether we have touched the true point of the Dharma or not is something we will know when we die. If we have no fear or anguish at the moment of death and are able to take the Dharma along the path—that is, to realize the dharmakaya—this is a sign that we have arrived at the essential point of the practice. But if, on the other hand, our "practice" has been the pursuit of exclusively worldly interests, we will die and leave a corpse in the same manner as any ordinary person. We will not have used this human existence to practice in accordance with the teachings: obtaining it will have been meaningless.

At death, one dies with regrets.

While we are alive, we might think that we have understood the view, that we are meditating on emptiness, that we are practicing the Great Perfection. But as it is said, "It is when practitioners have to face situations that their hidden faults show up," and in the face of death our shortcomings will become all too clear. If we have not gained confidence in our practice, we will feel great remorse when we come to die, and that remorse will not help us.

> *At that time, even if you regret, you will have run out of means.*

There will be no way to escape, for even if, stricken with remorse, you now start to think of practicing the Dharma properly, there will be no time to do so.

The Dharma practitioner is betrayed by his own name.

A practitioner who is truly worthy of the name is someone who has assimilated the teachings. But there is otherwise no benefit at all in simply being known as a hermit who has spent many years in retreat or as an erudite scholar of whom people say, "He has received many teachings and studied a lot."

> *Unless you have* truly *practiced the Dharma, being called a practitioner does not help. If* you have not transformed your being by

practicing the three trainings and *you act contrary to the Dharma, though you may be called a "spiritual friend," you will have become a counselor in evil.*[84]

One listens to empty sounds.

Like listening to a melodious song of praise, nothing will come from listening to the dry leaves of flattery and praise. One risks pointlessly wasting one's human life.

Someone who is reputed to be a realized being or Dharma practitioner but has not actually reached such a level belies his reputation. He is an impostor. People may say of us, "He is a highly realized being, he is a great meditator," but if we listen to such sweet-sounding praises and conceitedly believe them, we become impostors, for these are but empty names that we do not merit, and we risk seeing our lives run their course in vain.

If one acts contrary to the Dharma,

then despite adopting the appearance of a Dharma practitioner, spending many years in retreat, being reputed to have a high degree of realization, or being proud of one's learning,

After death, one cannot but go to the hells.

What then is the principal cause for these fifteen ways in which the practice goes wrong? It is that instead of being concerned with future lives we are only interested in achieving fame and status in this life. So it is important to recognize these faults within ourselves so that we can then apply the correct antidotes. Just as we would identify a thief in order to punish him, we must recognize our own defects so that we can correct them. As the Kadampa teachers used to say, "Recognize your own faults; do not go looking for others' defects." This is how we should avoid these fifteen wrong paths.

The root and source of all these is attachment and clinging to the things of this life, so recognize them as faults and get rid of them.

✦✦ 19 ✦✦

Showing, by means of twenty-six kinds of folly, where indulging in negative actions will lead.

These twenty-six kinds of folly are a sign that we are not acting skillfully in accordance with the Dharma. Instead of eagerly practicing the Dharma, which entails meaningful enthusiasm, we readily throw ourselves into worldly activities and negative actions, with misplaced enthusiasm.

Taking twenty-six examples of folly in ordinary life,

Son, there are twenty-six kinds of folly *in the holy Dharma.*

It is foolish not to fear an army whose arrival is inevitable,

that is, to have no fear of death.

To not be afraid when a huge army is about to invade one's country and to think, "I'll manage; I'm not afraid to give my life; I shall send them packing on my own" is very rash and stupid. The point of this metaphor is that, of all our enemies, the most deadly is death itself, and the only thing that will help us combat death is to practice the Dharma. So to indulge in worldly activities instead of practicing the Dharma and to still pretend we are not afraid of death is thoroughly foolish.

It is foolish not to repay a debt you have definitely incurred,

*that is, not to purify your karmic debts, negative actions,
and obscurations.*

When you borrow a lot of money, you have to gradually pay it back, a little bit each year. But if you were to suddenly find yourself having to pay it back all at once, you would be left destitute. It is the same with all the negative actions you have done with your body, speech, and mind throughout your past lives. They are like a letter of debt, and if you do nothing about it and do not gradually purify all your obscurations and negative actions in order to pay it off, it will drag you down to the lower realms of samsara.

**It is foolish to run toward an enemy who will surely take
you captive,**

that is, to cling to samsara unafraid.

If you run toward an enemy, it is quite certain that you will be captured, imprisoned, tortured, and dismembered. Likewise, if you fail to recognize that samsara is exclusively a place of difficulty and suffering, where one can only be the loser in the face of enemies such as birth, old age, sickness, and death, and instead of being afraid of these enemies you perceive them as pleasurable and are even attached to them, you are very foolish.

It is foolish to enjoy carrying a greater load than you can bear,

that is, to not shy away from the ripened effect of negative actions.

When you go somewhere carrying a load on your back, it is important to make sure it is a reasonable weight, one that you can easily carry a long way. To think, "I can carry a mountain" is thoroughly foolish. But it is no less stupid to act without steering clear of negative actions, ignoring the fact that they will inevitably lead you to the lower realms in your future lives.

It is foolish to be eager to go somewhere unpleasant.

Only an idiot would gladly go somewhere dry and barren rather than to a region where food is naturally plentiful and clothing easy to obtain. Likewise it is utterly stupid

to take pleasure in doing negative actions.

Even a very minor negative action will have serious consequences far into the future that one can scarcely imagine, as described by Nagarjuna in his *Letter to a Friend*:

> For one whole day on earth three hundred darts
> Might strike you hard and cause you grievous pain,
> But that could never illustrate or match
> A fraction of the smallest pain in hell.[85]

The hell realms are nothing other than the result of one's own negative actions. If we ignore this and happily go on committing negative deeds—taking life, telling lies, fooling and cheating people, and so on—we are being thoroughly stupid.

It is foolish to leap into an abyss where you are certain to die.

Nobody but a mad person would jump over the edge of a cliff with a sheer drop of several thousand meters into the jaws of certain death. Yet people in this world do things thinking only of fame and renown, or go to war with their minds full of hatred, thereby creating the causes for their future rebirth in the hells. Similarly, they greedily amass wealth and hoard it for themselves, neither giving to those in need nor making offerings to the Three Jewels: thus they create the causes for rebirth as pretas. They have no faith in the Buddha's teachings and ignore the law by which positive and negative actions give corresponding effects: their stupidity and lack of discernment cause rebirth in the animal realm. All these negative actions must be avoided, for to indulge in them is

> *to jump into the three lower realms*

ignoring the enormous harm that will result.

It is foolish to sow buckwheat and hope to grow barley,

> *that is, to hope that negative actions will result in happiness.*

Someone who tills a field and sows buckwheat seed in it expecting to harvest a crop of barley the following year can only be a fool. But we are no better. We spend this life pursuing honors and fame, building up wealth and property, and thinking how to get rid of our opponents and how to protect and favor our family and friends. To achieve all this, we throw ourselves into performing the ten negative actions such as killing and cheating others. When we are successful in these, we imagine we have attained greatness and we pride ourselves on the result, thinking this is something to be happy about. Yet we have only managed to build up a pile of negative actions that will bring us enormous suffering.

It is foolish to expect the sun to shine into a north-facing cave.

If you go to a cave that faces north expecting to enjoy yourself sunbathing, then you are going to have a long wait.[86] It is equally stupid

> *to expect the teacher's blessings to happen when you have no devotion.*

The teacher is a true Buddha. His compassion and blessings make no distinction between one being and another. But just as we cannot expect the sunlight to enter a house when all the doors are closed and the windows shuttered, we cannot hope to receive the teacher's blessings if we lack devotion and close ourselves to those blessings.

It is foolish to place your hope and trust in someone who is obviously going to deceive you,

that is, to be attached to the good things of this life.

Right now we are being fooled by the things we hanker after, like comfortable clothes, delicious food, and fame and renown. But they are no better than children's toys or the mimicking antics of a monkey. It is important to realize they are tricking us and to not be distracted by them or crave them. Otherwise, if we pursue ordinary pleasures like dancing, singing, gambling, recounting stories, and listening to others' gossip, we are wasting the opportunity we have to determine our future lives.

It is foolish for someone of humble origins to vie with one of royal blood,

like a common subject contending with a prince; that is, to hope to develop noble qualities when one is just an ordinary person.

One would never consider someone from a very humble family to have the same rank as a prince, however much he might try to act like him or rival him. In the same way, someone very ordinary who pretends he is a realized being but has none of the extraordinary qualities of supreme beings—such as having purified obscurations, attained perfection in study, reflection, and meditation, and overcome worldly distractions—cannot hope to develop those qualities.

It is foolish to hope to be rich when you possess nothing,

that is, to hope to be other people's master when you have no qualities yourself.

Someone who hopes to become wealthy without running a business and working hard will never get rich. Likewise, you can never expect to become a teacher and gain other people's admiration and respect if you have not acquired the necessary good qualities that come from practicing the Dharma.

It is foolish for a cripple to try to ride a horse,

that is, to make a promise you cannot keep.

A person with a broken leg who mounts a wild horse in the hope of having a pleasant ride will inevitably be thrown. It is equally foolish to promise yourself or anyone else that you will carry out a big task when you are unable to do so. Not only will you not complete the task, it will also bring shame on you.

It is foolish to say you have completed a task without having done any work,

that is, to disdain skillful means when you have not realized the natural state.

Unless you have gone through all the stages of the practice, to say, "I have realized the natural state; I have gained sound experience and realization" is just foolish prattling. You may think it is unnecessary to accumulate merit, to purify yourself, to have the determination to be free, to wish to get out of samsara, and to be content with little, but until you have truly realized the wisdom of no-self, such disregard for the methods of the practice is as foolish as a person with no legs thinking he will be able to walk great distances.

It is foolish, when you have still not recovered from an illness, to get fed up with the doctor and to take a liking to someone who has prepared a vial of poison,

that is, to have no respect for the doctor who cures the disease of the five poisons while relishing the company of those who indulge in negative actions.

Whether you are suffering from a phlegm disorder or an energy imbalance, you should undergo the full treatment and do everything the doctor says until your illness is cured. However difficult that may be, however unpleasant the taste of the medicine, or however painful the treatment, it is all for your own good. But if you are unable to endure the treatment and you do whatever you like—even happily taking things that are dangerous for you—you will end up causing your own death.

Likewise, if you do not want to take the medicine for the sickness of the five poisons by following the teachings expounded by the Buddha and, instead, you prefer to keep the company of people who indulge in negative actions and take you hunting and whoring, you will destroy yourself.

It is foolish for a merchant with nothing to sell to be a hearty eater,

that is, to teach others when you have not realized the meaning yourself.

A big merchant who abandons his business and does nothing but spend his time eating will soon exhaust his wealth and find himself destitute. In the same way, to want to teach others the Dharma when you have not attained liberation yourself is pure folly. You will not be able to benefit them if you have neither acquired a sound understanding of the teachings nor gained any realization through practice. Like a wooden mill,[87] you will make a lot of noise but produce nothing useful.

It is foolish to run off without listening to your father's advice,

that is, to take the wrong direction without listening to the teacher's instructions.

If we ignore the advice of our father who tells us, "This is how you should proceed if you want to succeed, overcome adversity, and protect your own interests," and we do not follow right ways even in worldly terms, but act rashly, get drunk, and do all sorts of mischief, we are surely being very foolish. The same is true if we do not do as our teacher says when he tells us, "If you practice in this way, if you avoid this and adopt that, then you will progress toward enlightenment."

It is foolish for a daughter to ignore her mother's advice,

for if mother and daughter quarrel, it will be to her detriment for a long time afterwards. Likewise, it is foolish

to prefer the pleasures of the senses in this life to what is beneficial for future lives.

It is foolish, having left the house naked and then found clothes, to return home again without them;

that is, having learned the Dharma, to get rich instead of practicing.

Having found the clothes of Dharma, we do not wear them—we do not study and meditate, but return to worldly activities like doing business and trying to become wealthy. This is a great waste.

It is foolish to take off your boots when there is no river;

that is, to interrupt the practice of Dharma when you do not have the confidence of realization.

Apart from when you have to ford a river, if you take off your boots, you will simply hurt your feet on the stones. Similarly, if you stop practicing the Dharma before gaining sound realization, you will only do yourself harm. This also applies to interrupting other people's practice in an untimely manner, when you do not have realization yourself. For example, you might say to them, "You should practice Mahamudra or the Great Perfection. There is no point in doing prostrations, in purifying your obscurations, or in accumulating merit." Or you might tell someone who is practicing to study, and someone who is studying to stop wasting their life learning things and to practice instead.

It is foolish to drink salty water that will never quench your thirst,

that is, to have desires and never know contentment.

The more one drinks salty water, the thirstier one gets. Likewise, if you indulge your thirst for sensual pleasures, you will never have enough. As it is said, desire is like a hungry dog that is never satiated.

It is foolish to be oblivious of the inside when the outside has collapsed;

your body is old yet your mind is still full of attachment and aversion.

It is the height of folly to remain inside a house unaware that it is deteriorating and needs urgent repairs—with the roof about to fall in and the walls collapsing. It is the same with our body: we do not realize that it is aging year after year, that it is slowly breaking down. And yet inside we have more attachment and aversion than ever, and we give no thought to our future lives.

It is foolish to be clever at counseling others while giving yourself the wrong advice.

You do not practice what you preach.

Some people are very good at giving other people advice. Their words are like rays of sunshine, helping people all over the country, and yet they do not know how to conduct their own lives properly. Similarly, if you teach others the Dharma but do not know how to apply it yourself, what you say is in contradiction with what you do.

It is foolish to scale a fortress without a ladder.

It would be unthinkable to try and enter a fortress with very high walls without using a ladder to reach the top of the wall. Likewise it is stupid

> *to boast of heading for liberation without completing the* two *accumulations.*

It is foolish for children to not want to do a job they will definitely have to do;

> *that is, for beginners to put off virtuous activities until later.*

Some people, instead of trying to learn something, to improve themselves, and to develop good qualities, waste their time like children playing useless games. Beginners in the Dharma are equally foolish if they remain idle and carefree instead of being diligent in practices such as accumulating merit, performing prostrations, making offerings, and practicing the generation and perfection phases.

It is foolish not to be worried about crossing an unfordable river,

> *that is, to be unconcerned by birth, old age, sickness, and death.*

If you were to arrive on the bank of a big river where there was no ford and you did not have a boat or other means for crossing the river, it would be ridiculous not to be worried about how you were going to get across. It would be similarly absurd not to be concerned about the four great rivers of birth, old age, sickness, and death, which are inherent to the samsaric condition and are unavoidable. If you do not use the Dharma to prepare yourself to face death and these other sufferings, and you simply get carried away by worldly activities, you are deluding yourself.

It is foolish to look elsewhere when *the Buddha's wisdom* **is already within you.**

You are like someone who has a wish-fulfilling gem but does not know it and puts all his effort into doing business, farming the land, and so on in the hope of becoming wealthy.

> *The above can all be summarized as five faults:*
>
> *(1) hankering after the things of this life;*

(2) wanting to have the result without the cause, that is, without accumulating merit and wisdom;

(3) not listening to the words of the teacher, that is, his instructions, and being a Dharma practitioner only in name;

(4) pledging yourself to the holy Dharma but then following ordinary ways that incorporate attachment and aversion; and

(5) not practicing what you preach, in other words, speaking in terms of the Dharma and acting in contradiction to the Dharma.

++ 20 ++

Nine pieces of personal advice for softening one's being.[88]

What do we mean by personal advice?

This is personal advice because it consists of oral instructions spoken directly—advice to be kept in the heart.

It is the well-intentioned advice, backed by experience, that a father gives his children. If they follow it, they are likely to succeed in whatever they do. Likewise, if we follow our teacher's instructions, we can obtain the ordinary and supreme accomplishments. As the great siddha Saraha said,

> When the teacher's words enter your heart,
> It is like seeing you have a treasure in the palm of your hand.

Son, there are nine pieces of personal advice.

The first one is

If you want to compete, take on the Buddha.

Look at the Capable One's life and train yourself following in his footsteps.

If you must compete with someone, vie with the Buddha. Take the example of Buddha Shakyamuni, who accumulated merit and wisdom over three measureless kalpas and, in order to receive teachings, gave his own limbs, his body, his kingdom, and his queen and children. He underwent incredible hardships such as piercing his body with a thousand nails. You should think, "I must do likewise." Once you have this intention to match the Buddha, to do as he did, although you may not be able to act on such a vast scale now, you will definitely be able gradually to progress toward Buddhahood.

If you want to backbite, slander the yidam.

People are fond of saying all sorts of things about others behind their backs, mentioning their names again and again. Instead of slandering others in this way, "slander" the yidam: utter his name repeatedly by reciting his mantra all the time.

> All the time, without fail, be diligent in the approach and accomplishment practices,

murmuring his name day and night in the continuous recitation of the mantra. If you constantly recite the *mani*, the mantra of Avalokiteshvara, it is as though you were continuously calling him by his name—"He who is endowed with the Jewel and the Lotus"—and there is no doubt that you will receive his guidance and blessings.

If you have to be mean, be so with the instructions.[89]

In ordinary life there are some who greedily hoard wealth, filling their coffers with diamonds and gold. They check regularly to see how much they have and think only of how they might acquire more. We should have the same sort of meanness and interest in the practice of the generation and perfection phases, constantly wondering how we can improve our practice while at the same time keeping these gems hidden away in the treasury of our minds.

> If you keep them secret and practice them, blessings, experience, and realization will swiftly come.

If you are going to be unkind, be unkind to your negative actions.

Do not look back at negative actions and friends who act negatively.[90]

Someone unkind may seem very pleasant and well-spoken the first time we meet him, but gradually his bad character will emerge and we will start to quarrel and fight. It is the same with negative actions and acquaintances who indulge in negative actions. Do not stay with them as you would do with your friends. Avoid them as much as possible by applying the antidote.

By all means be munificent—with the teacher.

Give unsparingly, particularly in making offerings to the teacher, to whom you should feel able to offer all your wealth and possessions, and even your own body.

*It is more beneficial than making offerings to the Buddhas
of the three times.*

The best kind of offering is that of our practice and realization. And though we may be unable to completely realize the Buddha's intentions through our practice, if we can at least have a good heart and help others, this will also fulfill the Buddha's wishes.

If you want to give someone the cold shoulder, make it samsara.

After a quarrel, we may turn our back on the other person. But our real quarrel should be with samsara.

Investigate your mind minutely;

if you find any flaws in your mind, get rid of them, and nurture any good qualities you have like respect, devotion, and confidence in the law of cause and effect—in short,

be diligent in the methods that will prevent your taking birth in samsara in the future.

If you are going to enumerate faults, list your own defects.

Look inwards and find fault with yourself: "I'm not meditating correctly; I'm not studying properly . . ." This is a good way to spur one's diligence.

Depart from the land of your hidden defects.

Bid farewell to your laziness, lack of diligence, and other faults. This also implies giving everything you own, your wealth and possessions, to other people and going somewhere else to live.

When you have the victory, give it to others.

Give everything you have unstintingly to others. As Milarepa said, "If you do something good for others, they will regard you as a celestial being." If you forget your own selfish motives and consider others more important, being kind to them and treating them with compassion, in the long-term it can only help you.

Ultimately it will be for your own good.

As for the sutras and tantras, tease them out like wool.

To make woolen cloth one first has to wash the wool and then tease it out into separate fibers before spinning it into yarn for weaving. If the wool is teased out properly, it is easy to make the yarn. Likewise,

Seeking the teachings impartially and integrating them with your mind, correct your practice and your own mind. This is very important.

++ 21 ++

Nine pieces of heartfelt advice for keeping a low profile.

Son, there are nine pieces of heartfelt advice.

Be a child of the mountains.

Being in a place where there are a lot of distractions leads to much attachment, to arguments, and to likes and dislikes. One's meditation becomes dispersed. On the other hand,

For the great meditator who never leaves the mountains, good quali-ties grow day by day, month by month.

And there is a saying: "Be the child of the mountains, drape yourself in mist."

Eat the food of famine-time.

Do not let food, clothes, and conversation get the upper hand.[91]

If you need lavish helpings of food or an unusual diet, you will have to spend much time and effort to get these, and this again will be a cause for distraction. Remember that whether or not the food you eat is delicious, it all ends up as excrement. Be content to make do with enough food, however plain, to take the edge off your hunger and sustain your body. The same applies to clothing and conversation: you should have little care for special clothes and reduce worldly conversation to a minimum.

Do the things that please the enemy.

If you do not cast your ordinary ways to the wind, you will never destroy the castle of desire and hatred.

If you do not resist or compete with your enemies and do not become attached to your friends,[92] any enemy you have will be delighted and think, "This guy's a pushover. He isn't even trying to contend with me. I shall easily get the better of him." By casting away all hopes of becoming rich in this life, of becoming a governor or someone powerful, you will be free from the eight ordinary concerns and you will destroy the citadel of attachment and aversion.

Wear clothes that no one wants.

Without any attachment it is easy to practice.

Dress yourself in clothes that are sufficient to protect you from the cold and wind, without caring whether they look nice. If you use clothes that have been thrown away because nobody wants them, you will not need to worry how you use them: they will simply serve to protect you from the cold. But having to find beautiful, expensive clothes will simply involve you in unnecessary effort and cause further distraction.

Flee the crowds, alone.

As with the example given earlier of the young maiden who removes the bangles from her wrists in order to make less noise when she washes her hands, if we get away from being surrounded by lots of people, our meditation will not be broken up by useless chatter.

Your virtuous activities will presently increase, there will be no obstacles, and you will get food and provisions as well.

Be without a handle for your relations,

that is, a handle by which they can take hold of you and pull you. If you are caught by ordinary attachment to home life, you will be preoccupied with becoming a rich and influential householder. So

> *Unless you give up your longing and affection* for your relatives and friends, *you will not be able to cut the ties*

that keep you bound to them. Therefore,

> *Do not let people take your nose rope.*[93]

Your attachment makes you like an animal with a rope through its nose: people can make it go wherever they want. As long as you do not leave that rope in the hands of others you will be free to make your own decisions, particularly for practicing the Dharma.

Tie your fickleness down with a rope.

> *The human mind, like water, goes wherever it is led, so tether your mind with the rope of mindfulness.*

People have fickle minds, they listen to everything other people say. They change their minds all the time and are unable to concentrate on anything or make firm decisions. If you tell them to study, they rush off to find a book and start studying. Then if you tell them to practice, they immediately stop studying and start practicing instead. And if you tell them to go and work and engage in ordinary activities, they immediately go and do that. But they will never achieve anything by acting this way.

The human mind is the same, constantly wavering and changing direction, like grass on a mountain pass, which bends as the wind blows. It is like water, which goes wherever you channel it: if you dig a ditch or break the earth in front of flood water, it immediately flows along the channel you have made for it. So instead of letting the mind go wherever it likes, you should tether it with the rope of mindfulness, just as one ties up a horse with a halter to prevent it from wandering off. Concentrate your mind one-pointedly on the Dharma instead of giving in to its whims and letting it do whatever occurs to it.

Abandon havens of delight.

Some places, such as beautiful gardens, may seem very delightful: everyone is dancing and singing or talking, and one feels thoroughly at ease. But this is where one's attachment and aversion will grow. Therefore,

Do not be attached to the pleasures of samsara. If you do not forsake them, you will never stop the constant stream of negative actions, misery, and bad talk.

Focus your mind on space.

It is important to thoroughly familiarize yourself with the two kinds of no-self.

Space is something one cannot take hold of. It is free of preference and partiality. It has no limits or dimensions. It cannot be defined; there is nothing in it that one can grasp. You should aspire to practicing like that, free from conceptual elaboration, and to realizing the two kinds of no-self, the no-self of the individual and that of phenomena. It is very important to get used to this meditation and to gain experience in it over a long period of time.

•• 22 ••

Instructions, through five beatitudes, on taking good and bad circumstances equally.

Son, there are five beatitudes.

Blessed are they who recognize samsara for what it is: a poisonous tree of suffering.

Having recognized that its very nature is suffering, they avoid it.

Samsara is like a poisonous plant. Enjoying it and indulging in samsaric actions will bring us ruin, just as eating a poisonous plant, attractive and delicious though it may be, will make one very ill and even kill one. Once we recognize it as being poisonous, we avoid taking it even though its leaves or flowers or fruit look beautiful; and thus we stay healthy. Likewise, once we recognize that there is nothing but suffering in samsaric activities, we will no longer be attracted to them. Instead, we will recoil and avoid them.

Blessed are they who see those that give rise to afflictive emotions as spiritual friends.

When they see an enemy, for example, he is a master making them develop patience.

What makes afflictive emotions arise in our minds is attachment to those we like and aversion to those we do not like. But if instead of hating those we consider are enemies, we think of helping them, and instead of being attached to friends and relatives we simply regard them as illusions or as people we meet in a dream, we will free ourselves of the notions of friends and enemies; we will feel relaxed and happy. When you see enemies, people who might harm you, try and develop patience. Regard them, moreover, as friends helping you to progress on the path. If they actually do harm you, think that this is retribution for negative actions you did in the past and that you are thus purifying yourself of those actions. When you are able to do this and bear such circumstances patiently, your enemies become teachers helping you to develop the precious bodhichitta.

> **Blessed are they who correctly view the master who has trained in the three wisdoms.**

> *By seeing the teacher as the Buddha and his instructions as nectar, they will be set on the path to lasting liberation.*

When you see a sublime master—sublime from having perfected wisdom through hearing, wisdom through reflection, and wisdom through meditation—you should realize that to emulate this teacher in the way he acts, speaks, and thinks will bring you happiness in this life and future lives. Seeing him as the Buddha in person, you must never tire of drinking the nectar of his teachings. In this way you will truly be set on the path to liberation.

> **Blessed are they who see everything—outer and inner things and circumstances—as being without origin.**[94]

> *By doing so they will realize the wisdom mind of the Buddha.*

When you see that external phenomena (forms, smells, sounds, tastes, and tangible things) and your inner reactions to them (attachment to those that are pleasurable, aversion to those that are not) have never come into existence, do not truly exist in the moment, and will not go anywhere when they cease to exist, you will realize the void nature of all these external and inner phenomena. At that time it will be impossible for your mind to be deceived by external perceptions. You will be free from the impulse to accept some things and reject others, and you will easily realize the Buddha's wisdom.

Blessed are they who postpone all activities and set out on the unmistaken path.

Such people understand that all the busy activities of body, speech, and mind are completely unnecessary and decide to drop them since they will soon be dead. They then set their minds to one-pointedly practicing the supreme Dharma, the unmistaken path to liberation, for the duration of this life. Such people are very close to liberation and are not distracted by ordinary activities.

> *In short, if they give up all the activities of this life and put the perfect instructions into practice, the sun of happiness is certain to rise in their minds.*

•• 23 ••

Avoiding the twenty causes of breaking the samaya, the samaya being a distinguishing point between sutra and tantra.[95]

Son, there are twenty things that lead to breaches of samaya.

Apart from in exceptional circumstances,

To be *deliberately*[96] **secretive about your teacher while extolling your own virtues leads to a breach of samaya.**

There might, on occasion, be an important reason for concealing the identity of our teacher, but if we do so simply because the teacher is a very humble person, or a wandering hermit, or because he is not a very learned scholar, and we extol our own qualities, boasting about the different teachings we have received and now hold, this will lead to a breach of samaya, as will showing contempt for our teacher.

> *Unless it is* specifically in order *to get rid of* afflictive emotions *or to acquire* disillusionment with samsara and determination to be free, for anyone[97] **to view an erudite scholar and an uneducated person as equals leads to a breach of samaya.**

Competition, *with self-seeking and hostile motives,* **between patrons and disciples leads to a breach of samaya.**

For example, a disciple who sees that the teacher has a generous patron might try and attract the patron's support, thereby diverting the patron's support away from the teacher.

> **To have the intention of offering** *the teacher your wealth, property, and so forth that are yours to dispose of*[8] **and to put off doing so leads to a breach of samaya.**

You might start by thinking, "I will offer my teacher a hundred dollars," and then think, "Maybe fifty will do." To reduce an offering in this way, to delay making it, or to regret it afterwards causes the samaya to degenerate and also exhausts your good fortune.

> **Receiving as many teachings as you can possibly hear** *without considering whether or not there are conflicts and suchlike in the lineage* **leads to a breach of samaya.**

Before receiving a teaching from a teacher, we should check whether the lineage or anything connected with the teacher has been stained by breaches of samaya in the past, because if this is the case, even if we practice that teaching, it will not give rise to the common and supreme accomplishments. If we simply take it for granted that there has been no breach of samaya and that everything is pure and correct, we will be stained by samaya breaches ourselves. Whatever our connection with such stained lineages, our own good fortune will diminish: even in ordinary terms we will become poor, and so on.

> *An alternative version appears in the* Commentary:[99] *"To receive the teachings unworthily . . ."* Any teachings you receive must be with the prior approval of the teacher.

If we receive teachings against the teacher's wish, or without first checking whether he has agreed, or we use various means to oblige the teacher to give us teachings without being sure whether he considers those teachings suitable for us, this will lead to a breach of samaya.

> *When the time is not ripe, using pressure or complaint*

> **To insist on getting the instructions leads to a breach of samaya.**

The teacher knows the disciple's capacity and therefore the most suitable teaching to give. So if we use different means such as cunning and insistence to get teachings against the teacher's wishes, we will cause our samaya to degenerate.

> *Using lies and cunning* **to deceive your teacher and fellow disciples,** whom you should consider as your father and as your brothers and sisters, respectively, **leads to a breach of samaya.**

> **To put the blame on the master for wrong** *that is not your own doing* **leads to a breach of samaya.**

It may somehow happen that a fault or something wrong is associated with us even though we have not really done it ourselves. But if we claim that the teacher or our Dharma friends are responsible, we will cause our samaya to degenerate.

> *In a spirit of competition,* **to treat the master as a rival leads to a breach of samaya.**

One might, for example, vie with one's teacher or Dharma brothers and sisters with the wrong kind of motivation, thinking, "Let's see if I am as learned as they are," or try to compete with them in terms of spiritual accomplishment.

> **To abuse the master's confidence,** *divulging secrets he has entrusted you with or keeping your own defects secret from the teacher,* **leads to a breach of samaya.**

If the teacher entrusts us with secret instructions and tells us not to disclose them to anyone else until we have practiced them and obtained signs of accomplishment and realization, and we then spread them to other people like wealthy patrons who come and make large offerings, we are breaking the samaya. This is also the case if we try to hide our own defects from the teacher.

> **To scorn his kindness,** *rather than repaying it when you are able,* **leads to a breach of samaya.**

When we are in a position to do so, we should not fail to repay our teacher's kindness. On the other hand, if we do not see that any progress we have made in the practice is entirely due to his kindness, and instead we scorn his kindness and think, "It is because I am so diligent and perfect that I have all these qualities," our samaya will degenerate.

To be intent on looking after your own interests by *being utterly self-centered, self-seeking, and proud* **leads to a breach of samaya.**

When we are following the teacher and serving him, if we behave too selfishly, the teacher and the other disciples will get tired of us. Likewise, if we are very proud, this too will upset the teacher. Instead we should maintain a humble position and be free of pride.

To steal instructions and books—*writing them down secretly without asking your teacher or fellow disciples or, worse still, obtaining them by actually stealing the texts*—**leads to a breach of samaya.**

Someone who copies secret instructions without permission or, even worse, actually steals books or notes is breaking the samaya, particularly if he also gives them to others. Furthermore, the instructions in question will bring them no benefit.

To secretly enumerate the master's faults—*the hidden defects of the teacher and his retinue*—**leads to a breach of samaya.**

If it happens that the teacher or some of the people in his retinue have defects or hidden faults and we tell others about them behind their backs, we are breaking the samaya.

To block another's aspiration, *discouraging someone who has faith,* **leads to a breach of samaya.**

If you frustrate the wishes of someone who wholeheartedly wishes to practice the Dharma or who has no desire to achieve anything in samsara, you will cause your samaya to degenerate.

To make an outer show of the inner practices, *performing the secret activities prematurely,* **leads to a breach of samaya.**

If the time is ripe and we are completely free from the ties of afflictive emotions, practicing the secret activities of the Mantrayana will enhance our practice. But performing these activities without the teacher's permission or authority and without our having gained complete confidence and stability in the view, meditation, and action will cause our samaya to degenerate. This applies also to making an outward show of the Mantrayana's inner practices.

To be jealous of vajra brothers and sisters—*one's general brothers and sisters and closest vajra siblings*[100]—and to act in such a way that one is always in conflict with everyone else **leads to a breach of samaya.**

To act indiscriminately without a teacher or instructions, *practicing just as one pleases without having obtained the teachings or, if you have obtained them, without approval,* **leads to a breach of samaya.**

Practicing teachings we have not received or, even if we have received them, practicing them without proper permission from the teacher—thus engaging in a version of the teachings we have made up ourselves—leads to our spoiling the samaya.

To masquerade as a teacher, *giving clever explanations of one's own invention with no aural lineage and without knowing anything oneself,* **leads to a breach of samaya.**

This refers to someone who is ignorant and has none of the qualities obtained through hearing the teachings, reflecting on them, and putting them into practice. He has not received the instructions through a genuine lineage but pretends to teach others, giving them instructions he has made up himself.

If the Buddha taught that one should not, with animosity or attachment, look down on even the Tirthikas, this is no less applicable in the case of the others. For this reason

To criticize teachings and those who practice them leads to a breach of samaya.

It is not proper to criticize other religions, or even the lower Buddhist vehicles, in a hostile or petty way, thinking that the teachings we have received are much more advanced. If it is wrong to criticize those who have false, non-Buddhist views, one need hardly mention how wrong it is to criticize other views included within the Buddha's teaching. So rather than speak ill of other teachings and practitioners, which would cause a breach of samaya, we should have pure perception with regard to all of them.

To exhibit[101] **the instructions to unsuitable vessels,** *giving the secret teachings literally*[102] *to those in the lesser vehicles and the like,* **leads to a breach of samaya.**

Those who practice the lesser vehicles may not have the necessary open-ness of mind to accept the teachings of the Great Vehicle—the profound teachings on the view of emptiness and so on—and they may not be fit vessels for these teachings. Therefore openly disclosing these teachings to them without first checking whether they have the capacity can lead to spoiling their practice and cause our own samaya to degenerate.

> *Furthermore, having learned the different categories of root and branch samayas that have to be kept, the causes that lead to their degenerating, the disadvantages of their degenerating, and the benefits of keeping them, you should maintain constant diligence with mindfulness and carefulness.*

There are many different categories of samaya—the root samayas of body, speech, and mind, the twenty-five branch samayas, and so forth. If we transgress the samaya by having wrong views concerning the teacher, for example, or by doubting the teachings of the Secret Mantrayana, we create the causes for suffering in this life and in future lives. We therefore need to know the causes of breaking the samayas and the difficulties that will result, as well as the benefits of keeping them. If we guard the samaya as well as we protect our own eyes, all the accomplishments will come without any effort. So it is necessary at all times to remind ourselves exactly what we should do and what we should avoid, remaining constantly watchful and concerned as to whether we are actually conducting ourselves accordingly.

> *This completes these instructions, which are like a mother who guides and cares for her child,* giving it good advice and teaching it the right way to behave. *Through them a faithful vessel will be inspired to practice the Dharma and, relying on the superior training in discipline in accordance with the general pitakas, will keep it as the basis of his practice and thereby transform his being.*

This was the second section from the *Eighty Chapters of Personal Advice,* **the instruction on perfect discipline, the basis.**

III. Concentration

Instructions on the superior training of the mind, the perfect means.

Of the three trainings—discipline, concentration, and wisdom—this section deals with concentration.

It contains seventeen chapters.

·· 24 ··

Showing how the four blessings help one's meditation.

The combination of the teacher's blessings, the student's devotion, and the profundity of the instructions makes experience grow swiftly.

If we want to progress on the path to liberation, we have to benefit from the teacher's blessings. Without them, no amount of learning, power, or wealth will ever help us reach liberation. However, unless we have such fervent devotion that we see the teacher as the Buddha himself, we will not receive his blessings. It is said,[103]

> Unless the sun of devotion shines
> On the snow peak of the teacher's four kayas,
> The stream of his blessings will never flow.
> So earnestly arouse devotion in your mind.

Moreover, we need the profound instructions, and to obtain them we should be prepared to give everything we have, even our lives. Through these three things—the teacher's blessings, the devotion that enables us to receive them, and the instructions, which we should value greatly—experience will grow swiftly. In the best case we will progress by fulfilling the teacher's wishes and by practicing, in the middling case by serving him with our body, speech, and mind, and in the least ideal case by making material offerings to him.

Son, there are four practices that confer blessing.

What are these four kinds of blessing?

When you know your mind to be the absolute nature, all objects are liberated in the absolute nature and you will be unaffected by external circumstances.

The teacher's blessings will show us the nature of our mind, though this is something we already have inherently. When we achieve stable recognition of this absolute nature, all outer phenomena, which normally give rise to emotions such as attachment and aversion, will reinforce our practice rather than harm it. They will become helpers for our practice. The mind will no longer be deceived by external circumstances, and as a result our concentration and our realization of the view, meditation, and action will swiftly grow.

This is **the blessing of yourself, as exemplified by the sole of a shoe.**

If you cover the soles of your feet with leather, the result will be the same as if you were to cover the whole earth with leather: you will not hurt your feet on things like thorns and stones. This is like blessing yourself.

Having received this "blessing of yourself," in the same way that one can transform iron into copper and then into gold by alchemy, you will realize that all phenomena are the naturally arisen primal wisdom. This realization will be unstained by ordinary concepts associated with the adventitious obscurations that veil this primal wisdom.

Once all phenomena are recognized as the naturally arisen primal wisdom, they are beyond adventitious conceptual characteristics.

This is **the blessing of perceptions, as exemplified by a mountain torrent in spate.**

A torrent in spate running down the mountainside carries away all the rocks and trees and other things in the valley. Likewise if all outer phenomena become helpers enhancing one's practice, then the blessings that come from perceiving things in such a way sweep away all the afflictive emotions from one's nature.

With one-pointed concentration, there is no interruption in the flow.

A great river is something that never ceases; it is never exhausted; it flows continuously. One will be able to reach the level of the yoga that is like a flowing river—meaning the practice will never have any interruption. Likewise, if one can maintain concentration day and night,

This is **the blessing of the mind, as exemplified by the middle of a great river.**

Karma and afflictive emotions will not be able to interrupt this continuous flow of concentration.

Like the black jackal, whose eyes see as well by night as by day, one is introduced to the nonduality of perceiver and perceived.

Having been introduced to the absolute nature, which is free from a subject that perceives and an object that is perceived,

This is **the blessing** of the realization **of nonduality, as exemplified by a jackal.**

Now, by recognizing that appearances are the mind, the mind is empty, emptiness is nondual, and nonduality is self-liberating, one clears away all misconceptions about the outer, inner, secret, and absolute.

In the process of recognizing the nature of one's mind, the natural state of mind, we begin by saying, "outer appearances are the mind." In other words, whether we perceive outer phenomena as pure or impure, in both cases they are the projection or product of our own minds. Outer objects are not inherently pure or impure. Next, when we turn inwards and examine the mind carefully, we cannot find any color, shape, or location for this mind: it is what we term "empty." Yet these two—outer phenomena that appear and mind that is empty—are not two separate things like the two horns of a goat. They are united: the mind appears as the perceptions of phenomena yet it is empty; it is empty yet it appears. Moreover, the realization of this intrinsically nondual nature of appearance and mind is itself free from grasping at the notion of nonduality. It is important to know how to let this natural liberation of nonduality take place: if we cling to the concept of emptiness, we have to liberate that clinging to emptiness; if on the other hand we cling to appearance, we should let that clinging dissolve. In this way, we should dispel all misunderstandings and doubts about the realization of the different levels of emptiness: outer emptiness, inner emptiness, secret emptiness, and absolute emptiness.

> *However, this alone is not much help if you have not liberated your own mind into the absolute nature, just as ice, despite being water, does not function as water unless you melt it. So it is important to meditate with intense devotion.*

The result of dispelling all misconceptions and doubts is that everything is liberated in the absolute nature. But unless you can free this mind, which has attachment and aversion, in the absolute nature, it will not help simply to think, "appearance is empty, emptiness and appearances are one." Your mind will be like ice. Although the ice that forms when water freezes in winter is essentially water, it does not behave like water. Until you melt it, it is hard and sharp; water is soft and fluid. Ice can support the weight of objects; water penetrates and always flows down to the lowest point. So it is important to meditate with intense devotion to the teacher. If you have fervent devotion, the blessings will enter, and it will be easy to travel the path to liberation.

> *Although a yogi currently on the path has truly realized the absolute nature of his mind, he has not yet liberated all phenomena in the absolute nature, and so qualities such as the twelve hundred qualities do not manifestly appear. Nevertheless, through gradual habituation to that realization, all phenomena are liberated or dissolved into the absolute nature, and at that time all the qualities up to the level of ultimate Buddhahood become manifest.*

As a result of the teacher's introduction, a yogi currently on the path realizes that the buddha nature is something that is truly within him. With the confidence of that direct realization of the ultimate nature of the mind, all subjective perceptions are liberated into the space of the absolute nature and the yogi actualizes what is called "liberating whatever arises as great wisdom." Someone who has seen the truth[104] gains twelve hundred qualities such as the ability in one instant to have a vision of one hundred Buddhas, to enter into and arise from one hundred concentrations, to turn one hundred wheels of the Dharma, and so on. These qualities are not manifest at present because one is obscured by the net of the body, but as the power of the view of emptiness increases, they become clearer and clearer.

This is why it is taught that while we are ordinary beings, as at present, our realization can both increase and decline. From the attainment of the first level onwards, realization increases but does not decline. On the level of Buddhahood it does neither.

We who are now on the path fluctuate in our practice. Our realization is not stable, and our practice increases and declines alternately. When you make some progress and realization and experiences are on the rise, do not be influenced by pride and conceit. When your practice declines, do not be discouraged and think, "I will never learn to meditate." Eventually the alternation of growth and decline becomes exhausted and, having completed the paths of accumulating and joining, one reaches the path of seeing. From that point onwards and until the tenth level one's realization of emptiness becomes vaster but it does not decline. Finally when one reaches the ultimate level, the level of Buddhahood, it does not increase either. At that point there is no decline, for there are no defects, neither is there any increase, for the development of qualities has reached its culmination.

++ 25 ++

Showing, by means of illustrations, how using things as the path helps the meditation.

The understanding of the absolute nature is something that has to be practiced with one-pointed concentration. How we practice will now be explained by means of illustrations.

Son, there are four instructions for using things as the path.

As it is said in the Six Prerequisites for Concentration:

On account of material possessions one suffers.
To own nothing is supreme bliss.
By abandoning all its food,[105]
The pelican becomes ever happier.

For someone engaged in a life of contemplation, possessions and material things are simply a disturbance, a cause of difficulties. To have no possessions is supreme bliss. When we have nothing, we have no enemies. We are happy because we do not have the problem of first acquiring wealth, then protecting it and trying to increase it. As we find in the saying:

> Base your mind on the Dharma,
> Base your Dharma on a humble life,
> Base your humble life on the thought of death,
> Base your death on an empty, barren hollow.[106]

So if we give up all possessions, practice becomes very easy and we will find sublime happiness, like the pelican. The pelican can collect a lot of fish in its bill, but it is prey to being chased by other birds that try to make it give up its catch. It does not get a moment's peace until it surrenders the fish to its pursuers. But once it has done so, it is much happier. Similarly, when we have no possessions, we are free to remain comfortably at ease. On the other hand, with possessions we become preoccupied with having more, and we worry that we might lose them to enemies and thieves.

Accordingly,

Make freedom from attachment the path, as exemplified by the pelican carrying fish.

Now, in order to actually progress on the path we have to be free from afflictive emotions, for it is afflictive emotions that bind us in ignorance.

Since afflictive emotions can arise as primal wisdom,

Make the five poisons the path, as exemplified by the recitation of mantras over poison.

This does not refer to the ordinary emotions as they normally present themselves. It refers to finding their true nature, the ultimate nature of wisdom in the depth of these afflictive emotions. Once wisdom has truly arisen within us and we recognize the empty nature of the afflictive emotions, they cannot harm us, just as when an accomplished yogi recites a mantra over poisoned food, the poison is rendered harmless. By recognizing the empty nature of the afflictive emotions, they are liberated as wisdom and we can use them as the path. If we experience afflictive emotions in the ordinary way, they can only bind us down in samsara. But if we can recognize these emotions as wisdom, they will become helpers in our practice.

Now afflictive emotions arise in the mind by means of the eight consciousnesses.

> *If we recognize the eight consciousnesses as unborn, we cut the root of existence, the notion of a self.*

This idea of a self, the thought of "I," is the very root of samsara. It is this that has to be cut. When a tree is cut at the roots, there is no need to cut the branches, leaves, and flowers: they all fall at the same time and dry up. At present we have not been able to realize that the eight consciousnesses are unborn and we have therefore been unable to cut the belief in an "I" at the root. But once we know how to get rid of this notion of an "I," then whatever happens to us—suffering, happiness, attachment, or revulsion— it will all help our practice progress:

> **Make the unborn nature of the eight consciousnesses the path, as exemplified by cutting a fruit tree at the roots.**

The unborn absolute nature is completely empty, like space, unstained by relative phenomena such as the notions of permanence or nihilism that constitute wrong views. The view of this absolute, spacelike nature is unblemished by such extremes, like the lotus flower, which grows above the surface of the lake and is unstained by mud:

> *As the unborn absolute nature is unaffected by relative phenomena,*

> **Make the great purity the path, as exemplified by the lotus growing from the mud.**

++ 26 ++

Showing by means of illustrations how knowledge helps the meditation.

Son, here are instructions on four things to be known.

If you are to meditate with one-pointed concentration, you need to know clearly what you have to meditate on.

> *All phenomena in samsara and nirvana are devoid of true existence.*

At present we perceive samsara as something we have to reject and nirvana as something we have to attain. Now while this is correct according to relative truth, according to absolute truth the nature of the afflictive emotions and actions that we are supposed to reject is nothing other than emptiness, and the nature of the kayas and wisdoms we have to achieve is also nothing other than emptiness. When we realize the dharmakaya, which is free from true existence, we will know that all perceptions are similar to a dream or an illusion and we will no longer crave these phenomena. As it is said, "While there is attachment, there is no view."[107] And absence of attachment is the supreme view.

Know freedom from attachment, as illustrated by the magician,

for a magician knows that the things he has created do not exist truly and he is therefore not attached to them.

When you ascertain the nature of all phenomena, everything comes down to the truth of emptiness. The entities of samsara that have to be rejected are emptiness; the qualities of nirvana that have to be attained are emptiness. Their emptiness is not of different kinds: phenomena have the same all-pervading nature, the one taste in multiplicity, the sole essence. Therefore,

As phenomena and their nature are not two separate things,

Know indivisibility, as illustrated by sandalwood or the musk deer.

Sandalwood cannot be separated from its fragrance, nor the musk deer from its smell. It is in this same way that you should recognize the essential indivisibility of samsara and nirvana.

Since there is no relying on conditioned phenomena with characteristics,

Know that relatives deceive, as illustrated by being let down by a friend.

One cannot rely on the conditioned things of samsara like fame, wealth, rank, and so forth. There are no relative phenomena in samsara and nirvana on which one can depend. It is important to know this. If, for example, you are traveling to a distant land in the company of a friend who then somehow lets you down, you will realize you can no longer trust that friend. In the same way you should know that attachment to relatives and friends is simply a cause of deception. Free yourself from clinging and do not rely on such things.

Since the absolute nature has been present in you from the beginning,

Know inseparability, as illustrated by a sesame seed or the flame of a lamp.

The absolute nature has been constantly present within you since the very beginning. It is not something that you have been given by the teacher's blessings, like a gift. Nor is it something that has been changed from something else, like a square of woolen cloth that is dyed a different color. It has not been newly fabricated. Rather, it is like the oil in a sesame seed: despite the sesame seed's tiny size, there is always oil present in it. Or like the flame of a lamp: whatever the size of the flame, the light it gives out is naturally part of it. In the same way, you should know that none of the qualities of nirvana is ever separate from your essential nature.

When one knows this, the bonds of belief in true existence and dualistic concepts are loosened by themselves, and immaculate wisdom is born in one's mind.

◆◆ 27 ◆◆

Showing by means of illustrations how the crucial instructions help the meditation.

Son, there are four crucial instructions.

Although the creative power of the empty absolute nature appears multifariously, from the moment phenomena manifest they have no inherent existence: appearance and emptiness are united.

Because everything is by nature empty, infinite manifestations can arise: from the natural creative potential of emptiness all the phenomena of samsara and nirvana can manifest as an infinite display. Although all these manifestations arise, it is not as if they are permanent when they are there and impermanent when they are no longer there. Everything arises as in a dream or like a magical illusion. It is like a rainbow, which, though it appears clearly in the sky, is not solid. It is apparent yet empty. But its emptiness and its appearance are not two separate aspects. It is not that the rainbow being present is one aspect and its being empty is another. The rainbow is simultaneously apparent and empty, and there is no other emptiness than the rainbow itself. The same is true for all the phenomena of samsara and nirvana: they are empty from the very moment they appear.

You need the crucial instruction that shows how to make a clear-cut decision regarding the unobstructed nature of appearances, as illustrated by a clean silver mirror.[108]

Take the example of a mirror. If you take a silver mirror and polish it thoroughly, many images will arise on its surface. But though they appear clearly on the surface, they are not in the mirror nor are they sticking to the mirror's surface. We cannot say that they are inside the mirror or outside. How then do they arise? It is simply the conjuction of there being, say, someone's face in the front of the mirror and the mirror being there. As a result of these different conditions, an image appears. Now anyone can understand that, although all sorts of images appear in a mirror, they do not exist in any solid way. But we have to understand that the same is also true for all the infinite manifestations of samsara and nirvana. The emptiness and the manifestation are indivisible: the emptiness cannot be separated from the manifestation. When we speak of emptiness and appearance, this does not mean that there are two things in the same way that we talk about the two horns of an animal. It means that there is no emptiness besides the manifestation and there is no manifestation besides emptiness. Once we are free from clinging to this sort of duality, our concepts of existence and nonexistence will naturally fall apart. It is important to have a clear understanding—free of doubts—of this unimpeded manifestation.

When one is not bound by clinging to what is not two as being two, phenomenal characteristics are freed by themselves.

You need the crucial instruction on not being bound by characteristics, as illustrated by a prisoner who has been released.

A prisoner who has just been set free is very concerned not to do anything wrong that might put him back in jail again. We should be similarly mindful and vigilant so that we are not bound by concepts of existence, nonexistence, eternalism, or nihilism; otherwise, we will be seriously tied down by ignorance.

What is the crucial point here? It is to know the meaning of the unborn nature of the mind. The mind does not have a color, shape, location, or any other characteristics. So although there is nothing solid and no characteristics on which to meditate, once you have gained stability and confidence in the realization of the unborn nature of mind, do not stray into distraction and wander from that recognition even for an instant. Simply remain in the state of nongrasping, which is free from mental activity.

> *Although there is not even an atom to meditate upon with regard to the unborn nature of your own mind, do not be distracted for an instant. Be free from mental activity and conceptualization:*

> **This is the crucial instruction you need on not being distracted from the unborn nature, as illustrated by shooting an arrow straight at the target.**

By aiming an arrow very straight, one is certain to hit the target. Likewise, when the realization of the unborn nature is aimed at the target of grasping at a self, it is impossible for it not to hit the mark.

> *With the realization of the triple space, do not move from the inseparability of the absolute space and awareness.*

There are three spaces: the outer space, the blue sky, which is like an ornament;[109] the inner space, which is the nature of the mind; and the space in between, the space in the eye channels that connects the outer and inner spaces. When these three spaces are blended together, one realizes the inherent union of the empty aspect, the absolute expanse, and the clarity aspect, one's awareness. Do not waver from that understanding.

> **You need the crucial instruction on resting in one-pointed concentration, as illustrated by an ophthalmic surgeon.[110]**

When people with an eye disease that is making them go blind find a doctor who can treat them, they listen carefully to the doctor and do everything necessary for the treatment to succeed. As a result of the treatment, their eyes open and they can see the mountains and all the other beautiful things in the universe. If we listen in the same way, with one-pointed attention, to our teacher's instructions and practice them exactly as he tells us, one day our eyes will open and we will see the absolute nature just as it is. All the deluded perceptions of samsara and nirvana will clear by themselves, for they are, after all, groundless by nature, unborn and empty. Then all our dualistic concepts of existence, nonexistence, and so forth will naturally fall apart.

> By this means deluded perceptions, being groundless, are cleared away and phenomenal characteristics fall apart by themselves.

•• 28 ••

Personal advice on how to cut conceptual constructs regarding mental and extramental phenomena.

Son, there are four "cuts."[111]

> *Whatever dualistic thoughts arise, there are none that are anything other than the absolute nature.*

Cut the stream of the arising of dualistic thoughts and the following after them, taking the example of a tortoise placed on a silver platter.

Of the many thoughts that arise in our minds, good or bad, none of them move away and separate from the absolute nature for even a moment. They are like a tortoise placed on a silver platter: it finds the feeling of the smooth silver surface underneath it so pleasurable that it does not move at all. So if we never depart from the absolute nature, even when thoughts arise in our mind, there will be no way they can chain together and give rise to delusion. Normally, when we think of something in the past, it leads to another thought, which again leads to the next thought, and we project into the future, creating an uninterrupted chain of deluded thoughts with each thought triggering the next. If we follow such chains of thoughts, they will never stop. But if, whenever a thought arises, we remain in the absolute nature without wavering, the flow of these thoughts will naturally cease.

> *Whatever appears, nothing has moved from the absolute nature.*

Decide that nothing is extraneous to the absolute nature, taking the example of gold jewelry.

Once we know how to remain in the absolute nature, the manifold thoughts that arise in the mind are no different from gold jewelry. One can make all sorts of things out of gold, such as earrings, bracelets, and necklaces, but although they have a variety of different shapes, they are all made of gold. Likewise, if we are able to not move from the absolute nature, however many thoughts we might have, they never depart from the recognition of the absolute nature. A yogi for whom this is the case never departs from that realization, whatever he does with his body, speech, and mind. All his actions arise as the outer display or ornament of wisdom. All the signs one would expect from meditating on a deity come spontaneously without him actually doing any formal practice. The result of mantra recitation is obtained without his having to do a large number of recitations. In this way everything is included in the recognition that nothing is ever extraneous to the absolute nature.

In that state one does not become excited at pleasant events or depressed by unpleasant ones. Everything,

> *The whole variety of joys and sorrows, is one within the state*
> *of awareness.*

> **Decide on its indivisibility, taking the example of molasses**
> **and its sweet taste.**

We usually think of molasses as one thing and sweetness as another, and we therefore have two names and concepts for these. But in fact it is impossible to separate the sweetness from the molasses itself. If we reach a similar clear-cut understanding that all phenomena in samsara and nirvana, all happiness and suffering, are included in the absolute nature, then

> *All of samsara and nirvana arises from the creative display of*
> *the spontaneous primal wisdom.*

> **Decide that it is naturally manifesting awareness, taking the**
> **example of the moon in the sky and its reflection in water.**

When the moon shines on a lake, it is reflected on the water and the moon appears in its reflection exactly as it appears in the sky. Similarly, when we have a glimpse of awareness, it is what we call the illustrative wisdom: it is an image of the actual wisdom, something that we can point to as an example of it. Even though it is only a glimpse, it is still of the same nature as the absolute wisdom, a true likeness of it. Through the recognition of this illustrative wisdom, one is led to the recognition of the absolute wisdom,[112] which is like the moon in the sky. Both arise by themselves, and we should understand clearly that there is no basic difference between the illustrative wisdom and the ultimate awareness or absolute wisdom. It is, rather, a question of one's realization becoming vaster, of one becoming more skilled in one's recognition. Just as there is no difference in nature between the moon seen in the water and the moon seen in the sky, so it is with the illustrative wisdom and the absolute wisdom.

•• 29 ••

Showing how dealing properly with samsara and nirvana helps the meditation.

Son, there are four views.

The essential nature being union, its display is arrayed as an ornament.

View thoughts and appearances as the ornament of the absolute nature, taking the example of a rainbow adorning the sky.

As we have already seen, the essential nature is the intrinsic union of emptiness and appearance. All the infinite manifestations of samsara and nirvana arise spontaneously as the creativity of the absolute nature. They arise as its ornament and not as something different and separate from the absolute nature or as something that interferes with it. When a rainbow appears in the sky, beautiful and multicolored, the sky is empty but the rainbow appears in it like an ornament. Similarly, for a yogi who has realized the wisdom of the absolute nature, all manifestations appear as its ornaments. All thoughts appear as ornaments of the absolute nature, and there is nothing, no meditational defect such as dullness or excitement, that can obstruct it.

When one knows thoughts to be the absolute nature, attachment and aversion are put to death,

and one no longer accumulates karma.

View thoughts as the absolute nature, taking the example of tempering and honing a sword.

With a sword that has been tempered and carefully sharpened, one can cut the toughest branches and even the trunk of a tree. Similarly, if the mind is tempered with the absolute nature, any thoughts that arise will be severed by themselves. As a result,

There are no traces accumulated as habitual tendencies,

and the tendencies of good and bad karma will not be perpetuated.

View thoughts as leaving no trace, taking the example of birds flying in the sky.

With a bird that flies all over the sky, this way and that, it is impossible to point out exactly where it has flown, for it leaves no trace of its flight. For a yogi, too, the many various thoughts, good or bad, that arise in his mind leave no trace because as soon as they arise they immediately dissolve in the absolute nature. Thoughts related to attachment, aversion, and bewilderment may well arise in his mind, but since they dissolve as soon as they arise they do not leave any trace. As a result, they do not lead to the accumulation of karma and suffering. Good thoughts also, like faith, devotion, and compassion, may arise but immediately dissolve in the absolute nature and therefore do not lead to pride or attachment developing in the mind.

Phenomena are freed in the absolute nature.

View existence as untrue, taking the example of waking from a dream.

In a dream one dreams of all sorts of things good and bad; but when one wakes up, there is nothing left of them. Just so, the whole display of the universe and beings continues to manifest infinitely; but once we have realized the absolute nature, we do not cling to notions such as good and bad, and we view all these manifestations as being without any solid existence.

•• 30 ••

Explaining the actual method of resting in meditation.

Son, there are four kinds of meditation.

Bringing together everything that favors concentration and mastering the crucial point of how to rest in meditation, diligently

Meditate with increasing habituation, taking the example of the waxing moon.

In order for the realization of this absolute nature to dawn, we need to gather favorable conditions—to be free from conditions that break up the meditation and from distraction and grasping. Unless they are free from distraction, beginners who try to meditate will not benefit much. Moreover it is important to find the right balance between being too tense and too relaxed. If we are too tense, we will suffer from disturbances of the subtle energies and the mind will become unbalanced. If we are too relaxed, we will lapse into ordinary states of mind. So we have to be well versed in the various methods of meditation. At the same time we need to have great diligence. If we try to realize the absolute nature day after day, our realization will gradually become vaster and more stable, like the waxing moon, which grows fuller each day between the first and fifteenth days of the lunar month.

This is the view of the Prajñaparamita (the Mother of the Victorious Ones), the sphere of the inexpressible, inconceivable, supreme primal wisdom.

The wisdom that we realize cannot be described. The more our realization grows, the more the qualities associated with it—spontaneous devotion and compassion—will bloom. And the emptiness aspect of this absolute nature is what we call the Mother of the Victorious Ones, that is, Prajñaparamita, who is the mother of all the Shravakas, Pratyekabuddhas, Bodhisattvas, and Buddhas.

Meditate on thoughts and appearances as the inexpressible great bliss, taking the example of having your mouth full of water.

When one's mouth is full of water, even if one wants to say, "Pet!,"[113] one cannot possibly do so. Similarly, when we realize the absolute nature, although the phenomena of samsara and nirvana are still experienced, it is impossible to express them in words. This is why Zurchungpa says, "meditate on great bliss."

Meditate that fame and the like—

that is, the thoughts of the eight ordinary concerns—

are not ultimately true, taking the example of mist, which does not truly exist.

When the sky is full of mist in the morning, it seems as if there is something veiling the sun, but in fact there is nothing one can catch hold of, and the mist does not affect the actual sky behind it. Similarly, practitioners who have realized the absolute nature are not affected by the eight ordinary concerns: they do not crave fame and glory, and even if they happen to get these, it does not make them proud. If they are criticized or blamed, they do not get depressed. Such things do not affect their minds. They are completely free from ordinary worldly concerns and they see everything as in a dream, as an illusion. So they meditate seeing fame and related manifestations as impure—in the sense of irrelevant—like mist, which has no true existence.

Meditate on the uncontrived nature as empty, taking the example of water and bubbles;

the nature of the mind is empty like space.

In a river there may be many eddies and bubbles, but they are never something other than the water in the river. They are formed from water, they remain no different from water, and they again dissolve back into the water. So too with all the manifestations and experiences that arise as the creativity of awareness: they never change into anything different from the absolute nature. The absolute nature is always present within them, like the empty space that is always present inside a bamboo stem.

✦✦ 31 ✦✦

Showing how conduct[114] should be endowed with experience and realization.

Son, there are four kinds of conduct.

In your conduct, turn your back on worldly ways: consider the examples of a bride and a madman:

in other words, make sure you are conscientious and considerate of others' opinions, like an anxious newly-wed bride; do not act contrary to the Dharma like a madman who does whatever occurs to him.

When a newly-wed bride arrives in her new home, she is very conscientious, well behaved, and concerned to create a good impression.[115] We practitioners should be just as careful in everything we do, and if we do things contrary to the Dharma, we should feel thoroughly ashamed, knowing that we are in the presence of the infinite Buddhas. At the same time, we must avoid the extreme of behaving like a madman, who does whatever comes into his mind and never stops to think, "This is not the right way to behave."

> In your conduct, *the multifarious phenomenal perceptions* should not move from the absolute nature: take the example of fish in the ocean.

Wherever they go, fish in the ocean always remain in it, for there is no end to the ocean. In the same way, the manifold appearances of samsara and nirvana should be perceived as never having been extraneous to the absolute nature.

> In your conduct, whatever appears—*the five poisonous emotions and so forth*—should be primal wisdom: take the example of fire raging through a forest.

In a forest fire, the stronger the wind, the further the fire spreads; the more wood it reaches, the more the fire blazes. And while the afflictive emotions bind an ordinary person, for a yogi any thoughts that arise in his mind simply fuel his realization, which grows even stronger and clearer, because he experiences whatever appears as the display of wisdom.

> In your conduct, the many should have the single taste— *phenomena and their nature or appearance and emptiness being inseparable:* take the example of salt dissolving in water.

The absolute nature and relative phenomena are indivisible, as are appearance and emptiness, just as when salt dissolves in water, the saltiness and the water are completely inseparable. Thus, when relative conditioned phenomena dissolve into the absolute nature and they blend in one taste, all deluded thoughts vanish and can no longer arise.

++ 32 ++

Showing different kinds of experience.

Son, there are four kinds of experience.

When we try to preserve the recognition of the absolute nature in this way, we will have various experiences. The first of these is:

The experience of no clinging to thoughts, as illustrated by a small child and a mirror:

although there are perceptions, there is no clinging.

Experiences *will* arise. If we did not have experiences on the path, we would be on the wrong path. But although they arise, we must be completely free of clinging to them, like a small baby in front of a mirror. Whatever the baby does, the mirror will reflect it. But the baby does not cling to it as being good or bad. Likewise, someone who is completely free from clinging is not caught by notions of good and bad.

The experience of wisdom taking birth where it has not previously arisen, as illustrated by a poor woman finding treasure:

experience and realization are newly born.

When a new experience or realization of wisdom arises in the mind, we should be joyful, and the joy we feel should inspire us to even greater diligence in the practice, just as when a woman who is destitute finds treasure buried underground. She is overjoyed, knowing that for seven generations to come there will be no need to worry about being poor, and she therefore takes great care of the treasure she has found.

The experience of neither apprehension nor esteem, as illustrated by a swallow *entering the nest* and a lion:

one has gained decisive confidence.

At one point we will gain a sense of certainty and confidence from having a clear idea of where we are on the path, of how antidotes work on the emotions, and of the view of emptiness. We will find that we have no hesitation, like a swallow coming to the nest. Before building its nest, the swallow looks carefully for a good site free from possible dangers. But once it has built the nest, it flies straight to it, without any hesitation. Likewise, having carefully built up our meditation, we will reach a point where we have no hesitation and we immediately recognize the nature of our experiences. Like the lion, the king of animals, which has no fear of other animals wherever it goes, a yogi has no apprehension, whatever experiences arise in his mind. At the same time, he is not proud or infatuated with his experiences. Neither does he esteem experiences, nor is he apprehensive about them.

The experience of being unafraid of philosophical views, as illustrated by the lion who is not scared of the fox:

there is no fear of the view and action of lower vehicles.

When we have realized the absolute nature, we will not be tied by the views and conduct of the lower vehicles. Like the lion, which is never afraid of the fox however much it barks, someone who has full realization of the Great Perfection is not affected by the numerous teachings on the view, meditation, and action of the gradual vehicles; they do not make him hesitate.

•• 33 ••

The signs that arise from experience.

Son, there are four kinds of signs.

When experience and realization bloom within, this is

The sign of awareness shining within, as illustrated by a butter lamp inside a vase.

When a butter lamp is placed in a vase, it is protected from the wind and therefore burns very steadily and brightly. Similarly, when clear awareness fills one's inner space, karma and afflictive emotions are immediately dispelled.

For this there are four ways in which objects of knowledge are freed in their own nature.

Once we have realized the absolute nature, all concepts are dispelled within that same absolute nature.

They are self-freeing, like iron cutting iron.

Just as iron can be cut by iron but not by wood, when the ultimate nature of the subject and object acts as the antidote for the same subject and object, all duality naturally dissolves.

Appearances and the mind being inseparable, they are freed through one single thing, like fire lighting a fire.

When there are many different afflictive emotions occurring in the mind, there is no need to search for a separate antidote for each one. The absolute nature serves as the antidote for them all, like fire lighting a fire. Once one has realized that mind and appearances are inseparable, the more firewood one adds the stronger the fire blazes.

By knowing one's own nature, they are freed into the fundamental reality, like space mixing with space.

Inside a vase there is space, and that space is basically the same as the space outside. When the vase is broken with a hammer, the space inside and the vast space outside blend as one and become indistinguishable.

Appearances are recognized as being manifestations of the mind, like a mother and child meeting.

Once we have recognized that all outer phenomena are simply the self-manifestation of our own awareness or absolute nature, outer conditioned phenomena cannot deceive our inner absolute nature. This recognition that outer phenomena are our own projections is like a mother and child meeting: between them there is certain recognition, without hesitation or mistake.

When there is no effort, this is

The sign of the mind not getting involved in the pleasures of the senses, as illustrated by a king seated on his throne.

A king who has complete dominion over his kingdom has no need to actively increase his authority, nor to involve himself in the day-to-day running of the state. Similarly, when we have confidence in the absolute nature, we will not be lured by attractions and sensory experiences outside. The mind will not run after objects of desire. This is a sign of stability.

When one curtails one's plans because there is no time to waste, or decides clearly that all phenomena are unborn, this is

The sign of focusing the mind on the unborn nature, as illustrated by a sick person and a cemetery.

There are two examples here, reminding us that although we may have this sort of realization, we must never feel complacent with regard to impermanence and death, and we must be decided about the unborn nature of phenomena.

The first example is that of someone who is terminally ill and knows that there is little time left before the final journey to the cemetery. Such a person does not feel like wasting time. The second example (pointing to the realization that all phenomena are unborn) is that of the sick person's corpse being carried to the cemetery. Just as one does not need to take care of a corpse as one did of the living person, once we have realized the absolute nature we do not need to pay special attention to "what is to be rejected"—afflictive emotions and so forth. We do not need any other antidote for them than the realization of the unborn nature. Other, ordinary antidotes become irrelevant.

If we are free from *both the things to be rejected and the antidotes* to be applied, we will gain the confidence of a hawk. When a hawk sees a pigeon flying quietly through the forest, it does not hesitate for a second in swooping down on its prey. Likewise, if we have the confidence of having gone beyond both things to be rejected and the need for antidotes, we will overwhelm the afflictive emotions without hesitation. This is

The sign of having stamped on the afflictive emotions,
as illustrated by the pigeon and the hawk.

++ 34 ++

Showing that without experience and realization one is powerless not to be reborn in samsara.

Son, there are four instructions related to optical illusions,

with examples of being fooled by illusions.

If you press your eye with a finger while looking at the moon, you will see two moons, but of course there has never been more than one moon. Similarly, neither the world outside nor your own body, your name, or your mind has ever existed in any true way. Yet you assume they exist truly and therefore you cling to them.

As in the example of perceiving a mirage as water,

believing there is something when there is nothing,

if you do not know that the pleasures of the senses are a delusion,
you will wander.

Because we have been accustomed for so long to believing the true exis-

tence of things, we err. We are like wild animals on a vast plain in hot weather
who see a mirage in the distance. Believing it is water they run toward it,
only to find as they approach that there is nothing there. In the same way,
if we do not realize that all the desirable things of samsara related to form,
feeling, smell, and taste are nothing other than delusions, we cling to them
and wander. We cling to things that appear very beautiful or pleasant and
feel averse to things we cannot bear. As a result of being thus deluded by our
perceptions, we get involved in all sorts of different activities.

We also cling to things that we believe to be other than what they are:

As in the example of perceiving a rope as a snake,

thinking it is, even though it is not,

if you do not know that you are being fooled, you will wander.

When one cannot see very well, one may mistake a rope for a snake and
get a terrible fright—simply because one has not looked at the rope properly. It is the same with the various desirable experiences we can have.
Because we believe that they truly exist, we go to a great deal of trouble to
fulfill our desires. Instead of recognizing the benefits of following a teacher
and practicing the Dharma, we are fooled by our perceptions and so we
wander endlessly in samsara.

As in the example of the parrot eating poison *(and, by thus imitating the peacock, causing its own death),*

*if you behave as if you have attained realization even though you have
not and*

you cling to things thinking that they truly exist, you will wander.

If we have not achieved the full realization of emptiness that allows us to
use emotions as the path, and we try to perform activities that are the
domain of realized beings, we will go astray. Take the example of the peacock and the parrot. The peacock can eat poisonous berries, and doing so
only makes its plumage more brilliant. But if a parrot tries to do the same,
it dies. Similarly, if we try to imitate the great siddhas in enjoying desirable
experiences, it will only tie us further to samsara, because we still have the
concept that the object of desire truly exists. Rather than enhancing our
practice and serving to transform our afflictive emotions into wisdom, it will
simply result in our being obscured by our afflictive emotions and actions.

Believing in existence where there is no existence, one is helplessly con-
fused by attachment and aversion.

As in the example of the child and the empty fist

tricking it into thinking it contains a treat,[116]

if you are fooled by your perceptions, you will wander in samsara.

There are no phenomena that exist truly. Yet we postulate the existence
of phenomena and cling to them. Once we are caught by such delusions,
clinging enters our being and we become helplessly attracted to things we
like and repelled by things we dislike. Thus we are fooled by the perceptions of the senses, like a small child who is approached by someone pretending he has something in his hand. The child holds out its hand happily
expecting to receive a gift, only to cry with disappointment when the person opens his hand and there is nothing in it. Just so are we fooled by our
senses, and this is how we wander in samsara. This is why we need to recognize that all phenomena have no true existence at all.

•• 35 ••

Son, there are ten ways of failing the Buddhas

in one's commitment, which must accord with one's level.

It is important that our conduct accords with our level of realization. If you
are a great siddha, you can act accordingly. If not, you should act according to your level. But if you do not have a high degree of realization and
you behave as if you did, you will end up betraying the Buddhas in ten ways.
As we said earlier, if the conduct follows the view too closely, the view will
become demonic.

> *The way to avoid failing in your commitment is to take the*
> *Buddhas of the three times as your witnesses; for the fault in*
> *breaking a promise knows no bounds, whereas if you do not break*
> *it, inconceivable good qualities will be yours: you will become the*
> *foremost child of all the Buddhas of the past, present, and future.*
> *Therefore, within each six-hour period of the day take a reckoning,*
> *and if you have broken your promise, make your confession and*
> *renew the promise with a firm vow.*

In order not to be caught in this way by your actions and afflictive emotions, take the Buddhas of the past, present, and future as your witnesses. The Buddhas, who have the eye of wisdom, know that if you experience delusion in an ordinary way, it is impossible to attain liberation and enlightenment. We fall under the power of delusion because we fail to recognize that phenomena have no inherent existence. If we make a promise not to fall into delusion and we then break that promise, there will be boundless negative consequences. If we manage to keep that promise, we will gain inconceivable qualities and become the foremost child of all the Victorious Ones. Since the path shown by the Enlightened Ones is without mistake, if we follow it properly, we too will be treading the right path without mistake. You must therefore be mindful, conscious of the good and bad elements within you, and take stock of your faults and qualities. If you find that you have transgressed the samaya, regret your mistake, confess it, and repair the samaya, promising not to commit the same mistake again. If you find, on examining yourself in this way, that you have not transgressed the samaya, rejoice and dedicate that source of good to all sentient beings.

> *Recognizing that all happiness and suffering is the manifestation of your own previous actions,*

Even if the whole world rises up in enmity against you, do not stray from the absolute nature. If you do, you will be betraying the Buddhas of the three times.

It is important to realize that all the happiness and suffering, joy and sorrow you are experiencing now have not been decided for you by gods such as Indra, Brahma, and Vishnu, nor have they come about on their own. They are the natural result of your own past actions. So make a promise that even if the whole world rises up as your enemy, you will not wander from the absolute nature. Then, even if someone appears to threaten your life, if you can remain in equanimity within the recognition of the absolute nature, that enemy will be unable to harm you. But if you fall into delusion, thinking that enemies exist truly, and as a result you react by trying to defeat them and to protect others who arouse attachment in you, then you will surely be betraying the Buddhas of the past, present, and future.

Be mindful at all times of what is right and what is not; and be vigilant as to whether you are actually acting accordingly. Mindfulness and vigilance will then be your teachers.

Constantly supported by mindfulness and vigilance,

Whatever you do, do not wander from the continuum of the unborn absolute nature. If you do, you will be betraying the Buddhas of the three times.

In terms of the relative truth, you should accumulate merit in accordance with the unfailing interdependence of cause and effect, while knowing that these are like a dream or illusion. At the same time, in your meditation, you should never move from the understanding of the empty nature, dharmata.

Whatever happens to you, apply the antidote, refresh yourself with faith, assimilate the instructions, be unhypocritical in discipline, and have confidence in the law of actions and their results. By these means,

Even if your life is at stake, never lose sight of the Dharma. If you do, you will be betraying the Buddhas of the three times.

Whatever circumstances occur, whether they are good things like praise, fame, comfort, and wealth or bad things like criticism, injury, and sickness, do not be influenced by believing that these circumstances truly exist. Use the antidote on them. Remember that suffering is the result of your past deeds and make a wish that with your own suffering you may be able to take others' sufferings upon yourself. If you become wealthy or encounter other favorable situations, regard these as though they were a dream or an illusion and enjoy them without being attached. If you can do this, the antidote will have been efficient.

All these circumstances should also help to revive or increase your faith in the Three Jewels and your devotion to the teacher, like rekindling a fire. At the same time you should recognize the value of the instructions more deeply, practice discipline without hypocrisy, and have a firm conviction as to how the law of cause and effect operates. This should lead you to resolve never to lose sight of the Dharma, that is, never to lapse into negative actions, even if it costs you your life.

Keeping in mind the related benefits and risks, and remembering your teacher's *kindness,*

Do not spoil even an atom's worth of your samaya with the sublime teacher. If you do, you will be betraying the Buddhas of the three times.

In ordinary life, a merchant who conducts his business may gain an enormous profit, but there is also a risk involved, especially if his methods are slightly irregular. He may lose everything or end up in trouble with the law. For us Dharma practitioners, too, there are great benefits and great risks—related to our root teacher. If we practice in accordance with what he tells us, there is no doubt that we will derive the greatest benefit and achieve all the qualities of liberation and ultimate omniscience. But our relationship with the teacher also entails great risk: if we do not practice according to his instructions but behave hypocritically, pretending to do as he says in his presence and doing the opposite behind his back, we risk falling into the vajra hell.

Remembering death and reflecting on the defects of samsara,

Rather than now accomplishing fame *and other goals related to the eight ordinary concerns* **in this life, put all your efforts into the task of training in the mind** *turned toward enlightenment.* **If you involve yourself in the affairs of this life and are not diligent in the mind training, you will be betraying the Buddhas of the three times.**

What should we do in order to practice wholly in accordance with the Dharma and avoid anything that goes against it? We must remember death—the certainty that death will come and the unpredictability of when it will come. We also need to bear in mind the shortcomings of samsara and how any inclination to samsaric activities simply perpetuates suffering in samsara. Reflect as follows: "Today I have this human body with its freedoms and advantages. I have met a spiritual teacher and crossed the threshold of the Dharma. I have been lucky enough to receive the instructions that can bring Buddhahood in one lifetime, so I must practice them. Otherwise, if I indulge in activities that are motivated by the eight ordinary concerns, I will be fooling myself." So instead of thinking that fame and other ordinary concerns are important, make every effort to train single-mindedly in bodhichitta, purifying the two obscurations with the intention of benefiting the whole infinity of sentient beings. On the other hand, if you are diligent only in the affairs of this life, if you do not cultivate mindfulness of what is right and what is wrong, and if you are not constantly vigilant in checking whether you are acting, speaking, or thinking accordingly, you will be transgressing the precepts of the Buddhas of the past, present, and future and betraying them.

As it is said in all the sutras and tantras,

See the noble teachers as Vajrasattva in person and have devotion.

In terms of qualities and accomplishment, the teacher is truly the equal of all the Buddhas. But in terms of kindness, he is far kinder. Bearing this in mind, we should be full of respect and devotion throughout the six periods of the day and night and deeply determined to do whatever the teacher says.

If you do not, you will be betraying the Buddhas of the three times.

Recognizing that everything that appears is the mind, that the mind itself is empty, and that the inseparable union of clarity and emptiness is primal wisdom,

Know that everything outside and inside is the mind, and do not have attachment or aversion. If you do, you will be betraying the Buddhas of the three times.

We speak of the deluded perceptions of samsara where everything is seen as impure, and, linked to these, the afflictive emotions and the workings of karma. We also speak of nirvana and the pure phenomena of the kayas and wisdoms. But who made these two, the impurity of samsara and the purity of nirvana? It is the mind. If we look at the basic nature of this mind and ask ourselves what it is like—what is its shape, color, or locality—it is impossible to find any. It is nothing but emptiness. At the same time, it is not a a blank nothingness like the emptiness of an empty pot. The mind also has the power to know everything. This is the mind's clarity aspect. In truth, the mind is clarity and emptiness united, and the inseparable union of clarity and emptiness is what we call nondual wisdom.

All the outer objects, the universe and beings, and the inner subject that knows these, that conceives of subject and object and creates the notions of enemies and friends—all these are the mind. If we do not know that they are all the projections of the mind and we fail to recognize the mind's empty nature, we will be fooled by the various emotions such as attachment and aversion that grow in the mind. We must therefore understand that the whole manifestation of samsara and nirvana is nothing but the play of the mind and that the nature of this mind is emptiness. Its essential nature is unborn emptiness and its natural expression is clarity, the faculty of knowing. When we know this, we are no longer alienated; we are not influenced by attraction to the desirable and aversion to the undesirable. But when we fall under the power of attraction and aversion, we betray the Buddhas of the three times.

> *Acknowledging beings as your mothers, remembering their kindness, and wishing to repay that kindness,*

Cultivate great compassion and work for the sake of sentient beings. If you *depart from bodhichitta and* **strive for your own sake alone, you will be betraying the Buddhas of the three times.**

Practicing the Dharma just for your own benefit is of little use. You should practice for the sake of all sentient beings, who are as numerous as the sky is vast. Acknowledge that all beings have been your parents and feel the same love and gratitude for them as you do for your actual parents in this life. Think how kind they have been to you, giving you life and then providing you with everything you needed such as food, clothes, and affection. We can see how strong parents' love is for their children: even the most cruel animals like hawks and wolves who eat nothing but flesh and blood manifestly love their young. It is important to realize what a debt of gratitude every sentient being owes its parents.

How can we repay this kindness? The best way to do so is through the Dharma, recognizing that all phenomena are like a dream or an illusion. Look at yourself and see if you are able to avoid even a single negative action and to undertake a single positive action. If you make it your concern to do more and more positive actions and fewer and fewer negative ones, and on top of that you have bodhichitta, the wish to benefit others, then you will truly be practicing the Great Vehicle. On the other hand, if you transgress bodhichitta, if you fail to recognize that all beings have been your kind parents and as a result you are preoccupied only with fulfilling your own selfish goals, you will betray the Buddhas of the three times, for you will actually be behaving in complete contradiction to what they have taught.

> **All dualistic concepts** *on account of clinging to everything outside and inside as truly existing* **are the work of demons, so know that there is no duality of subject and object. If you fail to do so, you will be betraying the Buddhas of the three times.**

Where does the delusion that makes us go counter to the Buddhas' teachings come from? It comes from the mistaken belief that the universe and the beings in it truly exist. As a consequence of this dualistic clinging, we become very pleased with things like success, fame, praise, and gain, and get very upset by loss, criticism, and obscurity. For us the eight worldly concerns are all-important. At the root of this is the duality of the inner subject, the grasping mind, and the outer object that is grasped. Because of this grasping relationship between subject and object we are attracted to things that are pleasant and desirable and feel averse to anything that harms us, people's criticism and so forth. Thus we divide the whole world into pleasant and unpleasant, and we do everything we can to keep the one and get rid of the other. It is this duality that makes us fall into deluded ways of acting, and it is these that are the work of the demon. What do we mean by "demon"? It is anything that obstructs the path of liberation from samsara and prevents one from attaining ultimate omniscience. The antidote for this is to recognize all the phenomena of samsara and nirvana as the nondual wisdom of awareness and emptiness. If we fail to recognize this nonduality, we betray the Buddhas of the three times.

> **With this body as a support, be careful—**
>
> *that is, maintain mindfulness in the four kinds of conduct, guarding the body and so forth—*
>
> **as you seek the fruit of Buddhahood. If you fail to do so, you will be betraying the Buddhas of the three times.**

At present you have this human existence, which is free from the eight unfavorable conditions and endowed with the ten advantages—the five individual advantages and the five circumstantial ones. With this human body as a support, there is no path in the Dharma's nine vehicles—those of the Shravakas, Pratyekabuddhas, and Bodhisattvas and the six vehicles of the Vajrayana—that cannot be practiced. Each of these paths, if practiced, leads to a corresponding result. It is like finding a wish-fulfilling jewel that grants every wish or prayer one makes. Were one to be in possession of a wish-fulfilling jewel, it would be foolish not to make use of it. Similarly, now that we have this human body we should be one-pointed in using it to practice the supreme Dharma in every one of our four kinds of activity—eating, sleeping, walking, and sitting. In all these we need to constantly examine our minds, watching like a spy and checking whether we are acting in a negative or positive way. At the same time we have to remember clearly what is positive and what is negative—what we have to undertake and what we need to avoid. This mindfulness is the most extraordinary form of protection. So do not waste this opportunity by being careless. Use mindfulness to maintain control over your body, speech, and mind so that you are not influenced by worldly concerns. To be mindful of what is right and wrong and vigilant as to whether one is behaving accordingly is the basis of Dharma practice. Not to be mindful and vigilant is shameful, for it is betraying the Buddhas of the three times.

•• 36 ••

Using instructions to meditate without distraction,

for the practice has to be done with full concentration.

Son, there are four ways not to be distracted.

Master the crucial point of the methods for settling in concentration, following the examples given in the Six Prerequisites for Concentration.[117]

As the first step in training the mind we need to pacify the mind, protecting it from excessive activity. This is achieved through the practice of sustained calm, which acts like a glass lantern protecting the lamp's flame from the wind. This practice makes the mind more tranquil so that it is less prone to being carried away by attachment and hatred. It is therefore important to become skilled in the crucial point of letting the mind rest in concentration. This entails avoiding any sorts of extreme. If you are too tense in trying to control the mind, your concentration will tire and your enthusiasm for the practice will wane. On the other hand, if you relax too much, you will simply stray into an ordinary state. For this reason it is said:

Tauten at times,
Ease off at others:
Here is a crucial point in the view.

Do not be distracted from the expanse of the mind free of grasping, like a straight arrow.

There are four ways of meditating that concern practitioners who do this sort of practice in mountain retreats. Regarding the first of these, in our ordinary state we conceive of phenomena and consciousness as truly existing. As long as we have such concepts, we are certain to accumulate karma in samsara. If on the other hand we are able to recognize the unborn nature of the mind and be free from these concepts and fixations, and we remain without straying in the expanse of the mind that is free of grasping, this is very powerful, like a perfectly straight arrow, which flies directly to the center of the target.

Without any mental grasping at the unborn nature,

Do not be distracted from the absolute space, which is free from thoughts, like a *champion* athlete

or like a painter of sacred art mixing his colors.

At all times we should be aware of the unborn nature of the mind. However, we must never cling to this unborn nature; we must remain completely free. The point is to remain in the absolute nature, where there is no such thing as a meditator, an object of meditation, or an act of meditating. As long as one still has these sorts of notions and concepts, even if one has a reputation as a "great meditator," one's meditation will not be in any way superior to the worldly concentrations.[118] So we must not stray from the absolute space, which is free from thoughts. "Thoughts" here refers to the constant alternation of likes and dislikes, being pleased with favorable situations and upset by unfavorable ones. Train in this total concentration like a champion athlete training with bow and arrow or with the sword. If he drops his mindfulness and vigilance and is distracted even for an instant, he will be struck by his opponent's weapon. A painter too has to be mindful and attentive when preparing his paints, mixing the pigments with the right base and diluting it correctly so that the paint spreads easily on the canvas and produces the fine lines, details, and delicate shades that will please the eye.

As no phenomena are extraneous to the absolute nature,

Do not be distracted from *their being indivisible, or from* **the expanse of evenness, like a hooked fish.**

As no relative phenomena ever depart from the absolute nature, they are naturally inseparable from it. Their not being two things is also called "the great evenness." It is important to know how to never wander from this expanse of evenness. Just as a hooked fish is certain to be hauled out of the water onto dry land, if we have constant mindfulness, we will definitely be taken out of the ocean of samsara.

With the view free from extreme beliefs and your meditation free from intellectual fabrication,

Do not be distracted from the state beyond all thought, as if you were removing a thorn.

The root of liberation from samsara is having the correct view, and the correct view is the view that is free from the different extremes. If one clings to the appearance aspect, one falls into the extreme of eternalism; if one clings to the emptiness aspect, one falls into that of nihilism. We have to be free from clinging to either of these extremes of existence and nonexistence. This cannot be achieved by intellectual fabrication. The absolute nature can only be recognized by direct experience. It is not a question of trying to isolate an empty aspect of the mind and to fix one's mind on it, or of isolating a clarity aspect of the mind and clinging to that. This sort of intellectual manipulation will never bring us to Buddhahood. Our meditation must therefore be free from the work of the intellect.

Do not be distracted from this state beyond all thought. And although there is no particular deity to meditate upon, no visualization details or attributes that you have to remember, no object for the mind to concentrate on, at the same time there must be no wandering, no lack of mindfulness. The close mindfulness and vigilance needed here are the same as those of someone trying to pull a thorn out of his skin—very carefully, without hurting himself. The real meditation is to simply remain in the absolute nature without obscuring the mind with all sort of intellectual constructs.

++ 37 ++

Meditation using the instructions on the method of "resting."[119]

Son, there are four instructions on the method.

To let go of the subject inside that apprehends the objects of the six consciousnesses—

We are talking here about the six sensory experiences—seeing forms, hearing sounds, smelling odors, tasting flavors, and feeling things.[120] When we perceive an object, our reaction is to cling to what we perceive. For example when we see a form, the object, the eye and the consciousness interact and we think, "This is beautiful, I need it," or "That is ugly, I don't want it." We thus have an infinite number of such thoughts—of good and unpleasant tastes, fragrant and offensive smells, pleasant and unpleasant tactile sensations, and so on. All these lead to actions, and that is how the wheel of samsara is set in motion.

How should we let go of these clingings? By establishing the empty nature of the perceiving consciousness. Once we establish the empty nature of the mind, it is not that we cease to see objects, but rather that the sight of them no longer gives rise to clinging. Therefore, we no longer experience the attraction and aversion that lead to delusion. Free of these clingings, we should remain in meditative equipoise, which only one's self-awareness can experience. It is a state that is completely limpid and empty, like a vast open space, quite free from the stains of fixation. This is

The instruction on the state of mind devoid of all ordinary perception and thought, like a dry skull,

which has no eyes, ears, and tongue, and therefore has no ordinary perceptions.

Now for the actual instruction on the method of "resting," which is sixfold:

It is said that in meditation an object on which one makes an effort to focus is the prison of the view, so

(1) Leave things effortlessly in the expanse free from references.

In meditation, in which the yogi's concentration is like the flow of a river, the natural state unfolds. Through it we may have a glimpse of the absolute nature, and even though this glimpse is not full realization, we will be sure that it is not something we have fabricated and that this nature has been ours since the very beginning. Once you have recognized the absolute nature, remain in it without modifying it in any way:

> *(2) Leave everything without contrivance in the uncompounded absolute space.*

If we do not remain in that state of simplicity but make all sorts of fabrications, these will obscure our recognition of the absolute nature. Constantly stirring water with a stick will never make the mud settle and allow the water to become clear. But if the water is left as it is without being agitated, gradually all the mud particles will sink to the bottom leaving the water perfectly pure, clear, and transparent. We should do the same with the mind, leaving it in its natural state without interfering, without stirring it up with fabrications.

> *(3) Though everything arises in your own mind, leave it without any notion of "I" or self.*

It is important to realize that all the phenomena of samsara and nirvana appear as projections of your own mind, like the various reflections that appear in a mirror. At the same time you must remain completely free of any concept of a self. When the phenomena of samsara and nirvana appear in the mind, you should not grasp at them, thinking, "This is my mind," or "This is the object," or "I have perceived that object as beautiful (or ugly)." All perceptions should be left as they are without entertaining any notion of "I" or self.

> *(4) Leave everything without conceptualization in the uncontrived expanse.*

The absolute nature is what we call the uncontrived state. This primordial, uncontrived nature is not a state that is blind to forms, deaf to sounds, and so on. On the other hand, it is completely free from attachment to what is called beautiful and from aversion to what is called ugly. This means that it is free from the notions of subject and object and the clingings associated with these notions:

> *(5) Leave things just as they are in the expanse free of subject and object.*

(6) Leave things in the ineffable unborn expanse.

By "unborn" we mean that this absolute nature is not something that has come into existence at one point and may cease to exist at another. It is completely beyond coming into existence and ceasing to exist. And it is not something distant, that you have to search for far away: it is present within the basic nature of your mind. How is this? If you do not prolong the past thought and do not encourage a future thought to arise, if you look between the past thought and the future thought that has not yet come and watch the nature of the present moment, you can recognize the primordial uncontrived nature of the mind, which has always been within you. This is the wisdom free from thought, which is between the thoughts. It is liberation itself. When one is able to see this vivid state, this is what we call profound insight, which is clear awareness.

The instruction on the mind that, watching, sees nothing, like someone who has eaten poison.

The example is that of the falling lines that appear to the eyes of someone who has eaten a poisonous plant. Its meaning is that by recognizing that the apparent objects of the six consciousnesses are devoid of reality one reverses the belief in true existence.

People, and even animals, that eat the fruit or seeds of the plant known in Tibet as *thang trom* experience all sorts of hallucinations. All about them they see scorpions, donkeys, and all sorts of terrifying beasts. Also, people who suffer from phlegm disorders experience visual aberrations and see lines and dots and so on. All these are pure hallucinations, deluded perceptions of things that have never truly existed. But our ordinary way of perceiving the six sensory experiences is no less deluded. We need to recognize them as delusions, as devoid of any solid existence. Once we do so, we will be free from our belief in the true reality of phenomena.

The actual instruction concerns the primordial unborn nature and comprises six points:

(1) The absolute nature is primordially unstained by clinging.

This primordial nature is like the lotus flower, which grows out of the mud but is not dirtied by it. Just as the lotus flower, with its beautifully colored petals enclosing the anther and the nectar inside, is unsullied by the mud, the primordial nature with all its qualities is completely unstained by the dualistic clinging to subject and object.

(2) The realization is naturally free from craving.

It is free from the strong attachment to the eight ordinary concerns. But that freedom from attachment is not achieved by applying a remedy: craving dissolves by itself, naturally.

(3) The way of arising is spontaneous and free from grasping.

It is something that happens on its own, unlike contrived meditation in which one makes an effort to maintain sustained calm and to prevent deluded thoughts from arising in the mind. It is the wisdom realization of the absolute nature arising spontaneously without trying to contrive it or trying to control the mind.

*(4) The experience is naturally present and not something
        that is made.*

The wisdom of the absolute nature is always present and has been since the beginning. It is not something that has been made. And the experience of the recognition of that natural presence is devoid of any clinging to the recognition itself.

*(5) The natural state is, from the very beginning, unborn and
        entirely devoid of self.*

The recognition of the natural presence is not something to be sought outside. It is the natural manifestation of what is within us. Therefore,

*(6) The display arises spontaneously and is not something
        to be sought.*

If we adulterate appearances with our clinging, delusion will never cease. Therefore,

For outer appearances not to be spoiled by inner clinging, there is

The instruction on the mind free from judgments, like an infant.

Sometimes we think, "Today my meditation went well. I managed to remain in the natural state." At other times we get depressed because we have been unable to keep our mind under control. It is important to be free of these sorts of judgment where we value certain states and not others. We should be like tiny infants. Babies do not feel attachment if something beautiful is put in front of them, nor do they think of feeling afraid if they are about to be killed by a butcher wielding a sword. They do not esteem good, they do not distrust bad.

The actual instruction:

(1) The absolute nature is the uncontrived mind.

The uncontrived mind is the Buddha's mind. If we look at the uncontrived nature of the mind, we will reach a state that is free from discursive thoughts:

(2) The view is the mind without thoughts.

It is the wisdom free from dualistic distinctions such as getting excited about good experiences and feeling uncomfortable about bad experiences:

(3) The primal wisdom is the mind without concepts.

It is the wisdom of the nondual mind.

(4) The meditation is the undistracted mind.

Although there is no particular object on which to focus, at the same time the mind should not wander.

(5) The essential nature of the mind is unwavering.

When our recognition of that nature becomes quite steady, it does not waver, like a mountain that is never moved by the wind. This is known as "leaving as-it-is like a mountain."[121]

(6) The samaya of the mind is the knowledge that nothing transcends the mind,

for none of the phenomena that exist in samsara and nirvana ever pass outside this absolute nature. When we realize that they are all the display of the nature of the mind, this is the true samaya of the mind.

(7) The activity of the mind is not to give up

—not to give up mindfulness in our actions, both in the meditation period and the postmeditation period, until we attain complete and firm realization of the absolute nature. Only then will the meditation be free from the defects of excitement and drowsiness.

For leaving the consciousness just as it is, relaxed in its own state, there is:

The instruction on leaving the mind as it is, as if stunned,
like someone whose heart has been removed.

The example is that of someone whose heart has been taken out:
there is no hope of revival and the continuous stream of thoughts
is cut. The instruction on "leaving as it is, as if stunned"[122] *is that*
by leaving everything as it is in the uncontrived natural state—
without a subject that leaves, without an owner, as if stunned—
one will settle at ease, free of grasping and effort, in the arising
of the multifarious phenomena.

If one removes the heart from someone's chest, there is no hope of his remaining alive. Likewise when one has permeated all one's perceptions with the view of the absolute nature, delusion has no hope of staying. "Leaving everything as it is" means that one does not apply all sorts of fabrications: one leaves things as they are in the mountainlike view. But it is not that there is a subject that leaves and something that is left. There is no question of taking possession of the state of meditation and thinking, "This is my meditation" or "This is your meditation." "As if stunned" implies that there is no owner. It is a neutral state in which there is a complete absence of grasping. With all the myriads of perceptions that arise in the mind, there is no fixation or clinging to these perceptions. They are just left in a completely relaxed state.

In this natural state of the inseparability of the two truths, leave
things in uncontrived simplicity, a state of clear, empty awareness
that is not produced by effort through different causes and conditions.

In short, the manifested aspect, which is the infinite display of phenomena arising interdependently in accordance with the laws of causality, is relative truth. And the fact that all these phenomena are permeated with the emptiness endowed with all supreme qualities is the absolute truth. The true nature is the essential unity of these two truths, relative and absolute. It is not a state that is produced artificially by means of different causes and conditions. It is something that is recognized by remaining in the great evenness, directly recognized through the blessings of the teacher. It is clear, empty awareness free from effort and not made to happen by a combination of causes and conditions. In that state there is no subject who meditates, no act of meditation, and no object of meditation: these three concepts are entirely absent.

++ 38 ++

The instruction on how to rest in the natural flow.

Son, there are four ways to stay.

Stay without thought in the clarity that is not acquired and can *never* be lost

for the Buddha's wisdom has been present within you from the very beginning.

What do we mean by the wisdom of the Buddha? It is the indivisible union of clarity and emptiness, the absolute nature that is uncompounded and uncreated, the nature of the primal wisdom. That primal wisdom, which is the essence of Buddhahood, has always been present in our minds, but in our present deluded condition it is obscured, like the sun obscured by clouds. However, from the point of view of that nature itself, there has never been any obscuration, just as from the sun's point of view the sun has never been obscured. Once this view of the absolute nature has been realized, it cannot be lost again, for it has always been there. Neither is it something that has to be looked for or acquired, because one has always had it. It is free from discursive thoughts.

Stay without thinking in the bliss that is not to be evoked and cannot slip away

for the mind from the very beginning is not caught and is not fettered.

In truth, the mind, since the very beginning, has never been caught or tied. It is the primordial state of enlightenment, which has never been bound or fettered. It is not something that one can lose, nor does one need to evoke it.

Stay in vivid clarity, undistracted in the state beyond distraction

for distracting objects have never been extraneous to the absolute nature.

Since even the objects of distraction remain within the absolute nature, it is impossible to stray from the absolute nature. This is the true undistracted state.

How does one stay like that? There are six ways to be without contrivance:

(1) If you look for mind, it is empty.

At present, because we do not investigate things properly, we happily take them for granted and assume that the mind actually exists. After all, the mind seems so powerful. With all its past, present, and future thoughts it manages to accumulate so much karma. And yet, if we start to look for the mind, it is impossible to find it anywhere—not in any part of the body nor anywhere else. Neither is it possible to attribute to it any color or shape. If you look for the mind, you will only find emptiness.

Nevertheless, despite its empty nature the mind does not stop producing thoughts. These thoughts must be recognized as being the mind's natural activity, its creativity, like the light constantly given out by the flame of a lamp. The reason we fall into delusion is because we fail to recognize that all these thoughts are, in fact, nothing other than the display of the absolute nature. So you must not think that true meditation is an absence of thoughts, a calm state of extinction in which nothing arises at all. If your idea is to prevent thoughts arising, you will simply not realize the absolute nature:

(2) Block it and you will spoil it.

(3) Contrive it and you will adulterate it.

If you try to fabricate this absolute nature, which has been there from the beginning, you will simply be mixing it with impurity, staining it with defects.

(4) Meditate and you will be bound.

In any purposeful meditation, where you have the concepts of a meditator and a meditation, you will be tied down by the very act of meditating.

(5) Look at it and it will disappear.

When you look at the nature of the mind, "there is no mind," as it says in the *Prajñaparamita Sutras*. You cannot find it; it vanishes, because there is no true existence to be found in it.

(6) Effort will obscure it.

Therefore, do not seek, do not block, do not contrive, do not meditate, do not look, do not make effort: leave it just as it naturally is.

There being nothing in the mind for it to act on, nor anything to do through the path of action, nor anything that is accomplished,

Remain unhurried, with nothing to do, perfectly poised,[123]

the practice neither overtaut nor slack, like the string of a bent bow.

You should not say, "This is what I will meditate on," for there is nothing—no definite object with characteristics—that you have to realize. This is because the nature of mind is uncompounded and empty. It is not produced by any action, for it is primordially present. Simply remain in the recognition of this nature, watching it directly. Your practice should not alternate between sometimes being too tense and at other times being too relaxed. It should be even, like a bowstring, which is equally taut along its whole length, not tighter at one point and looser at another.

✦✦ 39 ✦✦

Unobstructed natural arising, the crucial point of the mind.

In order to preserve the absolute nature, we should not try to modify the mind or to block it.

Son, there are six crucial points of the mind to be understood.

Awareness, the fourth moment beyond the three—that directly experi-
enced, uncontrived state that is not adulterated by the notions of sub-
ject and object—is the simplicity of the dharmakaya. So recognize the
mind with this instruction—the natural dissolution of concepts:

Relaxation is the crucial point of the mind, exemplified by some-
one who has completed a task.

What we call the fourth moment is that in which one does not follow
the past thought, one does not invite future thoughts, and one is not at
present distracted by anything. It is the fourth aspect of time that transcends those three moments. If you look into awareness, there is no object
to hold onto, neither any mind that clings. It is unstained by the concept
of subject and object. That direct experience is the natural dharmakaya
state. With the spontaneous mindfulness of the absolute nature, as if the
dharmakaya were looking at itself, one is neither narrowly concentrated as
in the effortful mindfulness of sustained calm nor distractedly ordinary.
This is the instruction for naturally dissolving concepts.

Recognizing the mind in this way one reaches a state similar to that of
someone who has successfully completed an enormous task and is now
utterly relaxed and calm, not busying himself in any way. Likewise, when
the mind sees its own nature, it is relaxed and does not make any deliberate effort.

Being free from the clinging to the true existence of things, one has
no concerns, thinking of things as good or bad:

Freedom from concern is the crucial point of the mind,
exemplified by someone who has recovered from an illness.

It is important to be free from clinging to the true existence of things.
Otherwise the mind will make distinctions—between good experiences
and bad ones, such as afflictive emotions and suffering. You should reach
the state in which the mind is unconcerned by good and bad thoughts, like
someone who has caught a disease and, having now recovered from it, is
no longer concerned about that disease.

As there is not a single thing that has not been pure and perfect since
the very beginning, be free of the dualistic fixation of blocking some
things and encouraging others.

Freedom from hesitation is the crucial point of the mind, exemplified by a madman jumping off a cliff.

There is not a single thing that is not by nature as primordially pure and perfect as a Buddha, so we should be free of different fixations such as stopping some things and accomplishing others. A Buddha is someone who has cleared away all obscurations and therefore does not need to prevent afflictive emotions and so on, which are no longer present in him. Similarly, he has all the qualities of the kayas and wisdoms, which are expressed naturally like the rays emitted by the sun, and so he does not need to deliberately accomplish or create these qualities. The crucial point, therefore, is to be free of concepts and to not evaluate one's meditation by wondering whether or not one is meditating correctly. Rather we should be like a mad person jumping off a precipice—without any hesitation.

Everything that appears is liberated as primal wisdom, so the view is free from duality, the meditation is free from fixation, the action is free from effort, and the result is free from aspiration.

Freedom from expectation and apprehension is the crucial point of the mind, exemplified by one's *having* **met a person** *one had been looking* **for.**

At this time, everything that arises through the six senses—visual, auditory, olfactory, gustatory, and so forth—will be understood as being the display of wisdom and will therefore be liberated in its own wisdom nature. The view will be free from clinging to the duality of subject and object. The meditation will be free from fixation such as concepts of existence, nonexistence, and the rest. The action will be completely spontaneous, with no efforts or goals such as cultivating generosity, contriving discipline, and so on. The result will be free from any expectation of achieving a result in the future, for our own awareness—this natural state of the present moment, the dharmakaya within ourself, the fresh state of Buddhahood that we hold in our hand—is not something to be obtained sometime in the future. So the mind should be relaxed, entertaining neither hopes nor fears, just as when we have met an old friend we had been looking for—we feel fully satisfied and do not need to search any further.

Uttering the specific language of Ati overawes those in the lesser vehicles.

Freedom from fear is the crucial point of the mind, exemplified by a lion walking among other savage beasts.

All these terms—freedom from hope and doubt, primordial simplicity, and so on—are the language of Ati, the Great Perfection, and they might alarm those with narrow minds who are following lesser vehicles. Just as the lion, when it comes upon other wild animals, has nothing to fear, the crucial point in the practice of the Great Perfection is that one is fully confident and has no fear of other views.

The natural state is naturally radiant; no veils obscure it.

Clarity with absence of thoughts is the crucial point of the mind, exemplified by the flame of a lamp filled with sesame oil,

which shines very brightly.

•• 40 ••

Showing that the view, meditation, action, and result are innate and not extraneous.

Son, there are four things you need not seek.

Since the wisdom of the absolute nature free of intellect dwells in you innately, there is no need to look for it anew using one-sided views that are the product of the intellect.

Having the view that has no dualistic fixation, do not seek one that has; take the example of the sun: it does not have to look for its rays.

Similarly, this view devoid of dualistic fixation is like the natural radiance of the sun.

Regarding the uncontrived natural flow, there is no need to meditate on it with dualistic fixation as if it were something new for you.

Having the meditation that has no object on which to focus, do not seek one that has; take the example of a wish-fulfilling gem: it does not have to look for the things one wants.

If you simply rest in the uncontrived natural flow, you do not need to look for new ways of meditating, applying the methods of sustained calm and so forth. Simply by being what it is, a wish-fulfilling gem is able to fulfill the wishes of everyone in the country, bringing wealth to the poor and so on. Likewise, there is no need to transform a meditation without supports into one with supports.

Since things to be rejected and antidotes—afflictive emotions and primal wisdom, for instance—have the same taste, there is no duality of deed and doer, so

Having the action free of adoption and rejection, do not seek one to adopt and reject; take the example of a person: he does not have to look for himself.

By achieving the even taste in which there is no need to get rid of afflictive emotions and apply antidotes or look for wisdom, you should realize this evenness in which there is no action involving rejection and adoption. Just as there is no need for a person to look for himself, follow the action in which there is nothing to give up and nothing to adopt.

The result, the primordial state of Buddhahood, dwells within you, so

Having the result free of hope and fear, do not look for one with hope and fear; take the example of a monarch: he does not have to reassert his royalty—

a king presiding on his throne depends on no one else.

The result, primordial Buddhahood, is within you and does not need to depend on anything else, just as a king seated on his throne does not depend on others to rule his kingdom. He is master and is answerable to no one. Neither does he need to be afraid of another equally powerful king: both are confident in their own power and dignity. In the same way, the result implies complete confidence, without a trace of expectation or apprehension. So you do not need to look for a state in which hopes and doubts are still present.

Thus, since all phenomena in samsara and nirvana are by nature
inseparable, do not move from the inconceivable *evenness of the*
absolute nature that is beyond hope and fear, concept and effort.

These chapters on the superior training of the mind have been
arranged in a different order in the Commentary *as follows. After*
the thirtieth chapter come Chapters Thirty-six to Thirty-nine,
at which point one jumps to Chapter Seventy-seven in the section
on the training in wisdom. Next, one returns to Chapters Thirty-one
to Thirty-five, followed by Chapter Forty. Here, however, I have
followed the exact order of the root text.

Although in the *Commentary* the chapters have been rearranged in the logical order of the subjects they deal with, in this present annotated edition, for the sake of clarity, the order has been kept as it is in the root text.

To sum up, I have used these chapters to give an explanation to suit
readers' individual capacities, so that relying on the superior training
in concentration according to the Prajñaparamita, *the* Epitome,
and the Magical Display, *they practice the view and meditation*
on the path in much the same way as one brings up a small child—
in stages—combining skillful means and wisdom like a bird flying
in the sky. This completes the instruction.

The different subjects have been expounded in order according to the *Prajñaparamita Sutras;* the *Epitome of Essential Meaning,* which is the *Gathering of the Great Assembly;*[124] and the *Net of the Magical Display of Peaceful and Wrathful Deities.* Relying on these three main sections, we should practice the view, meditation, and action on the path in the same way as one gradually brings up a child. In doing so, we need always to combine skillful means and wisdom, just as a bird needs both its wings to fly in the sky. All this has been explained to suit the different capacities of beings, some of whom are more intelligent than others.

This was the third section from the Eighty Chapters of Personal Advice, the instruction on one-pointed concentration, the means.

IV. Wisdom

Instructions on the superior training of wisdom, the perfect essence.

"Wisdom" here refers to the wisdom of no-self, which we have to realize.

There are thirty-eight chapters.

❖❖ 41 ❖❖

Twelve points that explain the view.

*The realization referred to in the Later Mind Section is like a slash
with a very sharp blade: with the wisdom devoid of the three concepts,
all afflictive emotions and discursive thoughts are severed at the root.
The way this happens is that since all phenomena of the ground, path,
and result—samsara and nirvana—arise as the play of one's own
unborn mind, they are free from ontological extremes, from good and
bad, like space. The mind is by nature unborn, its display is unobstructed, its essential characteristic is absence of duality, and so on.
In introducing this, the* All-Accomplishing King *states,*

> *Because all things are subsumed in the root, the mind,*
> *It is the root that has to be taught.*

THE GREAT PERFECTION is divided into the Mind Section, Expanse Section, and Section of the Pith Instructions. The Mind Section has eighteen
subsections, divided into what are known as earlier and later,[125] referring
to the order in which they were given. The explanation here follows the
later teachings. These are said to be like a very sharp sword. In what way?
In our present condition, we believe that subject, object, and action truly
exist. It is these three concepts that we have to cut through, using the sharp
blade of this instruction, which slices the root of all the afflictive emotions

and deluded thoughts. When one cuts a tree at the root, everything—the trunk, branches, leaves, flowers, and fruit—falls to the ground at the same time. Similarly, if we cut ignorance at the root, the whole delusion of samsara will be instantly felled.

How do we cut through delusion? From the point of view of the way things appear, the ground—that is, our present condition when we start on the path—can be considered as impure, the path as a mixture of pure and impure, and the result as perfectly pure. But from the point of view of the way things are, there are no such things as pure and impure. What appears as impurity is simply an adventitious, temporary obscuration that has no existence of its own. But fundamentally there is nothing that has ever become anything other than what it has always been, primordially pure. The difference lies in whether or not this primordially pure nature is obscured. From its own point of view, the nature has not become worse when impurity is perceived; neither has it improved when purity is seen at the time of the result. It is like space, which can contain all the different universes, continents, mountains, and so forth and yet is not affected in any way by these things: it is not made better by things being beautiful, nor made worse by things being ugly. Similarly, all the different phenomena of the ground, path, and result arise as the display of one's mind, not affected by concepts such as good and bad. By nature the mind is unborn, its display is infinite and unobstructed, and its characteristic is the union of clarity and emptiness. This is how the nature of the mind is introduced, as being unborn, unobstructed, and free of duality. As it is said in the *All-Accomplishing King*, one of the Mind Section tantras, everything can be brought back to the mind, because the root of delusion and nondelusion is to be found in the mind itself. It is this mind that will now be explained.

Son, there are twelve points.

The unborn ultimate nature of your own mind is **not concealed anywhere** *and yet* **nobody can see it** *as a concrete object with characteristics.*

An ordinary being who uses the conditioned intellect to search for the unborn nature of the mind, the dharmakaya, will find that there is nothing to be seen. It is impossible to assign any characteristic to this nature of the mind in the same way that one attributes combustion and heat to fire or a tendency to stay at the bottom of its container to water.

Though it has **never stopped being** *yours* **since the very beginning,** *hitherto you have* **not recognized it** *as your nature.*

In fact there is nothing to be seen, nothing to be sought, because the mind has been with you from the beginning. It has not been with you sometimes and separate from you at others. Like your shadow, it always accompanies you. The only problem is that you have not recognized the nature of mind, like a pauper who is unaware that he is in possesion of a precious gem.

Since nothing exists as such inherently, **when things are examined nothing is seen.** *However, when unexamined, they seem to exist: thus all the phenomena of samsara and nirvana* **appear in every possible way,** *unobstructedly.*

In terms of relative truth, we happily take it for granted that things exist and therefore believe in their existence. But as soon as we examine them in depth, everything collapses; we cannot find anything that truly exists. And yet they all—the deluded phenomena of samsara and the wisdom phenomena of nirvana—arise as an infinite display of the mind, appearing in every possible way, unobstructedly.

Though in fact there is nothing, deluded appearances **appear in all their variety, but** *since they do not intrinsically exist in any way,* **there is nothing real.**

In truth these are all deluded appearances. They appear but they do not truly exist, for though they manifest in one way or another, their ultimate nature is not something that one can seize with one's hand or touch with one's finger. Once we have realized the unborn absolute nature, we see that all these phenomena never separate from that nature and therefore have no true existence even though they appear. But they still arise multifariously, and even though from the point of view of the absolute nature they are nonexistent, when we perceive them in a deluded way we perpetuate karma.

Though you have wandered for kalpas *in existence,* **you have never lost or been parted** *from the buddha nature, sugatagarbha.*

Even though we have wandered in samsara for kalpas and kalpas, we have never once been parted from the essence of enlightenment. You might think that one is cut off from the buddha nature when one is in samsara and reunited with it when one attains nirvana, but there has never been any separation.

> **Though** *the ultimate nature* **appears** *in* **a variety of ways** *as samsara and nirvana,* **there has** *never* **been any change** *in what it is.*

The absolute nature pervades the whole of samsara and nirvana. Even deluded phenomena occur within the absolute nature, but it is not tainted by them. In other words, deluded phenomena do not occur outside the absolute nature, and yet the absolute nature does not intrinsically contain delusion. It is unchanging and has never been stained or limited, even when we are deluded, for despite delusion not happening outside the absolute nature, when it is dispelled and we realize the absolute nature, the latter does not grow better in any way; it remains as it has always been.

> **Without having** *as much as* **a part of the** *minutest* **atom**[126] *of solid existence,* **it pervades everything** *like space.*

> **Within emptiness,** *which is like space,* **the various** *phenomena that arise through the interdependent process of cause and effect* **appear** *unobstructedly.*

In this emptiness, which is like space, relative phenomena manifest interdependently, with causes giving rise to effects, so that negative actions lead inevitably to suffering and positive actions lead inevitably to happiness.

> *The mind is like an unbroken horse: if you are tense and agitated, you cannot control it; if you relax, you can control it. Therefore,*

> **When it is not held or tied, it stays wherever it is.**

We can never understand the nature of the mind through intense effort but only by relaxing, just as breaking a wild horse requires that one approach it gently and treat it kindly rather than running after it and trying to use force. So do not try to catch hold of the nature of the mind, just leave it as it is.

> *By uniting sustained calm and profound insight,* **one travels through the space** *of the absolute nature* **unsupported,** *like a soaring garuda.*

A garuda launching itself into space from the top of a cliff does so without the slightest apprehension: it does not need anything to support it as it soars into the sky. Likewise, with sustained calm and profound insight united we can fly unsupported in the space of the absolute nature.

From the absolute nature that is not anything, anything can arise, so

everything possible is accomplished without effort.

This absolute nature has no characteristics whatsoever. Neither is there any solidity to it that makes it existent, nor is it nonexistent in the sense of being a blank void. And it is precisely for this reason, its being devoid of all characteristics, that it can manifest in every way possible, in other words, everything possible is effortlessly accomplished.

Without *the mind having color, shape,* **form, or characteristics, whichever way one views it** *and meditates on it, in that way* **it appears.**

The mind, too, is intrinsically devoid of characteristics. We cannot say that it has a color, a shape, a form, and so on. Because of this it, too, can appear in every possible way. Whichever way one looks at it or meditates upon it, in that way it appears. It is this very fact that everything is empty that allows the whole multiplicity of phenomena to manifest.

To sum up, this is an introduction to the nature of the mind. As it is unborn, there is no real basis to it that can be found. As its display is unobstructed, unlimited, and infinite, *it arises in various ways,* manifesting as suffering, happiness, and neutral states. *As it is ultimately free of duality, there is nothing to cling to as true,* as existing or not existing; one cannot ascribe any solid existence to it. *When the conceptual mind is liberated in its essence, nothing ever moves from the dharmata.*

++ 42 ++

Twelve kinds of confidence confirming the view.

From having seen the ultimate truth in its full nakedness, the mind is free of doubt.

Once we have seen the dharmata, we no longer have the slightest doubt or hesitation. We do not need to ask ourselves, "Is this really the absolute nature?"

Son, there are twelve kinds of confidence:

The confidence that *just as* the whole of existence *is created and destroyed* in space, *everything in samsara and nirvana* is one and the same *in thatness* and therefore has no intrinsic nature.

It is in space that in the beginning the universe and beings are formed as a result of karma, it is in space that in the end they all dissolve and vanish, and it is in space that they remain in the meanwhile. Similarly, everything in samsara and nirvana is of one taste within the absolute nature. Once we know this, we gain the clear conviction that everything is devoid of true existence.

The confidence that since the root *of all things*—both delusory and pure—is subsumed in the mind, Buddhahood is not *to be sought* elsewhere than in the mind.

The confidence that since the mind *by nature* has no birth *and no cessation,* it is uncompounded.

The confidence that since everything that appears is delusory, in truth enemies and friends do not exist *inherently as different entities.*

Everything we perceive is like an illusion conjured up by a magician. Simply by blowing a spell on to a table or other prop the magician can make horses, chariots, and even an entire army appear, but there are no horses or chariots there: it is all an illusion. Similarly, when we gain the conviction that everything we perceive is an illusion—for though it appears it does not truly exist—we will see that friends and enemies too are not truly existent.

The confidence that since all actions *based on delusion* are suffering—*that is, they are the cause of suffering*—in truth, *in terms of the ultimate nature,* there is nothing to be done—

no action to be performed and therefore no suffering to be experienced.

The confidence that since *the unborn absolute space* is the nature of all *phenomena, the nature* is nondual.

The confidence that there is no traveling *the path,* for realizing *the unborn nature of your mind* is Buddhahood—

Buddhahood is simply realizing what you actually have.

The confidence that the mind cannot be troubled by attachment and aversion, for everything that appears is untrue *like a magical illusion.*

The confidence that *although mind and appearances are many* and multifarious, *they have one taste* in being the display of the mind, *and that therefore the thoughts related to the five poisons such as* attachment and aversion are *intrinsically* unborn.

The confidence that objects *such as friends and enemies* that arouse *afflictive emotions, apart from simply being labels assigned by the ordinary mind, do not have any essential existence of their own; they* all dissolve in the mind.

The objects that make afflictive emotions grow, namely enemies and friends, are simply labels created by the mind. They do not exist on their own. There is no such thing as an enemy that remains one's enemy all one's life and throughout one's series of lives. Neither is there such a thing as a friend who has been a friend from the very beginning and will remain a friend forever. "Friend" and "enemy" are just labels that the mind attaches to the relevant objects. Once we know that these notions have no true existence, we will become confident that they dissolve within the mind.

The confidence that as *the nature of mind,* emptiness, is the source of everything *in samsara and nirvana,* it is the Absolute Space—the Mother, Prajñaparamita.

The confidence that *the natural state of the mind* is the great immensity, *for, like space,* it is the place where everything dwells.

This is confidence in the vastness of the nature of the mind. Just as space can accommodate the whole universe—the mountains, continents, and so forth, the nature of the mind is so vast that it can accommodate the whole of phenomena.

✦✦ 43 ✦✦

An instruction on seeing the absolute nature in nine ways.

Son, there are nine things *that, as a yogi on the path,* **one sees.**

One sees that everything *in samsara and nirvana* **is empty.**

One sees that the root *of all phenomena* **is the mind.**

If one has not recognized the nature of mind, the mind is the root of delusion; if one does recognize it, it is the root of enlightenment.

One sees that the nature *of one's own mind* **is unborn.**

One sees that *since the seventeen kinds of perception and so forth are unobstructed in the way they arise,* **one's situation is unpredictable.**

The mind displays in different ways depending on different circumstances. There are seventeen major ways in which it manifests: six correspond to the six realms, two to eternalism and nihilism, and nine to the nine vehicles.

One sees that the nature *of all phenomena* **is devoid of true existence.**

One sees that *despite the multifariousness of appearances and perceptions,* **the natural state** *of the absolute space* **does not change.**

Phenomena never waver from the wisdom of the dharmakaya, so although the way they appear may differ, the way the expanse of the absolute nature is never changes.

One sees that *since it is spontaneously arisen and free of causes and conditions,* **the way-it-is is devoid of duality,**

because in the nature of mind there is no division into subject and object.

One sees that *while it displays multifariously because of conditions,* **the ground nature itself does not tend toward any particular direction.**

One sees that the fundamental nature is devoid of concepts, *for there are no thoughts of ontological extremes* such as existence and nonexistence.

++ 44 ++

Seeing seven aspects of sublimity.

The meditator is free, for his mind has no owner and no responsibility.

Son, there are seven sublime things.

To be free from intellectual meditation is the sublime "leaving things as they are":[127]

do not try to fixate on existence and nonexistence, appearance and emptiness, and so on.

To be free of *the ordinary mind's dualistic* references *with regard to the absolute nature, which is beyond all reference,* is the sublime reference.

Neither thought nor no-thought transcends the intellect, and intellectual activity obscures freedom from intellect; thus,

Not to meditate on absence of thoughts is the sublime absence of thought.

Whether one has thoughts or remains in a state where there are no thoughts, one is still within the domain of the intellect. But trying to stop conceptual thoughts is not the solution because the state free from the intellect remains obscured by intellectual fabrication. We need to be in a state that is beyond elaborations and concepts, free from thought, and, at the same time, without intentional meditation. This is the sublime absence of thought as opposed to a relative, limited, and artificial absence of thought.

Not to use any *object of knowledge* as a support is the sublime support.[128]

Not to meditate on anything, *such as the union of appearances and emptiness,* the union of clarity and emptiness, or the union of emptiness and awareness, *making it a mental object,* **is the sublime meditation.**

To remain undistracted, with no *deliberate* **attempt to stop the movements** *of the mind and mental factors,* **is the sublime concentration.**[129]

The sublime concentration is one in which the movements of the mind flow freely without obstruction, without any attempt to block them. One does not try to stop the mind and its functions, but at the same time one is never distracted from the recognition of its nature.

When the mind is not involved with any *of the objects of the eight consciousnesses,* seeing forms, scenting odors, tasting, and so on, **this is the sublime absorption.**[130]

In short, all these amount to leaving things as they are, unadulterated by dualistic fixation and contrivance.

•• 45 ••

An instruction on perceiving in a nondualistic way but without denying the experiences of *the six sense organs being distinct and different.*

Son, there are six wisdom sense organs

that arise from certainty concerning the absolute nature.

When one knows that perceived forms are unborn, one does not grasp at them, and therefore

One sees the forms of mind's projection with the wisdom eye.

One understands the meaning of emptiness—*the absolute nature*—**with the wisdom ear.**

One senses *the nature* **as unborn with the wisdom nose.**

One tastes *multifariousness* **in a nondualistic way with the wisdom tongue.**

One touches *the truth*, the absolute nature, with the wisdom body.[131]

One knows that all that arises as the mind's projection arises in the *unborn* nature of the mind with the wisdom mind.

++ 46 ++

Using the above modes of perception to perceive in a nondualistic way without denying things being distinct and different.

If your own mind is free in the absolute nature, everything that appears outside arises as the absolute nature.

When one has recognized the nature of mind and there is no clinging to any of the phenomena of samsara and nirvana, all outer phenomena arise as the display of that nature, as ornaments to it, and they thus enhance the realization of the absolute nature. They are realized as manifestations of the absolute nature and therefore do not obstruct its recognition. So here, instead of six delusory objects we shall consider six wisdom objects.

Son, there are six wisdom objects.

The absolute nature **seen as clarity and emptiness inseparable is the wisdom form.**

If one has the direct experience of seeing the absolute nature as the non-dual, intrinsic union of clarity and emptiness, this is what we call wisdom form.

Sound understood as spontaneously arisen, *like the voice heard in an echo that does not belong to anyone,* **is the wisdom sound.**

The voice you hear in an echo is not really somebody's voice, even though you hear it as a voice. It is simply a reflection; the echo has not actually been created by anyone. So when sound is perceived as the echolike resonance of emptiness, this is the wisdom sound.

The *teacher's* **instruction imbibed to satiety is the wisdom fragrance.**

It is the teacher's instructions that enable us to realize the absolute nature, so we should carefully savor even a single one of them again and again, listening to it, reflecting upon it, and then meditating on it over and over. When we delight in the teacher's instruction like this, that delight is the wisdom fragrance.

The experience of *all phenomena* **as unborn is the wisdom flavor.**

When, without any notion of subject and object, we directly experience all the phenomena of samsara and nirvana as being unborn, we experience the wisdom flavor. It is the true flavor of the meaning of the teachings and not merely of the words.

The great bliss—*the absolute nature***—touched is the wisdom texture.**

Within the absolute nature there is nothing but purity. It is impossible to find even a trace of impurity. There is therefore no suffering. Neither is there a cause of suffering such as an afflictive emotion or action. There is only the great bliss, which, when we attain it, is the object of the wisdom sense of touch.

The recognition *of the natural state, the dharmata,* **is the wisdom phenomenon.**[132]

The dharmata is something that has to be recognized, but in a nondualistic way and not as an object that is recognized by a subject. It can only be realized by Awareness.[133] This recognition is the "object" of the wisdom mind.

++ 47 ++

Upon investigation, things are seen to be nonexistent in six ways.

On a relative level, the phenomena of samsara and nirvana appear and seem to exist, but if we examine them properly, we find that they have no true existence. There are six ways of perceiving this nonexistence.

Son, there are six authentic experiences.[134]

Since all phenomena have no true existence as such,

To not see them at all is authentic sight.

Relative phenomena appear momentarily like a rainbow forming in the sky: in truth they have no intrinsic, permanent existence. And since they do not exist, there is nothing to see. To see that there is nothing to see is what is known as "the great seeing," or "authentic sight." Seeing the absolute nature is sight without a seer, an object seen, or an act of seeing. Nevertheless, we give this realization of the true nature of phenomena the name "sight."

Since there is no duality of a hearer and something to be heard regarding the absolute nature,

To not hear anything is authentic hearing.

There being in fact no duality of someone who senses and something to be sensed,

To not sense anything is the authentic perception (of smell).

In truth, in the absolute view, meditation, and action there is no object or action. One is beyond all such concepts. So the authentic perception is absence of perception with regard to the whole of phenomena, from form up to omniscience.

Similarly,

To not taste anything is the authentic taste.

If we experience happiness, pleasure, suffering, or pain, it is because the experience is tinged with clinging. But here we are talking about the experience that is a nonexperience, the supreme experience.[135]

Not mentally touching anything, *true or false or whatever,* **is the authentic contact.**

This is contact where the mind does not touch either the supposed truth of nirvana or the supposed falsity of samsara.

Not being aware of any *characteristics in the whole of phenomena* **is the authentic awareness.**

This is awareness that does not take the conditioned characteristics of phenomena as its object.

++ 48 ++

Explaining six kinds of effortlessness, there being nothing in the absolute nature to adopt or reject.

There is nothing to obtain through purposeful effort, so

If one knows how to leave all phenomena without deliberate action, one is liberated in the basic natural state:

Son, there are six declarations on effortlessness.

Because in the space of one's unborn mind there is not the duality of a viewer and something to be viewed, **one settles in the view** *without contrivance or modification, affirmation or negation,* **and one's mind remains** **in total rest without any concept of vastness or constraint.**

When we stay in the view of natural simplicity without trying to modify what we feel is bad by transforming it into something good or to prevent some things and accomplish others, the mind will rest in the infinite expanse of the absolute nature without any feeling of congestion or obstruction.

The meditation is the utter peace *of the absolute nature,* **radiance from the depth,** *free of grasping and devoid of rough edges—thoughts related to outer and inner phenomena.*

Within the absolute nature there is nothing to meditate on and no action of meditating. We are simply dealing with the spontaneous radiance of wisdom deep within. Like a flame, wisdom is inherently luminous. At the same time, it throws light on other things, yet remains free from clinging to them. The meditation is a state devoid of the spikes of thoughts related to outer and inner phenomena. It is the utter peace of the absolute nature.

The action, *uncontrived and natural,* **is joyful spontaneity, without** *the effort of* **adoption** *or abstention.*

In this kind of action there is nothing that has to be specially grasped or achieved, nothing one has to try to get rid of. It is natural and effortless, acted out in accord with a spontaneous joy.

Since the mode of being of things is actualized, **there is no hope** *of achieving* **the result or fear** *of not achieving it;* **there is all-pervading peace:** *dualistic concepts of subject and object dissolve by themselves.*

Once one has realized the nature of things, one no longer hopes to attain Buddhahood, neither is one apprehensive that one might not obtain it. One simply remains in the even state of all-pervading peace in which all notions of subject and object have been freed in their own sphere.

It is the universal evenness *in the continuum of the absolute nature:* *things are* **beyond all distinctions of quality or magnitude.**

In the absolute nature all relative phenomena, whatever they are, are the same. There is no good or bad, large or small. Only a universal evenness, with no difference either between meditation and postmeditation.

It is the utmost ease where the mind has no sorrow,

for samsara, without being rejected, is primordially free, beyond suffering.

There is no need to reject samsara. It is all nothing but wisdom, so one is free from the torments of conditioned existence. There is only the utmost ease.

✦✦ 49 ✦✦

An instruction on sixteen metaphoric practices.

Son, there are sixteen metaphoric practices.

Once the absolute nature is actualized, all the various phenomena become its symbols.

Always strip *the awareness* **naked** *so that it is unobscured by characteristics.*

This is what we need to realize, awareness divested of all obscurations related to characteristics of conditioned things.

Always perform the great ablution *of emptiness as the antidote for the belief in substantial existence and for clinging to true existence.*

It is the realization of emptiness that is the principal antidote for our belief in solid reality and our clinging to true existence.

Take the sun and the moon—*emptiness and compassion*—**in your hand.**

By holding the sun and the moon in our two hands we would dispel the darkness of the whole world. Similarly, when we realize the emptiness of phenomena and when, within that emptiness, there arises spontaneous compassion, the union of these two is the culmination of the Bodhisattva path.

Whirl the wheel *of view and meditation.*

Whirling the wheel of the view and meditation directly cuts through all deluded perception and confusion.[136]

Gaze in the *magical* **mirror** *of your mind.*

If you look at yourself in a clear mirror, you can see all the blemishes on your face and can then try to remove them. Likewise, by looking in the mirror of the mind you can see all the delusion that has occurred in it and thus remove that delusion.

Cure the sickness caused by the poison *of the* five *afflictive emotions.*

Untie the rope binding you—*that of the three poisons or* the notions *of subject and object.*

Flee *the company of evildoers: they are like* **savage beasts of prey.**

Keeping the company of negative friends who hold incorrect views is likely to make you stray off the path to liberation, so you should stay well away from them.

Having recognized the spontaneously arisen primal wisdom, **reside in the crystal vase** *of awareness—emptiness and clarity inseparable.*

Once we have recognized self-cognizing primal wisdom, all the vital points of the practice are contained within the vase of empty, clear awareness.

Climb the jewel stairs *from the bottom to the top, practicing the ten Dharma activities*[137] *and so on with faith, diligence, mindfulness, vigilance, and carefulness.*

With these five[138] we cannot but accomplish the activities of the sublime Dharma and we will not do any negative actions. So climb the steps of the ten Dharma activities, such as reading and writing, for whatever we undertake of the ten activities will lead to our accumulating an inconceivable store of merit and naturally acquiring excellent qualities.

Cut the tree *of belief in a self* **at the root.**

Sleep in the openness of space, *uncircumscribed awareness.*

Rest in the immensity of space, in the state of evenness, which has no edge or limit.

Let your own thought-movements **commit suicide.**

"Commit suicide" refers to the fact that the movements of deluded thought destroy themselves—that is, they dissolve by themselves—in the realization of the absolute nature.

Hasten to the golden isle *where everything that appears and is perceived arises as the absolute nature.*

Just as one would never find ordinary stones on a golden island, once one has realized the absolute nature everything that appears to the six senses arises as an ornament for the absolute nature and cannot cause that realization to decline.

Anoint your body with the balm *of concentration to allay the fever of desire and hatred.*

Anointing the body of a feverish patient with camphor or some other medicinal substance rapidly brings down the patient's temperature. Similarly, the cooling balm of concentration naturally causes the fever of attachment and aversion to abate.

Pick sky flowers: *in truth they do not exist; phenomena are but names.*

All phenomena—pillars, vases, mountains, and the rest—are simply names given to perceptions, the manifestations of things that do not exist, like the two moons one sees if one presses a finger on one's eye when looking at the moon. Through the interdependence of cause and effect, relative phenomena appear but they have no true existence, like a sky flower. When we speak of a sky flower, it is only a name: it has neither shape nor scent. You cannot pick it with your hands, neither can you make a garland with it.

✦✦ 50 ✦✦

There being nothing to adopt or reject, the view is free of affirmation or negation.

As there is no clinging to the notions of good and bad, there is nothing to reject and nothing to adopt.

Son, there are five views.

All thoughts that arise are the unborn absolute nature, so

Do not get angry at thoughts.

The primal wisdom of no-thought is not to be meditated on separately.

When one remains in the natural flow of the absolute nature, various thoughts may pass one after another through the past, present, and future but in truth they are never born, they never remain, and they never cease. They never leave the realm of the unborn absolute nature. With regard to thoughts, therefore, there is nothing to be angry at. Simply see them as the ornament of the absolute nature. Besides recognizing the absolute nature and seeing thoughts as its ornament, there is no wisdom of no-thought that has to be meditated on separately.

Primal wisdom or dharmata is not to be sought on some far shore rid of afflictive emotions and thoughts, so

Do not be attached to the absolute nature.

*As long as you have attachment you create the cause for wandering
in samsara.*

It is important to realize that wisdom and the afflictive emotions are not
two separate things, like a piece of gold and stains on it. The very nature
of desire, hatred, and the other afflictive emotions is wisdom. So wisdom
is not some distant land to be reached, leaving the afflictive emotions
behind. It is simply a question of dwelling in the recognition of the absolute nature. But if, in doing so, the thought occurs to you that you have
achieved the perfect view, you may fall into the error of attachment; as it
is said, "While there is attachment, there is no view,"[139] and attachment is
the cause of samsara.[140]

Knowing all phenomena to be equal,

Do not be proud of *your* concentration—

do not feel conceited or self-satisfied, priding yourself on your concentration being free from distraction and delusion.

*Everything unwanted and all wrong thoughts are a display of your
own mind, so*

Do not be resentful of anything wrong.[141]

Undesirable circumstances such as suffering and sickness, and wrong
thoughts like desire and attachment, are, all of them, simply the display of
your own mind, so you should recognize their nature rather than trying to
get rid of them. Here "resentful" of wrong thoughts means that when they
arise, you should not begrudge them and be obsessed with feeling you have
to get the better of them.

Since you yourself possess the spontaneously arisen primal wisdom,

Do not be confused with regard to wisdom:

Recognize it.

The self-arisen wisdom is not something you have to look for far away.
It is present within you. If you recognize this wisdom that you have, you
are no longer obscured by confusion.

++ 51 ++

Explaining ten aspects of complete confidence in the natural state.

Since all the dualistic perceptions of happiness, suffering, and so forth are freed in the absolute space, one cannot be benefited or harmed by anything:

Son, there are ten aspects to complete confidence.

Ordinary beings have the concepts of suffering and happiness: suffering is something they wish to get rid of; happiness and pleasure are something they want to keep. But for someone in whom everything has dissolved in the absolute space, happiness brings no benefit, suffering does not harm. The complete confidence one gains from remaining in such a state of evenness can cope with ten kinds of situations.

The self-arisen primal wisdom or bodhichitta has no cause or conditions and is therefore unchanging in the past, present, and future.

Everything possible[142] may pour down like rain,

but bodhichitta, the kingly doer-of-all, will never get wet or stained.

The self-arisen wisdom, which is also called bodhichitta, is not something that has been fabricated, a new product created by the conjunction of causes and conditions. It never has changed, never changes, and never will change. The absolute nature remains what it is, perfectly pure, at all times. Even if it appears obscured for impure beings at the start of the path, it has never actually been obscured. If it seems to be a mixture of pure and impure during the course of the path, it in fact always remains pure. And at the time of the result, perfect enlightenment, it is simply the same ground nature made evident and not something new that was not there before. So even though all the hallucinations that make up existence fall like rain from the sky, it cannot affect one's confidence: the kinglike bodhichitta that is the doer-of-everything will never be stained or dampened.

Similarly,

The three worlds may overflow, gushing forth **like a river** cascading over a cliff,

but it—the kingly bodhichitta—will not be carried away.

Even though the six mental states—the five poisons and miserliness— may blaze like fire,

it—the absolute nature—*will not be consumed.*

The one thousand million worlds may be buffeted as if by the wind,

but it will remain unmoved.

The universe of a thousand million worlds may shake as if buffeted by the wind, but the realization of the nature will remain unmoved, like a mighty mountain. As it is said, leaving things as they are is the measure of the perfect, mountainlike view.

The three poisons may gather like darkness,

but it will not grope in confusion.

The three poisons may obscure everything but they cannot obscure wisdom, which is inherently luminous and radiant from within.

The thousand million worlds may be filled by the sun,

but this will never illuminate the primal wisdom.

The sun may spread throughout the universe of a thousand million worlds, but this could never make wisdom brighter than it already is and has always been.

Whole continents may be plunged into darkness,

but the nature *can never be eclipsed by ignorance.*

Birth and death may be distinct,

but it cannot die.

Birth and death might appear different, but in truth there is no such thing as birth and death.

One may have karmic tendencies,

but from the very beginning the nature has never been affected, so there is nothing to discard now.

There is no need to get rid of habitual tendencies that come from having accumulated positive and negative actions, because they only exist from the point of view of the way things appear. From the point of view of the way things are, there have never been any habitual tendencies to stain the absolute nature, so there is no need to discard them now.

Phenomenal existence may be turned upside down,

but the nature will not be destroyed or separated.

As the "Prayer of Samantabhadra" says, "Even when the three worlds are destroyed, there is no fear." Neither is there attachment.

These are the vajra words on the wisdom—the total confidence and conviction— that cannot be crushed by anything.

++ 52 ++

An instruction that matches examples and their meanings to show how the absolute nature permeates everything.

These various examples give a general idea of the absolute nature.

Son, there are four examples and their meanings.

Take the example of a Sugata's body: whichever way one looks at it, it is beautiful. *Similarly,* **everything** *a realized being* **does, since it is permeated with the** *realization of the* **unborn nature, is bliss,** *for he does not have ordinary attachment and aversion.*

Whether one looks at a Sugata's face or any other part of his body, one never feels one has looked enough. It is an example of ultimate beauty. Similarly, those for whom everything is backed by the realization of the unborn nature no longer have ordinary attachment and aversion, and such persons can therefore act like enlightened beings: whatever they do is bliss. Since they have fully realized the absolute nature, there is no question of telling them, "This is the right thing to do; that is something you should not do." They have no concepts or limits, so they can act as they wish. Everything they do will be nothing but bliss.

Take the example of a smile and a scowl: two expressions but no more than *one* **face.** *Similarly,* **everything that appears, everything that exists—***all the manifestation of samsara or nirvana***—does so within the unborn absolute nature.**

Samsara and nirvana are like two expressions on the same face, one dark and sullen, the other light and smiling. But, whatever the expression, we are not talking about a different face. It is not degraded when smeared with the dirt of samsara, neither is it improved when the dirt of samsara is washed off. Samsara and nirvana remain within the expanse of the absolute nature in the same way that the universe with its different continents all appear in space.

Take the example of a blind person: it makes no difference whether one smiles at him or not. *Similarly, since everything that arises unobstructedly from the unborn absolute space is inseparable from it and has the same taste,* **in the absolute nature there is nothing to be adopted or rejected.**

If you smile at blind people, they do not think, "That person is happy with me." If you frown at them, they do not think, "He is upset with me." It is the same with phenomena: they are all of one taste, intrinsically one, appearing in an unobstructed way from the expanse of the unborn while remaining inseparable from it. For this reason, in the absolute nature there is nothing to adopt and nothing to give up.

Take the example of the trunk of a plantain tree: it has no core.[143] *Similarly,* **phenomenal existence has no essence,**

for when examined using such logical arguments as "Neither one nor many,"[144] *there is nothing to be found.*

The plantain tree is hollow inside: it has no solid core. It is also said that it is without essence, in the sense that it bears fruit only once. If you analyze phenomena with the aim of determining their ultimate nature, using the "neither one nor many" argument, you will find they have no true existence. Phenomenal existence is devoid of essence: it is emptiness endowed with supreme qualities.

++ 53 ++

When the four ontological extremes dissolve by themselves, it is
shown that phenomena are the mind's projections and do not
have to be abandoned.

Son, there are four dissolutions of extremes.

As regards all the phenomena of samsara and nirvana,

In the absolute truth they are unborn, so they are beyond the
extreme of existence.

Although samsara and nirvana appear, in truth they are devoid of solid
existence, of any existing entity. One cannot, therefore, say that they exist.

In relative truth,

the appearance aspect that is the interdependent gathering of
causes and conditions,

they are unceasing, so they are beyond the extreme of
nonexistence.

This empty nature, the lack of intrinsic existence in phenomena, does
not imply a blank naught in which there is nothing at all, as we find in the
view of the nihilists. According to relative truth, all phenomena arise as a
result of the interdependent conjunction of causes and conditions. This
enables us to explain not only how samsara is formed but also how it is
possible to progress toward nirvana. There is no contradiction between the
absolute nature and its infinite display and, because of this, one is free from
the extreme of *existence* and that of *nonexistence*.

Ultimately, the two truths, or appearance and emptiness, **do not exist**
as distinct phenomena: *there is no basis for such distinctions, they are*
inseparable—in other words, **they are not two, so they are beyond**
the extreme of both existence and nonexistence.

One cannot say that the two truths are distinct or that appearance and
emptiness are distinct, because if one examines the relative truth in depth,
one arrives at the absolute truth, and it is within the absolute truth that the
relative truth appears as its display. They are actually indistinguishable,

they cannot be separated, and they are thus not two. In this way one must be free from the extreme of *both existence and nonexistence.*

> *Intellectually apprehended,* "neither" arises as "both," so phenomena are beyond the extreme of neither existence nor nonexistence.[145]

One might, then, cling to the opposite notion and have an intellectual concept that phenomena neither exist nor do not exist. So one must be free of this extreme as well, the extreme of *neither existence nor nonexistence.*

> *Regarding this there are four faults that occur if one asserts that the two truths are one and the same:*

Ultimately we must be free of all kinds of ontological extremes and postulates. The two truths are neither two distinct things nor a single entity; they are beyond any concept of being one or two. To those who cling to the concept of a single entity and say that the two truths are one and the same, excluding even the possibility of its having two aspects, it can be shown that there are four faults in such an argument:

> *(1) it would follow that ordinary beings who see compounded phenomena could see the absolute truth;*

If there were no difference whatsoever between absolute truth and relative truth, this would mean that since ordinary beings can perceive the relative truth they must also be able to see the absolute truth. This is not the case.

> *(2) it would follow that the absolute truth could be an objective condition for afflictive emotions arising;*

Relative phenomena are the causes for afflictive emotions arising, so if relative and absolute were the same, absolute truth would also be a cause for the arising of afflictive emotions. This is not the case.

> *(3) it would follow that there was no distinction between relative and absolute;*

If they were the same, there would be no way to recognize absolute truth as distinct from relative truth, and this too is not correct.

(4) it would follow that the absolute truth would not depend on listening to the teachings and reflecting on them.

To experience the relative truth one does not need to practice the Dharma or gain any experience in it, so if the two truths were exactly the same, one would also be able to realize the absolute truth without listening to the teachings, reflecting on them, and meditating: such things would be unnecessary.

And there are four faults that occur if one asserts that they are different,

One might argue, on the other hand, that the relative truth and absolute truth are essentially separate and distinct. Such an argument also has four faults,

for it would then follow that:

(1) the mind that had realized the absolute could not dispel the belief that relative phenomena truly exist;

If relative and absolute were completely separate and unrelated, realizing the absolute truth would not help to dispel our clinging to relative phenomena as truly existent. But in fact when one realizes the absolute truth, the belief in the true existence of relative phenomena is simultaneously dispelled.

(2) absolute truth would not be the ultimate nature of relative phenomena;

If they were separate things, the ultimate nature of relative truth could never be absolute truth. But in reality, when we examine the nature of relative truth, we arrive at absolute truth.

(3) the absence of intrinsic existence in relative phenomena would not be the absolute truth;

The fact that the phenomena of relative truth have no true existence of their own *is* the ultimate truth. So we speak of absolute truth in relation to relative truth. If they were completely separate entities, we could not describe absolute truth in these terms.

(4) sublime beings would see them separately and would be bound
and liberated at one and the same time.

Seeing relative phenomena means being in a state of ignorance, while understanding absolute truth means being free. If, then, the two truths were separate, enlightened beings would see both separately; they would be at the same time enslaved in relative truth and liberated in absolute truth.

> *In our tradition there are none of these faults because we make*
> *no assertions at all about the two truths being either single or*
> *different. We establish two truths in relation to the conditions,*
> *deluded or nondeluded, of a single mind: in the deluded state the*
> *absolute truth does not appear to the relative, deluded mind, while*
> *in the nondeluded state the delusory relative does not appear to*
> *the mind that has realized the absolute truth. Thus the two truths*
> *are like light and darkness. On the one hand, they have one and*
> *the same nature but different aspects; on the other hand, their*
> *differences disallow their being one and the same. Both of these*
> *are explained in the* Commentary.

None of the above faults is to be found in our own tradition because we do not subscribe to the views that see the two truths either as a single entity or as two distinct entities. All we are saying here is that the relative and absolute truth are related to the condition of a single mind that is either deluded or nondeluded. When it is deluded, this is the relative truth, and the ultimate nature of things does not arise in the deluded mind. When the undeluded absolute truth is realized, the delusory perceptions of relative truth do not arise. In this way relative and absolute truths are like darkness and light. One cannot have darkness and light at the same time. Likewise, relative truth and absolute truth, though fundamentally of the same nature, are simply two aspects, one obscured and the other enlightened, each excluding the other. When the light manifests, darkness disappears. When darkness is present, there is no light. This is explained in the *Commentary*.

•• 54 ••

Four ultimate aspects that decisively establish the ultimate path.

Son, there are four ultimates.

Having recognized all outer and inner phenomena to be the play of your own mind,

like the things that appear in a dream,

to know that the mind is empty and immaterial is the ultimate reach of the view.

As exemplified by a person in a magical illusion,

While not blocking the five senses, to be free from notions of subject and object is the ultimate reach of meditation.

The illusions of people, soldiers, horses, and so forth that a magician creates are simply the result of his casting a spell or reciting some mantras, and the magician himself is not attached to the things he has projected. So to be free from any clinging to subject and object, while not blocking the perceptions of the five senses, is the ultimate reach of meditation.

As exemplified by the accumulation of merit and wisdom by a great emanation,

To know how to act uniting view and action is the ultimate reach of action.

Bodhisattvas work for the benefit of beings, make offerings, and so forth, and thus they accumulate great merit. At the same time they know that everything is like a dream and like an illusion. Although they are accumulating merit, they do not have any clinging and they know the illusory, void nature of that merit; thus, they accumulate wisdom. This is the ultimate reach of action, the ability to unite view and action.

As exemplified by an illusory being enjoying riches in a dream,

To be free of the belief that there is any truth in phenomenal existence is the ultimate reach of experience and realization.

However much wealth the illusory being may enjoy in the dream, when he wakes up, there is nothing left. Similarly, to have no clinging to the universe and beings as truly existing is the ultimate reach of meditative experience and realization.

++ 55 ++

An instruction on the five dharmakaya aspects of the mind,
with illustrations.

Son, there are five dharmakaya aspects of the mind,

the unobstructed, all-pervading primal wisdom or absolute nature,
emptiness and clarity inseparable.

The primal wisdom that is empty and radiant, unobstructed and all-encompassing, can also be called the absolute nature. It pervades the whole of samsara and nirvana, and at the same time it knows itself. This is the dharmakaya of the mind, and it has five aspects.

The unmoving dharmakaya,

the absence of movement in the absolute nature, the naked state of
awareness and emptiness inseparable,

illustrated by the oceanic deep—

it is very difficult to fathom; at the same time it is utterly still.

The unchanging dharmakaya,

the absolute nature in which there is no change,

illustrated by Mount Meru.

In the middle of the great ocean stands Mount Meru, made of five kinds of precious jewels. Neither the wind nor the waves of the ocean can shake it. Similarly, when a yogi rests in the meditation of the absolute nature without wavering, this is what we call dharmakaya.

The uninterrupted dharmakaya,

the continuous state of the absolute nature or radiant clarity,

illustrated by a great river.

A great, continuously flowing river has its origins in the ocean, being fed by the rain, and ends up flowing back into the ocean. In the same way that the river flows in an uninterrupted cycle, there is no interruption in the absolute nature.

The undimming dharmakaya,

the primal wisdom that neither grows brighter nor grows dimmer,

illustrated by the sun,

never changing, always shining and emitting rays of light.

The thought-free dharmakaya,

clear awareness devoid of thought,

illustrated by the reflection of the moon in water.

The moon's reflection on water appears without obstruction and seems to shine very brightly, yet it is simply the appearance of something that does not exist. There is no such thing as a moon in the water. Likewise, when one recognizes that thoughts have no true existence, one recognizes awareness, and this is dharmakaya.

•• 56 ••

An instruction using the symbolic language of the secret mantras.

Son, there are six primal wisdoms related to the mind.

The fresh nature just as it is, **unadulterated** *by thoughts, is* **free of the duality** *of subject and object; it* **is the wisdom of coalescence.**

With this first wisdom, dualistic notions are liberated as soon as one recognizes their nondual nature.

The mind **neither reaching out** *toward the object* **nor withdrawing, there is the wisdom of one taste** *with regard to the manifold perceptions and thoughts.*

Here, the mind neither reaches out to phenomena outside nor withdraws inside. It is the state of wisdom in which the outer perceptions of the six senses such as forms, sounds, smells, and tastes and the inner thoughts concerning the past, present, and future are all blended in one taste. All these things manifest in different ways. Ordinary beings alternate between positive and negative thoughts regarding them, but in truth they are never anything other than being one taste in the absolute nature. This wisdom, in which one is not scattered outwards nor withdrawn inwards, is all-penetrating and unobstructed. It is the knowledge that outer and inner perceptions are one within the nature of mind.

With no adoption or rejection *with regard to anything in samsara and nirvana,* **there is the wisdom with no hope or fear.**

Within our own buddha nature we naturally have all the qualities of nirvana, so we do not need to look for them and take possession of them outside. Neither do we need to get rid of anything, because the obscurations that are temporarily veiling our realization of the absolute nature are not inherent to that absolute nature. So with this third wisdom, doubts are completely absent: there is no wondering, "Will I be able to achieve all those qualities?" or "Will I succeed in getting rid of all these defects?"

Putting the seal *of the unborn absolute nature* **on the perceptions** *of the multifarious phenomena,* **there is the spontaneously arisen wisdom.**

Just as placing a yellow filter in front of a source of light makes everything look yellow, the self-arisen wisdom permeates and colors all the various manifestations of conditioned phenomena with the absolute nature. Once we have put the seal of the absolute nature on everything, however many relative phenomena arise they will not harm our realization of ultimate reality.

The nature of mind beyond all ontological extremes, **the union of appearances and emptiness, of awareness and emptiness, is the wisdom of union.**

The eight consciousnesses and their objects having been empty from the very beginning, **there is outer emptiness and inner emptiness: this is the wisdom of emptiness.**

•• 57 ••

Introducing the nature of the mind.

Son, there are seven ways in which the nature of the mind is introduced.

The Great Space *says:*

Its nature is not definitely any one thing:
Whichever way one looks at it, in that way it appears.

Even a single object, on account of one's own mind, appears
in various ways. For this reason, the outer object is devoid
of intrinsic existence, and thus,

The object is introduced as being the mind's projection.

As the *Tantra of the Great Space*, which is one of the tantras of the Great
Perfection, explains, one cannot define the mind as having any one definite nature. How it appears depends on how one looks at it. It is because
of the mind that any one object can be perceived in different ways. This
demonstrates that outer phenomena have no intrinsic existence and so
introduces the fact that an object's appearance is a projection of the mind.

The multifarious manifesting aspects of one's own mind arise unob-
structedly like reflections: their nature is never anything other than
emptiness. Thus,

The mind's projection is introduced as a reflection.

The mind projects appearances in many ways. To someone who has
done many positive actions, everything will appear as the blissful Buddhafield of Amitabha, where all is perfect. On the other hand, someone
who has mainly committed negative actions will perceive everything as a
hell realm, where all is suffering. All these various phenomena appear
unobstructedly like reflections; their nature is never anything other than
empty. This is the introduction to the mind's projection as being a reflection: it appears but there is nothing one can catch hold of.

The appearances of spontaneously arisen primal wisdom arise
without bias,

The self-arisen wisdom does not manifest in one particular direction
and not in the other. It pervades everything,

and thus,

Appearances are introduced as infinite.

By means of the pith instruction of the triple space,[146]

The consciousness is introduced as being without support.

By realizing the nature of one's own mind,

Awareness is introduced as being self-cognizing.[147]

Awareness is self-cognizing: it is not an awareness of objects outside like forms, sounds, smells, and the other objects of the six senses.

The objects that appear to the eight consciousnesses have never in fact come into existence, so

The object is introduced as being unborn.

The ultimate unborn nature is devoid of dualistic characteristics, so

The unborn is introduced as being free of conceptual constructions.

◆◆ 58 ◆◆

Placing a seal by introducing the ultimate nature of things that appear.

Son, there are six ways of introducing the ultimate nature of everything that arises,

everything being one in the absolute nature so that there is nothing to be adopted or rejected—

no distinction between samsara as something to be rejected and nirvana as something to be attained.

From the creativity of the nature of one's own mind the seventeen kinds of perceptions and appearances—the six kinds of perceptions of the beings in the six realms, the two Tirthika views of eternalism and nihilism, and the nine different viewpoints of the nine vehicles—arise indeterminately, so

Do not value existence

by considering anything to be truly existent.

The whole range of different ways of perceiving things can be summarized into seventeen kinds: six for the beings of the six realms, who each perceive things in their own way; two for the Tirthikas—the eternalists (who believe in the *atman*, or a permanent, intrinsically existent, and unchanging creator), and the nihilists (who deny that beings take rebirth in a continuous series of lives, reject the law of karma, and do not accept that samsara is essentially imperfect); and nine for the nine vehicles, which each have different viewpoints. And yet none of these perceptions and appearances are truly existent, so we should not cherish the notion of their so-called existence. Neither should we feel proud if we have realized that they are nonexistent.

> *Everything is the play of the absolute nature, so since you perceive things, good and bad,*

> **Do not prize nonexistence.**

> *Since phenomena do not fall into ontological extremes,*

> **Do not reconcile them in** *a conceptual* **inseparability** of existence and nonexistence.

While not falling into the extremes of existence and nonexistence, you should not conceptualize phenomena as not being either of these two, for their existence and nonexistence have been indivisible from the very beginning. Neither should you divide things up:

> **Do not differentiate things** *as good or bad.*

> **Do not conceive of anything** *as existent, nonexistent, or whatever by intellectual analysis.*

Avoid applying intellectual analysis to the absolute nature and thinking, "Is it existent, is it nonexistent . . .?"

> **Do not be distracted from the radiant deep**—*ultimate reality.*

✦✦ 59 ✦✦

Introducing the ultimate nature of things that appear.

Son, there are eight introductions.

The mind is perfectly clear, *like space, uncompounded awareness.*

The movements *of thoughts* **subside by themselves** *like ripples subsiding back into the water.*

Thoughts are levelled instantly, *the protuberance-like thoughts born from circumstances subsiding naturally the moment they arise.*

Different thoughts may arise on account of good circumstances that make us feel attached or proud, or of bad circumstances that make us feel depressed. They should all be left to dissolve naturally.

Awareness is naturally pure, *for it is* naturally *unobscured by the eight consciousnesses.*

It is not perceptible, *for there is nothing that one can grasp with certainty and say, "This is it."*

The object is naturally empty, *because what appears has no intrinsic existence.*

Like a dream, **it is there but it does not exist.**

Like the moon reflected in water, **it does not exist and yet it is there.**

◆◆ 60 ◆◆

Nine sayings introducing the unborn nature of things that appear.

Phenomena lack true origin, they are deceptive appearances: without considering them to be real, without clinging to their existence,

Son, the unborn nature is introduced in nine ways.

Since the very beginning, none of the phenomena of samsara and nirvana have ever been born as anything that truly exists. Their existence is false, like that of a dream or an illusion.

All phenomena that arise interdependently, when investigated with reasoning directed at their ultimate status, have no inherent birth, so

What is seemingly **born is unborn,** *like the horses and oxen in a magical illusion.*

"What is born" refers to all the phenomena that arise through interdependent production. If we carefully examine their true nature, we will find that they are unborn and therefore do not have any intrinsic existence. They are like the horses and oxen created by a skillful magician.

> **What** *is uncompounded and* **has not been born** *through causes and conditions* is **unborn,** *like space.*

"What has not been born" refers to uncompounded phenomena like space that have not been created through causes and conditions. One might think that such phenomena exist in some way even though uncompounded, but they have no true existence either.

> *Compounded phenomena do not exist as such, so*

> **What will never be born is unborn,** *like the son of a barren woman.*

Since compounded phenomena are all nonexistent by nature, they never will be born. Thus, they are unborn in the same way that the son of a barren woman is unborn.

> *Forms and suchlike have no intrinsic existence, so*

> **What appears is unborn,** *like a dream.*

> *There is nothing that can produce emptiness, so*

> **Emptiness is unborn,** *like the horn of a rabbit.*

There is no such thing as a rabbit's horn, so there could never be a cause for its coming into existence. The same is true of emptiness.

> *Since it cannot be grasped with certainty—one cannot say,*
> *"This is it"—*

> **Awareness is unborn,** *like the eight consciousnesses of a person in an illusion.*

A person created by a magician does not have any of the eight consciousnesses. It is therefore impossible to apprehend its eight consciousnesses. So it is with awareness.

> *Since the unborn—or emptiness—is not one-sided, it has the potential to appear in every possible way:*

The unborn appears, *like an optical illusion.*

One should not fall into the extreme of nihilism, taking only the side of emptiness and the unborn. Emptiness also has the ability to manifest in infinite ways, and we therefore speak of the manifestation of the unborn that is like a mirage. There is nothing there and yet it appears.

Since it is beyond intellectual investigation and has been unborn from the very beginning,

The unborn is primordially nonexistent, *like space, which has always been so.*[148]

When we speak of the unborn, this is not a mental fabrication, a label that we attach to things that we then call "unborn." It is beyond the realm of the intellect, primordially unborn like space, which has always been empty and is not something that suddenly became empty.

The unborn is not affected by the concepts of the eight extremes—existence, nonexistence, and so forth—just as one cannot say, "Space is this (or that),"[149] *so*

The unborn is free from extremes.

We cannot say that space exists because there is nothing one can take hold of. Neither can we say that it does not exist because there is something that we see that we call space.[150] In the same way, what we call the unborn is free of all concepts and extremes.

•• 61 ••

An instruction with four similes introducing the ultimate nature of things that appear.

Son, there are four similes,

conventional examples used to signify the absolute nature.

All phenomena arise from the state of inseparability of mind's triple space—the space above us, the space of the mind, and that of the absolute nature; there they dwell and into it they dissolve; they have never moved from it. So all intellectual assertions of tenets such as "they exist" or "they do not exist" are reduced to nothing. Therefore,

Taking the example of a mountain, *which is unmoved by circumstances,* by the wind, rain, and so on, **stamp your being with the view free from assertions.**

Since there is neither meditation nor anything to be meditated upon, there is no intentional movement:

Taking the example of a king seated on his throne, stamp your being with the meditation free of effort.

Once you have the view, you need to cultivate it through meditation. But in this case there is no meditating nor anything to meditate on. It is meditation devoid of subject and object, which does not involve any effort, in the same way that a king governs his kingdom and brings happiness to his people naturally by sitting on his throne, without any particular effort on his part.

Everything is the play of the absolute nature, and no conditioned phenomena are excluded, so

Taking the example of someone who has arrived on a golden island—even if they look for ordinary stones there, they will never find any—**stamp your being with the action free from dualistic perception,**

where there is nothing to adopt and nothing to abandon.

In the absolute nature, the basic way of being, which is naked and all-penetrating, freedom and nonfreedom are meaningless: there is no other so-called result to be sought.

Taking the example of a knot in a snake, stamp your being with the sole result in which there is freedom from hope and fear.

When a snake makes a knot in its body as it coils itself, it can undo that knot by itself without anyone else's help. In the same way, delusion naturally subsides by itself.

++ 62 ++

Five instructions on the ultimate nature of appearances.

Son, there are five instructions.

Ultimately, objects of knowledge, subject and object, are not born from causes and conditions; they do not depend on anything else; they are not the product of alteration, for example, by transforming bad into good; *they are intrinsically unborn from the very beginning. Therefore,*

Know that form and the consciousness of it are unborn.

Without clinging, be aware of what you perceive, *the objects of the eight consciousnesses.*

Remain without being distracted by the eight *ordinary* **concerns—** *praise, criticism, and so forth.*

With the view able to stand up to circumstances, the meditation immune to distraction, the action resistant to going off course, and with confidence in the result,

Remain without the consciousness being carried away by circumstances.

When we are resting in the view, it should not be disturbed by any situations, happy or unhappy, that may occur. And even if we have to be somewhere with a lot of distractions or a great many people, or we have to work, we should still be able to remain undistracted in meditation. Neither should we let our action be influenced by afflictive emotions and the results of our past actions. As for the result, we should have the firm conviction that it has been present within us since the very beginning.

Seal the mind

with the realization that your own mind is unborn,

and has always been from the very beginning, for it possesses the buddha nature.

++ 63 ++

The view of the one absolute nature without distinct aspects.

Son, there are five experiences of wisdom

that indicate that one has gone to the heart of the view and meditation.

The Six Points of Meditation *states,*

> *Whatever dualistic thoughts may arise,*
> *If you recognize that very thought as the absolute nature,*
> *There is no need to meditate on any other dharmadhatu.*

Accordingly,

Thoughts—good or bad—**are the absolute nature,**

they dissolve in the absolute nature devoid of dualistic thoughts of subject and object.

All the **characteristics** *of both samsara and nirvana* **are freed by themselves** *in the nondual expanse of evenness.*

Looking directly confirms *the recognition of the absolute nature in all perceptions, like meeting an old acquaintance.*

When one meets someone one knows, even if they are in the middle of a crowd of a thousand people, one recognizes them immediately. Similarly, once one is familiar with the absolute nature, one recognizes the absolute nature in everything that arises; one's recognition is confirmed by looking directly at one's perceptions.

> *Deluded* **clinging** *to friends, enemies, and so forth* **stops by itself.**

One naturally gives up one's desire to achieve one's own selfish aims and to avoid helping others.

> **The duality** *of blocking impure perceptions and developing pure perceptions* **vanishes by itself.**

All dualistic desires to block impure perceptions—those of ordinary beings—and to develop the pure perceptions of the Buddhas, Bodhisattvas, Pratyekabuddhas, and the Shravaka Arhats vanish by themselves.

++ 64 ++

A brief explanation of the way in which the indivisible absolute nature arises.

Son, there are four ways in which the nondual absolute nature arises.

The absolute nature is the sole essence, for it is not divided into good and bad:

In the absolute nature, *the fundamental view of* **the great** *evenness,* **there is no good or bad; this is the all-penetrating primal wisdom.**

By dwelling naturally without seeking anything—*which is the meditation of the all-penetrating wisdom*—**one remains in the state without conceptual constructs.**

Not adulterating or fabricating—*which is the spontaneous action with no goals or purposeful deeds*—**is the great impartiality.**

The result of actualizing the absolute nature is that, **as the ultimate nature of the mind arises spontaneously, primal wisdom unfolds in the expanse.**

++ 65 ++

Six ways in which the indivisible absolute nature arises.

Son, there are six ways in which the nondual absolute nature arises.

Since *the nature of mind, which is spontaneously arisen primal wisdom,* **arises in the state** of simplicity **free of contrivance from the very beginning, it is fresh.**[151]

Since everything is complete within the mind, it is spontaneous.

Since there is no blocking or encouraging, it is great primal wisdom.

It is great wisdom because when the natural presence of the infinite display of phenomena arises, it is beyond trying to prevent or accomplish it.

Since there is no *dualistic* division into concepts such as **samsara and nirvana,** *good and bad,* **it is the nondual vajra.**

Since mind is Buddha from the very beginning *without depending on causes and conditions,* **it is the self-born vajra.**

Since it is not caught by enemies *or by good or bad circumstances,* **it is the great evenness.**

++ 66 ++

Four ways in which indivisible absolute nature arises.

Son, there are four ways of arising without duality.

With the mind's concepts of past, present, and future severed, and the mind left in the natural flow,

It is clear and uncontrived, the natural radiance devoid of thoughts,

like an immaculate crystal.

Without any concepts whatsoever, it is the mirror of awareness,

like an untarnished mirror.[152]

It is the *realization of the radiant primal wisdom,* **self-cognizing awareness,** *like* **a wishing-gem** *that naturally produces everything one could desire.*

In the spontaneously arisen primal wisdom, there is no "other-elimination,"[153] *so*

Everything arising by itself, it is the unpremeditated wisdom.

++ 67 ++

Some instructions on the indivisible absolute nature.

Within absolute nature there is no division into good and bad, happiness and suffering.

Son, there are four instructions.

The absolute nature has no bias, so

In completely pervading all ten directions it is the great pervasion.

There is no direction associated with the absolute nature. One cannot say that it dwells more in the south or in the east or north or west. It is all-encompassing. That is why it is called the great pervasion.

Since it is without an outer gate and inner sanctum—*or periphery and center*— **it is the bodhichitta free of partiality.**

As anything arises *from that bodhichitta,* **it is the great unpredictability.**

One cannot classify it and put it in a definite category, because from the enlightened mind anything can happen and one cannot predict that this or that will occur.

Since it is neither lit nor dimmed *by circumstances, the absolute nature* **is the** *perfectly* **pure enlightened state.**

✦✦ 68 ✦✦

An instruction on seeing the unborn absolute nature by means of eight kinds of natural dissolution.

Son, there are eight kinds of natural dissolution.[154]

When one knows that the objects that appear have no true existence, one's belief in true existence naturally dissolves: the moment one rests with the mind undeluded in the direct perception of the absolute nature—seen directly, not merely apprehended intellectually—*everything that arises as the object of the six consciousnesses is ascertained as being appearance and emptiness inseparable, like a magical illusion or a dream. Thus,*

Forms seen by the eye—*whether beautiful or ugly*—**dissolve as they are seen.**

How does this happen?

They dissolve in the sphere of the unborn, *which is the intrinsic nature of both object and consciousness.*

As both the object and the consciousness that perceives it are intrinsically unborn, forms dissolve in the expanse of the unborn.

> *In the same way,* sounds heard by the ear—*pleasant, unpleasant,* words of praise, words of criticism, *and so forth*—fade away as they are heard; they fade away in the expanse of the unborn.

> Odors smelled by the nose—*fragrant, foul, and so on*—dissolve as they are smelt; they fade away in the sphere of the unborn.

> Tastes savored by the tongue—*sweet, sour, and so on*—dissolve as they are tasted; they fade away in the expanse of the unborn.

> Sensations felt through contact by the body—*smooth, rough, and so on*—dissolve as they are felt; they fade away in the expanse of the unborn.

> Perceptions too—*the seventeen kinds of perceptions*[155] *and others*—dissolve by themselves; they fade away in the sphere of the unborn, *appearance and emptiness inseparable.*[156]

> Words uttered, names, and categories—*whether of the Dharma or not*—dissolve by themselves; they dissolve in the expanse of the unborn, *sound and emptiness inseparable.*

> Thoughts too—*whether virtuous or not*—are free in themselves; they dissolve into the sphere of the unborn, *naturally pure awareness.*

•• 69 ••

Seeing how having the four stainless things prevents one going astray.

Son, there are four things that are stainless.

To recognize the unborn *absolute nature* in everything that appears, *the whole of phenomenal existence, illustrated by the eight similes of illusion,* is the stainless wisdom of the view.

Using the eight similes of illusion—a dream, a magic show, a mirage, a city of gandharvas, a flash of lightning, and so on—one realizes the unborn absolute nature in everything that appears, the universe and the beings in it. This is the stainless view.

Taking the unborn *nature* as the path *at all times* is the stainless path *of meditation.*

When one settles in the natural flow, in the unborn nature, an incapacity to express *this nature* is the stainless experience.

Not to stray from the unborn nature into ordinary thoughts *related to past, present, and future* is the stainless result.

•• 70 ••

Showing that the practitioner's insight will not find anything else other than the unborn nature.

Son, there are five things you will not find.

When one investigates using the "neither one nor many" reasoning,

There is no finding an object outside as something that truly exists:

things are like the bits of hair that appear to someone with an ophthalmic condition.

There is an eye condition that makes one see hairs in the air in front of one. Although the hairs appear to the patient, they do not exist.

Since there is neither a seeker nor anything to be sought,

There is no finding a mind inside.

That would be like space looking for space.

There is nothing to actually look for nor a subject that can look. Within this state of nonduality we will never find anything we can call a mind, just as if we try to find space there is nothing to be found.

When the body is *divided and subdivided into its limbs, digits, and so forth,* there is nothing left to call a body, so

There is no finding a body in between.

It is like the core of the plantain tree, for the plantain tree is hollow inside.

As there exists neither a place in which to circle nor anyone to go round in it,[157]

There is no finding the sentient being you do not want to be.

There is no samsara in which to go round and round, neither any beings to go round in it. None of this duality exists since there is nothing whatsoever that truly exists. So you will never find any being that exists in any solid way.

Beings are like a crowd in a dream.

Say you have a dream in which there is a great gathering. The people in it do not exist outside the dream; they all appear inside it, the dream of a single person. You can dream of all sorts of things—that nice things happen to you, or that someone kills you—but nothing has actually happened. And yet none of it is separate from you.

Apart from your own unborn mind, there exists no other Buddha, so

There is no finding the Buddha you would like to be.

The Buddha is not to be sought outside yourself.

++ 71 ++

How there is nothing to be found by someone on the path besides the absolute nature.

Son, there are five instances where there is nothing to be found.

From the beginning the nature of all phenomena, outer and inner, has never been anything but emptiness. **Whatever appears** *as an object outside* **is an appearance of something that does not exist.** *So even if you look for it,* **you will never find it** *in the past, present, or future:* **there is nothing to be found.**

Outer phenomena like the universe and beings and inner phenomena such as the eight consciousnesses have never been beyond the sphere of emptiness. They are like the two moons you see when you press one eye with your finger while looking at the moon: they are simply appearances of things that do not exist. So even if one looks for them, one never finds them. One never has found them and one never will.

> Awareness, *your own mind inside,* is awareness and emptiness inseparable, so you will not find it: there is nothing to be found.

It is the same with the inner mind, which holds on to outer things as truly existing entities. If you search for the nature of the mind, as it is actually the awareness nature, you will only find awareness and emptiness in union. You will not find any shape or color to this awareness.

> The body *composed of the six elements*—earth, water, fire, wind, space, and consciousness—has no essence, so you will not find it: there is nothing to be found.

For if you separate the skin, bones, blood, body cavities, and so on, they all divide up into their corresponding elements.

> *Deluded* beings *also* are, *in truth,* unborn, so you will not find them: there is nothing to be found.

Although all these things do not exist, they appear and are perceived by beings in a deluded way—with clinging to subject and object, with attachment and aversion. This deluded way of seeing things is like the perception of someone with jaundice for whom a brilliantly white conch is yellow. In fact, all things are unborn like a rainbow in the sky: they have never truly come into existence; they do not exist in any way at present; and they will never cease to exist, for if they have never been born, how could they ever cease? Thus one cannot find any so-called universe; one cannot find any so-called beings. They are all unborn.

> *As for* the undeluded Buddha state, it is your own mind, so you will not find it *anywhere else*: there is nothing to be found.

One might wonder whether there is a Buddha, an undeluded being, besides the mind. In truth the essence of Buddhahood has never been separate from us, so the Buddha too is not to be found elsewhere, outside. This buddha nature is none other than the profound, clear, and nondual primal wisdom. But even though it is within you, if you try to look for it, you will never find it as something that has form, color, or any other characteristic.

++ 72 ++

A detailed explanation of how the absolute nature arises non-dually,

that is, without notions of subject and object. This absolute nature dwelling forever within us is the primordial, continuous simplicity of the mind that has never been altered.

Son, there are five things to take as the path, *leaving the mind without contrivance in its own state* of primordial simplicity.

There is nothing whatsoever to focus on regarding the absolute nature, so

Do not conceive of its being anything.

As regards the absolute nature, there is nothing with a shape and color to meditate on as one does in the practice of sustained calm, where one concentrates on a small object or on a Buddha image. The nature of mind is devoid of any characteristics, so here one does not conceive of it as this or that.

Do not indulge in any object *outside—forms, sounds, and suchlike,*

distinguishing between beautiful and ugly, clinging to the one and feeling disgust for the other.

Mind is the Buddha, right now, so

Do not entertain any hope whatsoever—*such as a desire to obtain the qualities of the path and the result.*

Buddhahood is something that is already present, it has always been there. The result of the five paths is simply the recognition of the buddha nature that we already have. Once we recognize this fundamental nature, there is no need to look for any extra, separate qualities associated with the result, enlightenment—just as when we see the sun, we do not have to look for its rays. So do not feel that enlightenment is something far, far away that you might obtain in the distant future and that your present condition is different. The nature of mind is the Buddha at this very moment, so there is no need to wonder hopefully, "How can I obtain this result?"

*Nothing that you perceive, suffering or bliss, afflictive emotions
or primal wisdom, is extraneous to your own mind, so*

Do not regard anything as a defect.

In our present condition that is samsara we experience a lot of suffering. But if we were to examine this suffering, we would find that it is nothing but emptiness; and emptiness is pervaded by the supreme, unchanging great bliss. From the point of view of the way it is, suffering is nothing other than the wisdom of great bliss. From the point of view of the way it appears, suffering is suffering, and it appears thus because we have misconstrued our perception of the great unchanging bliss. Similarly, from the point of view of the way things appear to ordinary deluded beings, the five afflictive emotions experienced in a deluded way are the very cause of being bound in samsara. But if we realize their true nature directly, we will find that the nature of hatred is mirrorlike wisdom, that pride has the nature of the great evenness, that ignorance is the wisdom of the absolute expanse, that attachment is all-distinguishing wisdom, and that the nature of jealousy is all-accomplishing wisdom. In the same way, we will see that outer phenomena are nothing other than the play of the absolute nature. Inner thoughts and emotions are also the play of the absolute nature. Their nature is the wisdom of the great purity and great evenness, so they must not be seen as defects or as enemies that we have to get rid of.

*Give up thinking about past, present, and future, mulling over
one's memories, and so on:*

"Force"[158]—*meaning leave*—**the mind into its natural state.**

If we continue to nourish our past habits, one thought will lead to another in a continuous chain of delusion. We will remember our enemies and think, "They have wronged me in such-and-such a way, now I must retaliate." We will think of those to whom we are attached and give rise to even more attachment. This is something we must avoid. Nor should we give rise to all sorts of ideas for the future, thinking, "If I do that, I will earn a good living and lead a comfortable life . . ." In short, do not recollect the past or make projects for the future; in the present do not be affected by dullness and distraction. In this manner, give up the train of thoughts— past, present, and future—and simply watch the mind as it is, without change. This is the wisdom of seeing the very face of simplicity. It is present within us, always with us. There is nothing more to obtain.

++ 73 ++

An instruction on how the way-it-is endowed with triple emptiness arises by itself.

Son, emptiness is threefold,

the fundamental nature of all phenomena, for which from the very beginning there is no birth, no cessation, and no dwelling.

What do we mean by the threefold voidness? In general, what is the cause for the appearance of deluded phenomena? As it says in the *Guhyagarbha Tantra*, the buddha nature has been deluded because of thoughts and actions:

> Emaho, this wondrous reality
> Is the secret of all the perfect Buddhas.
> Within the unborn everything is born,
> In birth itself there is no birth.

> Emaho, this wondrous reality
> Is the secret of all the perfect Buddhas.
> Within no-cessation everything ceases,
> In cessation itself there is no cessation.

> Emaho, this wondrous reality
> Is the secret of all the perfect Buddhas.
> Within nondwelling everything dwells,
> In dwelling itself there is no dwelling.

> Emaho, this wondrous reality
> Is the secret of all the perfect Buddhas.
> Within nondiscernment everything is discerned,
> In discernment itself there is no discerning.

> Emaho, this wondrous reality
> Is the secret of the all the perfect Buddhas.
> Within there being no coming and going, everything comes and goes,
> In coming and going itself there is no coming and going.

When we say Emaho ("Wonder"), it is the wonder or surprise that comes from realizing the unborn nature. Phenomena have never been born in the past, they do not dwell in the present, and they will never cease in the future. They neither come nor go. This is the real meaning of the absolute truth, the primordial nature.

The threefold emptiness refers to emptiness of the past, present, and future. It is emptiness that has always been, since the very beginning. It is not a new emptiness produced by emptying something. If one were to make a pot out of clay and then break it with a hammer, one could not say one has made the pot become unborn or unproduced. That would be an artificial way of making something unproduced. But in the case of phenomena, they are naturally unborn:

Being intrinsically unborn from the beginning,

Phenomena outside are not born: they are empty.

Just as outer phenomena are empty, unborn, so too is the mind that perceives them:

Mind being without foundation or root,

The mind inside is empty: it is not born.

The aggregates "in between" are empty: they do not dwell.

Form that appears is like foam;

foam looks like something that has been produced on the surface of the sea, but it is soon dispersed by the breeze.

feeling experienced is like the plantain tree;

The plantain grows one year but dies the next, it does not propagate. There is nothing permanent either about the feelings: happiness turns into unhappiness, youth into old age, and so on. And even now, like the plantain, feelings have no essence.

perception is like a mirage;

it perceives the characteristics of pleasant or unpleasant feelings. But it is like the water one sees as a mirage in the middle of a plain when the earth becomes hot with the sun.

conditioning factors are like the plantain;

When feeling and perception come together, there arise conditioning factors;[159] these comprise the impulse to acquire that which is pleasant and get rid of that which is not. But these too are like the plantain, without any core or essence.

consciousness is like a magical illusion.

Consciousness is what is aware of these feelings, perceptions, and conditioning factors. But it is like an illusion: it has no truth, either now, or in the past, or in the future.

These five aggregates are the basis of all the manifested phenomena of samsara and nirvana. And yet if we investigate them, we will come to the conclusion that they are nothing other than emptiness.

++ 74 ++

Sealing phenomenal existence by taking groundlessness as the path.

By putting the seal of emptiness on all phenomena, the universe and beings, we will not fall into delusion.

Son, there are three things to take as the path.

Take as the path the absence of any ground *acting as a support for,* **or root** *that gives rise to, anything in samsara and nirvana.*

If you thoroughly investigate the different elements of samsara and nirvana, you will find they are devoid of any solid basis for being born or root from which to be born. It is as impossible for them to come into existence as it is to make a knot in the sky.

Stay without giving importance to things—*as true or untrue, to be hoped for or feared, and so on.*

As a result of believing that phenomena are solid and real, we try to get pleasant things like fame, praise, and enjoyable sensations, and we try to avoid unpleasant things like criticism. Such clingings arise only because of temporary conditions coming together, and they do not actually exist on their own. So you should not give any importance to things you hope to achieve and things you are afraid of experiencing.

Apply the seal *of the unborn to phenomenal existence.*

Why? Because if you do so, it will be impossible for you to experience delusion.

++ 75 ++

Severing ties—outer, inner, and in-between.

When outer phenomena (forms, smells, and so on), inner phenomena (the consciousness that perceives form, the consciousness that perceives sound, and the rest of the eight consciousnesses) and the sense organs in between (the eye, ear, tongue, and so on) come together, this connection makes us cling to anything that is beautiful, melodious, or sweet and reject anything that is the opposite of those. In other words, as long as they are connected, they give rise to delusion. So it is important to break this connection:

> *If you do not cut outer and inner ties before putting the instructions into practice, the practice will degenerate into a mere attempt to impress others—a hypocritical facade.*

Son, there are four ties to be severed.

Sever outer ties *such as distracting circumstances—crowds and bustle.*

What do we mean by severing outer ties? If we stay in a place where there are many people and much activity, we can easily be distracted by good circumstances—people praising us, being of service to us, and so forth. Unless we cut such ties, it will be very difficult for us to gain any genuine experience of sustained calm and profound insight.

Sever inner ties *such as enemies and friends—objects that arouse attachment and aversion.*

It is also important to cut through our attachment to those we like and our hatred for those we dislike. See enemies as your kindest parents, who have helped you throughout your series of lives. Develop great love for them, compassion, and bodhichitta. As for the few selected beings to whom you are attached, bear in mind that your attachment will make you postpone your Dharma practice and stray from the path.

Sever "in-between" ties *such as the things you cling to that concern this life—*

anything, such as the performance of village ceremonies, that involves you trying to become wealthy, famous, or powerful in this life.

These three ties, then, correspond to the world outside, the mind inside, and the body, the way we act.

Moreover, having first gained a deep conviction concerning the teachings you have heard, having then cut through your intellectual doubts and having ultimately destroyed misconceptions regarding the view, meditation, and action,

Rely constantly on lonely places.[160]

To begin with, you should perfect your learning by gaining a clear understanding of the unborn, nondwelling, and unceasing nature of phenomena. Then, once you are convinced of this, inwardly you will have no hesitation or doubt, you will not continue to wonder whether or not the mind is empty. Realizing this point is what we call the view. Experiencing the view again and again is meditation. And acting without letting the view and meditation lapse into the ordinary condition is proper action. So, ultimately, cut through all the many misconceptions that arise with regard to the view, meditation, and action of the nine vehicles and acquire all their qualities, always relying on a secluded place to practice.

++ 76 ++

This chapter has two parts: the eight activities to be performed and how the teacher remedies faults in one's meditation and confers happiness and blessings.

i) The eight activities to be performed.

As we have seen, when we are in meditation, we need to realize that phenomena are unborn, nondwelling, and unceasing. But when we arise from meditation, there are eight activities we need to undertake.

Son, there are eight activities to be performed.

At times such as the beginning of a practice, meditate on

The three protections—*outer, inner, and secret.*

In order to practice we need to get rid of all outer and inner distractions and find an isolated place in which to meditate one-pointedly. Then, when we begin the practice, we must meditate on the three protections. The outer protection is the visualization of the protection tent that guards us against interruptions and obstacle makers. The inner protection is the use of various medicines that remedy disorders related to the channels, energies, and essence, the five elements, and so forth. The secret protection is the realization of the unborn, nondwelling, and unceasing nature of the mind that protects us from falling into delusion.

Make provision, *gathering everything you will need in order to practice.*

You should make sure that you have everything you will need for doing the practice, and in the right amount. If you have collected all sorts of things that are unnecessary for the practice, that shows you do not know how to be satisfied with little. On the other hand, if you try to practice with nothing, you will not have what you need to keep yourself alive and in good health, and this will constitute an obstacle to your continuing to practice. Try and find the right balance between being distracted because you have too many things and not having the strength to practice because you do not have enough—enough food to keep hunger at bay and remain healthy and enough clothing to protect you from the cold. All these things should be prepared beforehand. Deciding you need different things once you have started the practice will create obstacles and lead to difficulties.

Simplify—*that is, remain in the natural state: leave your body, speech, and mind just as they are, and always have been.*

And make offerings *to the teacher and the Three Jewels.*

From within that state offer all you have, making the outer, inner, and secret offerings to the teacher and the Three Jewels, for it is thanks to their kindness that you have all your current happiness, well-being, and possessions.

Regarding the actions you have committed in the past, **confess your negative actions** *with the four powers.*

Before you started following the Dharma, you accumulated a multitude of negative actions, for at that time you did not have the teachings to help you avoid such actions. These negative actions will hinder you on the path, so you must now purify them using the four powers: the power of regret, the power of the support, the power of the antidote, and the power of resolution.

And pray *that experience and realization may be born in your being.*

Pray fervently and one-pointedly as follows: "May experience and realization arise where they have not yet come to be; and where they have arisen may they not diminish, but grow and flourish more and more."

Sit **on a comfortable seat** *in a secluded place,*

so that you are not distracted as you meditate,[161]

And **perform the yogic exercises,**[162] *controlling body and speech.*

It is important to adopt the correct posture related to the body and speech. Regarding the body, it is impossible to develop perfect concentration if one is lying carelessly or sitting in an unbalanced posture, leaning to either side or forwards or backwards. This is why we need to adopt the seven-point posture of Vairochana, for with it concentration will naturally increase. It is said that when Lord Buddha was meditating in the forest, the monkeys came and imitated him, sitting in the same perfect posture. As a result, their channels were straightened and, despite their having no understanding, this allowed the wisdom energy to increase naturally so that they began to have a glimpse of emptiness. So this is why physical posture is so important. The body contains channels and the mind is associated with the energies that flow through the channels. When the impure karmic energy associated with the deluded mind flows through impure channels, it gives rise to the three poisons—attachment, aversion, and bewilderment. If the karmic energy that creates these three poisons is purified, this allows the wisdom energy to arise. And when one's channels, energies, and essence become wisdom channels, wisdom energy, and wisdom essence, one obtains supreme concentration, perfect recollection, and confidence.

ii) How the teacher remedies faults in one's meditation and confers happiness and blessings.

To remedy the various problems—errors, obstacles, and the like—that can occur during meditation it is important to follow the advice of a qualified teacher who is himself thoroughly experienced. By clearing up such problems and receiving the blessings of that secret treasure, the Guru's heart, one can easily travel the authentic path.

In the Commentary, *this section appears after the seventy-ninth chapter, but here we shall follow the order in the original text.*

Visualize *your root teacher* **seated on a** *lotus and moon* **throne** *on the crown of your head.* **Begin by** *arousing bodhichitta and* **performing the seven branches.**

Consider your root teacher seated on a lotus and moon disc above your head and arouse bodhichitta, thinking that whatever practice you are going to do physically, verbally, and mentally will be dedicated to the ultimate enlightenment of all sentient beings. Then in order to complete the accumulation of merit and wisdom do the seven-branch offering, which is likened to preparing a fertile field for planting crops: the prostrations and offerings correspond to tilling the ground, and confession to removing weeds and stones.

Next examine samsara.

Reflect on the nature of impermanence, suffering, and so on.

In order to prepare the ground for the growth of experience and realization, reflect on the fact that from the very bottom of the hells to the pinnacle of existence there is nothing in samsara that escapes suffering. However high one's position, however great one's wealth and fame, these things are impermanent: they change every moment and are no less fleeting than a rainbow in the sky. And even if you have a comfortable situation for the time being, it has mostly been obtained by accumulating negative actions, to others' detriment. In doing so you have been buying your own future suffering. So reflecting on this again and again, you should develop a strong wish to get out of samsara.

Then recall the intermediate states.

There are six intermediate states. In the natural intermediate state one recognizes the absolute nature that one had not recognized, like an orphan meeting its mother.

By "intermediate state" is meant a condition in which one is uncertain what will happen. Our present ordinary condition, the fact of dwelling in samsara, is what we call the natural intermediate state. In order to dispel the delusion of this natural intermediate state, we need to recognize everything as the absolute nature, the primordial simplicity of the natural state that we have hitherto failed to recognize. For that we need the teacher's instructions. Wandering in the delusion of samsara, we are like a child that has lost its parents wandering aimlessly with no one to protect it, feeling hungry and cold, in danger of falling sick. But when we meet with a qualified teacher, receive the teachings of the Great Vehicle, put them into practice, and finally have the experience of recognizing the absolute nature, the tremendous joy and relief we feel is like that of the lost child if it were suddenly to meet its mother. We should practice until we have that experience of the absolute nature manifesting like the mother we had lost.

In the intermediate state between birth and death one recognizes the primal wisdom as if one held up a torch in a dark cave.

The intermediate state between birth and death lasts from the moment one is born until one dies. In order to destroy the delusory perceptions of this intermediate state we need to recognize the wisdom free from all delusion. This is like being cured of jaundice and seeing the whiteness of a conch as it has always been, or like lighting a torch in the darkness: even if it is in a place that has been in total darkness for thousands of years, the moment one lights the torch all that darkness will immediately be dispelled.

In the intermediate state of dream one recognizes everything that appears as the mind, just as on an island of sages one would not find other beings even if one looked.

When we fall asleep, the consciousness dissolves into the consciousness of the ground of all and we experience deep sleep. From this state dreams manifest. We might dream that we become immensely rich, but when we wake up, we have not even a single needle and thread. We might dream that we have been installed on Indra's throne, but we wake up only to find ourselves on our bed. All these dreams, whether good or bad, are simply the product of the subtle karmic energy that moves the mind. They are projections of our own mind and nothing else. Just as one would never find any other kind of people on an island of sages even if one looked, one will never find any dream appearances that are truly existent, that are anything other than projections of the mind.

> In the intermediate state of concentration one makes clear
> what is not clear, like a model looking in a mirror.

The intermediate state of concentration is the period between entering meditation and rising from it into the postmeditation period. It is important during this intermediate state to get rid of all mistakes in our concentration and to make clear what is not clear. This requires the attentiveness of a young woman looking in the mirror, examining her face carefully for blemishes so that she can remove them. Without a mirror she will never find those blemishes, even though they are on her own face. Similarly, for us the mirror of mindfulness is indispensable. Otherwise if we rise out of meditation and fall into delusion in our postmeditational conduct, the benefit we gained through meditation will be lost. So, like the beautiful woman looking in the mirror, during meditation we must check whether or not we are straying into dullness or distraction, and during the postmeditation period we must watch whether we are losing control, even in the middle of acting very quickly.

> In the intermediate state of becoming one connects with one's
> remaining stock of positive actions, like inserting a pipe into
> a broken irrigation channel.

Between death and the next rebirth we have a mental body, which is tossed about like a feather by the wind of karma, moving constantly from place to place. If in the life we have just left we started practicing the Dharma and gained some experience and realization but did not attain ultimate realization, it is now, in this intermediate state of becoming, that we must make a connection so that we can meet a teacher again and continue our progress on the path. The instruction we need in order to get rid of the delusion of this intermediate state—the bridge between the moment of death when the perceptions of this life fade away and the moment of rebirth when the perceptions of the next life appear—is like a pipe or canal joining a source of water to an unirrigated field.

> *In the intermediate state of the radiant absolute nature, primal wisdom appears all-penetrating, like a shooting star in the sky.*

At death all the senses, elements, and so on dissolve into radiant light, after which they again arise from it. This luminosity is the intermediate state that comes between the delusion of this life and the delusion that arises in the intermediate state between this life and the next. If we manage to recognize the luminosity, we will realize the undeluded wisdom that is all-penetrating, and which even a mountain cannot obstruct. It arises like a shooting star appearing brightly in space for a short instant, so in order to recognize it and attain liberation in its arising we need to receive the teacher's pith instructions.

> *The crucial points on these*—the methods for attaining liberation in the six intermediate states—*are condensed in the teacher's pith instructions. Put them into practice.*

++ 77 ++

Using seven concentrations to meditate.

Son, there are seven concentrations *in which one does not move away from the view and meditation.*

In order to cut the stream of birth, death, and the intermediate state we need to be diligent in concentration. First we must acquire the correct view and gain complete conviction in it. Then we have to repeatedly make an inner experience of the view by means of what we call meditation, and this meditation must be free from faults such as dullness and distraction. In this way we will reach a stage where the view and meditation are united. If we do not have the correct view, however hard we try to meditate we will encounter problems and make mistakes. If on the other hand our view is perfectly sound, our meditation will naturally follow suit. But unless we observe constant self-control in a place where there are no distractions, our meditation will be dissipated by external conditions. To help us avoid straying from meditation, there are seven concentrations.

The concentration of the emptiness of the inner,

that is, the consciousnesses of the sense organs, the eye being devoid of eye-ness, and so forth.

The eye organ is what sees forms outside. The eye consciousness is what, on seeing forms, thinks of them as being beautiful or ugly and accordingly clings to them or rejects them. Form is the object of the eye organ to which it appears. If we think of what we see as truly existing, then clinging to beautiful things and aversion to ugly things arise. But if instead we recognize that the object, the sense organ, and the consciousness are all three devoid of true reality and we realize their emptiness, we will recognize the inner consciousness as empty, for it does not dwell outside, inside, or in between.

The concentration of the emptiness of the outer,

that is, the six objects, form being devoid of form-ness, and so forth.

Recognition of the emptiness of forms outside is what we call the concentration of the emptiness of outer phenomena, for outer phenomena—the whole universe and beings—are completely impermanent. Not only will they be destroyed at the end of the kalpa, but with the passing of the seasons, and even with every second that goes by, nothing remains the same. This is equally true for the thoughts inside us. Past, present, and future thoughts seem to follow one another, but, when analyzed using Madhyamika reasoning, they can be seen to possess not even a particle's worth of existence. So when we realize that things outside are empty and things inside are empty, all of our afflictive emotions will be naturally and completely destroyed.

Regarding compounded phenomena there is

The concentration of the emptiness of both inner and outer,

compounded phenomena, the container and contents,[163] *or phenomena outside and the mind inside.*

And regarding uncompounded phenomena there is

The concentration of the emptiness of the *uncompounded* absolute.

Then there is

The concentration of the lion's imposing demeanor,

which overawes deluded perceptions.

The lion is the king of animals, feared by all other animals, large and small. In the same way, one's recognition of the emptiness of all phenomena will overawe all deluded perceptions, all clinging to subject and object, all attachment and aversion.

The concentration of clear wisdom,

that is, the recognition of *the natural state free from the duality of subject and object.*

When one destroys even the most subtle concepts and notions of subject and object, one arrives at the way things truly are. But this state of emptiness is not empty like an empty pot or void space. It is filled with the clarity of awareness. By attaining sound realization of this concentration of clear wisdom, one is able to destroy an entire mountain of negative actions and obscurations.

The vajralike concentration,

which cannot be overcome by afflictive emotions and ignorance, nor separated from us: it is

indestructible and inseparable.

++ 78 ++

Six preparatory branches of the practice.

Son, there are six preparatory practices.

The six practices described here are called in Tibetan *Jorwa druk*, but they are not the same as the well-known six-limbed yoga of the Kalachakra tradition.[164]

Sit on a comfortable seat

as is proper for practicing concentration.

If you do not sit properly in the correct posture and on a seat that is perfectly comfortable for the purposes of meditation, your concentration will be constantly disrupted. This is why it is important to adopt the seven-point posture of Vairocana, to avoid pointless chitchat, and to keep the mind from being excessively withdrawn or excessively dissipated in following external phenomena.

Then visualize the channels *and wheels*[165] *in the body, the container.*

As a support for concentration, use your own body, which is formed from the growth of the different channels. Within these channels the energies flow, carrying the essence. The object of the practice is to bring about the cessation of the impure channels, energies, and essence, which are permeated with ignorance, and to let the wisdom channels, energy, and essence become manifest. The three main channels are the *uma* in the center, the *roma* on the right, and the *kyangma* on the left. There are also the five wheels: the wheel of great bliss in the crown of the head, the wheel of enjoyment in the throat center, the wheel of dharmas in the heart center, the wheel of manifestation in the navel center, and the bliss-preserving wheel in the secret center. Visualize these one by one. This is the meditation on the "outer fence of voidness" of the body.[166]

Expel the *poisonous* **energies** *that are contained.*

The channels are like a path on which the energies travel. The impure karmic energies associated with delusion are mixed with the three poisons—attachment, aversion, and bewilderment—and as they flow through the channels the afflictive emotions grow stronger and stronger. We therefore need to dispel these impure energies related to delusion, for if the energies can be purified, the qualities of wisdom will naturally increase. To do this, make a vajra fist with each hand and expel the poisonous energies, first through the left nostril to expel the energy associated with attachment, then through the right nostril to expel the energy associated with aversion, and finally through both nostrils together to expel the energy associated with bewilderment. Do this three times, or in greater detail nine times. This is like cleaning a vessel very thoroughly.

Perform the *physical* **yogic exercises,** *filling with the upper and lower energies and dispelling obstacles.*

There are two kinds of energy, or *prana*, referred to here. The upper *prana*, which passes through one's nostrils and mouth, is the *prana* associated with great bliss, the skillful means aspect. The lower *prana*, which passes through the lower doors, is that connected with emptiness, the wisdom aspect. To train these two *pranas* there are four steps. The first is to inhale. The second is to fill the "vase," pressing the upper *prana* down and bringing the lower *prana* up so that they meet together in the region below the navel center. Hold the breath in this way as long as you can. When you cannot hold it any longer, take a small additional breath and turn the *prana* three times on either side and three times in the middle, below the navel. This is the third step. Fourth, expel the *prana*, shooting it out like an arrow.

While you are trying to train the *prana* like this, various obstacles and problems may occur, so in order to dispel these you should go through the different yogic exercises or *trulkhor*. If you do this practice over a long period of time, the channels will be straightened, the energies will be purified, and the door to the manifestation of wisdom opened.

Rid yourself of other *pointless thoughts,* **mental turbidity.**

To take an example, the mind is like a crippled person, the energy like a blind horse. Unless the horse is controlled by its crippled rider, it will take the latter anywhere it likes—that is, the mind will be overpowered by wild thoughts. But once the cripple can control the horse, everything will come under control. So it is important to give up unnecessary wandering thoughts, all those thoughts related to attachment and aversion that we constantly follow and perpetuate, rendering the mind turbid like water in a muddy pool that has been stirred. Holding the breath in the "vase" exercise helps reduce these meaningless thoughts.

Bring the mind into the one-pointed concentration *of bliss, clarity, voidness, and the like.*

Having dispelled the thoughts and purified one's channels, energies, and essence, when one rests without wavering in the empty nature of the mind, three different experiences may occur: experiences of bliss, clarity, or voidness, which correspond to the nirmanakaya, sambhogakaya, and dharmakaya, respectively. However, if these experiences are tinged with clinging, the bliss will lead to rebirth in the world of desire; the clarity, to rebirth in the world of form; and the absence of thought, to rebirth in the world of formlessness. So while these three experiences will, and indeed must, occur as a normal result of progress on the path, when they occur, you must not

have the slightest clinging to them but permeate them with the realization
that they are completely empty. Realize that they are simply manifestations
of your own mind. Even if you reach a stage where you are able to stay in
unwavering concentration for days and days without even feeling hungry
or thirsty, you must never feel proud or pleased with yourself. Stay free of
clinging and pride, pray with fervent devotion to the teacher, and practice
diligently. That way, you will easily develop these various kinds of concentration. As it is said, everything can be accomplished with a little hardship.
But if one remains idle and indifferent, it is difficult to achieve anything.
So in order to cultivate these experiences of bliss, clarity, and voidness you
should bring everything into one-pointed concentration.

++ 79 ++

The five-limbed main practice of the yogi on the path.

Son, there are five branches in the main practice,

branches for practicing the actual path.

The practice of these various concentrations is like a journey on a road.
The road changes all the time, sometimes ascending, at other times
descending. One moment it is straight, the next it is winding. One will thus
encounter different aspects of the path, branches such as sustained calm
and profound insight, or the generation and perfection phases. Here we
shall consider five main branches of the actual path.

Drop *ordinary* **activities, put them off**—*such things as business and
farming the land: there will never come a time when they are finished.*

All these ordinary activities are like children's games. If we continue
them, they will never end. But if we abandon them, that is the end of them.
And however successful one may be at such activities, they are completely
pointless for they are no exception when it comes to the four ends:

The end of all gathering is dispersing,
The end of all living is dying.
The end of all meeting is parting,
The end of all rising is falling.

The more you become involved in such distracting activities, the longer you will continue to postpone the practice of Dharma. So rather than putting things off until later, make an effort now to practice the concentration that will bring bliss, clarity, and absence of thoughts.

Once you leave them aside, virtuous activities will blossom and

Your body, speech, and mind will be extremely happy,

you will feel completely relaxed and blissful, like a smooth, level plain with no rocks or rough features. In this serene state, this well-prepared ground, concentration will easily grow:

As a result, inner concentration will grow and various experiences occur:

The mirror of awareness will shine within.

Concentration, or the realization of wisdom, is supported by the body, which is why one needs to straighten the channels, purify the energies, and free oneself of discursive thoughts. By doing so, it is certain that the experiences and realization of the path will come. If your mind is free from dullness and distraction, you will realize your own nature, as when you see your face in a clear mirror.

At that time **the Sugatas will bestow their splendor.**

In other words, you will acquire the thirty-two major and eighty minor marks of a Perfect Buddha, one by one.

The Buddhas, Bodhisattvas, and Vidyadharas will bless you, the guardians of virtue[167] will protect you, and because of the majesty you will have gained, hindrances, negative forces, and obstacle makers will be unable to do you any harm.

Gradually you will be able to meet all the Buddhas, Bodhisattvas, and Vidyadharas dwelling in the Buddhafields and receive their blessings and instructions so that all obstacles and problems on the path are cleared. Just as a son who takes care of his family's fields, tilling the soil and producing a good harvest, will greatly please his parents, so too by keeping your body, speech, and mind in tune with the Dharma and persevering on the path for the sake of all sentient beings, you will gladden all the Buddhas and Bodhisattvas and they will shower blessings upon you. You will be able to reach Buddhafields like Tushita and Dumataka and other celestial fields. And you will be protected by all those who abide by virtue—Buddhas, Bodhisattvas, and the various protectors. You will obtain the majesty of the Buddhas and Bodhisattvas, with all their blessings, so that no hindrances, negative forces, or obstacle makers will be able to do you any harm.

> **It will be impossible for conditioned thoughts** *such as the five*
> *or three poisonous emotions* **to arise.**

Why are the afflictive emotions called poisons? Just as swallowing poison can have mortal results, if you harbor these afflictive emotions in your mind, they will kill any chance of liberation and you will continue to wander in samsara. However, close examination of these poisons will reveal that they are nothing other than conditioned thoughts. As such, they are unborn, nondwelling, and unceasing. If you realize their empty nature, afflictive emotions will be unable to rear up in your mind.

> *In short, if you give up all ordinary activities, by practicing the*
> *profound path with no conflict between your mind and the three*
> *trainings you will temporarily and ultimately master infinite*
> *qualities, accomplishing your own and others' welfare according*
> *to your wishes.*

All our different activities are projections of the mind, created by our thoughts. If you follow these deluded thoughts, there will be no end to your mind being upset by delusion, just as when the wind blows over the surface of a lake, the crystal clarity of the water is masked by ripples. It is therefore important to control the mind by applying the view, meditation, and action, both in meditation and in postmeditation, for major situations and minor ones. If you can do this and do nothing that goes against the practice of the three trainings of discipline, concentration, and wisdom, ultimately you will attain omniscient Buddhahood; and in the meanwhile you will be reborn in the higher realms of samsara as a human or celestial being. While you are on the path, you will be unfettered by afflictive emotions. Without any selfish hopes of attaining the peace of nirvana alone, you will constantly keep the vow of bodhichitta in mind to bring all sentient beings to the essence of enlightenment. By thus accomplishing both your own and others' aims, you will naturally make the inconceivable qualities of perfect Buddhahood a reality.

These chapters on the superior training in wisdom have been arranged in a different order in the Commentary, *which explains the text as follows. After the forty-second chapter it jumps straight to Chapter Forty-eight. It then continues from Chapter Fifty to Fifty-four. After that come Chapters Sixty-three and Sixty-nine. Next, Chapters Forty-three to Forty-seven, after which come Chapters Sixty-eight, Seventy, Seventy-one, Forty-nine, and Fifty-five to Fifty-nine. Then Chapters Sixty to Sixty-seven, leaving out Chapter Sixty-three, which came earlier. Next, Chapters Seventy-two to Seventy-nine, omitting Chapter Seventy-seven, which came in the section on the training of the mind. Here, however, I have followed the order in the root text.*

To sum up, by using these chapters to realize the meaning of the Later Mind Section of the Great Perfection, one achieves certainty through "clearly distinguishing," and complete confidence. As if vanquishing an adversary with a razor-sharp blade, this is the path that eradicates samsara and establishes the unborn nature with certainty.

Of the three sections of Atiyoga, the Great Perfection, namely the Mind, Space, and Pith Instruction sections, we have here followed mainly the Mind Section. These instructions for clearly distinguishing between the ordinary mind and awareness and for acquiring complete confidence in awareness alone are like a sharp sword that routs the legions of samsara, cutting samsara at the root and establishing its unborn nature.

This concludes the instruction on this section, which I have explained to suit those with keen intelligence.

This was the fourth section from the *Eighty Chapters of Personal Advice*, the instruction on stainless wisdom, the essence.

V. Conclusion

++ 80 ++

A concluding instruction on examining the disciple and how the disciple should practice.

These teachings will not help disciples who hear them unless they are going to put them into practice. It is therefore important to check first whether the disciple is a suitable vessel.

Son, there are three points in conclusion.

In the first place, these instructions should not be given to people who are not suitable vessels. Not only will such people derive no benefit from them, but the profound instructions, whose purpose is to free one from the bonds of afflictive emotions, will themselves be wasted. So the teacher must identify any faults in the disciple.

i) The defects of disciples to whom the instructions should not be given.

Recognize defects in disciples who might be liberated by these profound instructions:

do not give the instructions to improper vessels who are not interested in the Dharma and only indulge in worldly activities, **whose natural disposition is unsuitable,**

being bad-tempered, ungrateful, and so on—unable to acknowledge and return kindness,

who are inconstant *and have fickle minds,*

who find fault *in their own teacher,* **in the Dharma, and in individuals,** who lack pure perception and have no respect and devotion,

and who, *having received the profound instructions,* **will not put them into practice.**

Even if you do give them the instructions, you will not do them any good, and divulging the secret teachings will result in criticism and retribution.

ii) Suitable vessels to whom the teachings may be given.

To those who are good-natured—*who acknowledge what is done for them, are grateful for kindness, and so on,* and are prepared to give their lives, their body, speech, and mind to repay their teacher's kindness—

who are stable—*their faith,* diligence, *and suchlike never change*—

who have very pure perception *with regard to the Dharma, people, and so forth,*

and who, not content with merely hearing the teachings, **are assiduous in the practice,** *accomplishing what they have heard,*

to them you can give the instructions.

By doing so you will ensure that they hold the lineage of the teachings and serve the doctrine, fulfilling the aims of many—attaining realization for *themselves and* benefiting *others.*

iii) As for how disciples who are suitable vessels should put the instructions they have been given into practice,

They should see the teacher as the Buddha.

As a result they will receive the blessings of the lineage.

Such suitable disciples see the teacher as the Buddha himself, considering him as the true embodiment of the knowledge, love, and ability of all the Buddhas of the past, present, and future. And because of their devotion they will receive the blessings of all the lineage teachers from Samantabhadra down to their own root teacher.

They should keep the instructions in their hearts,

for the view, meditation, and action of the Mantrayana are exceedingly profound.

> *If they are able to keep them secret and to practice them, the two accomplishments,* common and supreme, *will come without effort.*

> **Befriending solitude,** *far from crowds and bustle* that make it hard to develop stable concentration, **they should practice.**

> **As a result, experience and realization will bloom and they will become the snow lion's cubs.**

The true signs of accomplishment are that one becomes controlled and peaceful, completely free from afflictive emotions. Along with these, such accomplishments as the various forms of perfect recollection and clairvoyance will come naturally. As meditative experiences and realization increase, one becomes fearless, like a snow lion cub, which has no fear of other, ordinary animals.

> *This completes the explanation of the instructions on how to recognize suitable disciples and on how to give rise to excellent qualities in one's being.*

> **This was the fifth section from the** *Eighty Chapters of Personal Advice,* **the instruction on the vessel and a related teaching.**

⁖ Colophon ⁖

**This is the essence of the heart of Deshek Gyawopa, the Lord
who attained the summit of the view.**[168]

These instructions are the essence of the heart of Zurchung Sherab Trakpa
who brought to full realization the view of the Great Perfection and was
known as the Sugata (indicating that he had attained Buddhahood) of
Gyawo—the name of the mountain hermitage in which he lived and practiced.

**It covers the Three Pitakas and follows the texts of *Epitome*,
Magic, and *Mind*.**

These texts are the *Epitome of Essential Meaning* (referring to the *Great
Gathering*[169]); the *Net of the Magical Display*, related to the *Guhyagarbha
Tantra*; and the Eighteen Tantras of the Mind Section, which is the first of
the three sections of Atiyoga.

**It is an instruction that within a single lifetime liberates those with
faith, diligence, and wisdom** who practice one-pointedly.

Written down by Zurchungpa's disciple **Khyungpo Yamarwa
exactly as the Lord spoke it, it is the culmination and quintessence
of his profound teachings.**[170]

The Eighty Chapters of Personal Advice
By the glorious heruka, Zurchungpa—
Great victory banner of the teaching, the glorious heruka come
    in human form—
Who bestows the fruit of complete liberation
On all who hear his name or even think of him,
Is the sublime and extraordinary jewel of the Ancient Translation
    lineage,
A treasure of the profound tantras, commentaries, and pith instruc-
    tions,
An event as rare in the three times as the udumbara lotus
That I have come upon through no effort of my own.

Such is my delight and joy at my good fortune in being able
  to receive these teachings and reflect on them *that I have
  written these notes.*
*If I have made the slightest error therein (*and any of these notes
  contradicts the words and meanings of the teachings of the
  Victorious Ones*),*
I confess it to the teacher and supreme deities.
Through the merit may the great enlightenment be swiftly attained
  by all sentient beings, especially those who have made a
  connection with this teaching.
In all our lives may we never be parted from the sublime tradition
Of the glorious Zur,
May we hear the teachings, reflect on them, and put them into
  practice, bearing aloft the victory banner of this teaching,
And by correctly holding, preserving, and spreading it
*May we achieve both aims—our own and others'—*and may we all
  attain ultimate Buddhahood.

*Using as a basis the text and structural outline transmitted to me by the
Vajradhara Khyentse Wangpo (*who had received these teachings through
both the direct and long lineages*),*[171] *I, the kusali Jamyang Lodrö Gyamtso
Drayang,*[172] *wrote these few notes to make it clearer, thinking that they might
be useful for people of limited intellect like myself. They follow the explanation given in the detailed commentary* The Lamp of Shining Jewels. *I wrote
them at Demchok Tashi Gempel*[173] *at an auspicious time in the month of Kartika*[174] *in the Wood Mouse Year (1924). As a result of this, long may the sublime doctrine of the secret and ultimate essence endure.*
  Sarwada mangalam bhavantu.

Zurchung Sherab Trakpa's
Eighty Chapters of Personal Advice

Zurchung Sherab Trakpa (1014-1074)

I. Faith

1

Son, since it is a prerequisite for the whole of the Dharma,
It is important to recognize the fault in not having faith
And the virtues of having it.
There are six faults that come from not having faith.
Without faith one is like a rock at the bottom of the ocean.
One is like a boat without a boatman.
One is like a blind person who goes into a temple.
One is like a burnt seed.
One is like a sheep stuck in a pen.
One is like a maimed person who has landed on an island of gold.

Son, there are six virtues of faith.
Faith is like a very fertile field.
Faith is like a wishing-gem.
Faith is like a king who enforces the law.
Faith is like someone who holds the stronghold of carefulness.
Faith is like a boat on a great river.
Faith is like an escort in a dangerous place.

Son, there are ten causes that give rise to faith.
You need to know that there is no happiness in your present way of life
    and circle of friends.
You need to have confidence in the law of cause and effect.
You need to remember death and impermanence.

You need to remember that you will depart without your retinue
or wealth.
You need to bear in mind that you are powerless to choose your
next rebirth.
You need to remember how hard it is to obtain a fully endowed human
body such as this.
You need to bear in mind that the whole of samsara is suffering.
You need to see the immense qualities of the Three Jewels.
You need to look at the lives and deeds of the Holy Beings.
You need to keep the company of excellent friends who abide by virtue.

++ 4 ++

Son, there are thirteen things to be abhorred.
Unless you turn your back on your fatherland, you will not vanquish
the demon of pride.
Unless you give up the activities of a household, you will never find
the time to practice the Dharma.
If you do not practice the moment faith arises, there will be no end
to the jobs you have to do.
Do not blame others for your own lack of faith.
Unless you cast your possessions to the wind, you will never exhaust
your worldly ambitions.
Unless you distance yourself from your relatives, there will be no
interruption in your attachment and aversion.
Unless you act now, you cannot be sure where you will go next.
Doing nothing now when you have the means, the prayers you make
for future lives are empty chatter.
Without lying to yourself, practice the Supreme Dharma.
Forsake now what you will have to give up anyway, and it will
become meaningful.
Rather than concerning yourself with things you obviously cannot
complete, concern yourself with making an experience of what you
definitely can complete.
Instead of preparing for next year—when you cannot be sure whether
or not there will be a next year—prepare for death, which is certain
to happen.
As you practice, food and clothing will take care of themselves, so do not
have great hopes or fears.

++ 5 ++

Son, there are thirteen things that are very important.

To a teacher who has the three qualities, it is very important to be respectful.

It is very important to give instructions to disciples who are proper vessels.

It is very important to give up attachment to things, externally and internally.

In practicing the instructions, it is very important to think in the long-term.

It is very important to develop fervent devotion to the yidam deity and the Three Jewels.

It is very important to cultivate diligence in the practice of virtue.

It is very important to steer clear of negative actions.

It is very important to rely on the absence of thoughts in your mind.

In the postmeditation period, it is very important to rely on compassion and bodhichitta.

It is very important to develop the conviction that the instructions are unmistaken.

It is very important to observe the vows and samayas.

It is very important to establish the unborn nature of the mind.

It is very important not to give the secret pith instructions to an improper vessel.

This was the first section from the *Eighty Chapters of Personal Advice*, the instruction on firm faith, the gateway.

II. Discipline

++ 6 ++

Son, there are ten facts.

If the continued existence of the Buddha's teaching and your having
faith coincide, it is simply that you accumulated merit in past lives.

If you are interested in the Dharma and meet a master who possesses
the instructions, it is simply that the blind man has found the jewel.

If faith, diligence, and wisdom coincide in a body free of defects,
it is simply that these good qualities are the karmic result of
having trained in the Dharma.

If your being born in samsara coincides with relatives scolding you,
it is simply that you are being exhorted to practice.

If your having things and your being delighted to give them away
coincide with a beggar, it is simply that generosity is coming to
perfection.

If, when you are practicing, the dam of suffering bursts, it is simply
that you are purifying your negative actions.

If people are hostile with a Dharma practitioner who has done nothing
wrong, it is simply that they are setting him on the path of patience.

If your having consummate faith coincides with applying the
instructions, it is simply that you have come to the end of karma.

If your own fear of death coincides with other people dying, it is simply
that the time has come to turn your mind away from samsara.

If you think you will finish your projects for this life first and after that
practice a bit of Dharma, this is simply the demon's delaying tactics.

++ 7 ++

Son, there are thirteen instructions.

As a spur to diligence in the practice, consider your own death
and others'.

If you want to cultivate extraordinary respect, examine the teacher's
outer and inner qualities.

If you want your conduct to concord with all, do not obstruct the
efforts of others.

So as never to upset the teacher, practice hard.

If you want to attain accomplishment quickly, keep the vows and
samayas without letting them degenerate.

If you want to halt the four rivers, you must ascertain the unborn nature
of the ground-of-all.

If you want no obstacles to your accomplishing enlightenment, leave
behind the distractions of this life.

If you want to benefit others effortlessly, meditate on the four boundless
qualities.

If you are fearful of the three lower realms in your future lives, steer clear
of the ten negative actions.

If you want to be happy in this and future lives, be diligent in performing
the ten positive actions.

If you want your mind to engage in the Dharma, you must experience
the hardship of suffering.

If you want to turn away from samsara, strive for unsurpassable
enlightenment.

If you want to obtain the result, the three kayas, unite the two
accumulations.

++ 8 ++

Son, there are five things that are useless.

No need to say you are interested in the Dharma if you have not turned
your mind away from samsara.

No need to meditate on emptiness if you have not countered attachment
to the things you perceive.

No need to practice meditation if you do not turn your mind away
from desire.

No need for fine words if you have not assimilated the meaning yourself.
No need to apply the instructions if you do not have devotion.

++ 9 ++

Son, there are five things you need to do.
You need to have fervent devotion to the teacher, for then the blessings
    of the lineage will automatically rub off on you.
You need to accumulate exceptional merit, for then everything you wish
    for will work.
You need to make your mind fit, for then extraordinary concentration
    will be born in your mind.
You need to cultivate extraordinary concentration, for then the afflictive
    emotions will be overwhelmed.
You need to be free of afflictive emotions, for then you will quickly
    attain enlightenment.

++ 10 ++

Son, there are five things that become lies.
As long as you delight in the things of this world, saying you are afraid
    of birth and death becomes a lie.
Unless you are afraid of birth and death, going for refuge becomes a lie.
Unless you are rid of desire, saying you are a great meditator becomes
    a lie.
Unless you have understood the law of karma, saying you have realized
    the view becomes a lie.
Unless you have abandoned the abyss of existence, saying you are
    a Buddha becomes a lie.

++ 11 ++

Son, there are five things that are true.
It is true to say that without meditating one will never become a Buddha.
It is true to say that if you do not break the samaya, you will not go
    to hell.
It is true to say that if you separate skillful means and wisdom, you will
    fall to the Shravaka level.

It is true to say that if you do not know how to unite view and conduct,
you are on the wrong path.
It is true to say that the mind is by nature perfectly pure and clear,
unstained by defects.

++ 12 ++

Son, there are five things that are pointless.
There is no point in following a master who does not have the nectar
of the teachings.
There is no point in accepting a disciple who is not a proper vessel.
There is no point in making a connection with someone who will
not keep the samaya.
There is no point in performing positive actions that are mixed with
negative ones.
There is no point in knowing the teachings if you do not act accordingly.

++ 13 ++

Son, there are eight instructions.
As you practice, cross the pass of attachment and aversion.
When you are studying the texts, don the armor of forbearance.
When you are staying in sacred sites and secluded places, do not let
your mind hanker after food and wealth.
When you want the profound teachings, follow a master well-versed
in them.
When you meet a truly knowledgeable master, do all you can to please
him and never upset him.
When the Dharma gets difficult, stamp on your faint-heartedness.
When your family disowns you, cut all attachment in your mind.
When you are straying into ordinary thoughts, bring your consciousness
back to the essence.

++ 14 ++

Son, there are thirty-four pieces of advice.
As they are a source of obstacles, give up distractions.
There is no time to tarry: quickly, meditate!

Do not be concerned with how you live, be concerned with how you
    will die.
Practice alone without the luxury of attendants.
Deluded perception—cast it aside.
Do not indulge: too much activity gives rise to adverse circumstances.
You will be much happier having no one for company.
With no one to keep you company, there is no attachment or aversion.
It is impossible to make everyone happy, so stop trying to please people.
Stay alone like a corpse.
Do not enter a pit of thorns: stay in a place where you will be happy.
Enough with the past, now stop surrendering.
Do not consider people as enemies and friends; maintain primal
    wisdom.
Do not look to fame; watch your own mind.
Unless you are diligent, you will go down.
Give up your wandering ways of the past.
Go to the island in the ocean that has the riches you desire.
If you reach this island, you will never return.
Give your property to your father.
If you make your old father happy, he will give you his heartfelt advice.
He'll speak to his son straight from the heart.
Once you have found a gem, do not throw it away.
Turn back and correct yourself.
When your brothers and sisters are all together, listen to what they say
    and carry it out.
If you fear being scattered, fence yourself in.
If you fear you are running away, hold yourself with the hook.
Make your view stand firmly on its own.
Observe discipline without hypocrisy.
Give generously and impartially.
Patiently bear with adversity.
Put up with suffering when you are listening and reflecting.
Do not cast your meditation into the mouth of fame.
Your conduct should be such that you are not carried away
    by the demons.
You will be beguiled by the demon of appearances.

✦✦ 15 ✦✦

Son, do not discredit the house of your forefathers.

Do not taint your siblings and relatives.

Do not throw dust on other relatives, close or distant.

Without paying taxes to the king, you cannot hope to be his subject.

Do not race downhill.

Do not be clever in wrong ways.

✦✦ 16 ✦✦

Son, there are ten things that do no harm.

If you can cope with the place, there is no harm in staying in your
own country.

If you can cope with those with whom you are connected, there is
no harm in not leaving your family.

If you can cope with the question of clothing, there is no harm even
in going naked.

If you can cope with the problem of attachment and aversion, however
you conduct yourself outwardly, you will not come to any harm.

If you know how to handle the teacher, there is no harm in discontinuing
respect.

If you can cope with samsara, you will not come to any harm even if you
do not practice.

If you can cope with the lower realms, you will not come to any harm
even if you perform negative actions.

If you can cope with the hells, there is no harm in not keeping the
samayas even if you have entered the door of the secret mantras.

If you are confident in the view, there is no harm in taking things easy
and sleeping.

If you can cope with the problem of residence, it does not matter
where you live.

If you can cope with the problem of food, it does not matter what
you eat.

If you can cope with the problem of the body, even if you do not steer
clear of contagious diseases, you will come to no harm.

✦✦ 17 ✦✦

Son, there are eighteen objects of derision.
In the beginning when faith is born, one is ready to leap in the air.
Later, torn by doubts, one fills desolate valleys with one's footprints.
In the end, having completely lost faith, one becomes a mooring stone
   on the bottom of hell.
In the beginning, having found the master, one talks about all the
   teachings he has transmitted.
Later, one tires of the master and criticizes him.
In the end, one abandons the teacher and considers him as one's greatest
   enemy.
In the beginning, when one achieves a degree of concentration,
   one thinks, "There is no practitioner as good as I am."
Later, one gets tired of meditating and resembles an inmate in an
   open prison.
In the end, one gives up meditation and loiters in the villages.
In the beginning when experiences occur, one brags about them.
Later one gives up meditation and, as an expert in letters, takes
   to giving teachings.
In the end when one abandons one's body, one dies in a completely
   ordinary state.
In the beginning, one develops but a faint conviction in one's realization
   of the view.
Later, torn by doubts, one lies about one's knowledge and questions
   others.
In the end, far from having the view, one is completely dominated
   by errors and obscurations.
When the result is lost in error, the windows of liberation are shuttered.
By blocking the windows of liberation, one will never interrupt the
   stream of birth and death.
Unless one interrupts the stream of birth and death, one is powerless
   to choose where one will be reborn.

✦✦ 18 ✦✦

Son, there are fifteen ways in which the practice goes wrong.
The view rushes into uncertainty.

The meditation gets lost in idiot meditation.
The action strays into wild, inappropriate conduct.
The samaya gets lost in being undervalued.
The master is treated as one of one's own.
The disciple attends teachings unwillingly.
The practice is left for when one has the leisure.
One's experiences are ghost sightings.
The result is the achievement of worldly fame.
One receives the instructions inauthentically.
Having obtained a human body in Jambudvipa, one returns
    empty-handed.
At death, one dies with regrets.
The Dharma practitioner is betrayed by his own name.
One listens to empty sounds.
After death, one cannot but go to the hells.

•• 19 ••

Son, there are twenty-six kinds of folly.
It is foolish not to fear an army whose arrival is inevitable.
It is foolish not to repay a debt you have definitely incurred.
It is foolish to run toward an enemy who will surely take you captive.
It is foolish to enjoy carrying a greater load than you can bear.
It is foolish to be eager to go somewhere unpleasant.
It is foolish to leap into an abyss where you are certain to die.
It is foolish to sow buckwheat and hope to grow barley.
It is foolish to expect the sun to shine into a north-facing cave.
It is foolish to place your hope and trust in someone who is obviously
    going to deceive you.
It is foolish for someone of humble origins to vie with one of royal
    blood.
It is foolish to hope to be rich when you possess nothing.
It is foolish for a cripple to try to ride a horse.
It is foolish to say you have completed a task without having done
    any work.
It is foolish, when you have still not recovered from an illness, to get
    fed up with the doctor and to take a liking to someone who has
    prepared a vial of poison.

It is foolish for a merchant with nothing to sell to be a hearty eater.
It is foolish to run off without listening to your father's advice.
It is foolish for a daughter to ignore her mother's advice.
It is foolish, having left the house naked and then found clothes,
    to return home again without them.
It is foolish to take off your boots when there is no river.
It is foolish to drink salty water that will never quench your thirst.
It is foolish to be oblivious of the inside when the outside has collapsed.
It is foolish to be clever at counseling others while giving yourself the
    wrong advice.
It is foolish to scale a fortress without a ladder.
It is foolish for children to not want to do a job they will definitely
    have to do.
It is foolish not to be worried about crossing an unfordable river.
It is foolish to look elsewhere for something that is already within you.

◆◆ 20 ◆◆

Son, there are nine pieces of personal advice.
If you want to compete, take on the Buddha.
If you want to backbite, slander the yidam.
If you have to be mean, be so with the instructions.
If you are going to be unkind, be unkind to your negative actions.
By all means be munificent—with the teacher.
If you want to give someone the cold shoulder, make it samsara.
If you are going to enumerate faults, list your own defects.
When you have the victory, give it to others.
As for the sutras and tantras, tease them out like wool.

◆◆ 21 ◆◆

Son, there are nine pieces of heartfelt advice.
Be a child of the mountains.
Eat the food of famine-time.
Do the things that please the enemy.
Wear clothes that no one wants.
Flee the crowds, alone.
Be without a handle for your relations.

Tie your fickleness down with a rope.
Abandon havens of delight.
Focus your mind on space.

++ 22 ++

Son, there are five beatitudes.
Blessed are they who recognize samsara for what it is: a poisonous
   tree of suffering.
Blessed are they who see those that give rise to afflictive emotions as
   spiritual friends.
Blessed are they who correctly view the master who has trained in the
   three wisdoms.
Blessed are they who see everything—outer and inner things and
   circumstances—as being without origin.
Blessed are they who postpone all activities and set out on the
   unmistaken path.

++ 23 ++

Son, there are twenty things that lead to breaches of samaya.
To be secretive about your teacher while extolling your own virtues
   leads to a breach of samaya.
To view an erudite scholar and an uneducated person as equals leads
   to a breach of samaya.
Competition between patrons and disciples leads to a breach of samaya.
To have the intention of offering and to put off doing so leads to a
   breach of samaya.
Receiving as many teachings as you can possibly hear leads to a breach
   of samaya.
To insist on getting the instructions leads to a breach of samaya.
To deceive your teacher and fellow disciples leads to a breach of samaya.
To blame the master for wrong leads to a breach of samaya.
To treat the master as a rival leads to a breach of samaya.
To abuse the master's confidence leads to a breach of samaya.
To scorn his kindness leads to a breach of samaya.
To be intent on looking after your own interests leads to a breach
   of samaya.

To steal instructions and books leads to a breach of samaya.

To secretly enumerate the master's faults leads to a breach of samaya.

To block another's aspiration leads to a breach of samaya.

To make an outer show of the inner practices leads to a breach
of samaya.

To be jealous of vajra brothers and sisters leads to a breach of samaya.

To act indiscriminately without a teacher or instructions leads
to a breach of samaya.

To masquerade as a teacher leads to a breach of samaya.

To criticize teachings and those who practice them leads to a breach
of samaya.

To exhibit the instructions to unsuitable vessels leads to a breach
of samaya.

This was the second section from the *Eighty Chapters of Personal Advice*, the instruction on perfect discipline, the basis.

III. Concentration

++ 24 ++

Son, there are four practices that confer blessing.
The blessing of yourself, as exemplified by the sole of a shoe.
The blessing of perceptions, as exemplified by a mountain torrent
    in spate.
The blessing of the mind, as exemplified by the middle of a great river.
The blessing of nonduality, as exemplified by a jackal.

++ 25 ++

Son, there are four instructions for using things as the path.
Make freedom from attachment the path, as exemplified by the pelican
    carrying fish.
Make the five poisons the path, as exemplified by the recitation
    of mantras over poison.
Make the unborn nature of the eight consciousnesses the path,
    as exemplified by cutting a fruit tree at the roots.
Make the great purity the path, as exemplified by the lotus growing
    from the mud.

++ 26 ++

Son, here are instructions on four things to be known.
Know freedom from attachment, as illustrated by the magician.
Know indivisibility, as illustrated by sandalwood or the musk deer.
Know that relatives deceive, as illustrated by being let down by a friend.
Know inseparability, as illustrated by a sesame seed or the flame
    of a lamp.

++ 27 ++

Son, there are four crucial instructions.
You need the crucial instruction that shows how to make a clear-cut
   decision regarding the unobstructed nature of appearances,
   as illustrated by a clean silver mirror.
You need the crucial instruction on not being bound by characteristics,
   as illustrated by a prisoner who has been released.
You need the crucial instruction on not being distracted from
   the unborn nature, as illustrated by shooting an arrow straight
   at the target.
You need the crucial instruction on resting in one-pointed
   concentration, as illustrated by an ophthalmic surgeon.

++ 28 ++

Son, there are four "cuts."
Cut the stream of the arising of dualistic thoughts and the following
   after them, taking the example of a tortoise placed on a silver platter.
Decide that nothing is extraneous to the absolute nature, taking the
   example of gold jewelry.
Decide on its indivisibility, taking the example of molasses and its
   sweet taste.
Decide that it is naturally manifesting awareness, taking the example
   of the moon in the sky and its reflection in water.

++ 29 ++

Son, there are four views.
View thoughts and appearances as the ornament of the absolute nature,
   taking the example of a rainbow adorning the sky.
View thoughts as the absolute nature, taking the example of tempering
   and honing a sword.
View thoughts as leaving no trace, taking the example of birds flying
   in the sky.
View existence as untrue, taking the example of waking from a dream.

✦✦ 30 ✦✦

Son, there are four kinds of meditation.

Meditate with increasing habituation, taking the example of the waxing moon.

Meditate on thoughts and appearances as the inexpressible great bliss, taking the example of having your mouth full of water.

Meditate that fame and the like are not ultimately true, taking the example of mist, which does not truly exist.

Meditate on the uncontrived nature as empty, taking the example of water and bubbles.

✦✦ 31 ✦✦

Son, there are four kinds of conduct.

In your conduct, turn your back on worldly ways: consider the examples of a bride and a madman.

In your conduct, do not move from the absolute nature: take the example of fish in the ocean.

In your conduct, whatever appears should be primal wisdom: take the example of fire raging through a forest.

In your conduct, the many should have the single taste: take the example of salt dissolving in water.

✦✦ 32 ✦✦

Son, there are four kinds of experience.

The experience of no clinging to thoughts, as illustrated by a small child and a mirror.

The experience of wisdom taking birth where it has not previously arisen, as illustrated by a poor woman finding treasure.

The experience of neither apprehension nor esteem, as illustrated by a swallow and a lion.

The experience of being unafraid of philosophical views, as illustrated by the lion who is not scared of the fox.

++ 33 ++

Son, there are four kinds of signs.
The sign of awareness shining within, as illustrated by a butter lamp
    inside a vase.
The sign of the mind not getting involved in the pleasures of the senses,
    as illustrated by a king seated on his throne.
The sign of focusing the mind on the unborn nature, as illustrated
    by a sick person and a cemetery.
The sign of having stamped on the afflictive emotions, as illustrated
    by the pigeon and the hawk.

++ 34 ++

Son, there are four instructions related to optical illusions.
As in the example of perceiving a mirage as water, if you do not know
    that the pleasures of the senses are a delusion, you will wander.
As in the example of perceiving a rope as a snake, if you do not know
    that you are being fooled, you will wander.
As in the example of the parrot eating poison, if you cling to things
    thinking that they truly exist, you will wander.
As in the example of the child and the empty fist, if you are fooled
    by your perceptions, you will wander in samsara.

++ 35 ++

Son, there are ten ways of failing the Buddhas.
Even if the whole world rises up in enmity against you, do not stray
    from the absolute nature. If you do, you will be betraying the
    Buddhas of the three times.
Whatever you do, do not wander from the continuum of the unborn
    absolute nature. If you do, you will be betraying the Buddhas of
    the three times.
Even if your life is at stake, never lose sight of the Dharma. If you do,
    you will be betraying the Buddhas of the three times.
Do not spoil even an atom's worth of your samaya with the
    sublime teacher. If you do, you will be betraying the Buddhas
    of the three times.

Rather than now accomplishing fame in this life, put all your efforts
into the task of training the mind. If you involve yourself in the affairs
of this life and are not diligent in the mind training, you will be
betraying the Buddhas of the three times.
See the noble teachers as Vajrasattva in person and have devotion.
If you do not, you will be betraying the Buddhas of the three times.
Know that everything outside and inside is the mind, and do not
have attachment or aversion. If you do, you will be betraying
the Buddhas of the three times.
Cultivate great compassion and work for the sake of sentient beings.
If you strive for your own sake alone, you will be betraying the
Buddhas of the three times.
All dualistic concepts are the work of demons, so know that there is
no duality of subject and object. If you fail to do so, you will be
betraying the Buddhas of the three times.
With this body as a support, be careful as you seek the fruit of
Buddhahood. If you fail to do so, you will be betraying the Buddhas
of the three times.

++ 36 ++

Son, there are four ways not to be distracted.
Do not be distracted from the expanse of the mind free of grasping,
like a straight arrow.
Do not be distracted from the absolute space, which is free from
thoughts, like an athlete.
Do not be distracted from the expanse of evenness, like a hooked fish.
Do not be distracted from the state beyond all thought, as if you were
removing a thorn.

++ 37 ++

Son, there are four instructions on the method.
The instruction on the state of mind devoid of all ordinary perception
and thought, like a dry skull.
The instruction on the mind that, watching, sees nothing, like someone
who has eaten poison.
The instruction on the mind free from judgments, like an infant.

The instruction on leaving the mind as it is, as if stunned, like someone
whose heart has been removed.

++ 38 ++

Son, there are four ways to stay.
Stay without thought in the clarity that is not acquired and cannot
be lost.
Stay without thinking in the bliss that is not to be evoked and cannot
slip away.
Stay in vivid clarity, undistracted in the state beyond distraction.
Remain unhurried, with nothing to do, perfectly poised.

++ 39 ++

Son, there are six crucial points of the mind to be understood.
Relaxation is the crucial point of the mind, exemplified by someone
who has completed a task.
Freedom from concern is the crucial point of the mind, exemplified
by someone who has recovered from an illness.
Freedom from hesitation is the crucial point of the mind, exemplified
by a madman jumping off a cliff.
Freedom from expectation and apprehension is the crucial point
of the mind, exemplified by one's meeting a person one had been
looking for.
Freedom from fear is the crucial point of the mind, exemplified by
a lion walking among other savage beasts.
Clarity with absence of thoughts is the crucial point of the mind,
exemplified by the flame of a lamp filled with sesame oil.

++ 40 ++

Son, there are four things you need not seek.
Having the view that has no dualistic fixation, do not seek one that has;
take the example of the sun: it does not have to look for its rays.
Having the meditation that has no object on which to focus, do not
seek one that has; take the example of a wish-fulfilling gem:
it does not have to look for the things one wants.

Having the action free of adoption and rejection, do not seek one
to adopt and reject; take the example of a person: he does not have
to look for himself.

Having the result free of hope and fear, do not look for one with hope
and fear; take the example of a monarch: he does not have to reassert
his royalty.

This was the third section from the *Eighty Chapters of Personal Advice,* the
instruction on one-pointed concentration, the means.

IV. Wisdom

◆◆ 41 ◆◆

Son, there are twelve points.
Not concealed anywhere, the mind is invisible.
From the beginning never separate from you, it has not been recognized.
Invisible when examined, things appear in every possible way.
They appear multifariously, yet they are not real things.
Despite kalpas of wandering, it has never been lost or separated.
Though it appears in multifarious ways, it has never changed.
There is not an atom to it, yet it pervades everything.
Within emptiness, all sorts of things appear.
When it is not held or tied, it stays wherever it is.
Unsupported, one moves through space.
Without any effort, everything is accomplished.
With neither form nor characteristics, it appears as it is viewed.

◆◆ 42 ◆◆

Son, there are twelve kinds of confidence.
The confidence that the whole of existence is one and the same in space
    and therefore has no intrinsic nature.
The confidence that since the root is subsumed in the mind,
    Buddhahood is not elsewhere.
The confidence that since the mind has no birth, it is uncompounded.
The confidence that since everything that appears is delusory, in truth
    enemies and friends do not exist.
The confidence that since all actions are suffering, in truth there is
    nothing to be done.
The confidence that since it is the nature of everything, it is nondual.
The confidence that there is no traveling, for realization is Buddhahood.

The confidence that the mind cannot be troubled by attachment and
aversion, for everything that appears is untrue.
The confidence that attachment and aversion are unborn.
The confidence that objects that arouse all dissolve in the mind.
The confidence that as it is the source of everything, it is the Absolute
Space—the Mother.
The confidence that it is the great immensity, it is the place where
everything dwells.

++ 43 ++

Son, there are nine things one sees.
One sees that everything is empty.
One sees that the root is the mind.
One sees that the nature is unborn.
One sees that one's situation is unpredictable.
One sees that the nature is devoid of true existence.
One sees that the natural state does not change.
One sees that the way-it-is is devoid of duality.
One sees that the ground nature itself does not tend toward any
particular direction.
One sees that the fundamental nature is devoid of concepts.

++ 44 ++

Son, there are seven sublime things.
To be free from intellectual meditation is the sublime "leaving things
as they are."
To be free of references is the sublime reference.
Not to meditate on absence of thoughts is the sublime absence
of thought.
Not to use anything as a support is the sublime support.
Not to meditate on anything is the sublime meditation.
To remain undistracted, with no attempt to stop movements, is the
sublime concentration.
When the mind is not involved with anything, this is the
sublime absorption.

++ 45 ++

Son, there are six wisdom sense organs.
The wisdom eye, which sees the forms of mind's projection.
The wisdom ear, which understands the meaning of emptiness.
The wisdom nose, which senses the unborn.
The wisdom tongue, which tastes in a nondualistic way.
The wisdom body, which touches the absolute nature.
The wisdom mind, which recognizes the mind's projection as arising
    in the nature of the mind.

++ 46 ++

Son, there are six wisdom objects.
The absolute nature seen as clarity and emptiness inseparable is the
    wisdom form.
Sound understood as spontaneously arisen is the wisdom sound.
The instruction imbibed to satiety is the wisdom fragrance.
The experience of the object as unborn is the wisdom flavor.
The great bliss touched is the wisdom texture.
Recognition is the wisdom phenomenon.

++ 47 ++

Son, there are six authentic experiences.
To not see at all is authentic sight.
To not hear anything is authentic hearing.
To not sense anything is the authentic perception (of smell).
To not taste anything is the authentic taste.
Not mentally touching anything is the authentic contact.
Not being aware of anything is the authentic awareness.

++ 48 ++

Son, there are six declarations on effortlessness.
One settles in the view in total rest, without any concept of vastness
    or constraint.
The meditation is the utter peace, radiance from the depth.

The action is joyful spontaneity, without adoption.
The result is all-pervading peace, where there is no hope or fear.
It is the universal evenness beyond all distinctions of quality
    or magnitude.
It is the utmost ease where the mind has no sorrow.

◆◆ 49 ◆◆

Son, there are sixteen metaphoric practices.
Always strip naked.
Always perform the great ablution.
Take the sun and the moon in your hand.
Whirl the wheel.
Gaze in the mirror.
Cure the sickness caused by the poisons.
Untie the rope binding you.
Flee from the midst of savage beasts of prey.
Reside in the crystal vase.
Climb the jewel stairs.
Cut the tree at the root.
Sleep in the openness of space.
Commit suicide.
Hasten to the golden isle.
Anoint your body with balm.
Pick sky flowers.

◆◆ 50 ◆◆

Son, there are five views.
Do not get angry at thoughts.
Do not be attached to the absolute nature.
Do not be proud of concentration.
Do not be resentful of anything wrong.
Do not be confused with regard to wisdom.

++ 51 ++

Son, there are ten aspects to complete confidence.
Everything possible may pour down like rain.
The three worlds may overflow like a river.
The six mental states may blaze like fire.
The one thousand million worlds may be buffeted as if by the wind.
The three poisons may gather like darkness.
The thousand million worlds may be filled by the sun.
Whole continents may be plunged into darkness.
Birth and death may be distinct.
One may have karmic tendencies.
Phenomenal existence may be turned upside down.

++ 52 ++

Son, there are four examples and their meanings.
Take the example of a Sugata's body: whichever way one looks at it,
    it is beautiful. Similarly, everything one does, if it is permeated
    with the unborn nature, is bliss.
Take the example of a smile and a scowl: two expressions but no more
    than a face. Similarly, everything that appears, everything that exists,
    does so within the unborn absolute nature.
Take the example of a blind person: it makes no difference whether one
    smiles at him or not. Similarly, in the absolute nature there is nothing
    to be adopted or rejected.
Take the example of the trunk of a plantain tree: it has no core. Similarly,
    phenomenal existence has no essence.

++ 53 ++

Son, there are four dissolutions of extremes.
In the absolute truth, phenomena are unborn, so they are beyond the
    extreme of existence.
In relative truth, they are unceasing, so they are beyond the extreme of
    nonexistence.
Not existing as distinct phenomena, they are not two, so they are beyond
    the extreme of both existence and nonexistence.

"Neither" arises as "both," so phenomena are beyond the extreme of
neither existence nor nonexistence.

++ 54 ++

Son, there are four ultimates.

Having recognized all outer and inner phenomena to be your own mind,
to know that the mind is empty and immaterial is the ultimate reach
of the view.

While not blocking the five senses, to be free from notions of subject and
object is the ultimate reach of meditation.

To know how to act uniting view and action is the ultimate reach of
action.

To be free of the belief that there is any truth in phenomenal existence
is the ultimate reach of experience and realization.

++ 55 ++

Son, there are five dharmakaya aspects of the mind.

The unmoving dharmakaya, illustrated by the oceanic deep.

The unchanging dharmakaya, illustrated by Mount Meru.

The uninterrupted dharmakaya, illustrated by a great river.

The undimming dharmakaya, illustrated by the sun.

The thought-free dharmakaya, illustrated by the reflection of the moon
in water.

++ 56 ++

Son, there are six primal wisdoms related to the mind.

The fresh nature, unadulterated, free of the duality is the wisdom of
coalescence.

Neither reaching out nor withdrawing, there is the wisdom of one taste.

With no adoption or rejection, there is the wisdom with no hope or fear.

Putting the seal on perceptions, there is the spontaneously arisen wisdom.

The union of appearances and emptiness, of awareness and emptiness,
is the wisdom of union.

There is outer emptiness and inner emptiness: this is the wisdom
of emptiness.

++ 57 ++

Son, there are seven ways in which the nature of the mind is introduced.
The object is introduced as being the mind's projection.
The mind's projection is introduced as a reflection.
Appearances are introduced as infinite.
The consciousness is introduced as being without support.
Awareness is introduced as being self-cognizing.
The object is introduced as being unborn.
The unborn is introduced as being free of conceptual constructions.

++ 58 ++

Son, there are six ways of introducing the ultimate nature of everything
    that arises.
Do not value existence.
Do not prize nonexistence.
Do not reconcile them in inseparability.
Do not differentiate things.
Do not conceive of anything.
Do not be distracted from the radiant deep.

++ 59 ++

Son, there are eight introductions.
The mind is perfectly clear.
Movements subside by themselves.
Thoughts are levelled instantly.
Awareness is naturally pure.
It is not perceptible.
The object is naturally empty.
It is there but it does not exist.
It does not exist and yet it is there.

++ 60 ++

Son, the unborn nature is introduced in nine ways.
What is born is unborn.
What has not been born is unborn.
What will never be born is unborn.
What appears is unborn.
Emptiness is unborn.
Awareness is unborn.
The unborn appears.
The unborn is primordially nonexistent.
The unborn is free from extremes.

++ 61 ++

Son, there are four similes.
Taking the example of a mountain, stamp your being with the view free
     from assertions.
Taking the example of a king seated on his throne, stamp your being
     with the meditation free of effort.
Taking the example of someone who has arrived on a golden island,
     stamp your being with the action free from dualistic perception.
Taking the example of a knot in a snake, stamp your being with the sole
     result in which there is freedom from hope and fear.

++ 62 ++

Son, there are five instructions.
Know that form and consciousness are unborn.
Without clinging, be aware of what you perceive.
Remain without being distracted by the eight concerns.
Remain without the consciousness being carried away by circumstances.
Seal the mind.

++ 63 ++

Son, there are five experiences of wisdom.
Thoughts are the absolute nature.

Characteristics are freed by themselves.
Looking directly confirms.
Clinging stops by itself.
Duality vanishes by itself.

✦✦ 64 ✦✦

Son, there are four ways in which the nondual absolute nature arises.
In the absolute nature, there is no good or bad; this is the all-penetrating
    primal wisdom.
By dwelling naturally without seeking anything, one remains in the state
    without conceptual constructs.
Not adulterating or fabricating is the great impartiality.
As the ultimate nature of the mind arises spontaneously, primal wisdom
    unfolds in the expanse.

✦✦ 65 ✦✦

Son, there are six ways in which the nondual absolute nature arises.
Since it arises in the state free of contrivance from the very beginning, it
    is fresh.
Since everything is complete within the mind, it is spontaneous.
Since there is no blocking or encouraging, it is great primal wisdom.
Since there is no division into samsara and nirvana, it is the nondual
    vajra.
Since mind is Buddha from the very beginning, it is the self-born vajra.
Since it is not caught by enemies, it is the great evenness.

✦✦ 66 ✦✦

Son, there are four ways of arising without duality.
It is clear and uncontrived, the natural radiance devoid of thoughts.
Without any concepts whatsoever, it is the mirror of awareness.
It is the self-cognizing awareness, a wishing-gem.
Everything arising by itself, it is the unpremeditated wisdom.

++ 67 ++

Son, there are four instructions.

In completely pervading all ten directions, it is the great pervasion.

Since it is without an outer gate and inner sanctum, it is the bodhichitta
free of partiality.

As anything arises, it is the great unpredictability.

Since it is neither lit nor dimmed, it is the pure enlightened state.

++ 68 ++

Son, there are eight kinds of natural dissolution.

Forms seen by the eye dissolve as they are seen; they dissolve in the
sphere of the unborn.

Sounds heard by the ear fade away as they are heard; they fade away
in the expanse of the unborn.

Odors smelled by the nose dissolve as they are smelt; they fade away
in the sphere of the unborn.

Tastes savored by the tongue dissolve as they are tasted; they fade away
in the expanse of the unborn.

Sensations felt by the body dissolve as they are felt; they fade away
in the expanse of the unborn.

Perceptions too dissolve by themselves; they fade away in the sphere
of the unborn.

Words uttered dissolve by themselves; they dissolve in the expanse
of the unborn.

Thoughts too are free in themselves; they dissolve into the sphere
of the unborn.

++ 69 ++

Son, there are four things that are stainless.

To recognize the unborn in everything that appears is the stainless
wisdom of the view.

Taking the unborn as the path is the stainless path.

In the unborn nature, an incapacity to express is the stainless experience.

Not to stray from the unborn nature into ordinary thoughts is the
stainless result.

⁙70 ⁙

Son, there are five things you will not find.
There is no finding an object outside.
There is no finding a mind inside.
There is no finding a body in between.
There is no finding the sentient being you do not want to be.
There is no finding the Buddha you would like to be.

⁙ 71 ⁙

Son, there are five instances where there is nothing to be found.
Whatever appears is an appearance of something that does not exist.
    You will never find it: there is nothing to be found.
Awareness is awareness and emptiness inseparable, so you will not find
    it: there is nothing to be found.
The body has no essence, so you will not find it: there is nothing
    to be found.
Beings are unborn, so you will not find them: there is nothing
    to be found.
The undeluded Buddha state is your own mind, so you will not find it:
    there is nothing to be found.

⁙ 72 ⁙

Son, there are five things to take as the path.
Do not conceive of anything.
Do not indulge in any object.
Do not entertain any hope whatsoever.
Do not regard anything as a defect.
"Force" the mind into its natural state.

⁙ 73 ⁙

Son, emptiness is threefold.
Phenomena outside are not born: they are empty.
The mind inside is empty: it is not born.
The aggregates "in between" are empty: they do not dwell.

✦✦ 74 ✦✦

Son, there are three things to take as the path.
Take as the path the absence of any ground or root.
Stay without giving importance to things.
Apply the seal.

✦✦ 75 ✦✦

Son, there are four ties to be severed.
Sever outer ties.
Sever inner ties.
Sever "in-between" ties.
Rely constantly on lonely places.

✦✦ 76 ✦✦

Son, there are eight activities to be performed.
The three protections.
Making provision.
Simplifying.
Making offerings.
Confessing negative actions.
Prayer.
Sitting on a comfortable seat.
Performing the yogic exercises.

Visualize the teacher seated on a throne.
Begin by performing the seven branches.
Next examine samsara.
Then recall the intermediate states.

✦✦ 77 ✦✦

Son, there are seven concentrations.
The concentration of the emptiness of the inner.
The concentration of the emptiness of the outer.
The concentration of the emptiness of both inner and outer.

The concentration of the emptiness of the absolute.
The concentration of the lion's imposing demeanor.
The concentration of clear wisdom.
The vajralike concentration.

++ 78 ++

Son, there are six preparatory practices.
Sit on a comfortable seat.
Next, visualize the channels.
Expel the energies.
Perform the yogic exercises.
Rid yourself of other mental turbidity.
Bring the mind into one-pointed concentration.

++ 79 ++

Son, there are five branches in the main practice.
Drop activities, put them off.
Your body, speech, and mind will be extremely happy.
The mirror of awareness will shine within.
The Sugatas will bestow their splendor.
It will be impossible for conditioned thoughts to arise.

This was the fourth section from the *Eighty Chapters of Personal Advice*, the instruction on stainless wisdom, the essence.

V. Conclusion

Son, there are three points in conclusion.

Recognize defects in disciples who might be liberated by these profound
instructions: do not give the instructions to improper vessels whose
natural disposition is unsuitable, who are inconstant, who find fault
in the Dharma and in individuals, and who will not put the
instructions into practice.

To those who are good-natured, whose minds are stable, who have
very pure perception, and who are assiduous in the practice—
to them you can give the instructions.

They should see the teacher as the Buddha. They should keep the
instructions in their hearts. Befriending solitude, they should
practice. As a result, experience and realization will bloom and
they will become the snow lion's cubs.

This was the fifth section from the *Eighty Chapters of Personal Advice*, the
instruction on the vessel and a related teaching.

This is the essence of the heart of Deshek Gyawopa, the Lord who attained
the summit of the view.

It covers the Three Pitakas and follows the texts of *Epitome*, *Magic*,
and *Mind*.

It is an instruction that within a single lifetime liberates those with faith,
diligence, and wisdom.

Written down by Khyungpo Yamarwa exactly as the Lord spoke it, it is
the culmination and quintessence of his profound teachings.

Shechen Gyaltsap Rinpoche's
A Necklace of Jewels

An annotated edition of Zurchung Sherab Trakpa's
precious instructions on the three trainings,
Eighty Chapters of Personal Advice.

Pith instructions comprising the essence of the Pitakas
in general and the three inner tantra sections:
Epitome, Magic, and *Mind.*

Shechen Gyaltsap Pema Gyurme Namgyal (1871-1926)

NAMO RATNA GURU BHYA

I pay homage to the precious Teacher.

Bowing down to the teacher who is Vajrasattva in reality,
I shall thread a Necklace of Jewels,
The Eighty Chapters of Personal Advice
Laid out in detail with a structural outline—
A treasury of gems of the three trainings.

The Buddha, having considered the various mental capacities of sentient
  beings,
Taught the various vehicles of the Dharma.
From these Deshek Gyawopa teased out the wool of the sutras and the
  tantras.
He churned the milk of the Three Pitakas.
He drank the words of the learned ones like water.
He savored the realization and experience of former masters like salt.
Looking at appearances as in a mirror,
He saw that whatever one does there is nothing but suffering.
He saw that the concerns of this world are to be given up.
He saw that besides accomplishing something meaningful for future lives,
  nothing is of any use.
He saw that status and fame have to be thrown away like spit and snot.
He saw the need to rid himself of retinue and bustle—for it is hard to make
  everyone happy—and to meditate alone.
At Trak Gyawo he practiced intensively.
He himself made a living experience of these Eighty Chapters of Personal
  Advice *on how to practice the whole of the Dharma.*
For those who fear birth and death, this is a practice for today.
He gave this as a spontaneous teaching, out of love, as direct heartfelt advice.

There are five topics. As we find in the scriptures:

> *Having cultivated firm devotion,*
> *In the field of pure discipline*
> *Sow the seed of concentration,*
> *And see the harvest of wisdom ripen.*

Accordingly, there are the instructions on faith, the gateway;
The instructions on discipline, the basis;
The instructions on concentration, the means;
The instructions on wisdom, the essence;
And to conclude, a summary of the above.

I. Faith

This first section has five chapters.[175]

◆◆ 1 ◆◆

Showing the importance of faith as a prerequisite and the fault in not having faith.

Son, since it is a prerequisite for the whole of the Dharma, it is important to recognize the fault in not having faith and the virtues of having it.

The essence of faith is to make one's being and the perfect Dharma inseparable. The etymology of the word "faith" is: the aspiration to achieve one's goal. The categories of faith are three: vivid faith, yearning faith, and confident faith.

There are six faults that come from not having faith.

Without faith one is like a rock at the bottom of the ocean—*the Dharma will not benefit one's being.*

One is like a boat without a boatman—*one will not be able to cross to the other side of samsara.*

One is like a blind person who goes into a temple—*one will be unable to understand the words and their significance.*

One is like a burnt seed—*the sprout of enlightenment will not grow.*

One is like a sheep stuck in a pen—*there is no liberation from suffering.*

One is like a maimed person who has landed on an island of gold—*one will return empty-handed at the end of this precious human life.*

++ 2 ++

The virtues of faith.

Son, there are six virtues of faith.

Faith is like a very fertile field—*the whole crop of virtue will grow.*

Faith is like a wishing-gem—*it fulfills all one's own and others' desires.*

Faith is like a king who enforces the law—*he makes himself and others happy.*

Faith is like someone who holds the stronghold of carefulness—*he will not be stained by defects and he will gather qualities.*

Faith is like a boat on a great river—*it will deliver one from the suffering of birth, old age, sickness, and death.*

Faith is like an escort in a dangerous place—*it will free us from the fears of samsara and its lower realms.*

++ 3 ++

The causes that nurture faith and its qualities.

Son, there are ten causes that give rise to faith.

You need to know that there is no happiness in your present way of life and circle of friends. *Ultimately these are the cause of suffering.*

You need to have confidence in the law of cause and effect, *for it can never ever fail.*

You need to remember death and impermanence. *There is no certainty when you will die.*

You need to remember that you will depart without your retinue or wealth. *When you die, you have to leave them all behind, so they are no use to you.*

You need to bear in mind that you are powerless to choose your next rebirth. *There is no knowing where the force of your actions will take you.*

You need to remember how hard it is to obtain a fully endowed human body such as this. *It is difficult to bring together the freedoms and advantages and their multiple causes.*

You need to bear in mind that the whole of samsara is suffering. *It is never anything other than the three kinds of suffering.*

You need to see the immense qualities of the Three Jewels. *It is certain that they forever protect us from the suffering of samsara.*

You need to look at the lives and deeds of the Holy Beings. *The activities of their Body, Speech, and Mind are unstained by faults or defects.*

You need to keep the company of excellent friends who abide by virtue. *Their good ways will naturally rub off on you, and faith and other virtuous qualities will increase.*

✦✦ 4 ✦✦

Counseling yourself with thirteen teachings on things to be regarded with distaste.

Son, there are thirteen things to be abhorred.

Unless you turn your back on your fatherland, you will not vanquish the demon of pride. *Wholeheartedly adopt foreign lands.*

Unless you give up the activities of a household, you will never find the time to practice the Dharma. *Put aside the business of running a household.*

If you do not practice the moment faith arises, there will be no end to the jobs you have to do. *Cut through your indecision.*

Do not blame others for your own lack of faith. *Wind the nose rope around your head.*

Unless you cast your possessions to the wind, you will never exhaust your worldly ambitions. *Whatever you have, use it to make offerings to the teacher and to the Three Jewels.*

Unless you distance yourself from your relatives, there will be no interruption in your attachment and aversion. *Always rely on solitude.*

Unless you act now, you cannot be sure where you will go next. *Now, when all the favorable conditions have come together, you should do anything to get free from samsara.*

Doing nothing now when you have the means, the prayers you make for future lives are empty chatter. *If you have the ability and you do not act, you are letting yourself down.*

Without lying to yourself, practice the Supreme Dharma. *Take your own mind as a witness.*

Forsake now what you will have to give up anyway, and it will become meaningful. *Whatever you have, your body and wealth, give it away for the Dharma.*

Rather than concerning yourself with things you obviously cannot complete, concern yourself with making an experience of what you definitely can complete. *For the sake of the Dharma, be prepared for austerity and forbearance.*

Instead of preparing for next year—when you cannot be sure whether or not there will be a next year—prepare for death, which is certain to happen. *Time is short, curtail your plans.*

As you practice, food and clothing will take care of themselves, so do not have great hopes or fears. *For those who practice the Dharma it is very important to give up all concern for this life.*

◆◆ 5 ◆◆

Thirteen important points that show the unmistaken path.

Son, there are thirteen things that are very important.

His realization is like space, beyond all partiality. His experience is constant and level like the ocean. His compassion shines evenly, like the sun and the moon. To a teacher who has these three qualities, it is very important to be respectful. *As the teacher is the root of the path, follow him, pleasing him in the three ways. Do not do anything disrespectful, even in a dream.*

It is very important to give instructions to disciples who are proper vessels. *They will hold the lineage and benefit themselves and others, and the teachings and beings. Do not be miserly with the teachings.*

It is very important to give up attachment to things, externally and internally. *Remember the defects of attachment to the pleasures of the five senses.*

In practicing the instructions, it is very important to think in the long-term. *With regard to the Dharma, do not be impatient. You need to accompany the teacher for a long time. Do not be skittish.*

It is very important to develop fervent devotion to the yidam deity and the Three Jewels. *Without fervent devotion, blessings will not enter. At all times be diligent in taking refuge.*

It is very important to cultivate diligence in the practice of virtue. *Act like a beautiful woman whose hair has caught fire. Do not fall under the influence of laziness.*

It is very important to steer clear of negative actions. *Think of their fully ripened effect and avoid them as you would a speck of dust in your eye.*

It is very important to rely on the absence of thoughts in your mind. *Let the thoughts related to the five poisons dissolve by themselves.*

In the postmeditation period, it is very important to rely on compassion and bodhichitta. *This is the root of the Great Vehicle and is therefore indispensable. Train in considering others more important than yourself.*

It is very important to develop the conviction that the instructions are unmistaken. *If you have no doubts, accomplishment will be swift in coming.*

It is very important to observe the vows and samayas. *Do not let your mind be stained by the downfalls and faults related to the three vows.*

It is very important to establish the unborn nature of the mind. *As your mind and appearances are the display of the absolute nature, come to the clear conclusion that the nature of mind is unborn like space.*

It is very important not to give the secret pith instructions to an improper vessel. *Divulging the secret teachings leads to criticism, so be careful: take pains to check the worthiness of the disciple.*

This was the first section from the *Eighty Chapters of Personal Advice,* the instruction on firm faith, the gateway.

II. Discipline

The eighteen chapters that follow comprise the instructions on the jewel-like superior training in discipline, the perfect foundation.

✦✦ 6 ✦✦

An instruction on timeliness in the practice.

Son, there are ten facts.

If the continued existence of the Buddha's teaching and your having faith coincide, it is simply that you accumulated merit in past lives. *Now that for once you have acquired the freedoms and advantages, do not squander them.*

If you are interested in the Dharma and meet a master who possesses the instructions, it is simply that the blind man has found the jewel. *Later it will be hard to find such a teacher repeatedly, so stay with him for a long time without separating from him, like the eyes in your forehead.*

If faith, diligence, and wisdom coincide in a body free of defects, it is simply that these good qualities are the karmic result of having trained in the Dharma. *Be diligent in the methods for making these three grow.*

If your being born in samsara coincides with relatives scolding you, it is simply that you are being exhorted to practice. *Decide for yourself and practice the Dharma.*

If your having things and your being delighted to give them away coincide with a beggar, it is simply that generosity is coming to perfection. *Without being trussed by the knot of miserliness, give away impartially.*

If, when you are practicing, the dam of suffering bursts, it is simply that you are purifying your negative actions. *Rejoice and give up wrong views.*

If people are hostile with a Dharma practitioner who has done nothing wrong, it is simply that they are setting him on the path of patience. *Avoid grudges and ill will; keep in mind the benefits of patience.*

If your having consummate faith coincides with applying the instructions, it is simply that you have come to the end of karma. *In the future you will not be reborn in samsara. The whole of the Dharma should serve as the antidote to attachment and aversion.*

If your own fear of death coincides with other people dying, it is simply that the time has come to turn your mind away from samsara. *Do not be attached to happiness and comfort in this life.*

If you think you will finish your projects for this life first and after that practice a bit of Dharma, this is simply the demon's delaying tactics. *It is very important not to fall under the influence of such a demon.*

✦✦ 7 ✦✦

Thirteen instructions to put into practice.

Son, there are thirteen instructions.

As a spur to diligence in the practice, consider your own death and others'. *The time of death is uncertain, so give up all this life's pointless activities and projects.*

If you want to cultivate extraordinary respect, examine the teacher's outer and inner qualities. *Avoid thinking of defects. Seeing faults reflects your own impure perception.*

If you want your conduct to concord with all, do not obstruct the efforts of others. *As all the vehicles are true in their own terms, do not have rigid opinions about paths or philosophical schools.*

So as never to upset the teacher, practice hard. *You will acquire all good qualities without exception.*

If you want to attain accomplishment quickly, keep the vows and samayas without letting them degenerate. *All the precepts boil down to giving up the ten negative actions and the five poisons as they are ordinarily experienced.*

If you want to halt the four rivers, you must ascertain the unborn nature of the ground-of-all. *When you have understood the unborn nature of the ground-of-all, the continuous flow of birth and death will cease.*

If you want no obstacles to your accomplishing enlightenment, leave behind the distractions of this life. *Trying to help others without having the ability is yet another distraction. Do not try to benefit others when you yourself are not ready.*

If you want to benefit others effortlessly, meditate on the four boundless qualities. *If you train in bodhichitta, nothing you do will exclude others' welfare.*

If you are fearful of the three lower realms in your future lives, steer clear of the ten negative actions. *Be careful, all the time.*

If you want to be happy in this and future lives, be diligent in performing the ten positive actions. *Now, when you have the choice, do not confuse what is to be adopted with what is to be avoided.*

If you want your mind to engage in the Dharma, you must experience the hardship of suffering. *Reflect on the pointlessness of weary toil and develop deep determination. There has never been a spiritual path that is easy.*

If you want to turn away from samsara, strive for unsurpassable enlightenment. *It is important to recognize the benefits of liberation and enlightenment according to the three vehicles.*

If you want to obtain the result, the three kayas, unite the two accumulations. *This will cause the stains veiling the three kayas to be removed.*

++ 8 ++

Showing how to recognize what is not true practice: five things that are useless.

Son, there are five things that are useless.

No need to say you are interested in the Dharma if you have not turned your mind away from samsara. *If everything you do is for this life alone, you will not accomplish the Dharma. To practice the genuine Dharma, you have to counter attachment to samsaric perceptions.*

No need to meditate on emptiness if you have not countered attachment to the things you perceive. *One meditates on emptiness in order to release one's clinging, believing that things truly exist. Unless you are free from this, emptiness is no more than a word.*

No need to practice meditation if you do not turn your mind away from desire. *Great meditators who end up sidetracked by village ceremonies risk dying as ordinary men.*

No need for fine words if you have not assimilated the meaning yourself. *There are many who are fooled by smart talk about the view, so hit the crucial point of the natural state.*

No need to apply the instructions if you do not have devotion. *Any experiences, realization, or good qualities that occur depend on the teacher's blessing: without devotion the blessings can never possibly penetrate.*

++ 9 ++

Showing how to practice with determination and the great armor of diligence: five things one needs to do.

Son, there are five things you need to do.

You need to have fervent devotion to the teacher, for then the blessings of the lineage will automatically rub off on you. *The practice of the Secret Mantrayana is the path of devotion and blessings. The root and lineage teachers are of one essence. See the teacher as the Dharmakaya Buddha. That way the blessings of all the Buddhas will enter you.*

You need to accumulate exceptional merit, for then everything you wish for will work. *The wishes of someone who has merit will be accomplished. At all times offer the seven branches, backed by bodhichitta. That way you will necessarily acquire a good heart.*

You need to make your mind fit, for then extraordinary concentration will be born in your mind. *It is important to train perfectly in making the body and mind fit.*

You need to cultivate extraordinary concentration, for then the afflictive emotions will be overwhelmed. *Sustained calm crushes the afflictive emotions, profound insight eradicates their seeds.*

You need to be free of afflictive emotions, for then you will quickly attain enlightenment. *Besides your own mind divested of obscurations, there is no other enlightenment to be sought.*

++ 10 ++

Identifying counterfeit Dharma.

Son, there are five things that become lies.

As long as you delight in the things of this world, saying you are afraid of birth and death becomes a lie. *Unless you are truly free from attachment, it is impossible to gain liberation from birth and death.*

Unless you are afraid of birth and death, going for refuge becomes a lie. *The words alone will not help.*

Unless you are rid of desire, saying you are a great meditator becomes a lie. *Attachment to anything, inside or out, is a cage imprisoning you. Whether one is shackled with a golden chain or bound with a rope, it is the same.*

Unless you have understood the law of karma, saying you have realized the view becomes a lie. *You have to master the essential point that emptiness manifests as cause and effect.*

Unless you have abandoned the abyss of existence, saying you are a Buddha becomes a lie. *Without getting rid of the cause, the five poisonous emotions, you will never close off the abyss of samsara, their result. So be diligent in applying the antidote, the three trainings.*

++ 11 ++

Practicing over a long period with determination, the armor of diligence, and daring.

Son, there are five things that are true.

It is true to say that without meditating one will never become a Buddha. *If you do not put the path into practice, even the Buddha catching you with his hand cannot help you. This very universe rests on the palm of the Buddha Vairochana-Himasagara.*

It is true to say that if you do not break the samaya, you will not go to hell. *Always take your own mind as witness and never part from mindfulness and vigilance.*

It is true to say that if you separate skillful means and wisdom, you will fall to the Shravaka level. *One who trains in the Great Vehicle must* never separate skillful means and wisdom. Train in the path of the six transcendent perfections.

It is true to say that if you do not know how to unite view and conduct, you are on the wrong path. *Take heed that the view does not slide toward action, and that action does not slide toward the view.*

It is true to say that the mind is by nature perfectly pure and clear, unstained by defects. *Mind is intrinsically radiant and has never been contaminated by adventitious impurities, so its natural expression is the great purity. This is the very reason exerting oneself on the path is meaningful. If it were intrinsically impure, there would be no transforming it into something pure, and there would therefore be no point in striving on the path.*

•• 12 ••

Son, there are five things that are pointless: *you might do them but the result will be wrong.*

There is no point in following a master who does not have the nectar of the teachings. *It is important to check first whether he is authentic.*

There is no point in accepting a disciple who is not a proper vessel. *Even if he follows you like your shadow, do not give him instruction. It will benefit neither you nor him.*

There is no point in making a connection with someone who will not keep the samaya. *The fault of his breaking the samaya will rub off on you, and he will not benefit either.*

There is no point in performing positive actions that are mixed with negative ones. *The preparation and conclusion must not be mixed with negative action. It is the nature of mixed actions that they mature as happiness and suffering separately.*

There is no point in knowing the teachings if you do not act accordingly. *It is important, rather, to integrate everything you know with your being and to put it into practice.*

⋅⋅ 13 ⋅⋅

*Putting the instructions into practice over a long period with
determination, armor, and daring.*

Son, there are eight instructions.

As you practice, cross the pass of attachment and aversion. *Begin by
falling upon those bandits, the eight ordinary concerns.*

When you are studying the texts, don the armor of forbearance.
*Earnestly put up with physical hardships and your inner fears regarding the
profound meaning.*

When you are staying in sacred sites and secluded places, do not let
your mind hanker after food and wealth. *It is important to have few
desires and be content with what you have.*

When you want the profound teachings, follow a master well-versed
in them. *Do not relegate the instructions to superficial knowledge: clear up
all your doubts about them.*

When you meet a truly knowledgeable master, do all you can to please
him and never upset him. *By doing so, you will gain all the qualities of his
knowledge. Always be careful in your behavior.*

When the Dharma gets difficult, stamp on your faint-heartedness.
With no concern for body and life, serve the Teacher and act with one taste.

When your family disowns you, cut all attachment in your mind. *Treat
friends and enemies equally and let attachment and aversion be liberated
by themselves.*

When you are straying into ordinary thoughts, bring your
consciousness back to the essence. *If the mind strays onto the object,
afflictive emotions will grow, so tether them with the rope of faith, diligence,
mindfulness, and vigilance. Develop determination and endurance. Use the
antidote of primal wisdom to let deluded thoughts be liberated by
themselves. This is a crucial point.*

⋅⋅ 14 ⋅⋅

*How to practice by applying whatever is necessary in the particular
situation.*

Son, there are thirty-four pieces of advice.

If you are distracted outwardly by crowds and bustle, your virtuous activities will be dispersed. If you are distracted inwardly by thoughts, afflictive emotions will rise up. If you are otherwise distracted by your own magical powers and giving blessings, your own life will be threatened. For this reason, as they are a source of obstacles, give up distractions.

When you are struck by death's poison, nothing will be of any use. There is no time to tarry: quickly, meditate!

Do not be concerned with how you live *in this life, subduing enemies and protecting your kin;* be concerned with how you will die.

Taking the example of a young maiden's bangles, practice alone without the luxury of attendants. *In particular, avoid bad company.*

As attachment to family is your own mind's deluded perception, cast it aside.

Do not indulge *in physical activities, talking, and thinking:* too much of these gives rise to adverse circumstances.

There is no need to be concerned with trying to please people. You will be much happier having no one for company. *Thus attachment and aversion will not arise. So*

With no one to keep you company, there is no attachment or aversion.

Since sentient beings' desires are never satisfied, it is impossible to make *everyone* happy—*even the Buddha could not do so*—so stop trying to please people.

Here is a metaphor for being without thoughts related to attachment and aversion: stay alone like a corpse.

Avoiding the abodes of attachment and aversion and thus being free from clinging and desire, do not enter a pit of thorns: stay in a place where you will be happy.

Until now you have surrendered your bodies and lives to attachment and aversion. Enough with the past, now stop such surrender. *Now surrender your body and life to the Dharma.*

Since all beings are endowed with the buddha nature, do not consider people as enemies and friends; maintain primal wisdom. *Apply yourself eagerly to sameness.*

Do not look to fame *or to experiencing any other of the eight ordinary concerns;* watch your own mind.

Practice the ascetic discipline of guarding the mind. Unless you are diligent *in this,* you will go down. *Even a single instant of negative thought creates the cause for being thrown into the lower realms.*

From time without beginning, your belief in the reality of things has fettered you in samsara. So now give up your wandering ways of the past.

Of the seven noble riches, the foremost, the source of them all, is being content. Go to the island in the ocean that has the riches you desire.

Without the capacity to be content, even a king is no better off than a beggar. Be satisfied with simply enough food and other necessities to stay alive. If you reach this island, you will never return.

If you have property, give it to your father. *If you please your teacher by offering him everything you have, he will give you all the profound instructions.*

If you make your old father happy, he will give you his heartfelt advice.

The teacher too speaks to his son straight from the heart. *To a suitable vessel he gives the instructions in their entirety.*

The disciple should guard them like his own heart and put them into practice. So once you have found a gem, do not throw it away.

Turn *the mind* back *from the deluded perceptions that are samsara* and correct yourself. *Travel the highway to enlightenment.*

When your vajra brothers and sisters are assembled, think of yourself as the least important of them all. When your brothers and sisters are all together, listen to what they say and carry it out.

If you fear *your practice* is being scattered, fence it in. *Rely on mindfulness and vigilance and never be without them.*

If you fear you are running after *the objects of the six senses*, hold yourself with the hook: *employ the watchman that is mindfulness.*

Know that all perceptions are dharmakaya, and with that confidence— as though you had landed on an island of gold and jewels—make your view stand firmly on its own.

Do not be ashamed in front of the deity, the teacher, or your own mind. Observe discipline without hypocrisy.

Give generously and impartially, *and stop expecting anything in return or any karmic reward.*

Patiently bear with adversity, *providing help in return for harm.*

Put up with suffering when you are listening and reflecting: *readily accept such things as illness, pain, hunger, and thirst for the sake of the Dharma, and take others' suffering upon yourself.*

Do not cast your meditation into the mouth of fame, *with hopes and so on of distinction and renown.*

Your conduct should be such that you are not carried away by the demons *of the eight ordinary concerns. It is important to match it with your progress.*

If you chase after the things you perceive, the demons that are the five poisonous thoughts will arise and you will be beguiled by the demon of appearances. *It is important, therefore, that the mind does not chase after the object.*

++ 15 ++

Six instructions for warding off defects.

Son, do not discredit the house of your forefathers. *Do not bring shame on your own root teacher, nor on the teachers of the lineage.*

Do not taint your siblings and relatives. *Avoid conflicts that prevent you from keeping the samaya with your brothers and sisters—those who have the same teacher as you and those who have entered the Vajrayana.*

Do not throw dust on other relatives, close or distant. *Never speak harshly to others who practice the Dharma.*

Without paying taxes to the king you cannot hope to be his subject. *If you do not please the teacher, his compassion and blessings will not flow.*

Do not race downhill *toward negative actions.*

Do not be clever in wrong ways *such as craft and pretence.*

++ 16 ++

An instruction on ten good and bad situations that do no harm—if one can cope with them.

Son, there are ten things that do no harm.

Here "if you can cope" implies a choice: if you can cope, take it on; if you cannot cope, do not take it on. "Do no harm" means: if a particular situation does no harm, use it; if it is harmful, don't.

So when you are able to take all adverse situations on the path without them affecting you adversely, if you can cope with the place, there is no harm in staying in your own country.

If you can cope with those with whom you are connected, *and do not develop attachment to friends and hatred for enemies,* there is no harm in not leaving your family.

If you can cope with the question of clothing, *and have completely given up such things as worrying about how attractive you are or being embarrassed,* there is no harm even in going naked.

If you can cope with the problem of attachment and aversion *and are able to take joy and sorrow on the path as one even taste,* however you conduct yourself outwardly, you will not come to any harm.

When you realize your own mind as being the teacher, all notions of difference are liberated by themselves. Thus, if you know how to handle the teacher, there is no harm in discontinuing respect.

In realizing that there are no such things as the names of samsara and nirvana and that everything one perceives is self-arisen primal wisdom, if you can cope with samsara, even if you do not practice, you will not come to any harm.

If you can cope with the lower realms *by liberating the mind and appearances into the absolute nature, so that there is no trace of the habitual tendencies,* you will not come to any harm even if you perform negative actions. *If it is for the sake of others, whatever one does is permissible.*

The absolute nature is free from effort and activity;
The essential nature appears in different ways
Yet the natural expression is free and nondual.
When you know your own mind to be samsara and nirvana,
Beyond the observance of all samayas to be kept,

you can cope with the hells, and there is no harm in not keeping the samayas even if you have entered the door of the secret mantras.

If you are confident in the view *that is beyond intellect and free from activity, and recognize that activities are delusion,* there is no harm in taking things easy and sleeping.

If you can cope with the problem of residence *and are not attached to the quality of your dwelling,* it does not matter where you live.

If you can cope with the problem of food *and are free from dualistic concepts of food being good or bad, pure or polluted,* it does not matter what you eat.

If you can cope with the problem of the body *and have severed the ties of self-love,* even if you do not steer clear of contagious diseases, you will come to no harm.

++ 17 ++

Examining and deriding one's own faults and those of Dharma practitioners
in general.

Son, there are eighteen objects of derision.

These are, in general, derisory behavior, erroneous practices, foolishness,
and breaches of samaya; and there are eight things that prevent such faults
from occurring:

someone good-natured who is competent to guide one;

a good friend who is clever at leading one;

a concern for future lives that stems from remembering death;

careful avoidance of negative deeds stemming from the conviction that
happiness and suffering are the result of actions;

a sense of shame in one's own eyes;

a sense of decency in others' regard;

great determination;

and reliability, as in someone whose word can be trusted and who does
not break his promise.

From the eight faults that are the opposite of these come derisory
behavior and the rest.

An object of derision here is an object of scornful laughter or of contempt,
something to be ashamed of both from the conventional point of view and
from that of the holy Dharma.

In the beginning when faith is born, one is ready to leap in the air.
When one receives the teachings, one does all sorts of things such as tearing
one's hair out and weeping.

Later, torn by doubts, one fills desolate valleys with one's footprints.
Without having cleared up one's doubts about the instructions, one grows
hesitant and wanders all over the place.

In the end, having completely lost faith, one becomes a mooring stone
on the bottom of hell. *In the end one develops wrong views with regard to*
the Dharma and the teacher.

These are the three faults in not having firm faith.

In the beginning, having found the master, one talks about all the teachings he has transmitted. *Having entrusted body and soul to him, one proclaims the secret teachings for all to hear, saying, "These are the most profound of my teacher's words."*

Later, one tires of the master and criticizes him. *One regrets everything one offered before, and one spreads rumors, claiming he has hidden defects.*

In the end, one abandons the teacher and considers him as one's greatest enemy. *One makes new acquaintances and follows other teachers.*

These are the three faults of following the teacher in the wrong way.

In the beginning, when one achieves a degree of concentration, one thinks, "There is no practitioner as good as I am." *Priding oneself on some small experience one has in sustained calm, one gets the idea there is no greater meditator or better practitioner than oneself.*

Later, one gets tired of meditating and resembles an inmate in an open prison. *In the hermitage one becomes bored during the day and fearful at night; at sunset one is glad to eat and sleep.*

In the end, one gives up meditation and loiters in the villages. *If one does not integrate the Dharma with one's being, one ends up performing village ceremonies or working as a hired laborer, a servant, and so forth.*

These are the three faults of failing to go through the practice properly.

In the beginning when experiences occur, one brags about them *like someone deranged. One is contemptuous of relative truth.*

Later one gives up meditation and, as an expert in letters, takes to giving teachings. *Like someone who shows others the way when he himself has no idea which road to take, one explains the teachings to others without having any understanding or realization oneself.*

In the end when one abandons one's body, one dies in a completely ordinary state. *Like an ordinary being one dies without having really set out on the path.*

These are the three faults of not obtaining any stability in the experience of the practice.

In the beginning, one develops but a faint conviction in one's realization of the view. *Having merely gained a vague and general understanding, one prides oneself on one's superb realization. One looks down on others.*

Later, torn by doubts, one lies about one's knowledge and questions others. *Pretending to be knowledgeable when in fact one knows nothing, one pesters others with questions.*

In the end, far from having the view, one is completely dominated by errors and obscurations. *Having fallen under the influence of eternalistic and nihilistic views like those of the Tirthikas, one never realizes evenness, the union state free from elaboration.*

These are the three faults of not gaining the confidence of realization.

When the result is lost in error, the windows of liberation are shuttered. *By failing to unite skillful means and wisdom, one misses the crucial point of the path and closes the door to nirvana, the result.*

By blocking the windows of liberation, one will never interrupt the stream of birth and death. *Because of one's belief that everything that appears is real and the notion of one's body and mind as "I," one is fettered by karma and afflictive emotions, and there is no liberation.*

Unless one interrupts the stream of birth and death, one is powerless to choose where one will be reborn. *On account of one's actions and afflictive emotions, one cannot but take rebirth in existence.*

These are the three faults or objects of derision where the result is utterly wrong.

Therefore, recognize these faults that come from not blending your mind and the Dharma, and do your best to avoid them.

✦✦ 18 ✦✦

Clarifying errors and obscurations: fifteen ways in which the practice goes wrong.

Having turned away from the holy Dharma, one follows ordinary, worldly ways while retaining the appearance of Buddhadharma.

Son, there are fifteen ways in which the practice goes wrong.

The view rushes into uncertainty. *One repeats others' words without having transformed one's own being.*

The meditation gets lost in idiot meditation. *Without profound insight one does not destroy the foundation, afflictive emotions: experiences and realization cannot take birth.*

The action strays into wild, inappropriate conduct. *Acting in ways* contrary to the Dharma, one behaves like a madman. *One has not recognized the crucial point of accumulation and purification.*

The samaya gets lost in being undervalued. *Without knowing the precepts to be observed, one disdains the samaya, thinking there is no harm in spoiling it up to a point.*

The master is treated as one of one's own. *Thinking of him as an uncle, one fails to develop faith or respect.*

The disciple attends teachings unwillingly. *If you listen to keep others happy or for fear of people criticizing, you will never understand the teachings.*

The practice is left for when one has the leisure. *By falling under the power of sleep and indolence, one will never obtain the result.*

One's experiences are ghost sightings. *Like a clairvoyant, one sees spirits and thinks of them more and more.*

The result is the achievement of worldly fame. *The attachment and aversion of the eight ordinary concerns increase and one is no different from ordinary people.*

One receives the instructions inauthentically. *Without serving the teacher or putting the teachings into practice, one relies merely on having the texts and receiving the transmission. Thus one does not throw oneself with real diligence into experiencing the practice.*

Having obtained a human body in Jambudvipa, one returns empty-handed, *like coming back empty-handed from an island of jewels. From the bed of a Dharma practitioner they remove the corpse of an ordinary person. There was no point in obtaining a human body.*

At death, one dies with regrets. *At that time, even if you regret, you will have run out of means.*

The Dharma practitioner is betrayed by his own name. *Unless you have practiced the Dharma, being called a practitioner does not help. If you act contrary to the Dharma, though you may be called a "spiritual friend," you will have become a counselor in evil.*

One listens to empty sounds. *Like listening to a melodious song of praise, nothing will come from listening to the dry leaves of flattery and praise. One risks pointlessly wasting one's human life.*

If one acts contrary to the Dharma, after death one cannot but go to the hells.

The root and source of all these is attachment and clinging to the things of this life, so recognize them as faults and get rid of them.

✦✦ 19 ✦✦

Showing, by means of twenty-six kinds of folly, where indulging in negative actions will lead.

Taking twenty-six examples of folly in ordinary life,
Son, there are twenty-six kinds of folly *in the holy Dharma.*
It is foolish not to fear an army whose arrival is inevitable, *that is, to have no fear of death.*
It is foolish not to repay a debt you have definitely incurred, *that is, not to purify your karmic debts, negative actions, and obscurations.*
It is foolish to run toward an enemy who will surely take you captive, *that is, to cling to samsara unafraid.*
It is foolish to enjoy carrying a greater load than you can bear, *that is, to not shy away from the ripened effect of negative actions.*
It is foolish to be eager to go somewhere unpleasant, *that is, to take pleasure in doing negative actions.*
It is foolish to leap into an abyss where you are certain to die, *that is, to jump into the three lower realms.*
It is foolish to sow buckwheat and hope to grow barley, *that is, to hope that negative actions will result in happiness.*
It is foolish to expect the sun to shine into a north-facing cave, *that is, to expect the teacher's blessings to happen when you have no devotion.*
It is foolish to place your hope and trust in someone who is obviously going to deceive you, *that is, to be attached to the good things of this life.*
It is foolish for someone of humble origins to vie with one of royal blood, *like a common subject contending with a prince; that is, to hope to develop noble qualities when one is just an ordinary person.*
It is foolish to hope to be rich when you possess nothing, *that is, to hope to be other people's master when you have no qualities yourself.*
It is foolish for a cripple to try to ride a horse, *that is, to make a promise you cannot keep.*
It is foolish to say you have completed a task without having done any work, *that is, to disdain skillful means when you have not realized the natural state.*
It is foolish, when you have still not recovered from an illness, to get fed up with the doctor and to take a liking to someone who has prepared a vial of poison; *that is, to have no respect for the doctor who cures the*

disease of the five poisons while relishing the company of those who indulge in negative actions.

It is foolish for a merchant with nothing to sell to be a hearty eater, *that is, to teach others when you have not realized the meaning yourself.*

It is foolish to run off without listening to your father's advice, *that is, to take the wrong direction without listening to the teacher's instructions.*

It is foolish for a daughter to ignore her mother's advice, *that is, to prefer the pleasures of the senses in this life to what is beneficial for future lives.*

It is foolish, having left the house naked and then found clothes, to return home again without them; *that is, having learned the Dharma, to get rich instead of practicing.*

It is foolish to take off your boots when there is no river; *that is, to interrupt the practice of Dharma when you do not have the confidence of realization.*

It is foolish to drink salty water that will never quench your thirst, *that is, to have desires and never know contentment.*

It is foolish to be oblivious of the inside when the outside has collapsed; *your body is old yet your mind is still full of attachment and aversion.*

It is foolish to be clever at counseling others while giving yourself the wrong advice. *You do not practice what you preach.*

It is foolish to scale a fortress without a ladder, *that is, to boast of heading for liberation without completing the accumulations.*

It is foolish for children to not want to do a job they will definitely have to do; *that is, for beginners to put off virtuous activities until later.*

It is foolish not to be worried about crossing an unfordable river, *that is, to be unconcerned by birth, old age, sickness, and death.*

It is foolish to look elsewhere when *the Buddha's wisdom* is already within you.

The above can all be summarized as five faults: hankering after the things of this life; wanting to have the result without the cause; not listening to the words of the teacher; pledging yourself to the holy Dharma but then following ordinary ways; and not practicing what you preach.

∗∗ 20 ∗∗

Nine pieces of personal advice for softening one's being.

This is personal advice because it consists of oral instructions spoken directly—advice to be kept in the heart.

Son, there are nine pieces of personal advice.

If you want to compete, take on the Buddha. *Look at the Capable One's life and train yourself following in his footsteps.*

If you want to backbite, slander the yidam. *All the time, without fail, be diligent in the approach and accomplishment practices.*

If you have to be mean, be so with the instructions. *If you keep them secret and practice them, blessings, experience, and realization will swiftly come.*

If you are going to be unkind, be unkind to your negative actions. *Do not look back at negative actions and friends who act negatively.*

By all means be munificent—with the teacher. *It is more beneficial than making offerings to the Buddhas of the three times.*

If you want to give someone the cold shoulder, make it samsara. *Investigate your mind minutely; be diligent in the methods that will prevent your taking birth in samsara in the future.*

If you are going to enumerate faults, list your own defects. *Depart from the land of your hidden defects.*

When you have the victory, give it to others. *Ultimately it will be for your own good.*

As for the sutras and tantras, tease them out like wool. *Seeking the teachings impartially and integrating them with your mind, correct your practice and your own mind. This is very important.*

∗∗ 21 ∗∗

Nine pieces of heartfelt advice for keeping a low profile.

Son, there are nine pieces of heartfelt advice.

Be a child of the mountains. *For the great meditator who never leaves the mountains, good qualities grow day by day, month by month.*

Eat the food of famine-time. *Do not let food, clothes, and conversation get the upper hand.*

Do the things that please the enemy. *If you do not cast your ordinary ways to the wind, you will never destroy the castle of desire and hatred.*

Wear clothes that no one wants. *Without any attachment it is easy to practice.*

Flee the crowds, alone. *Your virtuous activities will presently increase, there will be no obstacles, and you will get food and provisions as well.*

Be without a handle for your relations. *Unless you give up your longing and affection, you will not be able to cut your ties. Do not let people take your nose rope.*

Tie your fickleness down with a rope. *The human mind, like water, goes wherever it is led, so tether your mind with the rope of mindfulness.*

Abandon havens of delight. *Do not be attached to the pleasures of samsara. If you do not forsake them, you will never stop the constant stream of negative actions, misery, and bad talk.*

Focus your mind on space. *It is important to thoroughly familiarize yourself with the two kinds of no-self.*

++ 22 ++

Instructions, through five beatitudes, on taking good and bad circumstances equally.

Son, there are five beatitudes.

Blessed are they who recognize samsara for what it is: a poisonous tree of suffering. *Having recognized that its very nature is suffering, they avoid it.*

Blessed are they who see those that give rise to afflictive emotions as spiritual friends. *When they see an enemy, for example, he is a master making them develop patience.*

Blessed are they who correctly view the master who has trained in the three wisdoms. *By seeing the teacher as the Buddha and his instructions as nectar, they will be set on the path to lasting liberation.*

Blessed are they who see everything—outer and inner things and circumstances—as being without origin. *By doing so they will realize the wisdom mind of the Buddha.*

Blessed are they who postpone all activities and set out on the unmistaken path. *In short, if they give up all the activities of this life and put the perfect instructions into practice, the sun of happiness is certain to rise in their minds.*

✦✦ 23 ✦✦

Avoiding the twenty causes of breaking the samaya, the samaya being a distinguishing point between sutra and tantra.

Son, there are twenty things that lead to breaches of samaya.

Apart from in exceptional circumstances, to be *deliberately* secretive about your teacher while extolling your own virtues leads to a breach of samaya.

Unless it is to get rid of or to acquire, to view an erudite scholar and an uneducated person as equals leads to a breach of samaya.

Competition, *with self-seeking and hostile motives,* between patrons and disciples leads to a breach of samaya.

To have the intention of offering *the teacher your wealth, property, and so forth that are yours to dispose of* and to put off doing so leads to a breach of samaya.

Receiving as many teachings as you can possibly hear *without considering whether or not there are conflicts and suchlike in the lineage* leads to a breach of samaya. *An alternative version appears in the* Commentary: *"To receive the teachings unworthily . . ." Any teachings you receive must be with the prior approval of the teacher.*

Using pressure or complaint to insist on getting the instructions *prematurely* leads to a breach of samaya.

Using lies and cunning to deceive your teacher and fellow disciples leads to a breach of samaya.

To put the blame on the master for wrong *that is not your own doing* leads to a breach of samaya.

In a spirit of competition, to treat the master as a rival leads to a breach of samaya.

To abuse the master's confidence, *divulging secrets he has entrusted you with or keeping your own defects secret from the teacher,* leads to a breach of samaya.

To scorn his kindness, *rather than repaying it when you are able,* leads to a breach of samaya.

To be intent on looking after your own interests *by being utterly self-centered, self-seeking, and proud* leads to a breach of samaya.

To steal instructions and books—*writing them down secretly without asking your teacher or fellow disciples or, worse still, obtaining them by actually stealing the texts*—leads to a breach of samaya.

To secretly enumerate the master's faults—*the hidden defects of the teacher and his retinue*—leads to a breach of samaya.

To block another's aspiration, *discouraging someone who has faith,* leads to a breach of samaya.

To make an outer show of the inner practices, *performing the secret activities prematurely,* leads to a breach of samaya.

To be jealous of vajra brothers and sisters—*one's general brothers and sisters and closest vajra siblings*—leads to a breach of samaya.

To act indiscriminately without a teacher or instructions, *practicing just as one pleases without having obtained the teachings or, if you have obtained them, without approval,* leads to a breach of samaya.

To masquerade as a teacher, *giving clever explanations of one's own invention with no aural lineage and without knowing anything oneself,* leads to a breach of samaya.

If the Buddha taught that one should not, with animosity or attachment, look down on even the Tirthikas, this is no less applicable in the case of the others. For this reason, to criticize teachings and those who practice them leads to a breach of samaya.

To exhibit the instructions to unsuitable vessels, *giving the secret teachings literally to those in the lesser vehicles and the like,* leads to a breach of samaya.

Furthermore, having learned the different categories of root and branch samayas that have to be kept, the causes that lead to their degenerating, the disadvantages of their degenerating, and the benefits of keeping them, you should maintain constant diligence with mindfulness and carefulness.

This completes these instructions, which are like a mother who guides and cares for her child. Through them a faithful vessel will be inspired to practice the Dharma and, relying on the superior training in discipline in accordance with the general pitakas, will keep it as the basis of his practice and thereby transform his being.

This was the second section from the *Eighty Chapters of Personal Advice,* the instruction on perfect discipline, the basis.

III. Concentration

The next seventeen chapters comprise the instructions on the superior training of the mind, the perfect means.

·· 24 ··

Showing how the four blessings help one's meditation.

The combination of the teacher's blessings, the student's devotion, and the profundity of the instructions makes experience grow swiftly.

Son, there are four practices that confer blessing.

When you know your mind to be the absolute nature, all objects are liberated in the absolute nature and you will be unaffected by external circumstances. This is the blessing of yourself, as exemplified by the sole of a shoe.

Once all phenomena are recognized as the naturally arisen primal wisdom, they are beyond adventitious conceptual characteristics. This is the blessing of perceptions, as exemplified by a mountain torrent in spate.

With one-pointed concentration, there is no interruption in the flow. This is the blessing of the mind, as exemplified by the middle of a great river.

Like the black jackal, whose eyes see as well by night as by day, one is introduced to the nonduality of perceiver and perceived. This is the blessing of nonduality, as exemplified by a jackal.

Now, by recognizing that appearances are the mind, the mind is empty, emptiness is nondual, and nonduality is self-liberating, one clears away all misconceptions about the outer, inner, secret, and absolute.

However, this alone is not much help if you have not liberated your own mind into the absolute nature, just as ice, despite being water, does not function as water unless you melt it. So it is important to meditate with intense devotion.

Although a yogi currently on the path has truly realized the absolute nature of his mind, he has not yet liberated all phenomena in the absolute nature, and so qualities such as the twelve hundred qualities do not manifestly appear. Nevertheless, through gradual habituation to that realization, all phenomena are liberated or dissolved into the absolute nature, and at that time all the qualities up to the level of ultimate Buddhahood become manifest.

This is why it is taught that while we are ordinary beings, as at present, our realization can both increase and decline. From the attainment of the first level onwards, realization increases but does not decline. On the level of Buddhahood it does neither.

++ 25 ++

Showing, by means of illustrations, how using things as the path helps the meditation.

Son, there are four instructions for using things as the path.
As it is said in the Six Prerequisites for Concentration:

> *On account of material possessions one suffers.*
> *To own nothing is supreme bliss.*
> *By abandoning all its food,*
> *The pelican becomes ever happier.*

Accordingly, make freedom from attachment the path, as exemplified by the pelican carrying fish.

Since afflictive emotions can arise as primal wisdom, make the five poisons the path, as exemplified by the recitation of mantras over poison.

If we recognize the eight consciousnesses as unborn, we cut the root of existence, the notion of a self. Make the unborn nature of the eight consciousnesses the path, as exemplified by cutting a fruit tree at the roots.

As the unborn absolute nature is unaffected by relative phenomena, make the great purity the path, as exemplified by the lotus growing from the mud.

++ 26 ++

Showing by means of illustrations how knowledge helps the meditation.

Son, here are instructions on four things to be known.

All phenomena in samsara and nirvana are devoid of true existence. Know freedom from attachment, as illustrated by the magician.

As phenomena and their nature are not two separate things, know indivisibility, as illustrated by sandalwood or the musk deer.

Since there is no relying on conditioned phenomena with characteristics, know that relatives deceive, as illustrated by being let down by a friend.

Since the absolute nature has been present in you from the beginning, know inseparability, as illustrated by a sesame seed or the flame of a lamp. *When one knows this, the bonds of belief in true existence and dualistic concepts are loosened by themselves, and immaculate wisdom is born in one's mind.*

++ 27 ++

Showing by means of illustrations how the crucial instructions help the meditation.

Son, there are four crucial instructions.

Although the creative power of the empty absolute nature appears multifariously, from the moment phenomena manifest they have no inherent existence: appearance and emptiness are united. You need the crucial instruction that shows how to make a clear-cut decision regarding the unobstructed nature of appearances, as illustrated by a clean silver mirror.

When one is not bound by clinging to what is not two as being two, phenomenal characteristics are freed by themselves. You need the crucial instruction on not being bound by characteristics, as illustrated by a prisoner who has been released.

Although there is not even an atom to meditate upon with regard to the unborn nature of your own mind, do not be distracted for an instant. Be free from mental activity and conceptualization. This is the crucial instruction you need on not being distracted from the unborn nature, as illustrated by shooting an arrow straight at the target.

With the realization of the triple space, do not move from the inseparability of the absolute space and awareness. You need the crucial instruction on resting in one-pointed concentration, as illustrated by an ophthalmic surgeon.

By this means deluded perceptions, being groundless, are cleared away and phenomenal characteristics fall apart by themselves.

✦✦ 28 ✦✦

Personal advice on how to cut conceptual constructs regarding mental and extramental phenomena.

Son, there are four "cuts."

Whatever dualistic thoughts arise, there are none that are anything other than the absolute nature. Cut the stream of the arising of dualistic thoughts and the following after them, taking the example of a tortoise placed on a silver platter.

Whatever appears, nothing has moved from the absolute nature. Decide that nothing is extraneous to the absolute nature, taking the example of gold jewelry.

The whole variety of joys and sorrows is one within the state of awareness. Decide on its indivisibility, taking the example of molasses and its sweet taste.

All of samsara and nirvana arises from the creative display of the spontaneous primal wisdom. Decide that it is naturally manifesting awareness, taking the example of the moon in the sky and its reflection in water.

✦✦ 29 ✦✦

Showing how dealing properly with samsara and nirvana helps the meditation.

Son, there are four views.

The essential nature being union, its display is arrayed as an ornament. View thoughts and appearances as the ornament of the absolute nature, taking the example of a rainbow adorning the sky.

When one knows thoughts to be the absolute nature, attachment and aversion are put to death. View thoughts as the absolute nature, taking the example of tempering and honing a sword.

There are no traces accumulated as habitual tendencies. View thoughts as leaving no trace, taking the example of birds flying in the sky.

Phenomena are freed in the absolute nature. View existence as untrue, taking the example of waking from a dream.

✦ 30 ✦

Explaining the actual method of resting in meditation.

Son, there are four kinds of meditation.

Bringing together everything that favors concentration and mastering the crucial point of how to rest in meditation, diligently meditate with increasing habituation, taking the example of the waxing moon.

This is the view of the Prajñaparamita (the Mother of the Victorious Ones), the sphere of the inexpressible, inconceivable, supreme primal wisdom. Meditate on thoughts and appearances as the inexpressible great bliss, taking the example of having your mouth full of water.

Meditate that fame and the like—*that is, the thoughts of the eight ordinary concerns*—are not ultimately true, taking the example of mist, which does not truly exist.

Meditate on the uncontrived nature as empty, taking the example of water and bubbles; *the nature of the mind is empty like space.*

✦ 31 ✦

Showing how conduct should be endowed with experience and realization.

Son, there are four kinds of conduct.

In your conduct, turn your back on worldly ways: consider the examples of a bride and a madman. *In other words, make sure you are conscientious and considerate of others' opinions, like an anxious newly-wed bride; do not act contrary to the Dharma like a madman who does whatever occurs to him.*

In your conduct, *the multifarious phenomenal perceptions* should not move from the absolute nature: take the example of fish in the ocean.

In your conduct, whatever appears—*the five poisonous emotions and so* forth—should be primal wisdom: take the example of fire raging through a forest.

In your conduct, the many should have the single taste—*phenomena and their nature or appearance and emptiness being inseparable:* take the example of salt dissolving in water.

++ 32 ++

Showing different kinds of experience.

Son, there are four kinds of experience.

The experience of no clinging to thoughts, as illustrated by a small child and a mirror: *although there are perceptions, there is no clinging.*

The experience of wisdom taking birth where it has not previously arisen, as illustrated by a poor woman finding treasure: *experience and realization are newly born.*

The experience of neither apprehension nor esteem, as illustrated by a swallow *entering the nest* and a lion: *one has gained decisive confidence.*

The experience of being unafraid of philosophical views, as illustrated by the lion who is not scared of the fox: *there is no fear of the view and action of lower vehicles.*

++ 33 ++

The signs that arise from experience.

Son, there are four kinds of signs.

When experience and realization bloom within, this is the sign of awareness shining within, as illustrated by a butter lamp inside a vase. *For this there are four ways in which objects of knowledge are freed in their own nature.*

(1) They are self-freeing, like iron cutting iron.

(2) Appearances and the mind being inseparable, they are freed through one single thing, like fire lighting a fire.

(3) By knowing one's own nature, they are freed into the fundamental reality, like space mixing with space.

(4) Appearances are recognized as being manifestations of the mind, like a mother and child meeting.

When there is no effort, this is the sign of the mind not getting involved in the pleasures of the senses, as illustrated by a king seated on his throne.

When one curtails one's plans because there is no time to waste, or decides clearly that all phenomena are unborn, this is the sign of focusing the mind on the unborn nature, as illustrated by a sick person and a cemetery.

The sign of having stamped on the afflictive emotions, as illustrated by the pigeon and the hawk—*the thing to be rejected and the antidote.*

++ 34 ++

Showing that without experience and realization one is powerless not to be reborn in samsara.

Son, there are four instructions related to optical illusions, *with examples of being fooled by illusions.*

As in the example of perceiving a mirage as water, *believing there is something when there is nothing,* if you do not know that the pleasures of the senses are a delusion, you will wander.

As in the example of perceiving a rope as a snake, *thinking it is, even though it is not,* if you do not know that you are being fooled, you will wander.

As in the example of the parrot eating poison *(and, by thus imitating the peacock, causing its own death),* if you behave as if you have attained realization even though you have not and you cling to things thinking that they truly exist, you will wander.

Believing in existence where there is no existence, one is helplessly confused by attachment and aversion. As in the example of the child and the empty fist *tricking it into thinking it contains a treat,* if you are fooled by your perceptions, you will wander in samsara.

++ 35 ++

Son, there are ten ways of failing the Buddhas *in one's commitment, which must accord with one's level.*

The way to avoid failing in your commitment is to take the Buddhas of the three times as your witnesses; for the fault in breaking a promise knows no bounds, whereas if you do not break it, inconceivable good qualities will be yours: you will become the foremost child of all the Buddhas of the past, present, and future. Therefore, within each six-hour period of the day take a reckoning, and if you have broken your promise, make your confession and renew the promise with a firm vow.

Recognizing that all happiness and suffering is the manifestation of your own previous actions, even if the whole world rises up in enmity against you, do not stray from the absolute nature. If you do, you will be betraying the Buddhas of the three times.

Constantly supported by mindfulness and vigilance, whatever you do, do not wander from the continuum of the unborn absolute nature. If you do, you will be betraying the Buddhas of the three times.

Whatever happens to you, apply the antidote, refresh yourself with faith, assimilate the instructions, be unhypocritical in discipline, and have confidence in the law of actions and their results. By these means, even if your life is at stake, never lose sight of the Dharma. If you do, you will be betraying the Buddhas of the three times.

Keeping in mind the related benefits and risks, and remembering kindness, do not spoil even an atom's worth of your samaya with the sublime teacher. If you do, you will be betraying the Buddhas of the three times.

Remembering death and reflecting on the defects of samsara, rather than now accomplishing fame *and other goals related to the eight ordinary concerns* in this life, put all your efforts into the task of training in the mind *turned toward enlightenment.* If you involve yourself in the affairs of this life and are not diligent in the mind training, you will be betraying the Buddhas of the three times.

As it is said in all the sutras and tantras, see the noble teachers as Vajrasattva in person and have devotion. If you do not, you will be betraying the Buddhas of the three times.

Recognizing that everything that appears is the mind, that the mind itself is empty, and that the inseparable union of clarity and emptiness is primal wisdom, know that everything outside and inside is the mind, and do not have attachment or aversion. If you do, you will be betraying the Buddhas of the three times.

Acknowledging beings as your mothers, remembering their kindness, and wishing to repay that kindness, cultivate great compassion and work for the sake of sentient beings. If you *depart from bodhichitta and* strive for your own sake alone, you will be betraying the Buddhas of the three times.

All dualistic concepts *on account of clinging to everything outside and inside as truly existing* are the work of demons, so know that there is no duality of subject and object. If you fail to do so, you will be betraying the Buddhas of the three times.

With this body as a support, be careful—*that is, maintain mindfulness in the four kinds of conduct, guarding the body and so forth*—as you seek the fruit of Buddhahood. If you fail to do so, you will be betraying the Buddhas of the three times.

++ 36 ++

Using instructions to meditate without distraction.

Son, there are four ways not to be distracted.

Master the crucial point of the methods for settling in concentration, following the examples given in the Six Prerequisites for Concentration.

Do not be distracted from the expanse of the mind free of grasping, like a straight arrow.

Without any mental grasping at the unborn nature, do not be distracted from the absolute space, which is free from thoughts, like a *champion* athlete *or like a painter of sacred art mixing his colors.*

As no phenomena are extraneous to the absolute nature, do not be distracted from *their being indivisible, or from* the expanse of evenness, like a hooked fish.

With the view free from extreme beliefs and your meditation free from intellectual fabrication, do not be distracted from the state beyond all thought, as if you were removing a thorn.

++ 37 ++

Meditation using the instructions on the method of "resting."

Son, there are four instructions on the method.

To let go of the subject inside that apprehends the objects of the six consciousnesses there is the instruction on the state of mind devoid of all ordinary perception and thought, like a dry skull.

Now for the actual instruction on the method of "resting," which is sixfold:

(1) Leave things effortlessly in the expanse free from references.

(2) Leave everything without contrivance in the uncompounded absolute space.

(3) Though everything arises in your own mind, leave it without any notion of "I" or self.

(4) Leave everything without conceptualization in the uncontrived expanse.

(5) Leave things just as they are in the expanse free of subject and object.

(6) Leave things in the ineffable unborn expanse.

The instruction on the mind that, watching, sees nothing, like someone who has eaten poison.

The example is that of the falling lines that appear to the eyes of someone who has eaten a poisonous plant. Its meaning is that by recognizing that the apparent objects of the six consciousnesses are devoid of reality one reverses the belief in true existence.

The actual instruction concerns the primordial unborn nature and comprises six points:

(1) The absolute nature is primordially unstained by clinging.

(2) The realization is naturally free from craving.

(3) The way of arising is spontaneous and free from grasping.

(4) The experience is naturally present and not something that is made.

(5) The natural state is unborn and devoid of self.

(6) The display arises spontaneously and is not something to be sought.

For outer appearances not to be spoiled by inner clinging, there is the instruction on the mind free from judgments, like an infant.

The actual instruction:

(1) The absolute nature is the uncontrived mind.

(2) The view is the mind without thoughts.

(3) The primal wisdom is the mind without concepts.

(4) The meditation is the undistracted mind.

(5) The essential nature of the mind is unwavering.

(6) The samaya of the mind is the knowledge that nothing transcends the mind.

(7) The activity of the mind is not to give up.

The instruction on leaving the mind as it is, as if stunned, like someone whose heart has been removed. *The example is that of someone whose heart has been taken out: there is no hope of revival and the continuous stream of thoughts is cut. The instruction on "leaving as it is, as if stunned" is that by leaving everything as it is in the uncontrived natural state—without a subject that leaves, without an owner, as if stunned—one will settle at ease, free of grasping and effort, in the arising of the multifarious phenomena. In this natural state of the inseparability of the two truths, leave things in uncontrived simplicity, a state of clear, empty awareness that is not produced by effort through different causes and conditions.*

✦✦ 38 ✦✦

The instruction on how to rest in the natural flow.

Son, there are four ways to stay.

Stay without thought in the clarity that is not acquired and can *never be lost, for the Buddha's wisdom has been present within you from the very beginning.*

Stay without thinking in the bliss that is not to be evoked and cannot slip away, *for the mind from the very beginning is not caught and is not fettered.*

Stay in vivid clarity, undistracted in the state beyond distraction, *for distracting objects have never been extraneous to the absolute nature.*

How does one stay like that? There are six ways to be without contrivance:

(1) If you look for mind, it is empty.
(2) Block it and you will spoil it.
(3) Contrive it and you will adulterate it.
(4) Meditate and you will be bound.
(5) Look at it and it will disappear.
(6) Effort will obscure it.

Therefore, do not seek, do not block, do not contrive, do not meditate, do not look, do not make effort: leave it just as it naturally is.

There being nothing in the mind for it to act on, nor anything to do through the path of action, nor anything that is accomplished, remain unhurried, with nothing to do, perfectly poised, *the practice neither overtaut nor slack, like the string of a bent bow.*

++ 39 ++

Unobstructed natural arising, the crucial point of the mind.

Son, there are six crucial points of the mind to be understood.

Awareness, the fourth moment beyond the three—that directly experienced, uncontrived state that is not adulterated by the notions of subject and object—is the simplicity of the dharmakaya. So recognize the mind with this instruction—the natural dissolution of concepts: relaxation is the crucial point of the mind, exemplified by someone who has completed a task.

Being free from the clinging to the true existence of things, one has no concerns, thinking of things as good or bad: freedom from concern is the crucial point of the mind, exemplified by someone who has recovered from an illness.

As there is not a single thing that has not been pure and perfect since the very beginning, be free of the dualistic fixation of blocking some things and encouraging others. Freedom from hesitation is the crucial point of the mind, exemplified by a madman jumping off a cliff.

Everything that appears is liberated as primal wisdom, so the view is free from duality, the meditation is free from fixation, the action is free from effort, and the result is free from aspiration. Freedom from expectation and apprehension is the crucial point of the mind, exemplified by one's *having* met a person *one had been looking* for.

Uttering the specific language of Ati overawes those in the lesser vehicles. Freedom from fear is the crucial point of the mind, exemplified by a lion walking among other savage beasts.

The natural state is naturally radiant; no veils obscure it. Clarity with absence of thoughts is the crucial point of the mind, exemplified by the flame of a lamp filled with sesame oil.

++ 40 ++

Showing that the view, meditation, action, and result are innate and not extraneous.

Son, there are four things you need not seek.
Since the wisdom of the absolute nature free of intellect dwells in you

innately, there is no need to look for it anew using one-sided views that are the product of the intellect. Having the view that has no dualistic fixation, do not seek one that has; take the example of the sun: it does not have to look for its rays.

Regarding the uncontrived natural flow, there is no need to meditate on it with dualistic fixation as if it were something new for you. Having the meditation that has no object on which to focus, do not seek one that has; take the example of a wish-fulfilling gem: it does not have to look for the things one wants.

Since things to be rejected and antidotes—afflictive emotions and primal wisdom, for instance—have the same taste, there is no duality of deed and doer. Having the action free of adoption and rejection, do not seek one to adopt and reject; take the example of a person: he does not have to look for himself.

The result, the primordial state of Buddhahood, dwells within you. Having the result free of hope and fear, do not look for one with hope and fear; take the example of a monarch: he does not have to reassert his royalty—*a king presiding on his throne depends on no one else.*

Thus, since all phenomena in samsara and nirvana are by nature inseparable, do not move from the evenness of the absolute nature that is beyond hope and fear, concept and effort.

These chapters on the superior training of the mind have been arranged in a different order in the Commentary *as follows. After the thirtieth chapter come Chapters Thirty-six to Thirty-nine, at which point one jumps to Chapter Seventy-seven in the section on the training in wisdom. Next, one returns to Chapters Thirty-one to Thirty-five, followed by Chapter Forty. Here, however, I have followed the exact order of the root text.*

To sum up, I have used these chapters to give an explanation to suit readers' individual capacities, so that relying on the superior training in concentration according to the Prajñaparamita, *the* Epitome, *and the* Magical Display, *they practice the view and meditation on the path in much the same way as one brings up a small child—in stages—combining skillful means and wisdom like a bird flying in the sky. This completes the instruction.*

This was the third section from the *Eighty Chapters of Personal Advice,* the instruction on one-pointed concentration, the means.

IV. Wisdom

The following thirty-eight chapters contain the instructions on the superior training of wisdom, the perfect essence.

✦✦ 41 ✦✦

Twelve points that explain the view.

The realization referred to in the Later Mind Section is like a slash with a very sharp blade: with the wisdom devoid of the three concepts, all afflictive emotions and discursive thoughts are severed at the root. The way this happens is that since all phenomena of the ground, path, and result— samsara and nirvana—arise as the play of one's own unborn mind, they are free from ontological extremes, from good and bad, like space. The mind is by nature unborn, its display is unobstructed, its essential characteristic is absence of duality, and so on. In introducing this, the All-Accomplishing King *states,*

> Because all things are subsumed in the root, the mind,
> It is the root that has to be taught.

Son, there are twelve points.

The unborn ultimate nature of your own mind is not concealed anywhere *and yet* nobody can see it *as a concrete object with characteristics.*

Though it has never stopped being *yours* since the very beginning, hitherto you have *not recognized it* as your nature.

Since nothing exists as such inherently, when things are examined nothing is seen. *However, when unexamined, they seem to exist: thus all the phenomena of samsara and nirvana* appear in every possible way, unobstructedly.

Though in fact there is nothing, deluded appearances appear in all their variety, but *since they do not intrinsically exist in any way,* there is nothing real.

Though you have wandered for kalpas *in existence,* you have never lost or been parted *from the buddha nature, sugatagarbha.*

Though *the ultimate nature* appears *in* a variety of ways *as samsara and nirvana,* there has *never* been any change *in what it is.*

Without having *as much as* a part of the *minutest* atom *of solid existence,* it pervades everything *like space.*

Within emptiness, *which is like space,* the various *phenomena that arise through the interdependent process of cause and effect* appear *unobstructedly.*

The mind is like an unbroken horse: if you are tense and agitated, you cannot control it; if you relax, you can control it. Therefore, when it is not held or tied, it stays wherever it is.

By uniting sustained calm and profound insight, one travels through the space *of the absolute nature* unsupported, *like a soaring garuda.*

From the absolute nature that is not anything, anything can arise, so everything possible is accomplished without effort.

Without *the mind having color, shape,* form, or characteristics, whichever way one views it *and meditates on it, in that way* it appears.

To sum up, this is an introduction to the nature of the mind. As it is unborn, there is no real basis to it. As its display is unobstructed, it arises in various ways. As it is ultimately free of duality, there is nothing to cling to as true. When the conceptual mind is liberated in its essence, nothing ever moves from the dharmata.

♦♦ 42 ♦♦

Twelve kinds of confidence confirming the view.

From having seen the ultimate truth in its full nakedness, the mind is free of doubt.

Son, there are twelve kinds of confidence:

The confidence that *just as* the whole of existence *is created and destroyed* in space, *everything in samsara and nirvana* is one and the same *in thatness* and therefore has no intrinsic nature.

The confidence that since the root *of all things* is subsumed in the mind, Buddhahood is not *to be sought* elsewhere.

The confidence that since the mind *by nature* has no birth *and no cessation*, it is uncompounded.

The confidence that since everything that appears is delusory, in truth enemies and friends do not exist *inherently as different entities.*

The confidence that since all actions *based on delusion* are suffering— *that is, they are the cause of suffering*—in truth, *in terms of the ultimate nature*, there is nothing to be done.

The confidence that since *the unborn absolute space* is the nature of all *phenomena, the nature* is nondual.

The confidence that there is no traveling *the path*, for realizing *the unborn nature of your mind* is Buddhahood.

The confidence that the mind cannot be troubled by attachment and aversion, for everything that appears is untrue *like a magical illusion.*

The confidence that *although mind and appearances are many, they have one taste, and that therefore the thoughts related to the five poisons such as* attachment and aversion are *intrinsically* unborn.

The confidence that objects *such as friends and enemies* that arouse *afflictive emotions, apart from simply being labels assigned by the ordinary mind, do not have any essential existence of their own; they* all dissolve in the mind.

The confidence that as *the nature of mind* is the source of everything *in samsara and nirvana*, it is the Absolute Space—the Mother.

The confidence that *the natural state of the mind* is the great immensity, *for, like space,* it is the place where everything dwells.

++ 43 ++

An instruction on seeing the absolute nature in nine ways.

Son, there are nine things *that, as a yogi on the path*, one sees.
One sees that everything *in samsara and nirvana* is empty.
One sees that the root *of all phenomena* is the mind.
One sees that the nature *of one's own mind* is unborn.
One sees that *since the seventeen kinds of perception and so forth are unobstructed in the way they arise*, one's situation is unpredictable.
One sees that the nature *of all phenomena* is devoid of true existence.
One sees that *despite the multifariousness of appearances and perceptions*, the natural state *of the absolute space* does not change.

One sees that *since it is spontaneously arisen and free of causes and conditions,* the way-it-is is devoid of duality.

One sees that *while it displays multifariously because of conditions,* the ground nature itself does not tend toward any particular direction.

One sees that the fundamental nature is devoid of concepts, *for there are no thoughts of ontological extremes.*

++ 44 ++

Seeing seven aspects of sublimity.

The meditator is free, for his mind has no owner and no responsibility. Son, there are seven sublime things.

To be free from intellectual meditation is the sublime "leaving things as they are": *Do not try to fixate on existence and nonexistence, appearance and emptiness, and so on.*

To be free of *the ordinary mind's dualistic* references *with regard to the absolute nature, which is beyond all reference,* is the sublime reference.

Neither thought nor no-thought transcends the intellect, and intellectual activity obscures freedom from intellect; thus, not to meditate on absence of thoughts is the sublime absence of thought.

Not to use any *object of knowledge* as a support is the sublime support.

Not to meditate on anything, *such as the union of appearances and emptiness, making it a mental object,* is the sublime meditation.

To remain undistracted, with no *deliberate* attempt to stop the movements *of the mind and mental factors,* is the sublime concentration.

When the mind is not involved with any *of the objects of the eight consciousnesses,* this is the sublime absorption.

In short, all these amount to leaving things as they are, unadulterated by dualistic fixation and contrivance.

++ 45 ++

An instruction on perceiving in a nondualistic way but without denying the six sense organs being distinct and different.

Son, there are six wisdom sense organs *that arise from certainty concerning the absolute nature.*

When one knows that perceived forms are unborn, one does not grasp at them, and therefore one sees the forms of mind's projection with the wisdom eye.

One understands the meaning of emptiness—*the absolute nature*—with the wisdom ear.

One senses *the nature* as unborn with the wisdom nose.

One tastes *multifariousness* in a nondualistic way with the wisdom tongue.

One touches *the truth,* the absolute nature, with the wisdom body.

One knows that all that arises as the mind's projection arises in the *unborn* nature of the mind with the wisdom mind.

⁕⁕ 46 ⁕⁕

Using the above modes of perception to perceive in a nondualistic way without denying things being distinct and different.

If your own mind is free in the absolute nature, everything that appears outside arises as the absolute nature.

Son, there are six wisdom objects.

The absolute nature seen as clarity and emptiness inseparable is the wisdom form.

Sound understood as spontaneously arisen, *like the voice heard in an echo that does not belong to anyone,* is the wisdom sound.

The *teacher's* instruction imbibed to satiety is the wisdom fragrance.

The experience of *all phenomena* as unborn is the wisdom flavor.

The great bliss—*the absolute nature*—touched is the wisdom texture.

The recognition *of the natural state, the dharmata,* is the wisdom phenomenon.

⁕⁕ 47 ⁕⁕

Upon investigation, things are seen to be nonexistent in six ways.

Son, there are six authentic experiences.

Since all phenomena have no true existence as such, to not see them at all is authentic sight.

Since there is no duality of a hearer and something to be heard regarding the absolute nature, to not hear anything is authentic hearing.

There being in fact no duality of someone who senses and something to be sensed, to not sense anything is the authentic perception (of smell).

Similarly, to not taste anything is the authentic taste.

Not mentally touching anything, *true or false or whatever,* is the authentic contact.

Not being aware of any *characteristics in the whole of phenomena* is the authentic awareness.

•• 48 ••

Explaining six kinds of effortlessness, there being nothing in the absolute nature to adopt or reject.

If one knows how to leave all phenomena without deliberate action, one is liberated in the basic natural state:
Son, there are six declarations on effortlessness.

Because in the space of one's unborn mind there is not the duality of a viewer and something to be viewed, one settles in the view *without contrivance or modification, affirmation or negation, and one's mind remains* in total rest without any concept of vastness or constraint.

The meditation is the utter peace *of the absolute nature,* radiance from the depth, *free of grasping and devoid of rough edges—thoughts related to outer and inner phenomena.*

The action, *uncontrived and natural,* is joyful spontaneity, without *the effort of* adoption *or abstention.*

Since the mode of being of things is actualized, there is no hope *of achieving* the result or fear *of not achieving it;* there is all-pervading peace: *dualistic concepts of subject and object dissolve by themselves.*

It is the universal evenness *in the continuum of the absolute nature: things are* beyond all distinctions of quality or magnitude.

It is the utmost ease where the mind has no sorrow, *for samsara, without being rejected, is primordially free, beyond suffering.*

++ 49 ++

An instruction on sixteen metaphoric practices.

Son, there are sixteen metaphoric practices.

Always strip *the awareness* naked *so that it is unobscured by characteristics.*

Always perform the great ablution *of emptiness as the antidote for the belief in substantial existence and for clinging to true existence.*

Take the sun and the moon—*emptiness and compassion*—in your hand.

Whirl the wheel *of view and meditation.*

Gaze in the *magical* mirror *of your mind.*

Cure the sickness caused by the poison *of the afflictive emotions.*

Untie the rope binding you—*that of the three poisons or of subject and object.*

Flee *the company of evildoers: they are like* savage beasts of prey.

Having recognized the spontaneously arisen primal wisdom, reside in the crystal vase *of awareness—emptiness and clarity inseparable.*

Climb the jewel stairs *from the bottom to the top, practicing the ten Dharma activities and so on with faith, diligence, mindfulness, vigilance, and carefulness.*

Cut the tree *of belief in a self* at the root.

Sleep in the openness of space, *uncircumscribed awareness.*

Let your own thought-movements commit suicide.

Hasten to the golden isle *where everything that appears and is perceived arises as the absolute nature.*

Anoint your body with the balm *of concentration to allay the fever of desire and hatred.*

Pick sky flowers: *in truth they do not exist; phenomena are but names.*

++ 50 ++

There being nothing to adopt or reject, the view is free of affirmation or negation.

Son, there are five views.

All thoughts that arise are the unborn absolute nature, so do not get angry at thoughts. *The primal wisdom of no-thought is not to be meditated on separately.*

Primal wisdom or dharmata is not to be sought on some far shore rid of afflictive emotions and thoughts, so do not be attached to the absolute nature. *As long as you have attachment you create the cause for wandering in samsara.*

Knowing all phenomena to be equal, do not be proud of *your* concentration.

Everything unwanted and all wrong thoughts are a display of your own mind, so do not be resentful of anything wrong.

Since you yourself possess the spontaneously arisen primal wisdom, do not be confused with regard to wisdom. *Recognize it.*

••• 51 •••

Explaining ten aspects of complete confidence in the natural state.

Since all the dualistic perceptions of happiness, suffering, and so forth are freed in the absolute space, one cannot be benefited or harmed by anything:
Son, there are ten aspects to complete confidence.

The self-arisen primal wisdom or bodhichitta has no cause or conditions and is therefore unchanging in the past, present, and future.

Everything possible may pour down like rain *but bodhichitta, the kingly doer-of-all, will never get wet or stained.*

Similarly, the three worlds may overflow like a river, *but it will not be carried away.*

Even though the six mental states may blaze like fire, *it will not be consumed.*

The one thousand million worlds may be buffeted as if by the wind, *but it will remain unmoved.*

The three poisons may gather like darkness, *but it will not grope in confusion.*

The thousand million worlds may be filled by the sun, *but this will never illuminate the primal wisdom.*

Whole continents may be plunged into darkness, *but it can never be eclipsed by ignorance.*

Birth and death may be distinct, *but it cannot die.*

One may have karmic tendencies, *but from the very beginning the nature has never been affected, so there is nothing to discard now.*

Phenomenal existence may be turned upside down, *but the nature will not be destroyed or separated.*

These are the vajra words on the wisdom—the total confidence and conviction— that cannot be crushed by anything.

++ 52 ++

An instruction that matches examples and their meanings to show how the absolute nature permeates everything.

Son, there are four examples and their meanings.

Take the example of a Sugata's body: whichever way one looks at it, it is beautiful. *Similarly,* everything *a realized being* does, since it is permeated with the *realization of the* unborn nature, is bliss, *for he does not have ordinary attachment and aversion.*

Take the example of a smile and a scowl: two expressions but no more than *one* face. *Similarly,* everything that appears, everything that exists— *all the manifestation of samsara or nirvana*—does so within the unborn absolute nature.

Take the example of a blind person: it makes no difference whether one smiles at him or not. *Similarly, since everything that arises unobstructedly from the unborn absolute space is inseparable from it and has the same taste,* in the absolute nature there is nothing to be adopted or rejected.

Take the example of the trunk of a plantain tree: it has no core. *Similarly,* phenomenal existence has no essence, *for when examined using such logical arguments as "Neither one nor many," there is nothing to be found.*

++ 53 ++

When the four ontological extremes dissolve by themselves, it is shown that phenomena are the mind's projections and do not have to be abandoned.

Son, there are four dissolutions of extremes.

As regards all the phenomena of samsara and nirvana, in the absolute truth they are unborn, so they are beyond the extreme of existence.

In relative truth, *the appearance aspect that is the interdependent gathering of causes and conditions,* they are unceasing, so they are beyond the extreme of nonexistence.

Ultimately, the two truths, or appearance and emptiness, do not exist as distinct phenomena: *there is no basis for such distinctions, they are inseparable—in other words,* they are not two, so they are beyond the extreme of both existence and nonexistence.

Intellectually apprehended, "neither" arises as "both," so phenomena are beyond the extreme of neither existence nor nonexistence.

Regarding this there are four faults that occur if one asserts that the two truths are one and the same:

(1) it would follow that ordinary beings who see compounded phenomena could see the absolute truth;

(2) it would follow that the absolute truth could be an objective condition for afflictive emotions arising;

(3) it would follow that there was no distinction between relative and absolute; and

(4) it would follow that the absolute truth would not depend on listening to the teachings and reflecting on them.

And there are four faults that occur if one asserts that they are different, for it would then follow that:

(1) the mind that had realized the absolute could not dispel the belief that relative phenomena truly exist;

(2) absolute truth would not be the ultimate nature of relative phenomena;

(3) the absence of intrinsic existence in relative phenomena would not be the absolute truth; and

(4) sublime beings would see them separately and would be bound and liberated at one and the same time.

In our tradition there are none of these faults because we make no assertions at all about the two truths being either single or different. We establish two truths in relation to the conditions, deluded or nondeluded, of a single mind: in the deluded state the absolute truth does not appear to the relative, deluded mind, while in the nondeluded state the delusory relative does not appear to the mind that has realized the absolute truth. Thus the two truths are like light and darkness. On the one hand, they have one and the same nature but different aspects; on the other hand, their differences disallow their being one and the same. Both of these are explained in the Commentary.

✦✦ 54 ✦✦

Four ultimate aspects that decisively establish the ultimate path.

Son, there are four ultimates.

Having recognized all outer and inner phenomena to be your own mind, *like the things that appear in a dream,* to know that the mind is empty and immaterial is the ultimate reach of the view.

As exemplified by a person in a magical illusion, while not blocking the five senses, to be free from notions of subject and object is the ultimate reach of meditation.

As exemplified by the accumulation of merit and wisdom by a great emanation, to know how to act uniting view and action is the ultimate reach of action.

As exemplified by an illusory being enjoying riches in a dream, to be free of the belief that there is any truth in phenomenal existence is the ultimate reach of experience and realization.

✦✦ 55 ✦✦

An instruction on the five dharmakaya aspects of the mind, with illustrations.

Son, there are five dharmakaya aspects of the mind, *the unobstructed, all-pervading primal wisdom or absolute nature, emptiness and clarity inseparable.*

The unmoving dharmakaya, *the absence of movement in the absolute nature, the naked state of awareness and emptiness inseparable,* illustrated by the oceanic deep.

The unchanging dharmakaya, *the absolute nature in which there is no change,* illustrated by Mount Meru.

The uninterrupted dharmakaya, *the continuous state of the absolute nature or radiant clarity,* illustrated by a great river.

The undimming dharmakaya, *the primal wisdom that neither grows brighter nor grows dimmer,* illustrated by the sun.

The thought-free dharmakaya, *clear awareness devoid of thought,* illustrated by the reflection of the moon in water.

✦✦ 56 ✦✦

An instruction using the symbolic language of the secret mantras.

Son, there are six primal wisdoms related to the mind.

The fresh nature, unadulterated *by thoughts, is* free of the duality *of subject and object; it* is the wisdom of coalescence.

The mind neither reaching out *toward the object* nor withdrawing, there is the wisdom of one taste *with regard to the manifold perceptions and thoughts.*

With no adoption or rejection *with regard to anything in samsara and nirvana,* there is the wisdom with no hope or fear.

Putting the seal *of the unborn absolute nature* on the perceptions *of the multifarious phenomena,* there is the spontaneously arisen wisdom.

The nature of mind beyond all ontological extremes, the union of appearances and emptiness, of awareness and emptiness, is the wisdom of union.

The eight consciousnesses and their objects having been empty from the very beginning, there is outer emptiness and inner emptiness: this is the wisdom of emptiness.

✦✦ 57 ✦✦

Introducing the nature of the mind.

Son, there are seven ways in which the nature of the mind is introduced.

The Great Space *says:*

Its nature is not definitely any one thing:
Whichever way one looks at it, in that way it appears.

Even a single object, on account of one's own mind, appears in various ways. For this reason, the outer object is devoid of intrinsic existence, and thus, the object is introduced as being the mind's projection.

The multifarious manifesting aspects of one's own mind arise unobstructedly like reflections: their nature is never anything other than emptiness. Thus, the mind's projection is introduced as a reflection.

The appearances of spontaneously arisen primal wisdom arise without bias, and thus, appearances are introduced as infinite.

By means of the pith instruction of the triple space, the consciousness is introduced as being without support.

By realizing the nature of one's own mind, awareness is introduced as being self-cognizing.

The objects that appear to the eight consciousnesses have never in fact come into existence, so the object is introduced as being unborn.

The ultimate unborn nature is devoid of dualistic characteristics, so the unborn is introduced as being free of conceptual constructions.

⁕⁕ 58 ⁕⁕

Placing a seal by introducing the ultimate nature of things that appear.

Son, there are six ways of introducing the ultimate nature of everything that arises, *everything being one in the absolute nature so that there is nothing to be adopted or rejected.*

From the creativity of the nature of one's own mind the seventeen kinds of perceptions and appearances—the six kinds of perceptions of the beings in the six realms, the two Tirthika views of eternalism and nihilism, and the nine different viewpoints of the nine vehicles—arise indeterminately, so do not value existence *by considering anything to be truly existent.*

Everything is the play of the absolute nature, so since you perceive things, good and bad, do not prize nonexistence.

Since phenomena do not fall into ontological extremes, do not reconcile them in *a conceptual* inseparability.

Do not differentiate things *as good or bad.*

Do not conceive of anything *as existent, nonexistent, or whatever by intellectual analysis.*

Do not be distracted from the radiant deep—*ultimate reality.*

⁕⁕ 59 ⁕⁕

Introducing the ultimate nature of things that appear.

Son, there are eight introductions.

The mind is perfectly clear, *like space, uncompounded awareness.*

The movements *of thoughts* subside by themselves *like ripples subsiding back into the water.*

Thoughts are levelled instantly, *the protuberance-like thoughts born from circumstances subsiding naturally the moment they arise.*

Awareness is naturally pure, *for it is unobscured by the eight consciousnesses.*

It is not perceptible, *for there is nothing that one can grasp with certainty and say, "This is it."*

The object is naturally empty, *because what appears has no intrinsic existence.*

Like a dream, it is there but it does not exist.

Like the moon reflected in water, it does not exist and yet it is there.

✦✦ 60 ✦✦

Nine sayings introducing the unborn nature of things that appear.

Phenomena lack true origin, they are deceptive appearances: without considering them to be real, without clinging to their existence,
Son, the unborn nature is introduced in nine ways.

All phenomena that arise interdependently, when investigated with reasoning directed at their ultimate status, have no inherent birth, so what is born is unborn, *like the horses and oxen in a magical illusion.*

What *is uncompounded and* has not been born *through causes and conditions* is unborn, *like space.*

Compounded phenomena do not exist as such, so what will never be born is unborn, *like the son of a barren woman.*

Forms and suchlike have no intrinsic existence, so what appears is unborn, *like a dream.*

There is nothing that can produce emptiness, so emptiness is unborn, *like the horn of a rabbit.*

Since it cannot be grasped with certainty—one cannot say, "This is it"— awareness is unborn, *like the eight consciousnesses of a person in an illusion.*

Since the unborn—or emptiness—is not one-sided, it has the potential to appear in every possible way: the unborn appears, *like an optical illusion.*

Since it is beyond intellectual investigation and has been unborn from the very beginning, the unborn is primordially nonexistent, *like space, which has always been so.*

The unborn is not affected by the concepts of the eight extremes— existence, nonexistence, and so forth—just as one cannot say, "Space is this (or that)," so the unborn is free from extremes.

✦✦ 61 ✦✦

An instruction with four similes introducing the ultimate nature of things that appear.

Son, there are four similes, *conventional examples used to signify* the absolute nature.

All phenomena arise from the state of inseparability of mind's triple space; there they dwell and into it they dissolve; they have never moved from it. So all intellectual assertions of tenets such as "they exist" or "they do not exist" are reduced to nothing. Therefore, taking the example of a mountain, *which is unmoved by circumstances,* stamp your being with the view free from assertions.

Since there is neither meditation nor anything to be meditated upon, there is no intentional movement: taking the example of a king seated on his throne, stamp your being with the meditation free of effort.

Everything is the play of the absolute nature, and no phenomena are excluded, so taking the example of someone who has arrived on a golden island, stamp your being with the action free from dualistic perception, *where there is nothing to adopt and nothing to abandon.*

In the absolute nature, the basic way of being, which is naked and all-penetrating, freedom and nonfreedom are meaningless: there is no other result to be sought. Taking the example of a knot in a snake, stamp your being with the sole result in which there is freedom from hope and fear.

✦✦ 62 ✦✦

Five instructions on the ultimate nature of appearances.

Son, there are five instructions.

Ultimately, objects of knowledge, subject and object, are not born from causes and conditions; they do not depend on anything else; they are not the product of alteration; they are intrinsically unborn from the very beginning. Therefore, know that form and consciousness are unborn.

Without clinging, be aware of what you perceive, *the objects of the eight consciousnesses.*

Remain without being distracted by the eight *ordinary* concerns— *praise, criticism, and so forth.*

With the view able to stand up to circumstances, the meditation immune to distraction, the action resistant to going off course, and with confidence in the result, remain without the consciousness being carried away by circumstances.

Seal the mind *with the realization that your own mind is unborn.*

•• 63 ••

The view of the one absolute nature without distinct aspects.

Son, there are five experiences of wisdom *that indicate that one has gone to the heart of the view and meditation.*

The Six Points of Meditation *states,*

> *Whatever dualistic thoughts may arise,*
> *If you recognize that very thought as the absolute nature,*
> *There is no need to meditate on any other dharmadhatu.*

Accordingly, thoughts are the absolute nature, *they dissolve in the absolute nature devoid of dualistic thoughts of subject and object.*

All the characteristics *of both samsara and nirvana* are freed by themselves *in the nondual expanse of evenness.*

Looking directly confirms *the recognition of the absolute nature in all perceptions, like meeting an old acquaintance.*

Deluded clinging *to friends, enemies, and so forth* stops by itself.

The duality *of blocking impure perceptions and developing pure perceptions* vanishes by itself.

•• 64 ••

A brief explanation of the way in which the indivisible absolute nature arises.

Son, there are four ways in which the nondual absolute nature arises.

In the absolute nature, *the fundamental view of evenness,* there is no good or bad; this is the all-penetrating primal wisdom.

By dwelling naturally without seeking anything—*which is the meditation of the all-penetrating wisdom*—one remains in the state without conceptual constructs.

Not adulterating or fabricating—*which is the spontaneous action*—is the great impartiality.

The result of actualizing the absolute nature is that, as the ultimate nature of the mind arises spontaneously, primal wisdom unfolds in the expanse.

++ 65 ++

Six ways in which the indivisible absolute nature arises.

Son, there are six ways in which the nondual absolute nature arises.

Since *the nature of mind, which is spontaneously arisen primal wisdom,* arises in the state free of contrivance from the very beginning, it is fresh.

Since everything is complete within the mind, it is spontaneous.

Since there is no blocking or encouraging, it is great primal wisdom.

Since there is no *dualistic* division into samsara and nirvana, *good and bad,* it is the nondual vajra.

Since mind is Buddha from the very beginning *without depending on causes and conditions,* it is the self-born vajra.

Since it is not caught by enemies *or by good or bad circumstances,* it is the great evenness.

++ 66 ++

Four ways in which indivisible absolute nature arises.

Son, there are four ways of arising without duality.

With the mind's concepts of past, present, and future severed, and the mind left in the natural flow, it is clear and uncontrived, the natural radiance devoid of thoughts, *like an immaculate crystal.*

Without any concepts whatsoever, it is the mirror of awareness, *like an untarnished mirror.*

It is the *realization of the radiant primal wisdom,* self-cognizing awareness, *like* a wishing-gem *that naturally produces everything one could desire.*

In the spontaneously arisen primal wisdom, there is no "other-elimination," so everything arising by itself, it is the unpremeditated wisdom.

++ 67 ++

Some instructions on the indivisible absolute nature.

Son, there are four instructions.

The absolute nature has no bias, so in completely pervading all ten directions it is the great pervasion.

Since it is without an outer gate and inner sanctum—*or periphery and center*—it is the bodhichitta free of partiality.

As anything arises *from that bodhichitta,* it is the great unpredictability.

Since it is neither lit nor dimmed *by circumstances, the absolute nature* is the *perfectly* pure enlightened state.

++ 68 ++

An instruction on seeing the unborn absolute nature by means of eight kinds of natural dissolution.

Son, there are eight kinds of natural dissolution.

When one knows that the objects that appear have no true existence, one's belief in true existence naturally dissolves: the moment one rests with the mind undeluded in the direct perception of the absolute nature, everything that arises as the object of the six consciousnesses is ascertained as being appearance and emptiness inseparable, like a magical illusion or a dream. Thus,

Forms seen by the eye—*whether beautiful or ugly*—dissolve as they are seen. *How does this happen?* They dissolve in the sphere of the unborn, *which is the intrinsic nature of both object and consciousness.*

In the same way, sounds heard by the ear—*pleasant, unpleasant, and so forth*—fade away as they are heard; they fade away in the expanse of the unborn.

Odors smelled by the nose—*fragrant, foul, and so on*—dissolve as they are smelt; they fade away in the sphere of the unborn.

Tastes savored by the tongue—*sweet, sour, and so on*—dissolve as they are tasted; they fade away in the expanse of the unborn.

Sensations felt by the body—*smooth, rough, and so on*—dissolve as they are felt; they fade away in the expanse of the unborn.

Perceptions too—*the seventeen kinds of perceptions and others*—dissolve by themselves; they fade away in the sphere of the unborn, *appearance and emptiness inseparable.*

Words uttered—*whether of the Dharma or not*—dissolve by themselves; they dissolve in the expanse of the unborn, *sound and emptiness inseparable.*

Thoughts too—*whether virtuous or not*—are free in themselves; they dissolve into the sphere of the unborn, *naturally pure awareness.*

⁂ 69 ⁂

Seeing how having the four stainless things prevents one going astray.

Son, there are four things that are stainless.

To recognize the unborn *absolute nature* in everything that appears, *the whole of phenomenal existence, illustrated by the eight similes of illusion,* is the stainless wisdom of the view.

Taking the unborn *nature* as the path *at all times* is the stainless path *of meditation.*

When one settles in the natural flow, in the unborn nature, an incapacity to express *this nature* is the stainless experience.

Not to stray from the unborn nature into ordinary thoughts *related to past, present, and future* is the stainless result.

⁂ 70 ⁂

Showing that the practitioner's insight will not find anything else other than the unborn nature.

Son, there are five things you will not find.

When one investigates using the "neither one nor many" reasoning, there is no finding an object outside: *things are like the bits of hair that appear to someone with an ophthalmic condition.*

Since there is neither a seeker nor anything to be sought, there is no finding a mind inside. *That would be like space looking for space.*

When divided and subdivided into its limbs, digits, and so forth, there is no finding a body in between. *It is like the core of the plantain tree.*

As there exists neither a place in which to circle nor anyone to go round in it, there is no finding the sentient being you do not want to be. *Beings are like a crowd in a dream.*

Apart from your own unborn mind, there exists no other Buddha, so there is no finding the Buddha you would like to be.

++ 71 ++

How there is nothing to be found by someone on the path besides the absolute nature.

Son, there are five instances where there is nothing to be found.

From the beginning the nature of all phenomena, outer and inner, has never been anything but emptiness. Whatever appears *as an object outside* is an appearance of something that does not exist. *So even if you look for it,* you will never find it *in the past, present, or future:* there is nothing to be found.

Awareness, *your own mind inside,* is awareness and emptiness inseparable, so you will not find it: there is nothing to be found.

The body *composed of the six elements* has no essence, so you will not find it: there is nothing to be found.

Deluded beings *also* are, *in truth,* unborn, so you will not find them: there is nothing to be found.

As for the undeluded Buddha state, it is your own mind, so you will not find it *anywhere else:* there is nothing to be found.

++ 72 ++

A detailed explanation of how the absolute nature arises nondually.

Son, there are five things to take as the path, *leaving the mind without contrivance in its own state.*

There is nothing whatsoever to focus on regarding the absolute nature, so do not conceive of its being anything.

Do not indulge in any object *outside—forms, sounds, and suchlike.*

Mind is the Buddha, right now, so do not entertain any hope whatsoever— *such as a desire to obtain the qualities of the path and the result.*

Nothing that you perceive, suffering or bliss, afflictive emotions or primal wisdom, is extraneous to your own mind, so do not regard anything as a defect.

Give up thinking about past, present, and future, mulling over one's memories, and so on: "force"—*meaning leave*—the mind into its natural state.

❖❖ 73 ❖❖

An instruction on how the way-it-is endowed with triple emptiness arises by itself.

Son, emptiness is threefold, *the fundamental nature of all phenomena, for which from the very beginning there is no birth, no cessation, and no dwelling.*

Being intrinsically unborn from the beginning, phenomena outside are not born: they are empty.

Mind being without foundation or root, the mind inside is empty: it is not born.

The aggregates "in between" are empty: they do not dwell. *Form that appears is like foam; feeling experienced is like the plantain tree; perception is like a mirage; conditioning factors are like the plantain; consciousness is like a magical illusion.*

❖❖ 74 ❖❖

Sealing phenomenal existence by taking groundlessness as the path.

Son, there are three things to take as the path.

Take as the path the absence of any ground *acting as a support for,* or root *that gives rise to, anything in samsara and nirvana.*

Stay without giving importance to things—*as true or untrue, to be hoped for or feared, and so on.*

Apply the seal *of the unborn to phenomenal existence.*

✦✦ 75 ✦✦

Severing ties—outer, inner, and in-between.

If you do not cut outer and inner ties before putting the instructions into practice, the practice will degenerate into a mere attempt to impress others.
Son, there are four ties to be severed.
Sever outer ties *such as distracting circumstances—crowds and bustle.*
Sever inner ties *such as enemies and friends—objects that arouse attachment and aversion.*
Sever "in-between" ties *such as the things you cling to that concern this life.*
Moreover, having first gained a deep conviction concerning the teachings you have heard, having then cut through your intellectual doubts and having ultimately destroyed misconceptions regarding the view, meditation, and action, rely constantly on lonely places.

✦✦ 76 ✦✦

This chapter has two parts: the eight activities to be performed and how the teacher remedies faults in one's meditation and confers happiness and blessings.

i) The eight activities to be performed.

Son, there are eight activities to be performed.
At times such as the beginning of a practice, meditate on the three protections—*outer, inner, and secret.*
Make provision, *gathering everything you will need in order to practice.*
Simplify—*that is, remain in the natural state: leave your body, speech, and mind just as they are.*
Make offerings *to the teacher and the Three Jewels.*
Regarding the actions you have committed in the past, confess your negative actions *with the four powers.*
Pray *that experience and realization may be born in your being.*
Sit on a comfortable seat *in a secluded place,*
And perform the yogic exercises, *controlling body and speech.*

ii) How the teacher remedies faults in one's meditation and confers happiness and blessings.

In the Commentary, *this section appears after the seventy-ninth chapter, but here we shall follow the order in the original text.*

Visualize *your root teacher* seated on a *lotus and moon* throne *on the crown of your head.* Begin by *arousing bodhichitta and* performing the seven branches.

Next examine samsara. *Reflect on the nature of impermanence, suffering, and so on.*

Then recall the intermediate states. *There are six intermediate states. In the natural intermediate state one recognizes the absolute nature that one had not recognized, like an orphan meeting its mother. In the intermediate state between birth and death one recognizes the primal wisdom as if one held up a torch in a dark cave. In the intermediate state of dream one recognizes everything that appears as the mind, just as on an island of sages one would not find other beings even if one looked. In the intermediate state of concentration one makes clear what is not clear, like a model looking in a mirror. In the intermediate state of becoming one connects with one's remaining stock of positive actions, like inserting a pipe into a broken irrigation channel. In the intermediate state of the radiant absolute nature, primal wisdom appears all-penetrating, like a shooting star in the sky. The crucial points on these are condensed in the teacher's pith instructions. Put them into practice.*

✦✦ 77 ✦✦

Using seven concentrations to meditate.

Son, there are seven concentrations *in which one does not move away from the view and meditation.*

The concentration of the emptiness of the inner, *that is, the consciousnesses of the sense organs, the eye being devoid of eye-ness, and so forth.*

The concentration of the emptiness of the outer, *that is, the six objects, form being devoid of form-ness, and so forth.*

The concentration of the emptiness of both inner and outer, *compounded phenomena, the container and contents.*

The concentration of the emptiness of the *uncompounded* absolute.

The concentration of the lion's imposing demeanor, *which overawes deluded perceptions.*

The concentration of clear wisdom, *the natural state free from the duality of subject and object.*

The vajralike concentration, *indestructible and inseparable.*

++ 78 ++

Six preparatory branches of the practice.

Son, there are six preparatory practices.

Sit on a comfortable seat *as is proper for practicing concentration.*

Then visualize the channels *and wheels in the body, the container.*

Expel the *poisonous* energies *that are contained.*

Perform the *physical* yogic exercises, *filling with the upper and lower energies and dispelling obstacles.*

Rid yourself of other *pointless thoughts,* mental turbidity.

Bring the mind into the one-pointed concentration *of bliss, clarity, voidness, and the like.*

++ 79 ++

The five-limbed main practice of the yogi on the path.

Son, there are five branches in the main practice, *branches for practicing the actual path.*

Drop *ordinary* activities, put them off—*such things as business and farming the land: there will never come a time when they are finished.*

Once you leave them aside, virtuous activities will blossom and your body, speech, and mind will be extremely happy.

As a result, inner concentration will grow and various experiences occur: the mirror of awareness will shine within.

At that time the Sugatas will bestow their splendor. *The Buddhas, Bodhisattvas, and Vidyadharas will bless you, the guardians of virtue will protect you, and because of the majesty you will have gained, hindrances, negative forces, and obstacle makers will be unable to do you any harm.*

It will be impossible for conditioned thoughts *such as the five or three poisonous emotions* to arise.

In short, if you give up all ordinary activities, by practicing the profound path with no conflict between your mind and the three trainings you will temporarily and ultimately master infinite qualities, accomplishing your own and others' welfare according to your wishes.

These chapters on the superior training in wisdom have been arranged in a different order in the Commentary, which explains the text as follows. After the forty-second chapter it jumps straight to Chapter Forty-eight. It then continues from Chapter Fifty to Fifty-four. After that come Chapters Sixty-three and Sixty-nine. Next, Chapters Forty-three to Forty-seven, after which come Chapters Sixty-eight, Seventy, Seventy-one, Forty-nine, and Fifty-five to Fifty-nine. Then Chapters Sixty to Sixty-seven, leaving out Chapter Sixty-three, which came earlier. Next, Chapters Seventy-two to Seventy-nine, omitting Chapter Seventy-seven, which came in the section on the training of the mind. Here, however, I have followed the order in the root text.

To sum up, by using these chapters to realize the meaning of the Later Mind Section of the Great Perfection, one achieves certainty through "clearly distinguishing," and complete confidence. As if vanquishing an adversary with a razor-sharp blade, this is the path that eradicates samsara and establishes the unborn nature with certainty.

This concludes the instruction on this section, which I have explained to suit those with keen intelligence.

This was the fourth section from the *Eighty Chapters of Personal Advice,* the instruction on stainless wisdom, the essence.

V. Conclusion

++ 80 ++

A concluding instruction on examining the disciple and how the disciple should practice.

Son, there are three points in conclusion.

i) The defects of disciples to whom the instructions should not be given.

Recognize defects in disciples who might be liberated by these profound instructions: do not give the instructions to improper vessels whose natural disposition is unsuitable, *being bad-tempered, ungrateful, and so on;* who are inconstant *and have fickle minds;* who find fault *in their own teacher,* in the Dharma, and in individuals; and who, *having received the profound instructions,* will not put them into practice. *Even if you do give them the instructions, you will not do them any good, and divulging the secret teachings will result in criticism and retribution.*

ii) Suitable vessels to whom the teachings may be given.

To those who are good-natured—*who acknowledge what is done for them, are grateful for kindness, and so on;* who are stable *(their faith and suchlike never change);* who have very pure perception *with regard to the Dharma, people, and so forth;* and who are assiduous in the practice, *accomplishing what they have heard*—to them you can give the instructions. *By doing so you will ensure that they hold the lineage of the teachings and serve the doctrine, fulfilling the aims of many—themselves and others.*

iii) As for how disciples who are suitable vessels should put the instructions they have been given into practice:

They should see the teacher as the Buddha. *As a result they will receive the blessings of the lineage.* They should keep the instructions in their hearts. *If they are able to keep them secret and to practice them, the two accomplishments will come without effort.* Befriending solitude, *far from crowds and bustle,* they should practice. As a result, experience and realization will bloom and they will become the snow lion's cubs.

This completes the explanation of the instructions on how to recognize suitable disciples and on how to give rise to excellent qualities in one's being.

This was the fifth section from the *Eighty Chapters of Personal Advice,* the instruction on the vessel and a related teaching.

✤ Colophon ✤

This is the essence of the heart of Deshek Gyawopa, the Lord who attained the summit of the view.

It covers the Three Pitakas and follows the texts of *Epitome, Magic,* and *Mind.*

It is an instruction that within a single lifetime liberates those with faith, diligence, and wisdom.

Written down by Khyungpo Yamarwa exactly as the Lord spoke it, it is the culmination and quintessence of his profound teachings.

The Eighty Chapters of Personal Advice
By the glorious heruka, Zurchungpa,
Who bestows the fruit of complete liberation
On all who hear his name or even think of him,
Is the sublime and extraordinary jewel of the Ancient Translation lineage,
A treasure of the profound tantras, commentaries, and pith instructions,
An event as rare in the three times as the udumbara lotus
That I have come upon through no effort of my own.
Such is my delight and joy that I have written these notes.
If I have made the slightest error therein,
I confess it to the teacher and supreme deities.
Through the merit may the great enlightenment be swiftly attained.
In all our lives may we never be parted from the sublime tradition
Of the glorious Zur,
And by correctly holding, preserving, and spreading it,
May we achieve both aims—our own and others'.

Using as a basis the text and structural outline transmitted to me by the Vajradhara Khyentse Wangpo, I, the kusali Jamyang Lodrö Gyamtso Drayang, wrote these few notes to make it clearer, thinking that they might be useful for people of limited intellect like myself. They follow the explanation given in the detailed commentary The Lamp of Shining Jewels. *I wrote them at Demchok Tashi Gempel at an auspicious time in the month of Kartika in the Wood Mouse Year (1924). As a result of this, long may the sublime doctrine of the secret and ultimate essence endure.*

Sarwada mangalam bhavantu.

Eighty Chapters of Personal Advice

++ List of Chapters ++

Notes

1 See Dudjom Rinpoche, *The Nyingma School of Tibetan Buddhism: Its Fundamentals and History*, 2 vols., translated by Gyurme Dorje and Matthew Kapstein (Boston: Wisdom Publications, 1991).

2 The following account of Dilgo Khyentse Rinpoche's life has been adapted from the Padmakara Translation Group, *Dilgo Khyentse Rinpoche* (Saint Léon-sur-Vézère, France: Editions Padmakara, 1990). A more detailed account is given in Matthieu Ricard, *Journey to Enlightenment* (New York: Aperture, 1996).

3 *Epitome*, *Magic*, and *Mind* (Tib. *mdo sgyu sems gsum*). These are the abbreviated titles of the root tantras of the three inner tantras: Mahayoga, Anuyoga, and Atiyoga. They refer to the *Epitome of Essential Meaning* (*mdo dgongs pa 'dus pa*), the root tantra of Anuyoga; the *Net of the Magical Display* (*sgyu 'phrul drva ba*), the root tantra of Mahayoga; and the Eighteen Tantras of the Mind Section (*sems sde bco brgyad*) of Atiyoga.

4 The Sanskrit *ratna* (lit. "jewel"), used with reference to the Three Jewels (Skt. *Tri-ratna*, i.e., Buddha, Dharma, and Sangha), was translated into Tibetan as *dkon mchog*, meaning "rare and supreme." In the Vajrayana the teacher is often referred to as the Fourth Jewel.

5 Pronounced "bey" by Tibetans.

6 In this translation of the Commentary, Zurchungpa's root text appears in bold typeface, Shechen Gyaltsap's introduction, notes, and structural outline in italics, and Khyentse Rinpoche's commentary in normal typeface. In the earlier parts of the book the different elements (root text, notes, and commentary) mostly appear separately, but in the later chapters they are largely intermingled.

7 The Tibetan verb *spel ba* includes among its many meanings: to thread (a necklace) and to compose (a literary work).

8 Ngok Loden Sherab (*rngog blo ldan shes rab*) (1059-1109) was one of the principal translators and masters of the New Translation tradition.

9 Tib. *ma chags mi chags chags pa med*.

10 Tib. *chags thogs*: *chags*, "to be stuck on something"; *thogs*, "to be prevented from moving forward."

11 The great translator Rinchen Zangpo (958-1055).

12 *lotsawa* (Skt.), a translator.

13 Samsaric action, any action performed with a samsaric goal in mind.

14 A full account of Zurchungpa's life is given in H.H. Dudjom Rinpoche's *History of the Nyingma School* (Part Two of Dudjom Rinpoche, Jikdrel Yeshe Dorje, *The Nyingma School of Tibetan Buddhism*, vol. 1, translated by Gyurme Dorje and Matthew Kapstein [Boston: Wisdom Publications, 1991], pp. 635-645).

15 Trak Gyawo was originally Zurpoche's hermitage, which he bequeathed to Zurchungpa, who meditated there for a total of fourteen years, and it was there that
he finally passed away.

16 The Sanskrit word *dharma* (Tib. *chos*) has a wide range of meanings, including:
(to name only a few): a thing, phenomenon, characteristic, attribute, mental
object, topic, teaching, scripture, religion, law, custom, usage. In this book
"Dharma" (in uppercase) refers exclusively to the second of the Three Jewels, the
Buddha's teaching and Buddhist path.

17 I.e., the scriptures (or Dharma of transmission, Tib. *lung*) are not the Dharma of
realization (Tib. *rtogs*).

18 "Our Teacher" probably refers in this case to the Buddha Shakyamuni, though of
course it could equally well refer to one's own lama.

19 Tib. *rnam dkar gyi chos*, lit. "the perfectly white (or virtuous) Dharma."

20 This note of Shechen Gyaltsap and the following line of root text were missing in
the edition that Khyentse Rinpoche taught from, which reads, "One is like a blind
person who goes into a temple: the sprout of enlightenment—devotion, diligence,
and compassion—will not grow." We have therefore inserted the missing text here
from the more reliable woodblock edition.

21 I.e., do not let others lead you (by the nose); practice the Dharma to find happiness and freedom by yourself.

22 The traditional retreat that the Sangha observes during the three summer months.

23 See Bibliography.

24 Tib. *mkha' spyod*.

25 Lobpön Pawo is usually identified as Ashvagosha.

26 The story of Shabkar Tsogdruk Rangdrol's life has been translated as *The Life of
Shabkar: The Autobiography of a Tibetan Yogin,* translated by Matthieu Ricard
(Albany: SUNY Press, 1994: Ithaca: Snow Lion Publications, 2001).

27 The Tibetan word *zhen log* indicates a feeling of disgust or aversion, feeling sick of
or fed up with something, a distinct lack of desire, such as that felt by a jaundiced
patient presented with greasy food. The words from which it is derived in Tibetan
signify simply "the opposite of attachment."

28 See the story of Sunakshatra in Patrul Rinpoche, *The Words of My Perfect Teacher,*
translated by the Padmakara Translation Group, 2nd edition (Walnut Creek,
Calif.: Altamira Press, 1998; Boston: Shambhala, 1998), p. 147.

29 Lit. "making the supports of the Three Jewels," i.e., making statues and paintings
(supports of the Buddha's body), printing the scriptures (supports of the Buddha's speech), building stupas (supports of the Buddha's mind), and so on.

30 Zangdopelri (*zangs bdog dpal ri*), the Buddhafield of Padmasambhava.

31 Tib. *'bri gang med pa*, lit. "it does not diminish or become fuller."

32 Tib. *gsal 'grib med pa*, lit. "it does not grow brighter or dimmer."

33 The eight great chariots refer to the eight lineages of accomplishment, Tib. *sgrub
brgyud shing rta chen po brgyad*, described in Dudjom Rinpoche's *History* (in vol.
1 of *The Nyingma School of Tibetan Buddhism*, pp. 852-853) as the Nyingmapa,
Kadampa, Path and Fruit, Marpa Kagyupa, Shangpa Kagyupa, Kalachakra,
Padampa Sangye's lineage of Pacification and Object of Cutting, and the Oddiyana
Tradition of Service and Attainment.

34 Nagarjuna's *Letter to a Friend* (*Suhrillekha*), v. 23.

35 I.e., who do not fade after a promising start.

36 As the Buddha's attendant, Ananda never had time to actually practice in retreat, and at the time of the First Council he had still not attained the state of Arhat. He was therefore not eligible to attend the Council, where the whole of the Buddha's teachings were to be recited and verifed, even though he had heard all the Buddha's words and was obviously a priceless repository of these teachings. His presence at the Council was essential, so he was urged to meditate. As a result of the blessings he had received during all his time in the Buddha's presence, he attained Arhathood in a single night. He then proceeded to join the Council and to recite the sutras in their entirety to the assembly.

37 Mipham Jamyang Namgyal Gyatso (1846-1912) recognized Dilgo Khyentse Rinpoche as an incarnation and bestowed on him the empowerment of Mañjushri.

38 Yamantaka is the wrathful form of Mañjushri.

39 It should be remembered that when Khyentse Rinpoche gave this teaching he was addressing an audience of retreatants on whom he had just bestowed a number of empowerments.

40 Tib. *yin pa*, lit. "it is . . ."

41 Alternative translation: "rely on the teacher as your wisdom eye for a long time, without separating from him."

42 Tib. *rgya gad zer*, scolding in the sense of telling you that practicing the Dharma is a waste of time and that you should be doing something more worthwhile.

43 Implicit in the Tibetan here is the notion of *offering* to superior beings above and *giving* to lesser beings below. See Glossary, s.v. "offering and giving" and "four guests."

44 *The Way of the Bodhisattva*, VI, 2.

45 Do Khyentse Yeshe Dorje (1800-?) and Jamyang Khyentse Wangpo (1820-1892). It is impossible to measure the beneficial extent of these two great masters' activities.

46 Tib. *mkhas grub*, lit. "learned and accomplished." Scholars who are not only fully versed in the teachings but have practiced them and attained a high level of realization.

47 One should not try to observe precepts that one cannot possibly keep. Giving one's limbs, for example, is only possible for a Bodhisattva who is on the Bodhisattva levels. Certain Vajrayana samayas can only be kept by practitioners who have attained full realization.

48 I.e., the five poisons as they are experienced by ordinary beings as opposed to the way in which they are experienced by Vajrayana practitioners who, rather than giving up the five poisons, experience them as the five wisdoms.

49 Tib. *kun gzhi*, Skt. *alaya*.

50 Tib. *zung 'jug rdo rje'i sku*, the union of the dharmakaya and rupakaya.

51 According to the Khenpo Ngawang Pelzang in his *Guide to The Words of My Perfect Teacher*, carefulness (Tib. *bag yod pa*) is to exercise the utmost prudence in doing what is right and avoiding what is wrong.

52 Tib. *dgos med nga*, lit. "five things one does not need," in contrast to the five things in Chapter Nine that one does need, *dgos yod lnga*.

53 "Fine words" here means saying things like, "Everything is empty, everything is awareness," without having true realization. According to Khyentse Rinpoche's

commentary, this line in the root text can also be translated, "No point in sweet words if you are self-centered."

54 "Illuminates the white path," i.e., opens the door to the Dharma.

55 Tib. *las kyi dbang mo*, the dakini Mahakarmendrani, who transmitted the Vajra-kilaya teachings to Prabhahasti.

56 Tib. *go cha*, can refer to armorlike diligence or to the armor of patience.

57 Our universe is said to be located in the pistil of the thirteenth lotus flower, level with Buddha Vairochana-Himasagara's heart.

58 A Khampa (Eastern Tibetan) term of affectionate respect, used in this case by the old hunter for his teacher.

59 The Copper-Colored Mountain, the Buddhafield of Guru Rinpoche.

60 Compassion (Tib. *thugs rje*) in this context refers not only to compassion in its usual sense (Tib. *snying rje*) but also to the inseparability of the essential nature (*ngo bo*) and the natural expression (*rang bzhin*), the union of appearance and emptiness.

61 I.e., to sculpt statues, paint thangkas, print books, build stupas, and so forth.

62 Tib. *go cha*, in this case, seems to refer to the armor of both diligence and patience.

63 *The Way of the Bodhisattva*, VI, 2.

64 Alternative translation: "To have no one for company is great bliss."

65 Tib. *drang por srong*, "to correct." An alternative translation, which matches the imagery in Shechen Gyaltsap's note, would be, "keep to the straight."

66 The practice of giving one's own happiness to others and taking their suffering upon oneself (Tib. *gtong len*) is mentioned in numerous Bodhisattvayana texts, and described in particular in Atisha's *Seven Point Mind Training*, on which a commentary by Dilgo Khyentse Rinpoche has been published in *Enlightened Courage* (Peyzac-le-Moustier: Editions Padmakara, 1992; Ithaca: Snow Lion Publications, 1994, 2006).

67 The case against the common misconception that eating meat is acceptable is presented by Patrul Rinpoche in *The Words of My Perfect Teacher*. It is explained in detail by Shabkar Tsogdruk Rangdrol in *Food for Bodhisattvas* (Boston: Shambhala, 2004).

68 Lit. "the bones of your father and forefathers," i.e., your family line.

69 Tibetan families are very conscious of the fact that a murder, for example, committed within the family (by another member of the family) taints all its members.

70 I.e., to be protected by the king and enjoy the advantages of being his subject.

71 The word "cope" (Tib. *theg pa*) is used here with the meaning "to deal successfully with something." It carries the sense that one's progress in the practice is not affected by things and situations that might normally distract one or hinder one's practice. The ten maxims in this chapter all use the same vocabulary in the Tibetan but have necessitated slight variations in their translation.

72 For a disciple who has true realization of the view, failure to make an outward show of devotion will have no adverse effects.

73 For example, by buying animals that are due to be slaughtered or buying a fisherman's catch and returning the fish to the water.

74 This statement can be understood in two ways. If an ordinary being has no fear of the hells, then failure to keep the samaya will make no difference. On a higher level,

for a practitioner who has recognized the absolute nature and is therefore beyond any notion of samayas to be kept or not kept, the concept of hell no longer exists and not keeping the samaya in a literal sense is permissible.

75 "Polluted," Tib. *rme*, includes the notion of food that has been tainted by the person preparing it or that is considered "unclean" with regard to custom or religion.

76 Tib. *blo snying brang*, lit. "mind, heart, and chest."

77 Lit. "a prisoner without a yoke," i.e., someone in a prison with few constraints and hardships.

78 Tib. *log chos*, lit. "wrong paths."

79 Lit. "paternal uncle or maternal uncle" (Tib. *a khu'am a zhang*).

80 Lit. "the stone does not meet the bone of experience." Without smashing a bone with a stone (an image for diligence), the marrow of experience cannot be extracted.

81 Jambudvipa, the name of our world according to the ancient Buddhist cosmology.

82 I.e., Gampopa, Milarepa's foremost disciple.

83 I.e., there is no sign of accomplishment at death.

84 Tib. *sdig pa'i bshes gnyen*, the opposite of the Tibetan *dge ba'i bshes gnyen* (or "spiritual friend"); literally, a friend in evil as opposed to a friend in virtue.

85 *Letter to a Friend*, v. 86.

86 Readers in the southern hemisphere will, of course, need to read "south-facing" in this example.

87 A mill that has wooden wheels instead of proper millstones and is therefore useless for grinding grain.

88 The Tibetan phrase *gyong bcag pa* is used for softening leather. It therefore here means improving or training oneself.

89 "Meanness" here means small-minded and malicious as well as stingy.

90 "Do not look back": rather than looking back as one would usually do when one bids one's friends farewell, one should leave directly without looking back.

91 Lit. "make food, clothes, and conversation be the three losers."

92 In other words, if you are a failure in worldly terms.

93 Yaks in Tibet have their noses pierced (like bulls in the West) and a rope passed through the hole.

94 Tib. *skye med*, see Glossary, s.v. "unborn."

95 On the sutra path there are precepts and vows, but no samayas as there are in the Mantrayana.

96 Lit. "from the depth of your heart."

97 To inspire someone else to view a scholar and an uneducated person as equals is also a breach of samaya.

98 Tib. *rang dbang yod*, possessions that one has full control over.

99 The commentary in question is referred to by Shechen Gyaltsap in his colophon and is entitled *The Lamp of Shining Jewels*. We have not been able to identify either this work or its author.

100 "General" may refer to Dharma students in general or to all sentient beings, who, according to Jigme Lingpa, are our general brothers and sisters (Tib. *spyi'i mched*) in that we all possess the buddha nature. Our closest vajra siblings (*'dres pa'i mched*) are those with whom we have received empowerment from the same teacher in the same mandala.

101 Tib. *gdams ngag ngom logs su gtab*: like a child showing everyone the sweet it has just been given.

102 Lit. "just as they sound," i.e., without explaining the inner, symbolic meanings.

103 This saying is attributed to Drikung Kyobpa Rinpoche.

104 I.e., someone who has reached the path of seeing.

105 The same Tibetan word, *zang zing*, is used in the first three lines. It generally means things, material objects, but it is also used to mean meat or fish as food.

106 In other words, die alone in a remote place where there are no disturbances.

107 This is one of the four lines in *Parting from the Four Attachments* by Jetsun Trakpa Gyaltsen (1147-1216).

108 Mirrors in ancient India and Tibet consisted of a polished metal disc rather than glass back-coated with silver.

109 The "ornament space" (Tib. *rgyan gyi nam mkha'*), the blue sky which is conventionally considered as a "thing" as opposed to space which is defined as the absence of anything.

110 Lit. "eye-opening doctor," one who removes cataracts.

111 In the first instruction the Tibetan word *bcad* (meaning "to cut") is used on its own and in its literal sense, but in the other three instructions it is employed in the compound word *thag bcad pa*, meaning "to decide."

112 Tib. *dpe'i ye shes* and *don gyi ye shes*, respectively.

113 The syllable *phat* used in practices such as the *Chö* and transference practices (see *The Words of My Perfect Teacher*), and in the *trekchö* practice of the Great Perfection.

114 Tib. *spyod pa*, action, activity, or conduct, the third point after view and meditation.

115 For fear, in traditional society at least, of upsetting her husband or her mother-in-law.

116 Lit. "a fistful of sweet-tasting dough," considered as a treat by Tibetan children.

117 The *Six Prerequisites for Concentration* gives six examples: (1) give up expectation, like a courtesan whose client has not kept his appointment; (2) give up possessions, like a pelican (see pages 157–8); (3) give up attachment to a household, like a snake seeking a quiet life in a hole someone else has made; (4) live in the forest, like a deer-stalker who finds the forest so peaceful that he gives up hunting; (5) concentrate like an arrow-maker, undistracted by the bustle around him; and (6) stay alone, like a single bangle on a young maiden's wrist (see also page 102).

118 The concentrations practiced even by non-Buddhists that result in rebirth in the form and formless realms.

119 Tib. *bzhag thabs*: *bzhag pa* means to settle, to leave things, let them be, and also to rest, i.e., to rest in meditation.

120 The sixth sensory experience is that of the mind, which is considered here to be the sixth "sense organ."

121 Tib. *ri bo cog bzhag*.

122 Tib. *cog bzhag hor rdol*; *hor rdol* implies a sudden absence of ordinary thoughts.

123 Tib. *thang nge sbreng nge*, a term applied to a bamboo stick or a violin string that springs back to its original position when bent or plucked.

124 Tib. *tshogs chen 'dus pa*, an Anuyoga tantra.

125 Tib. *stod smad*.

126 Tib. *rdul phra rab*, lit."infinitesimal particle," the smallest possible particle accord-ing to some Buddhist philosophical schools, produced by dividing matter into fragments until no further reduction is possible. One infinitesimal particle mul-tiplied by seven to the power of seven would give a dust particle just visible to the naked eye in a shaft of sunlight.

127 Tib. *yid bzhag*, lit. "intellectually leaving things as they are," to be distinguished from the fifth of the seven, "sublime meditation" (*sgom*).

128 I.e., not to use ordinary supports.

129 Tib. *bsam gtan*.

130 Tib. *ting nge 'dzin*.

131 Of the six sense organs, the body is the organ of touch.

132 I.e., the "object" of the wisdom mind (Tib. *shes rab kyi chos*). The meaning of "dharma" (*chos*) in this case is "something that can be known."

133 Awareness (Tib. *rigpa*).

134 Tib. *yang dag pa drug*, lit. "six authenticities." Having dealt with the six wisdom sense organs and their six wisdom objects, Zurchungpa now explains the authen-tic, ultimate, or perfect ways in which these objects are experienced.

135 In this section "taste" and "experience" translate the same Tibetan word, *myong ba.*

136 "Wheel" (Tib. *'khor lo*) is used here in the traditional Indian sense of a weapon.

137 Tib. *chos spyod bcu*. Copying the canonical texts, making offerings, giving gene-rously, listening to the Dharma, memorizing the teachings, reading them, explain-ing them, reciting prayers and sutras, reflecting on the meaning of the Dharma, and meditating on it.

138 I.e., faith, diligence, mindfulness, vigilance, and carefulness.

139 This is one of the four lines in *Parting from the Four Attachments*.

140 In these last two sentences Khyentse Rinpoche also appears to be commenting on the root verse that follows: "Do not be proud of your concentration."

141 Tib. *phrag dog*, which, as one of the five poisons, is more usually translated as "jeal-ousy."

142 Tib. *srid pa*, also translated as "existence," "samsara."

143 The Tibetan word *snying po* means heart, core, essence.

144 See Glossary.

145 Neither existence nor nonexistence, apprehended intellectually, comes to the same thing as both existence and nonexistence, so constituting a fourth extreme.

146 The triple space is explained in Chapter Twenty-seven.

147 Lit. "awareness (Tib. *rig pa*) is introduced as having no object."

148 The Nepalese edition has *skye med ye med* for the root text, while the woodblock gives *skye med skye med*, which would translate as "the unborn is unborn."

149 I.e., one cannot apply concepts such as existence or nonexistence to space.

150 It might be helpful here to bear in mind that the Tibetan word for space (*nam mkha'*) is also the word for sky.

151 "It" in this and the following five statements refers to the way in which the absolute nature arises.

152 Lit. "a mirror unstained by oxidation," mirrors in Tibet traditionally consisting of a polished metal plate.

153 "Other-elimination" (Tib. *gzhan sel*) refers to our ordinary tendency to establish

the existence of something by eliminating everything else that is other than it. In the present case, primal wisdom is not the result of eliminating other things.

154 The Tibetan word *grol*, often translated as "liberate" or "free," can also be translated as "dissolve, subside, fade, etc." and needs to be understood in the particular context of mind teaching. When we say that forms "are liberated," it is not the forms themselves that are freed, as it were, from a state of imprisonment, but rather the mind's attachment and conceptual activity with regard to forms and other phenomena. For the meditator there are no concepts of subject, object, or action, and so when something is seen, any concept of that thing naturally dissolves as it is seen, like ripples dissolving back into the water. The meditator sees forms, but any concept of them dissolves with the sight of them. The same applies to the way the meditator experiences all other sensory events, including thoughts. "Freedom" thus encompasses and transcends everything: the meditator, the phenomena he perceives, and the very perception of them.

155 See above page 233.

156 The same Tibetan word, *snang*, is used here for perception and appearance.

157 The Tibetan word for samsara is *'khor ba*, meaning to turn, circle, go round and round.

158 The Tibetan word *mthu* usually denotes power, including magical power and the ability to exorcise. As Shechen Gyaltsap notes, in this context (perhaps as dialect, or in an anachronistic usage) it means "leave."

159 Tib. *'du byed*, also called "volition."

160 This is the fourth "tie to be severed," the "severing" in this case appearing in Shechen Gyaltsap's note, which employs the Tibetan verb *bchad* (meaning "to cut") in three forms: *phug bcad*, to make a decision or become convinced; *the tshom bcad*, to clear one's doubts; and *sgro 'dogs bcad*, to destroy misconceptions. These three are respectively qualified as outer, inner, and ultimate (*don*), mirroring the first three ties to be severed above.

161 The commentary here applies to both place and seat. The seat should be sufficiently comfortable to enable one to stay in meditation for as long as possible.

162 Tib. *'khrul 'khor*, pronounced "trulkor."

163 I.e., the universe and the beings in it.

164 Tib. *sbyor ba drug*. The Tibetan word *sbyor ba* (pronounced "jorwa") has a number of different meanings. In this case it means preparation (the preparation for the "main practice" in the chapter that follows), but the well-known *jorwa druk* of the Kalachakra tradition refers to six kinds of yoga.

165 *Chakras* (Skt.).

166 In the practice of the channels and energies (*rtsa lung*), one usually visualizes oneself as the deity, that is to say, as appearance and emptiness inseparable. Nevertheless, although one's body is empty, for the purposes of the practice it is still visualized with a shape, and is therefore delimited from the empty space outside the body. This limit (the "skin" of the deity's body) is referred to as the outer fence of voidness (*phyi'i stong ra*).

167 Lit. "protectors of the white side," i.e., Dharma protectors.

168 Zurchungpa was one of the four disciples of Lharje Zurpoche known as the four summits. He was the one who had arrived at the summit of the view. (See H.H.

Dudjom Rinpoche's *History of the Nyingma School* [in *The Nyingma School of Tibetan Buddhism,* vol. 1], p. 622).

169 Tib. *tshogs chen 'dus pa.*

170 This colophon by Khyungpo Yamarwa, who wrote down Zurchungpa's teaching, is now followed by Shechen Gyaltsap Rinpoche's own colophon.

171 Dilgo Khyentse Rinpoche seems to be implying here that Jamyang Khyentse Wangpo (1820-1892), as well as receiving these teachings transmitted from master to disciple over the centuries, had also had a vision of Zurchungpa in which he received the transmission of this text directly.

172 Shechen Gyaltsap Rinpoche (1871-1926), who refers to himself by the Indian term kusali, meaning a beggar.

173 Shechen Gyaltsap Rinpoche's hermitage at Shechen Monastery.

174 The month of October-November, when the moon is in the lunar mansion of the Pleiades.

175 Here, in our translation of Shechen Gyaltsap's Annotated Edition, Zurchungpa's root text is shown in normal typeface and Shechen Gyaltsap's annotations in italics.

Glossary

Abhidharma (Skt.), *chos mngon pa*. One of the **Three Pitakas**; the branch of the Buddha's teachings that deals mainly with psychology and logic.

absolute nature, *chos nyid*, Skt. *dharmata*. Also ultimate reality, ultimate nature. The true nature of phenomena, which is emptiness.

absolute truth, *don dam bden pa*. The ultimate nature of the mind and the true status of phenomena, which can only be known by **primal wisdom**, beyond all conceptual constructs and duality. *See also* **relative truth**.

accomplishment. (1) *dngos grub*, Skt. *siddhi*. The result (and goal) of spiritual practice. Common accomplishments include supernatural powers, which a **Bodhisattva** may use to benefit beings. The principal goal, however, is the supreme accomplishment, which is enlightenment. (2) *sgrub pa*. In the context of the recitation of **mantras**, *see* **approach and accomplishment**.

afflictive emotions, *nyon mongs pa*, Skt. *klesha*. Mental factors that influence thoughts and actions and produce suffering. For the three and five principal afflictive emotions, *see* **three poisons** and **five poisons**.

aggregate, *phung po*, Skt. *skandha*. *See* **five aggregates**.

Amitabha (Skt.), *'od dpag med*. The Buddha of Infinite Light; the Buddha of the Lotus family.

Ananda, *kun dga' bo*. A cousin of the Buddha who became his attendant. Since he was able to remember everything that he had heard the Buddha say, it was he who ensured the preservation of the **sutra** teachings by reciting the sutras in their entirety at the First Council.

Ancient Tradition, *rnying ma pa*. The followers of the first teachings of the Secret Mantrayana propagated in Tibet by the great masters **Vimalamitra** and **Padmasambhava** in the eighth century.

Ancient Translations, *snga 'gyur*. The first teachings translated from Sanskrit and propagated in Tibet, those of the **Ancient Tradition**, as distinct from the teachings of the **New Tradition** that were translated and propagated from the tenth century onwards.

appearances, *snang ba*. The things that appear to us, that we perceive.

approach and accomplishment, *bsnyen sgrub*. Two steps in practices involving the recitation of a **mantra**. In the first, practitioners *approach* the deity that they are visualizing by reciting the deity's mantra. In the second they are familiar enough to identify themselves with the deity. *See also* **deity**.

Arhat (Skt.), *dgra bcom pa*. Lit. "one who has vanquished the enemy" (the enemy in this case being **afflictive emotions**): a practitioner of the **Basic Vehicle** who has attained the cessation of suffering, i.e., nirvana, but not the Perfect Buddhahood of the **Great Vehicle**.

Aryadeva, *'phags pa lha* (second century). The most famous disciple of **Nagarjuna**, whose teaching he commented upon in several treatises on **Madhyamika** philosophy. *See also* **Middle Way**.

Asanga, *thogs med* (fourth century). The founder of the Yogachara School and author of many important treatises, in particular the five teachings he received from **Maitreya**.

asuras (Skt.), *lha min*. Also called demi-gods or jealous gods: a class of beings whose jealous nature spoils their enjoyment of their fortunate rebirth in the higher realms and involves them in constant conflict with the **gods** in the god realms.

Atisha (982-1054). Also known as Dipamkara or Jowo Atisha (*jo bo a ti sha*): this great Indian master and scholar, one of the main teachers at the famous university of **Vikramashila**, was a strict follower of the monastic rule. Although he was an accomplished master of the **tantras**, the last ten years of his life that he spent in Tibet were mainly devoted to propagating the teachings on refuge and bodhichitta, and to contributing to the translation of Buddhist texts. His disciples founded the **Kadampa** School.

Atiyoga. The highest of the three inner yogas, the summit of the **nine vehicles** according to the classification of the **Nyingmapa** School. *See also* **Great Perfection**.

Avalokiteshvara (Skt.), *spyan ras gzigs*. Chenrezi, the Bodhisattva of Compassion and essence of the speech of all the Buddhas.

awareness, *rig pa*, Skt. *vidya*. The original state of the mind: fresh, vast, luminous, and beyond thought.

Basic Vehicle, *theg dman*, Skt. *hinayana*. Lit. "lesser vehicle" (in relation to the Mahayana or **Great Vehicle**): the vehicle of the **Shravakas** and **Pratyekabuddhas**.

beginning. This word has been used to translate the Tibetan *ye* in expressions like *ye nas*, "from the very beginning," or *ye dag*, "pure from the beginning." However it should be understood that this does not refer to a first moment of origin or creation in the distant past, but rather to the fact that the pure nature has always been intrinsically present.

bodhichitta (Skt.), *byang chub kyi sems*. Lit. "the mind of enlightenment": on the relative level, it is the wish to attain Buddhahood for the sake of all beings, as well as the practice of the path of love, compassion, the **six transcendent perfections**, etc. necessary for achieving that goal; on the absolute level, it is the direct insight into the ultimate nature.

Bodhisattva (Skt.), *byang chub sems dpa'*. A follower of the **Great Vehicle** whose aim is enlightenment for all beings.

Brahma (Skt.), *tshangs pa*. Lit. "pure": the name given to the principal god in the **world of form**.

brahmin (Skt.). A member of the priestly caste in Indian society.

Buddha (Skt.), *sangs rgyas*. One who has dispelled (Tib. *sangs*) the darkness of the **two obscurations** and developed (Tib. *rgyas*) the two kinds of omniscience (knowing the nature of phenomena and knowing the multiplicity of phenomena).

Capable One, *thub pa*, Skt. *Muni*. An epithet of the Buddha Shakyamuni, often translated as "Mighty One." He was called "capable" because, when he was a **Bodhisattva** and there was none who had the courage to tame the most unfortunate beings, with extremely gross views, **afflictive emotions**, and actions, he, our kind Teacher, was the only one, of all the 1,002 Buddhas of this Excellent Kalpa, who had the strength or capacity to vow to benefit them.

Causal Vehicle of Characteristics, *rgyu mtshan nyid theg pa*. The vehicle that teaches the path as the cause for attaining enlightenment. It includes the vehicles of the **Shravakas**, **Pratyekabuddhas**, and **Bodhisattvas** (that is, those Bodhisattvas practicing the Sutra path and not that of the Mantras). It is distinct from the Resultant Vehicle of the Mantras, or **Secret Mantrayana**, which takes the result (i.e., enlightenment) as the path.

channels, *rtsa*, Skt. *nadi*. Subtle veins in which the subtle energy (*rlung*, Skt. *prana*) circulates. The left and right principal channels run from the nostrils to just below the navel, where they join the central channel. *See also* **energy**.

channels and energies (exercises of), *rtsa rlung gi 'phrul 'khor*. Exercises combining visualization, concentration, and physical movements, in which the flow of subtle energies through the subtle channels is controlled and directed. These practices should only be attempted with the proper transmission and guidance, after completing the **preliminary practice** and achieving some stability in the **generation phase**.

Chenrezi, *spyan ras gzigs*. The Tibetan name for **Avalokiteshvara**.

circumambulation, *skor ba*. An act of veneration that consists of walking clockwise, concentratedly and with awareness, around a sacred object, e.g., a temple, stupa, or holy mountain, or the residence, and even the person, of a spiritual master.

clinging, *'dzin pa*. Also means "to have a belief": thus "ego clinging" can also be interpreted as "believing in an 'I.'"

concentration, *bsam gtan*, Skt. *dhyana*. Meditative absorption, a state of mind without any distraction, essential for all meditative practices, the result of which depends on the motivation and view of the meditator. Non-Buddhist meditative concentration leads to rebirth in the **worlds of form and formlessness**. The concentrations of the **Shravakas** result in their attaining the level of **Arhat**, while only those of the **Bodhisattvas** can result in Perfect Buddhahood.

conceptual obscurations, *shes bya'i sgrib pa*. The concepts of subject, object, and action that prevent one from attaining omniscience.

conditioned, *'dus byas*. Produced (*byas*) by a combination (*'dus*) of causes and conditions.

crown protuberance, *gtsug tor*, Skt. *ushnisha*. The prominence on the head of a Buddha, one of the thirty-two major marks.

dakini (Skt.), *mkha' 'gro ma*. Lit. "moving through space": the feminine principle associated with wisdom and with the enlightened activities of the **lama**. This term has several levels of meaning. There are ordinary dakinis, who are beings with a certain degree of spiritual power, and wisdom dakinis, who are fully realized.

deity, *lha*, Skt. *deva*. This term designates a Buddha or wisdom deity, or sometimes a wealth deity or **Dharma protector**, as distinct from a nonenlightened god in the **world of desire**, the **world of form**, or the **world of formlessness**. See also **gods**.

demon, *bdud*, Skt. *mara*. In the context of Buddhist meditation and practice, a demon is any factor, on the physical or mental plane, that obstructs enlightenment. *See also* **four demons**.

determination to be free, *nges 'byung*. Also translated as "renunciation": the deeply felt wish to achieve liberation from **samsara**.

dharani (Skt.), *gzungs*. A **mantra** that has been blessed by a Buddha or Bodhisattva and has the power to help beings. Several of the **sutras** contain dharanis, often quite long.

Dharma (Skt.), *chos*. The Buddha's doctrine; the teachings transmitted in the scriptures and the qualities of realization attained through their practice. Note that the Sanskrit word *dharma* has ten principal meanings, including "anything that can be known." Vasubandhu defines the Dharma, in its Buddhist sense, as the "protective dharma" (*chos skyobs*): "It corrects (*'chos*) every one of the enemies, the afflictive emotions; and it protects (*skyobs*) us from the lower realms: these two characteristics are absent from other spiritual traditions."

dharmakaya (Skt.), *chos sku*. Lit. "Dharma body": the emptiness aspect of Buddhahood; also translated as "body of truth," "absolute dimension."

Dharma protector, *chos skyong*, Skt. *dharmapala*. The Dharma protectors fulfill the enlightened activities of the **lama** in protecting the teaching from being diluted and its transmission from being disturbed or distorted. Protectors are sometimes emanations of Buddhas or **Bodhisattvas**, and sometimes spirits, **gods**, or **demons** who have been subjugated by a great spiritual master and bound under oath.

dharmata (Skt.), *chos nyid*. The absolute or ultimate nature; the empty nature of all phenomena.

dualistic, *gnyis 'dzin*. Lit. "grasping at" or "apprehending two": the concept of "I" and "other."

duality. The mental state that conceives of subject and object, of an "I" that perceives and a phenomenon that is perceived.

Dzogchen. *See* **Great Perfection.**

eight freedoms, *dal ba brgyad*. The eight states of freedom from the **eight unfavorable conditions**, such freedom being essential in order to hear and practice the Buddha's teachings.

eight incompatible propensities, *ris chad blo'i mi khom pa brgyad*. Eight propensities that prevent one from practicing the Dharma and thus making effective use of a **precious human body**: (1) excessive attachment to family, worldly commitments, success, and so forth, (2) a basically bad character, (3) a lack of fear or dissatisfaction with regard to the sufferings of samsara, (4) a complete absence of faith, (5) a propensity for harmful or negative actions, (6) a lack of interest in the Dharma, (7) the fact of having broken one's vows, and (8) the fact of having broken the Vajrayana samayas.

eight intrusive circumstances, *'phral byung rkyen gyi mi khom pa brgyad*. Eight circumstances that prevent one from practicing the Dharma and thus making effective use of a **precious human body**: to be (1) overwhelmed by the five poisons, (2) extremely stupid, (3) to have a false teacher who has wrong views, (4) to be lazy, (5) to be overwhelmed by the results of one's previous bad karma, (6) to be someone's servant and thus lack the autonomy to practice, (7) to follow the Dharma merely in order to be fed, clothed, and to avoid other difficulties in life, and (8) to take up the Dharma only in order to win wealth and prestige.

eight ordinary concerns, *'jig rten chos brgyad*. The normal preoccupations of unrealized people without a clear spiritual perspective. They are: gain and loss, pleasure and pain, praise and criticism, fame and infamy.

eight unfavorable conditions, *mi khom pa brgyad*. The eight conditions in which sentient beings lack the opportunity to hear and practice the Buddha's teachings. These are: to be born (1) in the **hells**, (2) as a **preta**, (3) as an animal, or (4) as a long-lived god; or as human being but (5) in a world where no Buddha has appeared, or (6) in a barbaric region where the Buddha's doctrine is unknown, or (7) as someone holding wrong views, or (8) as someone mute or mentally deficient.

empowerment, *dbang bskur*, Skt. *abhisheka*. Lit. "transfer of power": the authorization to hear, study, and practice the teachings of the **Vajrayana**; this takes place in a ceremony which may be extremely elaborate or utterly simple.

emptiness, *stong pa nyid*, Skt. *shunyata*. The absence of true existence in all phenomena.

energy, *rlung*, Skt. *prana, vayu*. Lit. "wind," being described as "light and mobile": any one of a number of subtle energies that regulate the functions of the body and influence the mind, which is said to ride or be carried on the *rlung* like a rider on a horse. Mastery of these subtle energies in the **perfection phase** greatly enhances the practitioner's realization. *See also* **channels and energies**.

enlightenment, *byang chub*, Skt. *bodhi*. Purification (*byang*) of all obscurations and realization (*chub*) of all qualities.

essence, *thig le*, Skt. *bindu*. Lit. "drop": the essence or seed of the great bliss; in the **channels** there are different kinds, pure or degenerate. The term *thig le* has a number of different meanings according to the context and type of practice.

eternalism, *rtag par lta ba*. The belief in an eternally-existing entity, a soul for instance. This is one of the extreme views refuted by the proponents of the **Middle Way**.

evenness, *mnyam pa nyid*, Skt. *samata*. Also sameness, equality: all things equally have the nature of **emptiness**.

five aggregates, *phung po lnga*, Skt. *pañchaskandha*. The five psycho-physical components into which a person can be analyzed and which together produce the illusion of a self. They are form, feeling, perception, conditioning factors, and consciousness.

five circumstantial advantages, *gzhan 'byor lnga*. The last five of the **ten advantages**: (1) a Buddha has appeared in the world in which one is, (2) he has taught the doctrine, (3) his teaching has endured until now, (4) there are spiritual friends who can teach it, and (5) one has been accepted as a disciple by such a teacher.

five individual advantages, *rang 'byor lnga*. The first five of the **ten advantages**: (1) to be born a human, (2) in a region where the Buddha's doctrine is taught, (3) with all one's sense organs complete, (4) with a propensity for positive deeds, and (5) with faith in the Dharma.

five paths, *lam lnga*. Five successive stages in the path to enlightenment: the paths of accumulating, joining, seeing, meditation, and the path beyond learning.

five poisons, *dug lnga*. The five principal **afflictive emotions**: (1) bewilderment, ignorance, or confusion (Tib. *gti mug*), (2) attachment or desire (Tib. *'dod chags*), (3) aversion, hatred, or anger (Tib. *zhe sdang*), (4) jealousy (Tib. *phra dog*), and (5) pride (Tib. *nga rgyal*).

five wisdoms, *ye shes lnga.* Five aspects of the wisdom of Buddhahood: the wisdom of the absolute space (Tib. *chos dbyings kyi ye shes*), mirrorlike wisdom (Tib. *me long gi ye shes*), the wisdom of equality (Tib. *mnyam nyid kyi ye shes*), discriminating wisdom (Tib. *so sor rtog pa'i ye shes*), and all-accomplishing wisdom (Tib. *bya ba grub pa'i ye shes*).

four boundless qualities, *tshad med bzhi.* Unlimited love (Tib. *byams pa*), compassion (Tib. *snying rje*), joy (Tib. *dga' ba*), and equanimity (Tib. *btang snyoms*).

four demons, *bdud bzhi.* The demon of the **aggregates,** the demon of **afflictive emotions,** the demon of the Lord of Death, and the demon of the sons of the gods (or demon of distraction). *See also* **demon.**

Four Great Kings, *rgyal chen rigs bzhi.* The protectors of the four directions, who dwell in the first of the six god realms of the **world of desire.**

four guests, *mgron bzhi.* (1) The Buddhas and Bodhisattvas, (2) the **Dharma protectors,** (3) the beings of the six realms, and (4) those with whom we have karmic debts. *See also* **offering and giving.**

four kayas, *sku bzhi.* The **three kayas** plus the svabhavikakaya (Tib. *ngo bo nyid kyi sku*), the kaya of the nature as it is, representing the inseparability of the first three kayas.

Gampopa, *sgam po pa.* Gampopa Sönam Rinchen (1079-1153), also known as Dagpo Rinpoche, was the most famous disciple of **Milarepa** and the founder of the **Kagyupa** monastic order.

gandharva (Skt.), *dri za.* Lit. "smell eater": a spirit that feeds on smells. Also used for a being in the **intermediate state** who inhabits a mental body and therefore feeds not on solid food but on odors.

garuda (Skt.), *khyung.* A mythical bird symbolizing **primal wisdom,** of great size and able to fly as soon as it is hatched. The five colors in which it is sometimes represented symbolize the **five wisdoms.** It is the enemy of the **nagas,** and is depicted with a snake in its beak, symbolizing consuming the **afflictive emotions.**

Gelugpa, *dge lugs pa.* One of the schools of the **New Tradition,** founded by Je Tsongkhapa (1357-1419).

generation phase, *bskyed rim,* Skt. *utpattikrama.* The meditation associated with sadhana practice in which one purifies oneself of one's habitual clingings by meditating on forms, sounds, and thoughts as having the nature of deities, mantras, and wisdom. *See also* **perfection phase.**

geshe, *dge bshes.* Spiritual friend. The usual term for a **Kadampa** teacher, later used as the title for a doctor in philosophy in the **Gelugpa** School.

gods, *lha,* Skt. *deva.* A class of beings who, as a result of accumulating positive actions in previous lives, experience immense happiness and comfort, and are therefore considered by non-Buddhists as the ideal state to which they should aspire. Those in the **worlds of form and formlessness** experience an extended form of the meditation they practiced (without the aim of achieving liberation from samsara) in their previous life. Gods like Indra in the **world of desire** have, as a result of their merit, a certain power to affect the lives of other beings, and they are therefore worshipped, for example, by Hindus. The same Tibetan and Sanskrit term is also used to refer to enlightened beings, in which case it is more usually translated as "**deity.**"

Great Perfection, *dzogs pa chen po.* Another name for **Atiyoga.** *Perfection* means that the mind, in its nature, naturally contains all the qualities of the three bodies: its nature is emptiness, the **dharmakaya;** its natural expression is clarity, the sambhogakaya; and its compassion is all-encompassing, the **nirmanakaya**. *Great* means that this perfection is the natural condition of all things.

Great Vehicle, *theg pa chen po*, Skt. *mahayana*. The vehicle of the **Bodhisattvas**, referred to as "great" because it aims at full Buddhahood for the sake of all beings.

ground-of-all, *kun gzhi*, Skt. *alaya*. An abridged form of *kun gzhi rnam par shes pa*, the ground consciousness in which the **habitual tendencies** are stored. It is the basis for the other consciousnesses. In certain teachings, *kun gzhi* is used to signify the original nature, the primordial purity (*ka dag*).

Guru Rinpoche, *gu ru rin po che*. The name by which **Padmasambhava** is most commonly known in Tibet.

habitual tendencies, *bag chags*, Skt. *vasana*. Habitual patterns of thought, speech, or action created by one's attitudes and deeds in past lives.

Heaven of the Thirty-three, *gsum cu rtsa gsum*. The second of the six gods' realms in the **world of desire**. The abode of **Indra** and his thirty-two ministers.

hell, *dmyal ba*, Skt. *naraka*. One of the **six realms**, in which one undergoes great suffering, mainly in the form of intense heat or cold. Beings in the hell realm mostly experience the effects of actions rather than creating new causes.

Hell of Ultimate Torment, *mnar med*, Skt. *Avichi*. The most terrible of the hells, also called the Hell of Torment Unsurpassed.

higher realms, *mtho ris*. The **gods'** realms, the **asuras'** realm, and the human realm.

Indra (Skt.), *brgya byin*. The ruler of the **Heaven of the Thirty-three**.

intermediate state, *bar do*. The term used for the various stages of experience between death and the next rebirth, with a wider interpretation that includes the various states of consciousness in life.

Jambudvipa (Skt.), *'dzam bu gling*. The southern continent according to Buddhist cosmology, the world in which we live.

Jamgön Kongtrul Lodrö Thaye, *'jam mgon kong sprul blo gros mtha' yas* (1813-1899). Also known as Jamgön Kongtrul the Great. An important teacher of the nonsectarian movement, responsible, with Jamyang Khyentse Wangpo, for compiling several great collections of teachings and practices from all traditions, including the Treasury of Rediscovered Teachings (*rin chen gter mdzod*).

Jetsun Milarepa, *rje brtsun mi la* (1040-1123). Tibet's great yogi and poet, whose biography and spiritual songs are among the best loved works in Tibetan Buddhism. One of the foremost disciples of **Marpa**, he is among the great masters at the origin of the **Kagyupa** School.

Jigme Gyalwa'i Nyugu, *'jigs med rgyal ba'i myu gu*. One of **Jigme Lingpa**'s four principal disciples, and the root teacher of **Patrul Rinpoche**.

Jigme Lingpa, *'jigs med gling pa* (1729-1798). The discoverer of the Longchen Nyingtik teachings, revealed to him in a vision he had of **Longchenpa**. He is considered to be a combined emanation of **Vimalamitra** and King **Trisong Detsen**. **Patrul Rinpoche** is often considered to be the emanation of Jigme Lingpa's speech.

Kadampa, *bka' gdams pa*. The first of the schools of the **New Tradition**, which followed the teachings of **Atisha**. It stressed compassion, study, and pure discipline. Its teachings were continued by all the other schools, in particular the **Gelugpa**, which is also known as the New Kadampa School.

Kagyupa, *bka' brgyud pa.* One of the schools of the **New Tradition,** which followed the teachings brought to Tibet from India by **Marpa** the Translator in the eleventh century and transmitted to **Milarepa.** The Kagyu School has a number of branches.

kalpa (Skt.), *bskal pa.* A unit of time (of inconceivable length) used in Buddhist cosmology to describe the cycles of formation and destruction of a universe, and the ages of increase and decrease within them.

Kangyur, *bka' 'gyur.* Lit. "the translated word": the Tibetan translations of the original canonical works that recorded the Buddha's teachings of the **Tripitaka** and the **tantras.** The Kangyur comprises a collection of more than one hundred volumes.

karma (Skt.), *las.* Although this term simply means "action," it has come to be widely used to signify the result produced by past actions (Tib. *las kyi 'bras bu*), often with the implication of destiny or fate and of something beyond one's control. In the Buddhist teachings, the principle of karma covers the whole process of actions leading to results in future lives, which is something that is very definitely within one's control. *See also* **law of cause and effect.**

karmic energy, *las kyi rlung.* The subtle energy determined by one's karma, as opposed to *ye shes kyi rlung,* the energy connected with wisdom.

karmic obscurations (obscurations of past actions), *las kyi sgrib pa.* Obscurations created by negative actions. *See also* **obscurations.**

lama, *bla ma,* Skt. *guru.* (1) A spiritual teacher, explained as the contraction of *bla na med pa* (lit. "nothing superior"); (2) often used loosely for Buddhist monks or yogis in general.

law of cause and effect, *las rgyu 'bras.* Lit. "action, cause, and result": the process by which every action inevitably produces a corresponding effect. *See also* **karma.**

Lesser Vehicle, *theg dman,* Skt. *hinayana. See* **Basic Vehicle.**

liberation. (1) *thar pa:* freedom from samsara, either as an **Arhat** or as a **Buddha;** (2) *bsgral las byed pa:* a practice performed by a fully realized being in order to liberate the consciousness of a malignant being into a Buddhafield.

Lilavajra, *sgeg pa'i rdo rje* (eighth century). One of the most important **Vidyadharas** of the Kriya and Yoga **tantras,** and a major holder of the transmission of the Guhyagarbha tantra in the **Mahayoga** lineage.

Longchenpa, *klong chen rab 'byams pa* (1308-1363). Also known as the Omniscient Sovereign or King of Dharma: one of the most influential spiritual masters and scholars of the **Nyingmapa** School. He wrote more than two hundred and fifty treatises covering almost all of Buddhist theory and practice up to the **Great Perfection,** including the Seven Treasures (*mdzod bdun*), the Nyingtik Yabzhi (*snying tig ya bzhi*), the Trilogy of Rest (*ngal gso skor gsum*), the Trilogy of Natural Freedom (*rang grol skor gsum*), the Trilogy of Dispelling Darkness (*mun sel skor gsum*), and the Miscellaneous Writings (*gsung thor bu*).

lower realms, *ngan song.* The **hells,** the **preta** realm, and the animal realm.

Madhyamika (Skt.), *dbu ma.* The philosophical doctrine propounded by **Nagarjuna** and his followers, the **Middle Way** that avoids the extremes of existence and nonexistence.

Mahamudra (Skt.), *phyag rgya chen po.* Lit. "Great Seal": the Great Seal means that the seal of the absolute nature is on everything, that all phenomena belong to the wisdom mandala. The term is used to denote the teaching, the meditation practice, or the supreme accomplishment.

Mahayana (Skt.), *theg pa chen po. See* **Great Vehicle.**

Mahayoga (Skt.). The first of the three higher **yogas** according to the classification of the Dharma into **nine vehicles.** In this yoga, the main stress is put on the **generation phase** (*bskyed rim*).

Maitreya (Skt.), *byams pa.* The Buddha to come, the fifth in this present **kalpa.** He is one of the eight principal **Bodhisattva** disciples of Buddha Shakyamuni.

mani (Skt.). The **mantra** of **Avalokiteshvara,** *om mani padme hum.*

Mañjushri (Skt.), *'jam dpal dbyangs.* A tenth-level **Bodhisattva,** one of Buddha Shakyamuni's eight principal Bodhisattva disciples. He embodies the knowledge and wisdom of all the Buddhas and is usually depicted holding the sword of wisdom in his right hand and a book on a lotus in his left.

mantra (Skt.), *sngags.* A manifestation of supreme enlightenment in the form of sound: syllables which, in the **sadhanas** of the **Secret Mantrayana,** protect the mind of the practitioner from ordinary perceptions and invoke the wisdom deities.

Mantrayana. *See* **Secret Mantrayana.**

Marpa, *lho brag mar pa* (1012-1097). A great Tibetan master and translator, disciple of Drogmi, **Naropa,** Maitripa, and other great **siddhas.** He brought many **tantras** from India to Tibet and translated them. These teachings were passed down through **Milarepa** and his other disciples, and are the basis of the teachings of the **Kagyu** lineage.

merit, *bsod nams,* Skt. *punya.* The first of the **two accumulations.** "Merit" is also sometimes used loosely to translate the Tibetan terms *dge ba* (virtue, positive action) and *dge rtsa* (sources of good for the future).

Middle Way, *dbu ma'i lam,* Skt. *madhyamika.* A teaching on emptiness first expounded by **Nagarjuna** and considered to be the basis of the **Secret Mantrayana.** "Middle" in this context means that it is beyond the extreme points of view of nihilism and eternalism. *See also* **Madhyamika.**

Milarepa. *See* **Jetsun Milarepa.**

Mount Meru, *ri rab.* Lit. "the supreme mountain": the four-sided mountain in the form of an inverted pyramid that is the center of our universe according to Buddhist cosmology.

Nagarjuna, *klu sgrub* (first-second century). A great Indian master who expounded the teachings of the **Middle Way** and composed numerous philosophical and medical treatises.

nagas (Skt.), *klu.* Serpentlike beings (classed in the animal realm) living in the water or under the earth and endowed with magical powers and wealth. The most powerful ones have several heads.

Nalanda. The birthplace near Rajagriha of the Buddha's disciple **Shariputra,** which much later, starting in the time of the Gupta kings (fifth century), became one of the great centers of learning in Buddhist India. It was destroyed around A.D. 1200.

Naropa, *na ro pa* (1016-1100). An Indian **pandita** and **siddha,** the disciple of **Tilopa** and teacher of **Marpa** the Translator.

negative action, *sdig pa* or *mi dge ba.* Also harmful action, unwholesome act, evil: an action—physical, verbal, or mental—that produces suffering.

neither one nor many (argument of), *gcig du bral gyi gtan tshigs.* One of the four great arguments used by the Madhyamika School in investigating the nature of phenomena. It demonstrates that no phenomenon can truly exist either as a single, discrete thing or as a plurality of such things.

New Tradition, *gsar ma pa*. The followers of the **tantras** that were translated and propagated from the tenth century onwards by the translator **Rinchen Zangpo** and others. It designates all the schools of Tibetan Buddhism except for the Nyingmapa,
or **Ancient Tradition**.

New Translations. *See* **New Tradition**.

nihilism, *chad par lta ba*. The view that denies the existence of past and future lives, the
principle of cause and effect, and so on. One of the extreme views refuted by the
proponents of the **Middle Way**.

nine vehicles, *theg pa dgu*. The three vehicles of the Sutrayana (those of the **Shravakas**,
Pratyekabuddhas, and **Bodhisattvas**) and the six vehicles of the **Vajrayana** (Kriy-
atantra, Upatantra, Yogatantra, **Mahayoga**, Anuyoga, and **Atiyoga**).

nirmanakaya (Skt.), *sprul sku*. Lit. "body of manifestation": the aspect of Buddhahood
that manifests out of compassion to help ordinary beings.

nirvana (Skt.), *mya ngan las 'das pa*. Lit. "beyond suffering": while this can be loosely
understood as the goal of Buddhist practice, the opposite of samsara, it is important to realize that the term is understood differently by the different vehicles: the
nirvana of the **Basic Vehicle**, the peace of cessation that an **Arhat** attains, is very
different from a Buddha's nirvana, the state of perfect enlightenment that transcends both samsara and nirvana.

no-self, *bdag med*, Skt. *anatman, nairatmya*. Also egolessness: the absence of independ-
ent or intrinsic existence, either of oneself (Tib. *gang zag gi bdag med*) or of external phenomena (Tib. *chos kyi bdag med*).

Nyingmapa. *See* **Ancient Tradition**.

obscurations, *sgrib pa*, Skt. *avarana*. Factors that veil one's buddha nature. *See also* **two
obscurations**.

obscurations of afflictive emotions, *nyon mongs kyi sgrib pa*. Thoughts of hatred,
attachment, and so on that prevent one from attaining liberation. *See* **obscurations**.

offering and giving, *mchod sbyin*. The distinction is usually made, particularly in such
practices as the incense offering (Tib. *gsang*) and burnt offerings (Tib. *gsur*),
between *offering* to sublime beings "above," such as the Buddhas and Bodhisattvas,
and *giving* (as part of the practice of generosity) to ordinary beings "below," including animals and spirits. *See also* **four guests**.

omniscience, *thams cad mkhyen pa*. A synonym for Buddhahood.

Padampa Sangye, *pha dam pa sangs rgyas* (eleventh-twelfth century). An Indian **siddha** who established the teachings of the Shijepa (Tib. *zhi byed pa*) School. Teacher
of Machik Labdrön, to whom he transmitted the Chö teachings. He travelled to
Tibet several times.

Padmasambhava of Oddiyana, *o rgyan padma 'byung gnas*. The Lotus-born Teacher
from Oddiyana, often known as Guru Rinpoche. During the reign of King **Trisong
Detsen**, the great master subjugated the evil forces hostile to the propagation of
Buddhism in Tibet, spread the Buddhist teaching of **Vajrayana** in that country, and
hid innumerable spiritual treasures for the benefit of future generations. He is venerated as the Second Buddha, whose coming was predicted by the first one, Buddha Shakyamuni, to give the special teachings of Vajrayana.

pandita (Skt.). A scholar, someone learned in the five traditional sciences (crafts, medicine, philology, logic, and philosophy). The term is particularly used to refer to
Indian scholars.

path of seeing, *mthong lam*. The third of the **five paths**; the stage at which a **Bodhisattva** in meditation gains a genuine experience of **emptiness**.

paths of accumulating and joining, *tshogs lam, sbyor lam*. The first two of the **five paths** that prepare the **Bodhisattva** for attaining the **path of seeing**.

Patrul Rinpoche, Orgyen Jigme Chökyi Wangpo, *dpal sprul rin po che* (1808-1887). A major holder of the Longchen Nyingtik teachings and exponent of Shantideva's *Bodhicharyavatara (The Way of the Bodhisattva)*, famed for his simple lifestyle and as the author of *The Words of My Perfect Teacher*. He is often considered to be the emanation of **Jigme Lingpa**'s speech.

perfection phase, *rdzogs rim*, Skt. *sampannakrama*. (1) "With characteristics" (Tib. *mtshan bcas*): meditation on the **channels and energies** of the body visualized as a vajra body; (2) "without characteristics" (Tib. *mtshan med*): the meditation phase during which the forms visualized in the **generation phase** are dissolved and one remains in the experience of emptiness.

pitaka (Skt.), *sde snod*. Lit. "basket": a collection of scriptures, originally in the form of palm leaf folios stored in baskets. The Buddha's teachings are generally divided into three pitakas: **Vinaya**, **Sutra**, and **Abhidharma**.

pith instructions, *man ngag*, Skt. *upadesha*. Instructions that explain the most profound points of the teachings in a condensed and direct way for the purposes of practice.

positive action, *dge ba*. Also beneficial act, virtue, good: an action—physical, verbal, or mental—that produces happiness.

Pratimoksha (Skt.), *so sor thar pa*. Lit. "individual liberation": the collective term for the different forms of Buddhist ordination and their respective vows, as laid down in the **Vinaya**.

Pratyekabuddha (Skt.), *rang sangs rgyas*. A follower of the **Basic Vehicle** who attains **liberation** (the cessation of suffering) without the help of a spiritual teacher.

precious human body, *mi lus rin po che*. Rebirth as a human being free from the **eight unfavorable conditions** and possessing the **ten advantages**. This is the only situation in which it is possible to hear and practice the Buddha's teachings properly. According to the Omniscient Longchenpa, the precious human body requires sixteen further conditions in order to be fully effective, namely freedom from the **eight intrusive circumstances** and **eight incompatible propensities**.

preliminary practice, *sgnon 'gro*. The traditional preparation a practitioner needs to complete before the main practice of the Mantrayana. It comprises five principal sections—refuge, **bodhichitta**, purification (meditation on Vajrasattva), offering of the mandala, and guru yoga—each performed one hundred thousand times.

pretas (Skt.), *yi dvags*. Also known as hungry ghosts or spirits: a class of beings whose attachment and miserliness in previous lives result in constant hunger and the frustration of their desires.

primal wisdom, *ye shes*, Skt. *jñana*. The knowing (*shes pa*) that has always been present since the beginning (*ye nas*), awareness, clarity-emptiness, naturally dwelling in all beings.

profound insight, *lhag mthong*, Skt. *vipashyana*. The perception, through wisdom, of the true nature of things.

prostration, *phyag 'tshal ba*. A gesture of reverence, in which the forehead, the two hands, and the two knees touch the ground.

protectors. *See* Dharma protectors.

pure perception, *dag snang.* The perception of all the world and its contents as a pure Buddhafield, as the display of kayas and wisdoms.

refuge. (1) *skyabs yul,* the object in which one takes refuge; (2) *skyabs 'gro,* the practice of taking refuge.

relative truth, *kun rdzob bden pa.* Lit. "all-concealing truth": the apparent truth perceived and taken as real by the deluded mind, which conceals the true nature of phenomena. *See also* **absolute truth.**

Rinchen Zangpo, *rin chen bzang po* (958-1055). The most famous translator of the second propagation of Buddhism in Tibet, when the **New Tradition** began.

ringsel **relics,** *ring bsrel.* Pearl-like relics found in the bodily remains or ashes of someone who has attained a high degree of realization during his or her lifetime.

rishi (Skt.), *drang srong.* A sage, hermit, or saint; particularly the famous sages of Indian myth, who had enormous longevity and magical powers.

rupakaya (Skt.), *gzugs sku.* The body of form, which includes the **sambhogakaya** and **nirmanakaya** together.

sadhana (Skt.), *sgrub thabs.* The method for accomplishing the level of a particular **deity,** for example, the **lama, yidam,** or **dakini.**

Sakyapa, *sa skya pa.* One of the schools of the **New Tradition,** founded by Khön Könchok Gyalpo (1034-1102).

Sakya Pandita. An important **Sakyapa** master (1182-1251), also known as Kunga Gyaltsen.

samadhi (Skt.), *bsam gtan.* Meditative absorption of different degrees. Generally translated as "concentration."

Samantabhadra (Skt.), *kun tu bzang po.* (1) The original Buddha (Adibuddha), the source of the lineage of the **tantra** transmissions of the **Nyingma** School; he who has never fallen into delusion, the **Dharmakaya** Buddha, represented as a naked figure, deep blue like the sky, in union with Samantabhadri, as a symbol of awareness-emptiness, the pure, absolute nature, ever present and unobstructed; (2) the Bodhisattva Samantabhadra, one of the eight principal **Bodhisattva** disciples of Buddha Shakyamuni, renowned for the way in which, through the power of his concentration, he miraculously multiplied the offerings he made.

samaya (Skt.), *dam tshig.* Lit. "promise": sacred links between the teacher and disciple, and also between disciples, in the **Vajrayana.** The Sanskrit word *samaya* can mean: agreement, engagement, convention, precept, boundary, etc. Although there are many detailed obligations, the most essential samaya is to consider the teacher's body, speech, and mind as pure.

sambhogakaya (Skt.), *longs spyod rdzogs pa'i sku.* Lit. "body of perfect enjoyment": the spontaneously-luminous aspect of Buddhahood, only perceptible to highly realized beings.

samsara (Skt.), *'khor ba.* Lit. "wheel": and therefore also translated as "cyclic existence"; the endless round of birth, death, and rebirth in which beings suffer as a result of their actions and **afflictive emotions.**

Samye, *bsam yas.* Lit. "inconceivable": the first monastery in Tibet, in the Tsangpo Valley southeast of Lhasa, built during the time of King **Trisong Detsen.**

Sangha (Skt.), *dge 'dun.* The community of Buddhist practitioners.

Saraha, *sa ra ha.* An Indian mahasiddha, author of three cycles of *dohas* (songs of realization).

Secret Mantrayana, *gsang ngags kyi theg pa.* A branch of the **Great Vehicle** that uses the special techniques of the **tantras** to pursue the path of enlightenment for all beings more rapidly. Synonymous with **Vajrayana.**

sense of decency, *khrel yod.* Also modesty, consideration of others: to be ashamed because of what others might think if one commits negative actions. This is one of the **seven noble riches.**

sense of shame, *ngo tsha shes.* Also conscientiousness, honesty: to be ashamed of oneself if one commits negative actions. This is one of the **seven noble riches.**

seven branches, *yan lag bdun.* A form of prayer comprising seven parts: prostration, offering, confession, rejoicing, requesting the teachers to turn the wheel of Dharma, requesting them not to pass into nirvana, and dedication of merit.

seven noble riches, *'phags pa'i nor bdun.* Faith, discipline, generosity, learning, a sense of decency, a sense of shame, and wisdom.

seven-point posture of Vairochana, *rnam snang chos bdun.* The seven points of the ideal meditation posture: legs crossed in the vajra posture, back straight, hands in the gesture of meditation, eyes gazing along the nose, chin slightly tucked in, shoulders well apart "like a vulture's wings," and the tip of the tongue touching the palate.

Shakyamuni, *sha kya thub pa.* The Buddha of our time, who lived around the fifth century B.C.

Shantarakshita, *zhi ba mtsho.* Also called the Bodhisattva Abbot. A great Indian **pandita** of the Mahayana School who was abbot of the Buddhist university of **Nalanda** and author of a number of philosophical commentaries, such as the *Adornment of the Middle Way* (*dbu ma rgyan,* Skt. *Madhyamakalankara*). He was invited to Tibet by King **Trisong Detsen** to consecrate the site of the first Tibetan monastery at **Samye** and to ordain the first Tibetan monks.

Shariputra, *sha ri'i bu.* One of the two foremost **Shravaka** disciples of Buddha Shakyamuni.

Shravaka (Skt.), *nyan thos.* Lit. "one who listens": a follower of the **Basic Vehicle** whose goal is to attain liberation for himself as an **Arhat.**

siddha (Skt.), *grub thob.* Lit. "one who has attained the accomplishments": someone who has attained the fruit of the practice of the **Secret Mantrayana.**

siddhi (Skt.), *dngos grub. See* **accomplishment.**

six consciousnesses, *rnam shes tshogs drug.* The consciousnesses related to vision, hearing, smell, taste, touch, and mentation.

six realms of existence, *'gro drug.* Six modes of existence caused and dominated by particular mental poisons: the **hells** (anger), and the realms of the **pretas** (miserliness), animals (bewilderment or ignorance), humans (desire), **asuras** (jealousy), and **gods** (pride). These correspond to deluded perceptions produced by beings' **karma** and apprehended as real.

six sense organs, *dbang po drug.* The eye, ear, nose, tongue, body, and mind.

six transcendent perfections, *pha rol tu phyin pa drug.* Transcendent generosity, discipline, patience, diligence, concentration, and wisdom.

skillful means, *thabs,* Skt. *upaya.* Spontaneous, altruistic activity born from wisdom.

Songtsen Gampo, *srong btsan sgam po* (617-698). The first of Tibet's three great religious kings. It was during his time that the first Buddhist temples were built.

source of good, *dge rtsa*. A positive or virtuous act that serves as a cause propelling one towards happy states.

spiritual companions, *chos grogs*. Students of the same teacher, or with whom one has received teaching. It is considered vital to have harmonious relations with such people, particularly in the **Vajrayana**.

spiritual friend, *dge ba'i gshes gnyen*, Skt. *kalyanamitra*. A synonym for spiritual teacher.

stupa (Skt.), *mchod rten*. Lit. "support of offering": a symbolic representation of the Buddha's mind. The most typical Buddhist monument, which often has a wide square base, a rounded midsection, and a tall conical upper section topped by a sun and a moon. Stupas frequently contain the relics of enlightened beings. They vary in size from tiny clay models to the vast stupas at Borobodur in Indonesia and Baudha in Nepal.

sublime being, *'phags pa*, Skt. *arya*. A **Bodhisattva** on one of the ten Bodhisattva levels.

Sugata (Skt.), *bde bar gshegs pa*. Lit. "one who has gone to bliss": an epithet of a Buddha.

supreme accomplishment, *mchog gi dngos grub*. *See* **accomplishment**.

sustained calm, *zhi gnas*, Skt. *shamatha*. The basis of all concentrations; a calm, undistracted state of unwavering concentration.

sutra (Skt.), *mdo*. (1) A scripture containing the teachings of the Buddha; (2) the Sutrapitaka (*mdo sde*), the one of the **Three Pitakas** that deals with meditation.

tantra (Skt.), *rgyud*. Any one of the texts on which the **Vajrayana** teachings are based. They reveal the continuity between the original purity of the nature of mind and the result of the path, which is the realization of that nature.

Tathagata (Skt.), *de bzhin gshegs pa*. Lit. "one who has gone to thusness": an epithet of a Buddha.

ten advantages, *'byor ba bcu*. The ten conditions that enable one to hear and practice the Buddha's teachings. They are divided into **five individual advantages** and **five circumstantial advantages**.

Three Jewels, *dkon mchog gsum*, Skt. *triratna*. The Buddha, Dharma, and Sangha.

three kayas, *sku gsum*, Skt. *trikaya*. Lit. "the three bodies": the three aspects of Buddhahood: **dharmakaya**, **sambhogakaya**, and **nirmanakaya**.

three kinds of suffering, *sdug bsngal gsum*. The three fundamental types of suffering to which beings in samsara are subject: the suffering of change, suffering upon suffering, and the suffering of everything composite (or all-pervading suffering in the making).

Three Pitakas, *sde snod gsum*, Skt. *tripitaka*. *See* **pitaka**.

three poisons, *dug gsum*. The three afflictive emotions of bewilderment, attachment, and aversion. *See also* **five poisons**.

three seats, *gdan gsum*. The aggregates and elements, ayatanas (the sense organs and their corresponding sense objects), and limbs of one's body, whose true nature, according to the pure perception of the **Mantrayana**, is the mandala of the male and female **Tathagata**s, the male and female **Bodhisattva**s, and other deities.

three sweet foods, *mngar gsum*. Sugar, molasses, and honey.

three trainings, *bslabs pa gsum*, Skt. *trishiksha*. The threefold training in discipline, concentration, and wisdom.

three vehicles, *theg pa gsum*, Skt. *triyana*. The vehicles of the **Shravakas**, **Pratyekabuddhas**, and **Bodhisattvas**.

three ways of pleasing the teacher, *mnyes pa gsum.* (1) Making material offerings, (2) helping him through physical, verbal, or mental tasks, and (3) practicing what he teaches.

three white foods, *dkar gsum.* Milk, butter, and curd, which are traditionally considered to be very pure foods.

three worlds, *khams gsum.* The **world of desire**, the **world of form** and the **world of formlessness**. Alternatively (Tib. *'jig rten gsum, sa gsum, srid gsum*): the world of **gods** above the earth, that of **humans** on the earth, and that of the **nagas** under the earth.

Tilopa, *ti lo pa.* One of the eighty-four mahasiddhas of India; teacher of **Naropa**.

Tirthika (Skt.), *mu stegs pa.* A proponent of extreme philosophical views such as nihilism and eternalism. This term is often used to imply non-Buddhist religious traditions in India.

Trakpa Gyaltsen, *grags pa rgyal mtshan* (1147-1216). One of the five great scholars of the **Sakyapa** School, who are known as the Sakya Gongma.

transcendent perfection, *pha rol tu phyin pa*, Skt. *paramita.* A term used to describe the practice of a **Bodhisattva**, which combines **skillful means** and wisdom, the compassionate motivation of attaining enlightenment for the sake of all beings and the view of emptiness. *See* **six transcendent perfections**.

Tripitaka, *sde snod gsum.* The three collections of the Buddha's teachings: **Vinaya**, **Sutra**, and **Abhidharma**. The **Vajrayana** teachings are sometimes considered as a fourth pitaka. *See also* **pitaka**.

Trisong Detsen, *khri srong sde'u btsan* (790-844). The thirty-eighth king of Tibet, second of the three great religious kings. It was due to his efforts that the great masters came from India and established Buddhism firmly in Tibet.

Tushita Heaven, *dga' ldan.* Lit. "The Joyous": one of the realms of the gods in the **world of desire**, in which Buddha Shakyamuni took a final rebirth before appearing in this world. The future Buddha, **Maitreya**, is currently in the Tushita Heaven teaching the **Mahayana**.

two accumulations, *tshogs gnyis.* The accumulation of **merit** (Tib. *bsod nams*) and the accumulation of **wisdom** (Tib. *ye shes*).

two obscurations, *sgrib gnyis.* The obscurations of **afflictive emotions** and **conceptual obscurations**. *See also* **obscurations**.

two truths, *bden pa gnyis.* The **absolute** and **relative truth**s.

unborn, *skye med.* Not produced by anything, having no origin, that which has not come into existence. As Dilgo Khyentse Rinpoche explains, "By 'unborn' we mean that this absolute nature is not something that has come into existence at one point and may cease to exist at another. It is completely beyond coming into existence and ceasing to exist."

universal monarch, *'khor lo sgyur ba'i rgyal po*, Skt. *chakravartin.* (1) A king ruling over a world system; (2) an emperor.

Vairochana, *rnam par snang mdzad.* One of the five Tathagatas; the Buddha of the Buddha family.

Vairotsana, *bai ro tsa na.* Tibet's greatest translator and one of the first seven monks to be ordained in Tibet. He was one of the principal disciples of **Padmasambhava** and of Shri Singha.

Vaishravana (Skt.), *rnam thos sras*. One of the Four Great Kings (whose god realm is the first in the **world of desire**); guardian of the North and god of wealth.

vajra (Skt.), *rdo rje*. Also diamond, adamantine thunderbolt: a symbol of unchanging and indestructible wisdom capable of penetrating through everything; a ritual instrument symbolizing compassion, **skillful means**, or **awareness**, and always associated with the bell, the symbol of wisdom or **emptiness**.

vajra brothers and sisters, *rdo rje spun*. Students of the same teacher, or with whom one has received **Vajrayana** teachings. *See also* **spiritual companions**.

Vajradhara (Skt.), *rdo rje 'chang*. Lit. "vajra holder": in the **New Tradition**, he is the primordial Buddha, source of all the **tantras**. In the **Ancient Tradition**, Vajradhara represents the principle of the Teacher as enlightened holder of the **Vajrayana** teachings.

Vajrasattva (Skt.), *rdo rje sems dpa'*. The Buddha who embodies the forty-two peaceful and fifty-eight wrathful deities. The practice of Vajrasattva and recitation of his **mantra** are particularly effective for purifying **negative action**s. In the lineage of the **Great Perfection** he is the **Sambhogakaya** Buddha.

Vajrayana (Skt.), *rdo rje theg pa*. Also called the Diamond Vehicle or Adamantine Vehicle. *See* **Secret Mantrayana**.

vase empowerment, *bum dbang*. The first of the four **empowerments**. Receiving this empowerment purifies the defilements of the body, enables one to meditate on the **generation phase**, and sows the seed for obtaining the vajra body and the **nirmanakaya**.

vehicle, *theg pa*, Skt. *yana*. The means for traveling the path to enlightenment.

Vehicle of Characteristics, *mtshan nyid theg pa*. *See* **Causal Vehicle of Characteristics**.

Victorious One, *rgyal ba*, Skt. *jina*. A general epithet for a Buddha.

Vidyadhara (Skt.), *rig 'dzin*. Lit. "knowledge holder": one who through profound means holds the **deities**, **mantras**, and the wisdom of great bliss.

Vikramashila. One of the most famous Buddhist universities of India, destroyed in the twelfth century.

Vimalamitra, *dri med bshes bnyen*. An important Indian master who held an important place in the lineages of the **Great Perfection**. He went to Tibet in the eighth century, where he taught extensively, and composed and translated numerous Sanskrit texts. The quintessence of his teaching is known as the *Vima Nyingtik*.

Vinaya (Skt.), *'dul ba*. One of the **Three Pitakas**; the section of the Buddha's teaching that deals with discipline, and in particular with the vows of monastic ordination.

virtuous activities, *dge sbyor*. The practice of Dharma in general, but often used to refer to activities such as prostrations, circumambulation, reciting the scriptures, and so on.

wisdom. *See* **primal wisdom**.

wish-fulfilling jewel, *yid bzhin nor bu*, Skt. *chintamani*. A fabulous jewel found in the realms of the **gods** or **nagas** that fulfills all one's wishes.

world of desire, *'dod khams*, Skt. *kamaloka* or *kamadhatu*. The first of the three worlds, comprising the **hells**, and the realms of the **pretas**, animals, humans, **asuras**, and the six classes of kamaloka gods (Four Great Kings, Heaven of the Thirty-three, Heaven Free of Conflict (Yama), The Joyous Realm (Tushita), Enjoying Magical Creations, and Mastery over Others' Creations).

world of form, *gzugs khams*, Skt. *rupadhatu*. The second of the three worlds, comprising the twelve realms of the four concentrations and the five pure abodes.

world of formlessness, *gzugs med khams*, Skt. *arupyadhatu*. The third of the three worlds, at the peak of existence. It comprises the spheres of Infinite Space, Infinite Consciousness, Utter Nothingness, and Neither Existence nor Nonexistence.

wrong view, *log lta*, Skt. *mithyadrishti*. A false belief, particularly a view that will lead one to courses of action that bring more suffering.

yidam, *yi dam*, Skt. *devata, istadevata*. A **deity** representing enlightenment, in a male or female, peaceful or wrathful form, that corresponds to the practitioner's individual nature. The yidam is the source of **accomplishments**.

yoga (Skt.), *rnal 'byor*. Lit. "union (Tib. *'byor*) with the natural state (Tib. *rnal ma*)": a term for spiritual practice.

yogi (Skt.), *rnal 'byor pa*. A person practicing a spiritual path.

Bibliography

Eighteen Tantras of the Mind Section – *sems sde bco brgyad,* a collection of tantras of the Great Perfection.

Epitome of Essential Meaning – *mdo dgongs pa 'dus pa,* the root tantra of Anuyoga.

Four Themes of Gampopa – *dvags po'i chos bzhi,* a famous work by the Kagyu master Gampopa Sönam Rinchen condensing the Kadampa and Mahamudra teachings.

Great Space – *nam mkha' che,* a tantra.

Guhyagarbha Tantra – *rgyud gsang ba snying po, Tantra of the Secret Essence,* the root tantra of Mahayoga, also called the *Root Tantra of the Net of the Magical Display.*

The Hundred Verses of Advice – *zhal gdams ding ri brgya rtsa ma,* by Padampa Sangye (translated by the Padmakara Translation Group: *The Hundred Verses of Advice: Tibetan Buddhist Teachings on What Matters Most.* Boston: Shambhala, 2005).

History of the Nyingma School – *rnying ma'i chos 'byung,* by Dudjom Rinpoche, Jikdrel Yeshe Dorje (translated by Gyurme Dorje and Matthew Kapstein in *The Nyingma School of Tibetan Buddhism,* vol. 1. Boston: Wisdom Publications, 1991).

Lamp of Shining Jewels – *rin po che gsal ba'i sgron me,* an unidentified commentary on Zurchung Sherab Trakpa's *Eighty Chapters of Personal Advice.*

Letter to a Friend – *Suhrillekha, bshes pa'i spring yig,* by Nagarjuna (translated by the Padmakara Translation Group: *Nagarjuna's Letter to a Friend.* Ithaca, N.Y.: Snow Lion Publications, 2005).

Net of the Magical Display – *sgyu 'phrul drva ba,* the root tantra of Mahayoga.

Ornament of the Sutras – *Sutralankara, mdo sde rgyen,* one of the five great treatises that Maitreya transmitted to Asanga (translated by L. Jamspal et al., *The Universal Vehicle Discourse Literature.* New York: American Institute of Buddhist Studies, 2004).

Parting from the Four Attachments – *zhen pa bzhi bral,* an important instruction by the Sakya master Jetsun Trakpa Gyaltsen (1147-1216). (A commentary by Chogye Trichen Rinpoche on this instruction has been published as *Parting from the Four Attachments: Jetsun Drakpa Gyaltsen's Song of Experience on Mind Training and the View.* Ithaca, N.Y.: Snow Lion Publications, 2003.)

Six Points of Meditation – *bsgom don drug pa.*

Six Prerequisites for Concentration – *Dhyanasaddharma-vyavasthana, bsam gtan gyi chos drug rnam par gzhag pa,* a Madhyamika shastra by Avadhuti-pa.

Sutra in Repayment of Kindness – *Mahopaya-kaushalyabuddha-pratyupakaraka-sutra, thabs mkhas pa chen po sangs rgyas drin lan bsab pa'i mdo.* The teachings the Buddha gave his mother when he visited the Heaven of the Thirty-three, where she had been reborn.

Treasury of Knowledge – shes bya mdzod, by Jamgön Kongtrul Lodrö Thaye (1813-1899), an encyclopedic work that covers all the teachings of both the sutras and tantras. (A translation of the entire *Treasury* is being published by Snow Lion Publications.)

The Way of the Bodhisattva – Bodhicharyavatara, byang chub sems dpa'i spyod pa la 'jug pa, by Shantideva (translated by the Padmakara Translation Group: *The Way of the Bodhisattva,* Boston: Shambhala, 1997, 2006).

The Words of My Perfect Teacher – kun bzang bla ma'i zhal lung, by Patrul Rinpoche (translated by the Padmakara Translation Group: *The Words of My Perfect Teacher,* 2nd edition. Walnut Creek, CA: AltaMira Press, 1998; Boston: Shambhala, 1998).

RECOMMENDED READING

Patrul Rinpoche. *The Words of My Perfect Teacher.* Translated by the Padmakara Translation Group. 2nd edition. Walnut Creek, CA: AltaMira Press, 1998; Boston: Shambhala, 1998.

Longchen Yeshe Dorje, Kangyur Rinpoche. *Treasury of Precious Qualities.* Translated by the Padmakara Translation Group. Boston: Shambhala, 2001.

Gampopa. *The Jewel Ornament of Liberation.* Translated by Khenpo Konchog Gyaltsen Rinpoche. Ithaca, N.Y.: Snow Lion Publications, 1998.

The Padmakara Translation Group

The Padmakara Translation Group is devoted to the accurate and literary translation of Tibetan texts and spoken material into Western languages by trained Western translators, under the guidance of authoritative Tibetan scholars, principally Taklung Tsetrul Pema Wangyal Rinpoche and Jigme Khyentse Rinpoche, in a context of sustained study and discussion.

TRANSLATIONS INTO ENGLISH

The Excellent Path of Enlightenment, Dilgo Khyentse, Editions Padmakara, 1987; Snow Lion Publications, 1996.

The Wish-Fulfilling Jewel, Dilgo Khyentse, Shambhala, 1988.

Dilgo Khyentse Rinpoche, Editions Padmakara, 1990.

Enlightened Courage, Dilgo Khyentse, Editions Padmakara, 1992; Snow Lion Publications, 1994, 2006.

The Heart Treasure of the Enlightened Ones, Dilgo Khyentse and Patrul Rinpoche, Shambhala, 1992.

A Flash of Lightning in the Dark of Night, the Dalai Lama, Shambhala, 1993.

Wisdom: Two Buddhist Commentaries, Khenchen Kunzang Pelden and Minyak Kunzang Sönam, Editions Padmakara, 1993, 1999.

The Words of My Perfect Teacher, Patrul Rinpoche, International Sacred Literature Trust—HarperCollins, 1994; 2d edition, AltaMira Press, 1998; Shambhala, 1998.

The Life of Shabkar: The Autobiography of a Tibetan Yogin, SUNY Press, 1994; Snow Lion Publications, 2001.

Journey to Enlightenment, Matthieu Ricard, Aperture, 1996.

The Way of the Bodhisattva (Bodhicharyavatara), Shantideva, Shambhala, 1997, 2006.

Lady of the Lotus-Born, Gyalwa Changchub and Namkhai Nyingpo, Shambhala, 1999.

Treasury of Precious Qualities, Longchen Yeshe Dorje, Kangyur Rinpoche, Shambhala, 2001.

Counsels from My Heart, Dudjom Rinpoche, Shambhala, 2001.

Introduction to the Middle Way, Chandrakirti and Mipham Rinpoche, Shambhala, 2002.

Food of Bodhisattvas, Shabkar Tsogdruk Rangdrol, Shambhala, 2004.

A Guide to The Words of My Perfect Teacher, Khenpo Ngawang Pelzang, (transl. with Dipamkara), Shambhala, 2004.

The Hundred Verses of Advice, Dilgo Khyentse Rinpoche and Padampa Sangye, Shambhala, 2005.

The Adornment of the Middle Way, Shantarakshita and Mipham Rinpoche, Shambhala, 2005.

Nagarjuna's Letter to a Friend, Kangyur Rinpoche, Snow Lion Publications, 2005.